99 Adventures

Various methods of evangelism have been presented and used over the years. If the Bible's redemptive story is taught chronologically, it will enable unbelievers and believers to understand the completed picture, the metanarrative of the Bible. There certainly is room for other types of gospel presentations. If the goal of sharing Christ with unbelievers is for them to cling to the gospel, then chronological Bible teaching as a method of evangelism should be pursued. Unbelievers will understand who the God of the Bible is and what He did when they see whole picture painted for them. That is what Jesus did for the two men on the road to Emmaus. He explained to them the things about Himself from the Law and the prophets. May God bless your chronological Bible teaching as you expose the great truth of redemption.

Jim Cook

Table of Contents

Time Line	Adventures	Page
Beginnings	1-16	3-84
Beginnings of a Nation	17-35	85-179
Possessing the Land	36-38	180-194
A United Kingdom	39-42	195-214
A Divided Kingdom	43-45	215-229
Taken from Home	46-48	230-244
Returning to Home	49-50	245-254
The Early Life of Jesus Christ	51-54	255-274
The Ministry of Jesus Christ	55-67	275-339
Betrayal and Death	68-74	340-374
Victory and Life	75-78	375-394
The Church	79-90	395-454
Future Events	91-99	455-499

Teaching Process

The teacher's guide is divided into five key segments. Each part of the teaching process is important and all five should be followed for effective teaching. Chronological Bible teaching is a great way to evangelize and disciple children. As children come to know the stories of the Bible, they will understand the God of the Bible and how to respond to Him by faith.

Each of the five steps to teaching these lessons is a vital part of the lesson. Preparation before the lesson is extremely important and takes place in the days leading up to class. Then when class time starts, introduce the lesson with ideas or methods that will encourage students to become involved in the learning process. Teaching the story will take on several forms: through telling, through singing, through Scripture memory, and through activity. Be sure to review the lesson as well as previous lessons. Last, and probably most important, give your class something to apply or live out as a result of the lesson.

Adventure Number 1
Genesis 1:1

Story Line: God is very strong.

1) Study the Lesson (before class)

- God—the name of the Supreme Being, signifying in Hebrew, "Strong," "Mighty." It is expressive of omnipotent power; and by its use here in the plural form, is obscurely taught at the opening of the Bible, a doctrine clearly revealed in other parts of it, namely, that though God is one, there is a plurality of persons in the Godhead—Father, Son, and Spirit who were engaged in the creative work.[1]

- The Bible makes no attempt to prove that there is a God. It takes this fact as self-evident.

- Thirty-two times in thirty-one verses in Genesis 1 God is mentioned by name. Eleven times, He is referred to by use of personal pronouns.

- Heaven and earth have not existed from all eternity, but had a beginning; nor did they arise from a substance, but were created by God out of nothing.

- It is no accident that God is the subject of the first sentence in the Bible. This word dominates the whole chapter and catches the eye at every point in the page.[2]

- God created -- not formed from any pre-existing materials, but made out of nothing.

- The heavens and the earth -- the universe. This first verse is a general introduction to the Bible, declaring the great and important truth that all things had a beginning.

Footnotes - Adventure 1

1. Robert Jamieson, A.R. Fausset, and David Brown, Jamieson-Fausset-Brown Bible Commentary (Austin: Wordsearch, 2013), Genesis 1.

2. Derek Kidner, Genesis (Downers Grove: Inter-Varsity Press, 1967), 43.

2) Begin the Lesson

"God is real, even though you can't see God." (Hold up a piece of fabric and have several kids together blow on the fabric to make it move.) Say: **"What made the cloth move?"** (The air we blew out.) **"Could you see the air?"** (No.) **"How do you know there was air coming out?"** (We saw the cloth move, that is, we saw the result of the air) Say: **"The same thing is true of God. We can't actually see God because He is a Spirit, but we can see what God has done; and we know that He is real."** Alternate method: Use a piece of paper, a leaf, or anything that can be easily blown.

Explain that we can't fully understand eternity, but that is all right because our God is so great and powerful, He is bigger than anything we can comprehend. Part of this greatness is that He had no beginning, and He has no end.

Words that appear in bold type are words that the teacher could use to introduce the lesson.

3) Teach the Lesson

Tell The Story

Before there were ever birds, trees, stars, or even man and woman, there was God. God always existed. It is hard for all of us to understand how God always was and that He never had a beginning, but that is exactly what the Bible says about God. He is eternal and that means He has no beginning and He has no end.

God also does not try to prove that He exists. Many people want to know proofs about how God exists. The Bible does not describe God with proofs of His existence. It describes Him as the One who was always there.

Not only was God always there, He is described as being very powerful. The word that is used in Genesis 1:1 for God is "Elohim" which refers to God as powerful or very strong. He was always present and He is very powerful. So, we have learned a lot about God in just the first few words of the Bible. We will learn more about God later but right now we should remember that God

These verses talk about the eternal God.

- Psalms 19:1-4
- Romans 1:20
- Isaiah 46:9-10

is strong and that God is eternal.

The book of Genesis is the book of beginnings: the beginning of the world, the beginning of humans, the beginning of sin, the beginning of God's redemptive plan, and other beginnings. But the Bible is clear: God did not have a beginning. He always existed as the Powerful One. It is His massive power that He is known for, even before creation. In creation, we will see His great power, but the first thing we know about God is this: God is very powerful!

After Genesis 1:1, the rest of Genesis takes place on the earth. But the first verse in the Bible does not take place on the earth. It tells us about who God is. The God of the Bible alone is the powerful eternal One. No other gods exist. No one else has existed forever. Only the God of the Bible is powerful and eternal.

Teacher Helps

Ask the children: **"What are some things you know God has done that show you He is powerful?"** (Possible answers: creation, healing the sick, answered prayer, any story from the Bible, fulfilled prophecy.)

Praise and Worship

Praise and Worship styles vary greatly around the world. It is the intent of this curriculum that praise and worship songs be selected that best fit the content of this lesson. Recommendations for praise and worship are given and this music can generally be located at www.itunes.com. However, the teacher can feel free to select a similar praise and worship song.

"You Are God Alone" by Christ for the Nations Music is recommended for this lesson.

Bible Memory Activity: Phrases

Phrases. Say Genesis 1:1 in three phrases. Designate each part of the class to learn just one phrase. After they have learned one phrase, rotate until all kids have learned all three phrases.

1. In the beginning

2. God created

3. the heavens and the earth.

Bible Activity

This activity helps to emphasize that God is eternal: Together with the class, make a two-sided list of things that have a beginning (examples: time, people, the earth, etc. on one side) and things with no beginning (only God on the other side).

Genesis 1:1 (ESV) - In the beginning, God created the heavens and the earth.

4) Review the Lesson

The Birthday Game

Have kids tell when their birthday is and something special about one of their birthdays.

- What would they like to receive as a gift on their birthday?

- What do they like to eat, if they are given a choice, on their birthday?

- What is the best present they have ever received on their birthday?

5) Apply the Lesson

Eight essential truths emerge from the Bible's Story of Hope.

1. God. In the beginning, there was a very powerful God.

2. Man. God created many things. He created man and woman to be His special friends.

3. Sin. Man and woman disobeyed God. They did not do what He told them to do.

4. Death. God punished man and woman for their disobedience. Death, in the Bible, refers to separation.

5. Christ. God sent His one and only Son, His unique Son, who lived a perfect life.

6. Cross. Jesus died on the cross for the sins of the world.

7. Faith. If anyone places their faith in Christ, God welcomes them.

8. Life. God gives eternal life to those who put their faith in Him.

Teacher Helps

The Birthday Game:

If kids have some good ideas on how to celebrate God's power, it would be good to use or implement the ones that are most helpful.

Now tell kids that God does not have a birthday because He always existed. Not only did He always exist, He is very powerful. Ask kids, **"If you could celebrate God's power, how would you celebrate His power?"**

Tell children to go home and ask a friend or family member about the most powerful person that they know. It could be somebody who lifts weights, it could be somebody who exercises a lot, or it could be somebody who is very big. Why did they choose that person? Now, have children tell a family member that God is the most powerful Person in the world. He created the whole universe; He has to be very powerful.

Tell children to draw a picture of what they think God looks like. What does He look like? Have them explain their picture to you.

Story Line: God is very strong.

Teacher Helps

Adventure Number 2
Colossians 1:16 and Job 38:4-7

Story Line: God created angels.

1) Study the Lesson (before class)

- A great number of angels were created; Matthew 26:53.

- Angels are referred to in masculine terms but are not able to marry; Mark 12:25 and Luke 20:34-35.

- Angels have great power but they are not capable of being redeemed by God; Psalm 8:12, Hebrews 2:9, 1 Peter 1:12, and Ephesians 3:10-11.

- Angels can appear to us and we may not even recognize them; Hebrews 13:2. They can also appear and have great impact; Matthew 28:4 and Luke 1:11-13.

- There are ranks among angels. Michael is referred to as the archangel in 1 Thessalonians 4:16 and Jude 1:9. *Arche* is a noun that denotes order or rank.[1]

- From Colossians 1:16, Jesus Christ is the instrumental cause of creation, the final cause of creation, and the conserving cause of creation.[2]

- The cherubim are powerful angels who were chosen to guard the entrance to Eden after the Fall; Genesis 3:24. They are constantly represented as being near the throne of God; Ezekiel 10:5, 12 and 20.

- In Isaiah 6:2, seraphim are described as being above the throne on which the Son of God sat. They are repeatedly saying, *"Holy, holy, holy is the Lord God Almighty. The whole earth is full of His glory."*

Footnotes - Adventure 2

1. James Strong, Strong's Exhaustive Concordance (Austin: Wordsearch, 2010), 746.

2. John Walvoord and Roy Zuck, Bible Knowledge Commentary: New Testament (Wheaton: Scripture Press Publications, 1983), 673.

2) Begin the Lesson

It is hard to imagine what angels do. Gather your class of children in a circle with a small ball. Have children take turns rolling the ball gently to each other. When a child catches the ball, have each child name one thing that they think the angels do. At this point, do not correct children if they give a wrong answer. Let each child who wants to participate describe what they think angels do.

3) Teach the Lesson

God created thousands of angels. Can you remember any of their names? (Michael, Gabriel, Lucifer, seraphim, cherubim, archangel)

Ask, **"What do you think angels do most of the time?"** Explain that in the story today, we are going to find out who angels are and what they do.

Tell The Story

Before anything else existed, there was God. The name that describes God is a name of power. We know that God is and was powerful. He did not have to create anything for Him to be powerful. But He chose to create the heavens and the earth and all that is in them. Before God created the heavens and the earth, He created angels.

He did not create a few angels. He created many angels ... millions of them. The angels that God created were very smart and they could do many unusual things. But, they were not God. They did not know everything, like God does, but they did know a lot. They were powerful, but not as strong as God.

These angels worshipped and adored God. Many angels stood around the throne of God and said, *"Holy, holy, holy, is the Lord God almighty. The whole earth is full of His glory."*

Teacher Helps

The teacher should make sure that children do not throw the ball at one another. The purpose of the game is to get everyone thinking about angels and what they do.

Verses to look up about angels can be found in these passages:

- Exodus 14:19 - Angel went before Israel

- Daniel 10:13, 21 - Angels watch over Israel

- Luke 1:19, 26 - Gabriel announces good news

- Acts 10:3 - Angel sent to Cornelius

- Hebrews 1:13-14 - Angels as ministering spirits

- Revelation 6:3-7 - Angels directed John's attention

The angels also served God. If God had a job to do, like give a message to Abraham (or anybody else), angels did the job.

Angels also had the ability to choose. They could choose to worship and serve God or they could choose not to do this.

Praise and Worship

Praise and Worship styles vary greatly around the world. It is the intent of this curriculum that praise and worship songs be selected that best fit the content of this lesson. Recommendations for praise and worship are given and this music can generally be located at www.itunes.com. However, the teacher can feel free to select a similar praise and worship song.

"You Are God Alone" by Christ for the Nations Music is recommended for this lesson.

Bible Activity

The Praise Bucket. One of the major jobs that angels do is to praise God; see Psalm 148. Have children sit in a circle with a bucket in the middle. Pass out buttons or coins to the children. Have each child give a praise to God. When they give a praise to God, they should throw their button or coin into the bucket. In this way, kids will learn ways to praise God and they will think of different things for which to praise God. Have kids continue to praise God until they run out of ideas.

Things for which children could praise and thank God (family, church, friends, angels, Jesus Christ, salvation, blessings, answered prayer, Bible, a teacher, heaven).

Memory Verse

Colossians 1:16 (ESV) - For by him all things were created, in heaven and on earth, visible and invisible, whether thrones or dominions or rulers or authorities—all things were created through him and for him.

Teacher Helps

Bible Activity: The Praise Bucket

The Praise Bucket is designed to get children actively involved in learning what angels do. The same bucket could be used for serving or choosing to do right which are also things that angels do.

Memory Verse Activity: The Telephone Game

Memorize this verse using The Telephone Game. Have your class form one line, then whisper to the first person in line a phrase of this verse, have that person repeat the phrase to the next person. Do this until all have quoted the first phrase. Then do the same thing with the second phrase, the third phrase, and so on until they have memorized the verse.

4) Review the Lesson

Questions

1. How many angels has God created? (millions)

2. What do angels do? (serve and worship God)

3. Can angels choose to do right or wrong? (Yes, they can choose.)

4. When were angels created? (before the foundation of the earth)

5. The theme for last week's lesson was "God is very strong." What is the theme or main thing to remember from this lesson? (God created angels.)

Teacher Helps

Review questions will focus on the major ideas in the lesson. Let kids answer the questions without you giving them the answers, if possible.

5) Apply the Lesson

Read Psalm 148 to your class. Tell them that angels were created to praise the name of the Lord. Ask them, **"What are some things that we can praise the Lord for?"** List their praises and then let whoever would like to praise God.

Eight essential truths emerge from the Bible's Story of Hope. From this lesson about God, we learn that God created angels.

Story Line: God created angels.

The application step of the lesson is sometimes one of the most difficult. Your class should always have a takeaway or something to do as a result of listening to this story.

Adventure Number 3
Genesis 1:1-25

Story Line: God made everything.

1) Study the Lesson (before class)

- The Bible does not discuss evolution. Rather, it begins with the creation of the world by God. The worldview of the Bible begins with a Creator, not the creation.

- Since God is the Creator and the entire universe is His creation, it must be under His control. God was before all things, therefore, nothing else can be His equal. There can be no other gods because He was before anyone or anything else.

- When God created the world, He created it "out of nothing." The verb here, "created," is used throughout the Bible. However, it is used only when God is the subject.[1]

- The Genesis 1 account of God reveals that He is a redeeming God. It was His plan for man to have a vital, significant relationship with God. No other part of creation could boast of a redeeming God, only man and woman.

- The statement "the earth was without form and void" (Genesis 1:2) provides the setting for the rest of creation. On the second and third days of creation, God gave the earth form. On the third, fourth, and fifth days of creation, God filled the earth.

- "The importance of Genesis 1 is emphasized by the constant use of a significant figure of speech which always shows up by the multiple use of the word. Count up the "ands" in Genesis 1—there are almost one hundred of them. This figure of speech is used to slow us down and draw our attention to each phrase or word thus joined together."[2]

- At the end of creation, God gave man the incredible blessing and opportunity of being made in His image. No other creature or created thing had this given to them.

Footnotes - Adventure 3

1. John Walvoord and Roy Zuck, *Bible Knowledge Commentary: Old Testament* (Wheaton: Scripture Press Publications, 1983), 28.

2. John Phillips, *Exploring Genesis: An Expository Commentary* (Austin: Wordsearch, 2009), 35.

2) Begin the Lesson

Ask, **"What was the main idea that we learned from the last lesson?"** (God created angels). **"What was the theme from the week before that?"** (God is very strong.)

Have kids tell what they can remember from the last two lessons.

3) Teach the Lesson

The power of God to speak the world into existence has to be incredible. Discuss this concept with your children: since God created everything by just speaking it into existence, He is very strong and very powerful. Ask students, **"Have you ever made anything? Have you ever made something out of nothing?"**

Tell the Story

This is how the beginning of the heavens and the beginning of the earth happened. The earth was formed but it did not have much shape to it and there was nothing living on the earth. It was like a big empty pool of nothing and it was dark. The Spirit of God hovered over the earth and saw what it was like.

Because it was very dark, God spoke and said, *"Let there be light."* Guess what? Immediately, there was light! It didn't take a bunch of years and it wasn't a process. Out of nothing, God created light for the earth and it wasn't dark anymore. Where there was light, God called that day and where there was darkness, God called that night. That is how it was on the first day of creation.

The second day of creation was awesome! There was a lot of water on the earth and God made the sky. So, there was water above the earth and there was water on the earth. The water above the earth, our atmosphere, is

---

Teacher Helps

Review the last two lessons. Possible questions to ask your class could include:

- Not only did God always exist, He is very powerful. If you could celebrate God's power, how would you celebrate His power?

- How many angels has God created? (millions)

- What do angels do? (serve and worship God)

- Can angels choose to do right or wrong? (Yes, they can choose.)

- When were angels created? (before the foundation of the earth)

Day 1: Genesis 1:3-5. God names day and night.

Day 2: Genesis 1:6-8. God names heaven.

what makes the earth different from all the other known planets. The other planets do not have a covering like the earth does. This atmosphere is very important for us to exist right now. So, on day two of creation, God named the sky "heavens." After two days, God had named three things: day, night, and heavens. But, the story of creation gets even better.

On the third day of creation, God created land on the earth and He collected all the waters and called them ocean. For the dry land, He told it to bring forth all kinds of seed bearing plants. Now there was day and night or light and darkness. There was the atmosphere above the earth and there was dry ground as well as oceans. On the land were plants of all different kinds. It was really beautiful and God saw that it was good.

On the fourth day, God made lots of lights for the universe. He especially made two lights. The sun would be the earth's main source of light for the day and the moon would be the earth's main source of light for the night. He also made all the stars. So, when you look up and see the sun, moon, and stars, you can remember that God made all these on the fourth day. This is also how God made the earth to have different seasons. These lights would serve to help us know days, weeks, months, and years. Again, God saw that it was good.

On the fifth day of creation, God made all the birds of the air, all the fish of the sea, and other underwater creatures. God made all the huge fish of the sea like whales and all the small fish. He made colorful birds to fly in the air and majestic birds that were quite large. He told them to be fruitful. Every species of birds and every species of fish were created by God on the fifth day. All of these birds and fish were created out of nothing, they did not evolve like some people would like to tell us.

On the sixth day of creation, God made the animals to fill the earth and God made man and woman to take care of the earth. So, on the sixth day, there were bugs, reptiles, cattle, and all different kinds of wild animals. There was also man and woman. God told the man that He was giving to him all the plants and trees for food. The sixth day was very special to God and He said it was very good.

On the seventh day, God rested. He did not need to rest. But, He set aside a special day so that people could remember who God is and what God did. He rested as an example for us.

Teacher Helps

Day 3: Genesis 1:9-13. God names the ocean and the land.

Day 4: Genesis 1:14-19. God names the sun, moon, and stars.

Day 5: Genesis 1:20-23. God creates the birds of the air and fish of the sea but does not name them.

Day 6: Genesis 1:24-31. God creates the animals to fill the earth. God also creates man and woman to rule the earth.

Day 7: Genesis 2:1-3. God rested.

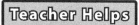

Praise and Worship

Praise and Worship styles vary greatly around the world. It is the intent of this curriculum that praise and worship songs be selected that best fit the content of this lesson. Recommendations for praise and worship are given and this music can generally be located at www.itunes.com. However, the teacher can feel free to select a similar praise and worship song.

"You Are God Alone" by Christ for the Nations Music is recommended for this lesson.

Bible Activity

Graffiti (writing that is placed on a bulletin board or chalk board). The teacher should write on a piece of paper or on the board: Day 1, Day 2, Day 3, Day 4, Day 5, Day 6, and Day 7. Then on separate pieces of paper, all the things mentioned in creation that were created (day, night, heaven, ocean, land, sun, moon, stars, birds, fish, animals, people, and rest) should be written down. Then the kids should match up which parts of creation happened on each specific day.

Memory Verse

Genesis 2:2 (ESV) - And on the seventh day God finished his work that he had done, and he rested on the seventh day from all his work that he had done.

Bible Activity: Graffiti

Graffiti prompts children to listen more intently to what happened on each day of creation. Children will become more involved in the learning process when they know they will have this activity.

Graffiti can also be used to help children memorize Genesis 2:2. Write each word of this verse on a separate piece of paper. Then have children put the words in order in groups of 2 or 3. When each group can put the verse together in order, they will probably have this verse memorized.

4) Review the Lesson

Have children simplify the lesson into 10 words or less using their own words. What are their answers? When children simplify the story of the lesson into ten words or less, they will probably say something like these possibilities:

- God made heaven, earth, and everything in them.
- God made people, animals, land, water, and air.
- God made everything.
- God is so powerful that He made all things.
- God spoke things into existence.
- God is a really big God.
- The Bible and evolution cannot both be true.

Review the Lesson Activity: Simplify

Simplify can even become a game for the children. The teacher can give each team of 2 or 3 kids about 1-2 minutes to come up with the most significant 10 words of this lesson.

5) Apply the Lesson

Eight essential truths emerge from the Bible's Story of Hope. From this story about God, we learn that God is the all-powerful Creator of everything.

Let children make their own creation. You can give them any materials that you have close at hand or they can gather materials of their own. Tell them to make their own creation, name their creation, then describe their own creation to the rest of the class. From this lesson we learn that God is powerful and creative.

Adventure Number 4
Genesis 1:26-31 and 2:7-25

Story Line: God made man and woman to be His special friends.

1) Study the Lesson (before class)

- God crowned man in three ways; first by bestowing upon him a posterity—*"Be fruitful and multiply"* (1:28a). God crowned Adam with a position (1:28b) giving him dominion over the fish of the sea, over the fowl of the air, and over every living thing. Finally, God crowned Adam with a possession (1:29-31). He gave him paradise to enjoy.[1]

- Man was the last creature that God created. He did not evolve, he was created.[2] Man was not created in the image and likeness of the beasts. No animal shows any desire to worship. No animal shows any consciousness of the judgment to come. No animal has the hope of immortality beyond the grave. No animal ever learned to read and write or admire a beautiful sunset.

- God describes the creation of man as "very good." No other part of creation was described as such.

- God's image was given only to humans. No other part of creation received the image of God. God does not have a human form. Being created in His image means that humans can experience His nature (like love, holiness, justice, truth, and wisdom).

- When God breathed into the nostrils of Adam the breath of life (Genesis 2:7), man became a living being. This made man a spiritual being (different from the animals of creation) with abilities to fellowship with God, know Him personally, and serve Him.

- The creation of man meant both male and female.

Footnotes - Adventure 4

1. Ibid, 46.

2. John Walvoord and Roy Zuck, *Bible Knowledge Commentary: Old Testament*, 29.

2) Begin the Lesson

Tell your class that they are learning the one big story of the Bible. While there are many stories in the Bible, they are linked to one major theme or story in the Bible. It is a story of hope. So, to help your class know that story and be able to put all the lessons together, we are going to review the lessons from the past.

- From the first lesson, what is the name for God in Genesis 1:1 and what does that name signify? (Elohim = God is very powerful)

- From the second lesson, we learned that angels have certain jobs to do. What are those jobs? (serve and worship God)

- From the third lesson, we learned about the creation of the universe. What did God create on each day? (Day 1 = day and night; Day 2 = heavens or atmosphere; Day 3 = oceans and land; Day 4 = sun, moon, and stars; Day 5 = birds in the air and fish in the sea; Day 6 = land animals, man, and woman)

Teacher Helps

Review is a significant part of learning. Many will have forgotten past lessons or they may not have been present when previous lessons were taught.

Divide the class into 3 teams:

- Team 1 Responsibility = tell the rest of the class what happened on Day 1.

- Team 2 Responsibility = tell the rest of the class what happened on Day 2.

- Team 3 Responsibility = tell the rest of the class what happened on Day 3.

3) Teach the Lesson

Ask students, **"What is the most beautiful place you have ever been? Say one word of what you would think Paradise is like?"**

The first place Adam and the woman lived was a beautiful place. When we read Genesis 2:8-9, what makes you think it was a beautiful place?

Tell the Story

On the sixth day of the creation week, God made man. His name was Adam. He made man by forming him from the dirt of the ground and then God breathed life into Adam. Adam became a living soul, much different than the animals, the birds, and the fish that God had created. As a living soul, Adam was created to have a special relationship with God. Adam had life and God placed him in the middle of a garden that had been made by God. The name of the garden was the garden of Eden. In the middle of the garden was a very special tree. The name of that tree was the tree of the knowledge of good and evil. This was the first time that God commanded Adam to do anything. That command was about life and death, good and evil. There were positive blessings from God in this command. Adam could enjoy almost anything in the garden. God also said, "Don't eat from that one tree." Man could eat freely from the fruits of the garden but he would surely die if he ate from the tree of the knowledge of good and evil.

At that point in time, there was no rain. The garden and all that was in it was watered by underground springs. Adam was to take care of the garden; he was kind of like a farmer who took care of all the trees and bushes in the garden. In that same garden were four large rivers so it must have been a very big garden. In the garden, God told Adam to name all the birds, all the cattle, and all the animals. When Adam did this, he realized that he did not have anyone like him to be his helper. God saw this and caused a deep sleep to come on Adam. While Adam was asleep, God took a rib from Adam and made a special friend for Adam. When Adam woke from his sleep and saw what God had made, Adam was so happy. He called his special friend "woman," because she was made from man.

So, Adam had no parents, no brothers, no sisters, and no other friends. But, now he had a very special friend. He must have had many conversations with his special friend, woman. He must have told her about the garden and what his jobs were. He must have told her that God said not to eat of the tree of the knowledge of good and evil. They felt no shame, no guilt, and no fear.

The man and the woman were special friends with each other and they were special friends with God. The relationship that they had with God was unique because they were created in his image; they were created to have fellowship with God. It was a wonderful beginning for man and woman.

Teacher Helps

Psalm 8:6-8 (ESV)

6 You have given him dominion over the works of your hands; you have put all things under his feet,

7 all sheep and oxen, and also the beasts of the field,

8 the birds of the heavens, and the fish of the sea, whatever passes along the paths of the seas.

Praise and Worship

Praise and Worship styles vary greatly around the world. It is the intent of this curriculum that praise and worship songs be selected that best fit the content of this lesson. Recommendations for praise and worship are given and this music can generally be located at www.itunes.com. However, the teacher can feel free to select a similar praise and worship song.

"You Are God Alone" by Christ for the Nations Music is recommended for this lesson.

Bible Activity

Give each child a piece of play dough about the size of an egg. Tell the children to make a clay sculpture of an animal. Give them about 4-5 minutes to work on their project, then give a few children a chance to tell what their project is. Ask them: "Is this alive?" (Kids laugh and say "Of course not!") Ask: "Well, have you ever seen a sculpture or statue that was VERY realistic looking?" (Most will say "yes.") "Some artists are so talented; they can make a sculpture that looks EXACTLY like a certain person or animal. Only God can create life. Not only that, but when people make sculptures or other art, they have to start with all the materials. When God created the heavens and the earth, He only SPOKE and it came into being. He is so great and powerful, His WORDS make great things happen. When God created Adam, He only used the dust of the earth.

No Fuss Play Dough

- 1 cup cold water
- 1 cup salt
- 2 teaspoons vegetable oil
- 2 cups flour
- 2 tablespoons cornstarch
- Food coloring (optional)

In a large bowl, mix together water, salt, oil and a few drops of food coloring. Mix flour and cornstarch and add 1/2 cup at a time, stirring constantly (you may need a little more or a little less than 2 cups flour so make sure you stir until it is the right consistency). Knead for a few minutes with flour on your hands.

Teacher Helps

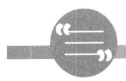

Memory Verse

Genesis 1:27 (ESV) - So God created man in his own image, in the image of God he created him; male and female he created them.

Bible Memory Activity: Scramble

Write each word on a piece of paper and scramble the words. Let children come up to the front of the class to put the words in order. You can time them to see who can put these words in order the fastest.

4) Review the Lesson

Have children put their hand or foot in something that will leave a mark like play doh or sand. When children leave their mark in the play dough, sand or something else, ask them, "What makes your handprint or footprint unique?"

Now, ask them how God has left His unique image on them. **"How has God left His own image with you?"**

5) Apply the Lesson

God has given us the ability to have personal, lifelong relationships or friendships with others and with God. Therefore, people have infinite personal worth and value. God loves you so much that He created you to be His personal special friend whom He loves very much. Do you know you can have a personal relationship with God?

Eight essential truths emerge from the Bible's Story of Hope. From this story in the Bible, we learn that God is a personal God who wants to have a relationship with every person.

> **Story Line: God made man and woman to be His special friends.**

Teacher Helps

Ask children,

"On the sixth day, what did God create?" (animals and people)

"Are animals God's special friends also?" (No. Animals are special to God, but they are not His special friends.)

"Why not?" (Because the animals were not created in the image of God.)

Assignment for next week: kids should bring a decoration for the "fun room." The fun room is where we will learn an important lesson next week. See the next lesson for suggestions to give the kids.

Adventure Number 5
Genesis 2:8-15

Story Line: Life in the garden was full of pleasure.

1) Study the Lesson (before class)

- The name of the tree of the knowledge of good and evil implies that evil already existed, either in the garden or at Satan's fall.[1]

- The bountiful garden, the rivers, and the precious stones all indicate that Eden was a place of beauty.

- The tree of the knowledge of good and evil, in the middle of the garden, probably reveals that the fall of Satan had already occurred.

- "Good and evil" is a merism (a rhetorical term for a pair of contrasting words). Good and evil refers to things that bring life or good and things that bring death or evil.[2]

- From Genesis 3:22, we learn that another tree produced fruit that would nourish a body to live forever.

- Because of the location of the rivers, the garden was probably located near Mesopotamia (Assyria and Babylon).

- In Revelation 22, the tree of life reappears and is a picture of people enjoying eternal life with God.

- God gave Adam a choice to work or care for the garden of Eden. Man was in the middle of the garden and now had a responsibility. His work was described as his service to God.

- The choice to eat from the right trees and the choice to not eat from the tree of the knowledge of good and evil is a choice that Adam faced. wWe also have choices to make, whether we will obey God or not obey Him.

Footnotes - Adventure 5

1. James Galvin, *Life Application Bible Notes* (Carol Stream: Tyndale House Publishers, 1986), 8.

2. John Walvoord and Roy Zuck, *Bible Knowledge Commentary: Old Testament*, 30.

2) Begin the Lesson

- The book of Genesis is the book of beginnings. Read the first chapter of Genesis and see how many beginnings you can name. Let children all take a turn so that they can name something from Genesis 1.

- On Day 1, God created light (Genesis 1:3).

- On Day 2, God created sky (1:6).

- On Day 3, God created land and vegetation. The dry land was separated from the waters and the waters were called seas. (1:9).

- On Day 4, God created the sun, moon and stars (1:14-18).

- On Day 5, God created the fish and birds (1:20-22).

- On Day 6, God created animals (1:24) and humans (1:26).

- Before the creation week, God created angels.

- God never had a beginning and He was never created.

Teacher Helps

Before children tell something that begins from Genesis 1, let them try to act out what they could say. For instance, if a child said this was the beginning of fish, that child would demonstrate a fish swimming and the others would try to guess what the child was acting out. Also, the teacher could give out slips of paper with things that were created in Genesis 1 and the kids could each pick one and see if the others could guess their creation.

3) Teach the Lesson

Ask students, **"What is the most special place you have ever lived? What made it special?"** Then, tell children the place we are going to learn about today is a very special place where there was only happiness.

Tell the Story

The teacher will want each child to feel like the garden was a very special place to live. You may want to tell about a very special place or a happy place where you have lived or visited.

Life in the garden was wonderful for Adam. There was tremendous beauty because of the four rivers that God placed in this area. These rivers probably served to keep the trees and bushes green and growing. At least two of the rivers were very big rivers.

Not only were there four beautiful rivers, there were lots of trees and bushes that provided all kinds of food for Adam to eat. Adam had his choice to eat of all kinds of fruits and vegetables. If Adam wanted to eat his favorite fruit, it was there. The garden of Eden had to be a fairly large garden so there would be plenty to eat. Whatever he wanted to eat and lots of it, that is what Adam had as breakfast, lunch, supper, and even snacks.

Not only was the garden beautiful and had lots of good food, there were very special stones like gold (yellow), pearls (white), and onyx or perhaps lapis lazuli (blue). These stones were gorgeous to view. Truly, God had placed Adam in a lush, bountiful, and precious garden.

As you can see in the picture, the animals were at peace with each other. The garden was also a peaceful place to live. While Adam had the responsibility of working the garden, it was not hard work. It is hard for us to think of work as not being hard, but for Adam, it was fun for him to take care of the garden. Imagine it like this, choose to do whatever you would like to do as a job and then you get to do it. That was Adam. The only thing he couldn't do was eat from the tree of the knowledge of good and evil.

The place God gave Adam to live was a wonderful place that was full of pleasure. You would have loved this place, if you had a chance to live here. It was peaceful and pleasant. It was rich and precious. It was bountiful and fruitful. And it was lush and green. What a great place God had prepared for Adam to live in close fellowship with Him.

 # Praise and Worship

Praise and Worship styles vary greatly around the world. It is the intent of this curriculum that praise and worship songs be selected that best fit the content of this lesson. Recommendations for praise and worship are given and this music can generally be located at www.itunes.com. However, the teacher can feel free to select a similar praise and worship song.

"You Are God Alone" by Christ for the Nations Music is recommended for this lesson.

Bible Activity

The Fun Room. Give each child the responsibility for this fun project. The teacher will want to make the classroom as beautiful as possible with the help of the kids and maybe their parents. Each child should have one of these responsibilities:

1. Find and bring everyone's favorite food to class this week.

2. Decorations should be made for the class to beautify the classroom.

3. Precious rocks or valuable possessions should be brought to the classroom this week.

4. Everyone who comes to this classroom has to be friendly and kind. No room for unkind comments or actions in this room.

After the class beautifies the classroom, the teacher should explain to the children that the garden of Eden was even better. It was a perfect place to be where there was lots of good food, lots of precious gems or rocks, lots of beautiful trees, and best of all, it was peaceful and pleasant.

Memory Verse

Genesis 2:8 (ESV) - And the LORD God planted a garden in Eden, in the east, and there he put the man whom he had formed.

Teacher Helps

Bible Activity: The Fun Room

Kids can decorate their room and bring stuff to it so that this is the best place to be. Let the kids be part of making their classroom "the fun room." Assignments can be made the week before so that this lesson takes on new meaning when they see and participate in making this room a great place to be.

Bible Activity: Memorize with Pictures

Have children memorize this verse using pictures for any word in the verse. For instance, the teacher may use a triangle for "the LORD God" or a leaf for the "garden." The teacher could simply put E for "east" and a stick figure of a man for "the man."

4) Review the Lesson

Teacher Helps

Bible Activity: The Boring Room

The Boring Room. After children have made their classroom a beautiful place to be, take down the decorations as a class, remove the delicious foods that were brought in, and return the classroom to the way it was. The teacher could even make the room messy and bring in food that was not delicious.

Emphasize to the kids that Adam's classroom, the garden, was beautiful but we are going to learn next week how Adam messed it up.

Take down all decorations, remove all food, and anything that was brought in to beautify the room should be out of view. The goal of the teacher is to let children get a small taste of what the garden was like and what life will be like for Adam very soon.

5) Apply the Lesson

Eight essential truths emerge from the Bible's Story of Hope. From this story in the Bible, we learn that God is a personal God Who wants to provide a place of pleasure for you to live. He is a generous and loving God.

The greatest pleasures in life are the pleasures that God brings. God can bring pleasure to your life in the form of nature, special possessions, peace in your home, and many other ways. But the best way to enjoy life is to let God be in control of your life. Ask children, **"What are some ways that you can let God be in control of your life?"**

Possible ways to let God be in control of your life:

- Choosing friends
- Choosing loving actions
- Choosing kind words

> **Story Line: Life in the garden was full of pleasure.**

Adventure Number 6
Ezekiel 28:11-17 and Isaiah 14:12-15

Story Line: Satan is God's enemy.   Satan was proud. God threw Satan out of heaven.

1) Study the Lesson (before class)

- Ezekiel did not use the word "king" very much. Apart from King Jehoiachin (Ezekiel 1:2) he did not use the title "king" of any of Israel's monarchs.[1]

- In Ezekiel 28:11-19, Ezekiel described the king in terms that could not apply to a man. This "king" had appeared in the Garden of Eden (v. 13), had been a guardian cherub (v. 14), had possessed free access to God's holy mountain (v. 14), and had been sinless from the time he was created (v. 15).

- "God had anointed Lucifer as a guardian cherub (Ezekiel 28:14). The cherubim (pl. of cherub) were the 'inner circle' of angels who had the closest access to God and guarded His holiness (cf. 10:1-14). Lucifer also had free access to God's holy mount (28:14), heaven, and he walked among the fiery stones (cf. v. 16)."[2]

- Ezekiel also told about the original beauty of Lucifer, as God created him in verses 12-15. Nine of the 12 precious stones of the breastplate worn by priests were used by Ezekiel to describe Lucifer himself.

- When Lucifer was created by God, he was blameless until wickedness was found in him (verses 14-15).

- From Isaiah 14, Lucifer means "morning star" and implies that Satan is trying to imitate Jesus Christ, "the bright and morning star."

Footnotes - Adventure 6

1. John Walvoord and Roy Zuck, *Bible Knowledge Commentary: Old Testament*, 1283.

2. Ibid.

2) Begin the Lesson

Adventure 1

    1. What is one thing we know about God?

    2. Read Genesis 1:1.

    3. God is very powerful.

    4. Praise God for His power.

Adventure 2

    1. What do angels do most of the time?

    2. Read Job 38:4-7.

    3. Angels worship and serve God.

    4. Pray that we would worship and serve God also.

Adventure 3

    1. How did the creation of the universe happen?

    2. Summarize Genesis 1:1-25. God spoke things into existence.

    3. The ability of God to speak everything into existence is powerful.

    4. Praise God for His creation.

Adventure 4

    1. How do we know that God wants us to be His special friends?

    2. Read Genesis 1:26-27.

    3. People were created in the image of God.

    4. Praise God that we can be His special friends.

Adventure 5

    1. What was life in the garden like?

    2. Read Genesis 2:8-15.

Teacher Helps

Review Activity: Ask, Read, Talk, Speak

A good review strategy of the first 5 lessons will focus on four main elements.

1) Ask a question.

2) Read the Bible.

3) Talk about it.

4) Speak to God.

3. Life in the garden was full of pleasure.

4. Thank God for all the good things He has provided.

3) Teach the Lesson

Teacher Helps

Follow the Leader Activity

Ask the children to play "Follow the Leader" (a bad leader).

Tell children to draw a picture of how they would picture Satan. If paper is unavailable, have the children tell how they picture Satan. After the children draw their picture, let them describe how they visualize Satan and why.

Say, **"Today, we will learn about Lucifer and what he was like."**

Tell the Story

All of the angels that God created were beautiful. He created millions of angels and they all worshipped God. Some of the angels had a higher rank. But, the most beautiful of all those angels was Lucifer. Lucifer was also a very high ranking angel. In fact, God said this about Lucifer,

"You were perfect in wisdom, perfect in beauty,
Walking my mountain, performing your duty,
An angel so special, sparkling like gold, and silver,
Precious stones elegance untold."

So, we know that Lucifer was one of the most special angels in heaven, maybe the most special of all the angels.

One day, a long time ago, pride entered Lucifer. Lucifer said that he was ascending to heaven to make his throne higher than all God's stars and he alone would sit on that throne!

"Ruling over all the gods on that utmost of heights,
I'll be the brightest of the lights, I'll be the sight of sights.
I will ascend above the clouds—the very tops of them.
I'll make myself like the Most High and never bow again!"

God resists the proud and so He had to punish Lucifer for this sin. He made Lucifer, or Satan, leave heaven permanently because of pride. Unfortunately,

When the bad leader says something mean, the class should say something mean.

When the bad leader says to misbehave, the class should misbehave.

When the bad leader says to question God, everyone in the class should say, **"Did God really say?"**

Have they ever done that? Why? That is exactly what one third of the angels did.

one third of all the angels that God had created followed Satan. God punished them also and expelled them from heaven. Satan and the angels who followed him will experience eternal punishment. We will hear more about that later.

Satan is now the enemy of God. Satan tries to influence people to resist God. Satan is a deceiver and he is proud. He knows that his eternal home will be in hell. Billions of years from now, Satan will still be suffering for his pride. Satan is leading a rebellion against God. Other angels have followed Satan in this rebellion. Many people have followed Satan in this rebellion. Because God is a holy God, He will not allow rebellion to go unpunished. If the most beautiful and powerful angel ever created will suffer eternal punishment for his pride, so will anyone else who follows Satan's example.

Praise and Worship

Praise and Worship styles vary greatly around the world. It is the intent of this curriculum that praise and worship songs be selected that best fit the content of this lesson. Recommendations for praise and worship are given and this music can generally be located at www.itunes.com. However, the teacher can feel free to select a similar praise and worship song.

"You Are God Alone" by Christ for the Nations Music is recommended for this lesson.

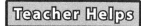

Bible Activity

Make a poster showing the superior power of God over Satan. Kids can read verses for each.

1. God is _____. He never sins. (Leviticus 19:2)
2. In Revelation 22:16, God is called the _____ _____.
3. God created all the _____ angels. (Genesis 1:31)
4. God is _____ all the time.
5. God has always existed, even before creation. He is _____.

1. holy/evil
2. bright and morning star/morning star
3. good/rebelled
4. everywhere/one
5. eternal/the lake of fire

1. Satan is _____ and loves sin. (Ezekiel 28:15)
2. Isaiah talks about Lucifer's title of _____ _____ as he imitates God's power, but falls short. (Isaiah 14:12)
3. Lucifer along with many other angels _____ against their Creator and were cast out of heaven.
4. Satan can only be in ___ place at a time. (Job 1:6-7)
5. Satan was created by God and will one day be cast into _____ _____ ____ ____ by God. (Revelation 20:10)

Poster Activity

If posters are available, use them. If not, use a blackboard. If nothing else is available, just ask the kids these questions and have them answer these statements about the superior power of God.

Memory Verse

Isaiah 14:12 (ESV) - How you are fallen from heaven, O Day Star, son of Dawn! How you are cut down to the ground, you who laid the nations low!

Memory Verse Activity: Balloon Pop

Write each word of the memory verse on a balloon, if balloons are available. Teach Isaiah 14:12 to the children and let them take turns popping balloons when they know each word of the memory verse.

4) Review the Lesson

Invite children to be part of a club. Make invitations for each child and hand deliver them. You could call your club something like "The Obedience Club." There is one rule for the obedience club: you have to do exactly what the teacher says. Those who talk when they are not supposed to talk or misbehave in some way are not permitted to be a part of "The Obedience Club." You may want to have special treats for this special invitation and those who participate.

Now comes the hard part. Without humiliating the child who disobeys, each child who does not follow the rules for "The Obedience Club" must sit in a different part of the room and they cannot have fun or enjoy treats with the rest of the class.

Tell the children this is exactly what happened to Lucifer. Only, he did not get to sit in another part of the classroom and his punishment was and is very real.

Review the Lesson Activity: The Obedience Club

It is very important not to humiliate or embarrass any child. This is only a pretend club to demonstrate a point, not to make any child feel lonely or ostracized.

5) Apply the Lesson

Give kids one minute to build the tallest tower they can build with anything they can find in your classroom. Whoever has the tallest tower should place their Bible on it.

Eight essential truths emerge from the Bible's Story of Hope. From this story in the Bible, we learn that God makes judgements. He judges those who are proud.

Apply the Lesson Activity: The Tallest Tower

Ask kids how they would feel if they were on top of the tallest tower? (proud) How would they feel if they fell? Explain that Satan fell from a high place because of his pride.

> **Story Line: Satan is God's enemy. Satan was proud. God threw Satan out of heaven.**

Adventure Number 7
Genesis 3:1-6

Story Line: Satan tempted Adam and the woman. They disobeyed God.

1) Study the Lesson (before class)

- The tempter was Satan in the form of a serpent. Adam and the woman's temptation came in the form of a disguise and was not expected.

- Satan is identified as that "old serpent" in some parts of Scripture and "evil" in other parts of Scripture; John 8:44; Romans 16:20; 2 Corinthians 11:3; 1 Timothy 2:14; Revelation 12:9; Revelation 20:2.

- The woman did not know the command of God very well or did not want to remember it. Satan's plan of attack in the Garden of Eden was based on subtlety. It was God's intention that headship should be invested in Adam. The woman was created second, not first. She was not made for headship; her inmost center of rule was not her head but her heart. Adam, on the other hand, was made to rule; his inmost center of rule was his intellect. Satan twisted God's order.[1]

- Look at the woman's choices: She looked, she took, she ate, and she gave.[2]

- The tempter cast doubt over God's character, suggesting that He was jealous and holding something back from Adam and the woman (Genesis 3:5).

- When compared with God's original commands (Genesis 2:16-17), Eve weakened, changed, and added to God's words (Genesis 3:3).

- Satan was a liar from the beginning (John 8:44). This is his lie: one can sin and get away with it. But death is the penalty for sin; Genesis 2:17.

Footnotes - Adventure 7

1. John Phillips, *Exploring Genesis*, 56.

2. James Galvin, *Life Application Bible Notes*, 10.

2) Begin the Lesson

Let's review the first six lessons with a game. Let kids tell which lesson the statement given was taught.

- Satan is God's enemy (Lesson 6). Ask, **"Why did Lucifer become God's enemy?"** (pride)

- Life in the garden was full of pleasure (Lesson 5). Ask, **"What made the garden full of pleasure?"** (lots of good food, beautiful stones and rivers, trees, everyone and everything was peaceful)

- God made man and woman to be His special friends (Lesson 4). Ask, **"What made the man and woman God's special friends?"** (They were created in His image)

- God made everything (Lesson 3). Ask, **"When God created the world, He made everything out of nothing. What does that mean?"** (It means that He spoke all of creation into existence.)

- God made the angels (Lesson 2). Ask, **"What are the main jobs of the angels?"** (to worship and serve God)

- God is very strong (Lesson 1). Ask, **"How do we know that God is very strong?"** (because that is what His name means and because of what He did in creation)

Teacher Helps

The teacher may want to keep score and let kids answer by team. Each right answer gets one point for the team. Always compliment the child's answer, even if it is not correct. Never belittle a child.

3) Teach the Lesson

1. Temptation is Satan's invitation to give in to his kind of life and give up on God's kind of life. Why does Satan want to tempt us?

2. To sin means to "miss the mark." That mark is the perfect standard of a holy God.

3. Satan tempted Adam and the woman to sin and he succeeded. How did he do that?

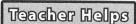

Tell the Story

Some time after Lucifer was expelled from heaven for his sin of rebellion, he went to the earth in the form of a serpent. Normally, animals don't talk but this serpent had very special abilities. So, he talked to the woman that God had created to be man's helper. Lucifer, now called Satan, wanted the man and woman to sin against God. Satan wanted them to rebel against God, just like he did. That is Satan's desire ... to get as many followers as possible. He wanted the man and woman to rebel against God and he wants us to rebel against God.

Satan didn't just come right out and say, "Rebel against God." He got the woman to question what God said. Satan said to the woman, "Did God actually say you shall not eat of any tree in the garden?" The serpent, Satan, was really clever and tricky. In fact, he was at his best when he was luring the woman away from what God said.

The woman talked back to the serpent and said, "We may eat of the fruit of the trees in the garden, but God said, 'You shall not eat of the fruit of the tree that is in the midst of the garden, neither shall you touch it, lest you die.'" The woman messed up what God said. God told them they couldn't eat of that one tree ... the tree of the knowledge of good and evil. He said nothing about not touching it.

Satan got the woman to question whether God would really punish sin. Satan told her, "You will not surely die." Satan was trying to convince her that God really would not punish disobedience like He had promised. Satan knew that God punished sin. That is why he was not in heaven anymore, because of his selfish choice.

Right after that, Satan suggested that God was only saying this because He was selfish or jealous. Satan told her, "God knows that when you eat of it your eyes will be opened, and you will be like God, knowing good and evil." So, Satan made selfish choices and he tried to persuade the woman to be selfish also. After all, Satan reasoned to her, God is selfish and would be jealous of you if you were just like Him.

In the end, Satan wanted the man and woman to doubt what God said, to deny what God promised, and to believe that God was selfish. Satan persuaded the woman to believe these lies. She ate of the fruit from the tree of the knowledge of good and evil. Then, she gave some to her husband and he also ate with her.

Praise and Worship

Praise and Worship styles vary greatly around the world. It is the intent of this curriculum that praise and worship songs be selected that best fit the content of this lesson. Recommendations for praise and worship are given and this music can generally be located at www.itunes.com. However, the teacher can feel free to select a similar praise and worship song.

"You Are God Alone" by Christ for the Nations Music is recommended for this lesson.

Bible Activity

Narrator: Adam and the woman had been given a beautiful garden to live in, with lovely trees and flowers, animals of all kinds, and lots of good food to eat. These were all good gifts from their loving creator, God. God had told them they could eat from every tree of the garden except for one. If they ate from the forbidden tree, God said they would surely die.

The scene begins with Adam and the woman walking around in the garden, talking about all the lovely things God has created, especially the wonderful fruit trees. (Encourage the children to be creative as they notice things on their walk, they love to use their imagination!)

Narrator: One day, as they were walking through the garden, a beautiful serpent appeared and began to talk to the woman. What she didn't know was that Satan, God's evil enemy, was actually speaking THROUGH the serpent. He was going to try to trick her and Adam into disobeying God.

The serpent, followed closely by Satan, enters the scene. Satan leans over the serpent (to show it is really Satan who is talking through the serpent) and says: "Did God really say you couldn't eat any fruit in the garden?"

The woman (innocently): "Oh no, we can eat from any tree in the garden, except the one in the middle. God said don't eat from it or even touch it or we will die."

Teacher Helps

Bible Activity

To review the lesson, children will "act out" the story in dramatic fashion. The teacher needs to coach the children all through the process, and practice several times. The narrator can read his/her part if he/she is old enough, or the narrator can be played by an adult.

Drama Parts:
- Adam
- The woman
- Serpent
- Satan
- Narrator

Satan (in a very convincing voice): "You won't die! God knows that the day you eat from it your eyes will be opened and you'll be like Him, knowing good and evil."

Narrator: The woman looked at the fruit and smiled. She thought about what Satan had said. Of course she didn't know it was Satan, she thought the serpent was her friend. She believed the lies and doubted the words of God. Then she reaches out her hand and picks the fruit. (If possible, bring a real piece of fruit to use as a prop. The Bible doesn't say what the fruit was, so use whatever is readily available to you.) After taking a bite, she hands it to Adam. He smiles and takes a bite. Suddenly they look very afraid. As the narrator describes the scenario, the characters should do the actions described.

The woman: Oh Adam, what have we done?! I feel so ashamed!

Adam: I feel the same way, woman! How could we have doubted what God told us? We can't let God see us like this! (Adam and woman run off the stage, looking scared).

Memory Verse

Genesis 3:6 (ESV) - She took of its fruit and ate, and she also gave some to her husband who was with her, and he ate.

4) Review the Lesson

This lesson revolves around three main facts:

1. Satan took the form of a serpent and spoke to the woman in the Garden of Eden.

2. Satan misquoted God's words and caused the woman to doubt that God would really punish her. Satan also suggested that God was selfish and jealous.

3. The woman ate the forbidden fruit and influenced her husband to eat also. This was the beginning of human sin and we refer to it as "the fall."

Bible Memory Activity

The teacher should think of motions to go along with the memory verse. Motions fit most naturally with action words in the verse. One or two actions per phase is sufficient. Motions will help children remember the verse and can be used as reminders by the teacher as reminders as the class is learning the verse.

Review Activity

Tell children to write down one main thing that they learned from this lesson. Then, have them share with one person in the class.

5) Apply the Lesson

Key concept: Ask kids, **"Do you think there is anyone in this class that has never sinned or disobeyed God?"**

Eight essential truths emerge from the Bible's Story of Hope. From this story in the Bible, we learn that God judges sin.

1. <u>God</u>. In the beginning, there was a very powerful God.

2. <u>Man</u>. God created people to be His special friends.

3. <u>Sin</u>. Man and woman disobeyed God.

4. <u>Death</u>. God punished man and woman for their disobedience. Death, in the Bible, refers to separation.

5. <u>Christ</u>. God sent His one and only Son who lived a perfect life.

6. <u>Cross</u>. Jesus died on the cross for the sins of the world.

7. <u>Faith</u>. If anyone places their faith in Christ, God welcomes them.

8. <u>Life</u>. God gives eternal life to those who put their faith in Him.

Story Line: Satan tempted Adam and the woman. They disobeyed God.

Teacher Helps

Review Activity (continued)

what they learned. They should write down each new thing they add to what somebody learned in the class. Repeat this process several times. Then, form a master list of what the kids learned from the lesson.

Key Concept

The teacher does not need to ask for specifics of sin. The teacher only needs to help children understand that they have said or done something that God will judge.

Adventure Number 8
Genesis 3:7-13 and Genesis 5:5

Story Line: Sin separated Adam and the woman from God.

1) Study the Lesson (before class)

- When God speaks of death, He is really speaking about separation. Three kinds of death happen as a result of sin: spiritual death, physical death, and an eternal death.

- The opening of Genesis 3:7 forces the reader to examine the meaning of death. The serpent's promise of eyes that would be opened came true in its fashion.[1]

- The shame that they experienced was a direct result of their sin.

- Adam and the woman tried to cover themselves with fig leaves that they had sewn together, but God had a different and better plan for them.

- In the evening, God spoke to Adam and the woman. They hid from God, probably because of the great amount of guilt they felt.

- Adam and the woman were foolish to think they could escape from God. God and Adam had a conversation in which God asked who had told Adam that he had no clothes. He also asked if they had eaten from the tree. God was not ignorant of these facts, He knew they had eaten and that they were naked.

- Adam blamed God. As the woman had been given him for his companion and help, he had eaten of the tree out of love for her; and perceiving she was ruined, was determined not to survive her.[2]

- When Adam and the woman sinned, it was not merely that they ate of the fruit. It was their love of self and their dishonor of God that brought shame on them.

- Choosing the created thing rather than the Creator resulted in sin.

Footnotes - Adventure 8

1. Derek Kidner, *Genesis*, 69.

2. Robert Jamieson, A.R. Fausset, and David Brown, *Jamieson-Fausset-Brown Bible Commentary*, Genesis 1.

2) Begin the Lesson

- As we discuss what happened in Scripture, we will talk about periods of time or eras. This will help us know what happened and in what time frame it happened. It is very difficult to put dates on Biblical events so we have not done that. However, we will learn periods of time.

- What was the first beginnings we studied? (creation)

- What were some of the themes that we learned from the period of time we call creation? (God is strong. God made all things. God made people to be His special friends.)

- What other period of time have we discussed? (fall)

- What are some of the lessons that we learned from the period of time we call the fall? (Satan was thrown out of heaven, Satan tempted Adam and Eve, and Adam and Eve sinned.)

3) Teach the Lesson

Ask children, **"If Satan tempts you, can you resist his temptations? What is the best way to avoid temptation?"** Ask children to give an explanation for their answers.

Ask children, **"What are some ways in which Satan tempts you?"** Help children see that everyone is tempted by Satan to disobey God.

Teacher Helps

Chronology of the Bible

The Table of Contents, located at the begining of the curriculum has a complete list of all periods of time or eras in the Bible. For the complete list, turn to the Table of Contents. For the current period of time or era, look at the bottom of any page and the teacher will see where this adventure is on the timeline of events. In this lesson, the timeline is "Beginnings".

As the grand story is told, the timeline or chronology of events becomes very important. The teacher and the student will see the Bible's Big Story more clearly.

Tell the Story

Satan did it. He convinced Adam and Eve to disobey God. When Satan told them, "You won't die," he knew he was lying to them. He knew man and woman were going to die but he convinced them that they wouldn't die. He also convinced Adam and the woman that God didn't really tell them not to eat from the tree of the knowledge of good and evil.

Immediately, Adam and the woman knew they had done wrong. They felt guilty and tried to hide from God. They even tried to make clothes for themselves out of fig leaves. How silly! They were the only ones in the garden of Eden but they tried to make clothes out of fig leaves. It did not work. In the evening, they thought they could hide from God. That was because they felt guilty for the disobedience they had committed. God called out and asked them where they were. He knew where they were, He only wanted to hear their response. He could have gone right to them and talked to them but He wanted them to come forward, talk to Him directly, and admit their sin.

God asked Adam another question, "Who told you that you were naked?" Again, God knew the answer to this question but He wanted Adam and his wife to come forward and talk to Him directly. God knew that Satan, or the serpent, had tempted them to do wrong. God never tempts anyone to do wrong. Only Satan does that.

Then, God asked the woman this question, "What is this that you have done?" Again, God knew the answer to this question but He wanted the woman to come forward and talk to Him directly. This time, the woman got it right. She told God that the serpent tempted her and she ate. But that was not the whole story. It was true that the serpent tempted her but the woman was blaming the serpent for her sin. That was wrong. God wanted her to admit her wrong to Him. Instead, she blamed the serpent. She hoped that God would accept her explanation. But, as with the fig leaves, God did not accept her explanation.

So, the man and woman lived for awhile longer and then they died. They died because of their sin. It was not God's will that either of them should die. They were supposed to live forever. But their disobedience in the garden of Eden came with a punishment and that punishment was death. Death in the Bible refers to separation, separation from God. Those who die in sin will never again be able to live with God in perfect peace in heaven. Death was the punishment for their disobedience. Separation from God was that punishment.

Teacher Helps

Read out loud the Bible passage for today, Genesis 3:7-13 and 5:5. Ask children to volunteer to listen for any mention of God, man, the woman, and the serpent. When they hear something, have them raise their hand and volunteer: what is going on right now?

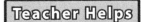

Praise and Worship

Praise and Worship styles vary greatly around the world. It is the intent of this curriculum that praise and worship songs be selected that best fit the content of this lesson. Recommendations for praise and worship are given and this music can generally be located at www.itunes.com. However, the teacher can feel free to select a similar praise and worship song.

"You Are God Alone" by Christ for the Nations Music is recommended for this lesson.

Bible Activity

Discuss these True or False statements with the children. Let them answer each question and tell you whether it is True or False. If they answer False, have the children tell you why it is False.

The tempter, Satan, will cast doubt on the character of God. He will suggest that God is withholding something good from us.

The tempter, Satan, will not tell us about the consequences of our disobedience.

The tempter, Satan, will try to minimize Who God is and what He expects from us.

The tempter, Satan, will deceive us into thinking we can become like God.

Satan's promises always come true.

God will always punish sin or disobedience.

Satan wants us to doubt God's Word and His goodness.

Bible Activity

Have children answer these true/false questions. Let them explain their answer, if time permits. The correct answer is underlined.

T or F

T or F

T or F

T or F

T or F

T or F

T or F

Memory Verse

Romans 5:12 (ESV) - Therefore, just as through one man sin entered the world, and death through sin, and thus death spread to all men, because all sinned.

Teacher Helps

Bible Memory Activity

Write words of the verse on a piece of paper using large letters. Cut the verse into individual phrases or words. Hide the strips around the room, out of view. Review the verse a few times. Let the children find the pieces. As they find them, let them gather in front of the room and place themselves in the proper order. Read the verse aloud.

4) Review the Lesson

Let's do a skit to review today's lesson. Have one child be the voice of God asking these three questions: 1) Where are you? 2) Who told you that you were naked? and 3) What is this that you have done?

- Have one child do a reenactment of how Satan tempted Adam and the woman.

- Have one boy be Adam and give the response that Adam gave.

- Have one girl be the woman and give the response she gave.

- You can read the story from the Bible and let the kids do the reenactment or drama of the story.

Review Skit

Let kids volunteer for the various roles in this skit: the voice of God, the serpent, Adam, and the woman. Coach the kids to make their skit look real or believable to the other kids.

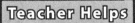

5) Apply the Lesson

Ask kids, **"Last week we talked about the eight essential truths from the Bible's Story of Hope. Do you remember those eight truths?"**

1. <u>God</u>. In the beginning, there was a very powerful God.

2. <u>Man</u>. God created people to be His special friends.

3. <u>Sin</u>. Man and woman disobeyed God.

4. <u>Death</u>. God punished man and woman for their disobedience. Death, in the Bible, refers to separation.

5. <u>Christ</u>. God sent His one and only Son who lived a perfect life.

6. <u>Cross</u>. Jesus died on the cross for the sins of the world.

7. <u>Faith</u>. If anyone places their faith in Christ, God welcomes them.

8. <u>Life</u>. God gives eternal life to those who put their faith in Him.

Death, or separation from God, is the essential truth that this lesson tells us about. God does not want you to be separated from Him. Yet, Satan will tempt you to do wrong. Satan will tempt you to disobey God. When Satan tempts you to do wrong, ignore His bad advice, and listen to God. God is always truthful and Satan will not tell you the whole truth. Practice listening to God in His Word and submitting to Him in obedience.

Story Line: Sin separated Adam and the woman from God.

Apply the Lesson Activity

Have children divide up into two teams. Have each team match the truth with the definition of the truth. For instance, "God" would be matched with "In the beginning, there was a very powerful God." "Man" would be matched with "God created people to be His special friends."

Time the kids. Winning team gets a prize. You may want to do this two or three times. Allow enough time for all to participate.

Adventure Number 9

Genesis 3:14-15

Story Line: God promised to send a special person who would crush Satan.

 ## 1) Study the Lesson (before class)

- Three punishments were given. The first punishment was for the serpent. The second punishment was for the woman. The third punishment was for Adam.

- The curse fell upon the serpent for having tempted the woman.

- The serpent wounds the heel that crushes him; and so Satan would be permitted to afflict the humanity of Christ and bring suffering and persecution on His people. The serpent's poison is lodged in its head; and a bruise on that part would be fatal. Christ's blow to Satan would be fatal.[1]

- The phrase "you will strike his heel" refers to Satan's repeated attempts to defeat Christ during his life on earth. 'He will strike your head' foreshadows Satan's defeat when Christ rose from the dead. A strike on the heel is not deadly, but a blow to the head is.[2]

- God told them of the continual struggle between satanic forces and people. The "offspring" of the serpent includes demons and anyone who serves the kingdom of darkness. The offspring of the woman would be someone born from her descendants.

- Adam and the woman's punishments show how seriously God views sin of any kind.

- The book of Genesis contains many stories of lives ruined by the serpent.

Footnotes - Adventure 9

1. Ibid, Genesis 3.

2. James Galvin, *Life Application Bible Notes*, 12.

2) Begin the Lesson

Teacher Helps

Let's think back over the last eight lessons that we have studied and see if we can put the lessons in order. Here are the themes for the first eight lessons:

- 1) God is very strong.
- 2) God created angels.
- 3) God made everything.
- 4) God made man and woman to be His special friends.
- 5) Life in the garden was full of pleasure.
- 6) Satan is God's enemy. Satan was proud. God threw Satan out of heaven.
- 7) Satan tempted Adam and Eve. Adam and Eve disobeyed God.
- 8) Sin separated Adam and Eve from God.

The teacher should write these eight statements on cards and then mix them up. Divide the children into 2 or 3 teams, depending on the size of the class. Time how long it takes each team to put the eight statements in the correct order. Do not number the slips of paper.

3) Teach the Lesson

Victory and winning are special times. Everyone loves to win and almost no one likes to lose. Ask children, **"What are some special times that you can remember when your team has won? What was it like? When are some times when your team lost? How did you feel?"**

This lesson is about a wonderful victory. It is the victory of a very special Person who will deliver a crushing blow to the tempter, Satan himself.

Many children already know who this special person is; of course, it is Jesus Christ. This lesson is very significant for children to understand the one story of the Bible. Now, we begin to see the plan of God to deliver His special friends from death.

Tell the Story

Imagine what it would be like to live in a perfect home. Nothing ever went wrong and everybody was happy. This place would be a fun place full of great times ... no bad things would ever happen. That is how life was for Adam and his wife. God had given them a few instructions. All of God's instructions were easy to do.

But, when the tempter tempted Adam and the woman, they both sinned and God had to punish them for that sin. They gave up a lot when they did this awful thing. When God judged them for their sin, He not only judged them, He judged the one who started the whole thing, Satan.

The first judgment was on Satan. God did not ask him any questions and God did not tolerate anything from this tempter. In fact, God declared war on Satan at this time. His judgment on Satan was that one day, Satan would be crushed and forever lose this battle of disobeying God and causing others to do the same. Not only did God declare war on Satan, God caused a curse to come on Satan. When God causes a curse to come on someone, He does not change His mind. As God pronounced judgment on Satan, Adam and the woman listened and it gave them hope. There was some really good news. God was going to send someone who would crush Satan. It would be one of their offspring. They felt awful about sinning. But now, God gave them a lot of hope. This began the Bible's big story of hope. It was the first time in all of the Bible that God gave a prophecy and when He did, it was awesome!

After God finished dealing with Satan, He turned to the woman and told her what her punishment would be ... not near as severe, but still there would be punishment. Bearing children would be difficult. There would be sorrow in what should have been her greatest delight ... having children. Also, now man would rule over her and sometimes she would not enjoy it.

Lastly, God issued His punishment against Adam. There was going to be lots of hard work that was very unrewarding. In the past, there was hard work but it was always very rewarding ... you might even say it was fun. Not now. Not only that, but God told Adam that he would die and return to the ground. He was given life from the ground and now that life would be taken from him. It was an announcement of death. It was not supposed to be like that. Adam and Eve were going to live forever and be happy. Now, work was hard and someday they were going to die.

Teacher Helps

Tell the Story Activity: The Throne and the Three Judgments

The teacher should designate a chair to be a "throne." Maybe bring in a special cloth to cover the chair. Invite a special speaker to come in and be the voice of God. He should not be seen. This person is to issue three judgments:

1) To the serpent

2) To the woman

3) To the man

The teacher should get volunteers for the serpent, the woman, and the man. They should react with fear when their judgment is pronounced.

Memory Verse

Genesis 3:15 (ESV)- I will put enmity between you and the woman, and between your offspring and her offspring; he shall bruise your head, and you shall bruise his heel."

Bible Memory Activity

Review the verse a few times then divide the children into two or more teams. Have the teams form lines across from a chalk or white board or piece of paper on a chair. Place something to write with at the board in front of each team. Have the first child of each team run to the board and write the first word of the verse, then run back to the line. The next child of the team will write the next word and it will continue until the verse is completed. Allow all teams to finish before playing again.

Praise and Worship

Praise and Worship styles vary greatly around the world. It is the intent of this curriculum that praise and worship songs be selected that best fit the content of this lesson. Recommendations for praise and worship are given and this music can generally be located at www.itunes.com. However, the teacher can feel free to select a similar praise and worship song.

"You Are God Alone" by Christ for the Nations Music is recommended for this lesson.

Bible Activity

Fishing for Snakes

Have a bag full of various objects. The student should reach into the bag and try to fish out something from the bag of various objects. One of the things that should be in the bag is a snake. The snake should be a cartoon snake, not a real snake. Go fishing and pull up various things that you have put in the bag. When you pull the snake out of the bag, have someone imitate the snake tempting Adam and Eve to sin. Now tell the kids that Satan is trying to get everyone to fish for him and follow what he says. God wants us to resist temptation and not give in to Satan. Adam and the woman did not do this.

Bible Activity: Fishing for Snakes

The teacher may want to put several toy snakes in the bag and let each snake offer a new temptation for the children to do wrong. Temptations such as lying, stealing, or cheating could be used.

4) Review the Lesson

Agree/Disagree Statements (If you disagree, why do you disagree?)

1. God punished the serpent. (Agree)

2. God said there would be war between the woman's descendant and Satan's descendant. (Agree)

3. Satan will bruise the woman's descendant's head and the woman's descendant will crush Satan's heel. (Disagree. Satan will bruise the woman's descendant's heel and the woman's descendant will crush Satan's head)

4. The descendant of this woman will be a male. (Agree)

5. The man and woman understood immediately how awful the consequences of their sin were. (Disagree. It would take many years and even then they would not fully understand it all.)

6. God said the woman would experience pain and suffering when her babies were born. (Agree)

7. Man would not have to work hard for his food to grow. (Disagree. He would have to work very hard.)

Review Activity: Agree and Disagree Statements

Kids will have fun disagreeing or agreeing with these seven statements. You may want to make up some statements of your own for them to agree or disagree with.

5) Apply the Lesson

Sin separates us from God. The evil one will try to convince us that his way is better than or different from God's way. But God has provided a "Satan Crusher." That person is Jesus Christ Who conquered death. If anyone will put their faith in Jesus Christ, the "Satan Crusher," Jesus Christ will welcome them and love them. You can put your faith and trust in the great "Satan Crusher."

Apply the Lesson Activity

The teacher may want to give more explanation from the New Testament that Jesus is that "Satan Crusher."

<u>Verses to look up are:</u>

- 1 Corinthians 15:57

- Romans 5:12-21

- John 11:25

Adventure Number 10
Genesis 3:16-19

Story Line: Sin affected God's creation in many negative ways.

1) Study the Lesson (before class)

- Adam and the woman learned from personal experience that God is holy and that He hates sin.
- The rest of the Bible contains accounts of people's experiences who have been affected by sin.
- The childbearing experience for a woman may have pain even if the woman had not sinned. But now, because of the sin, the pain in childbearing would increase significantly.
- Part of the woman's punishment would be frustration in her relationship to her husband. She would seek to dominate him and they would have problems because of this. Before the sin of Adam and the woman, this would not have happened.
- God does not tell Adam to dominate his wife. But, because of their sin, there would be conflict in their marriage relationship.
- God does not pronounce judgment on Adam for listening to his wife. Scripture is full of advice for the man to listen to his wife. (Genesis 21:12; Judges 13:23; 2 Kings 4:9-10)
- Adam was to gain his livelihood by tilling the ground; but what he did before the fall, he did with ease and pleasure. After the fall, it was painful and difficult work.[1]
- It is better to translate the verse "Your desire was for your husband." Having overstepped her bounds in this, she would now be mastered by him.[2]

Footnotes - Adventure 10

1. Robert Jamieson, A.R. Fausset, and David Brown, *Jamieson-Fausset-Brown Bible Commentary*, Genesis 3.

2. John Walvoord and Roy Zuck, *Bible Knowledge Commentary: Old Testament*, 33.

2) Begin the Lesson

In this lesson, we will learn what was lost in the Garden of Eden because of sin. Let's remember what life was like in the garden <u>before</u> Adam and Eve sinned.

1) Paradise

2) Close personal relationship with God

3) Protected place

4) Delight, pleasure, and abundance

5) No sin

6) Peace and harmony

7) Lots of freedom

8) Work that was not hard to do

Teacher Helps

Life in the Garden Activity

Children can review with the teacher what they remember about the Garden of Eden. This list is a few of the things that happened in the garden. The teacher may ask the kids to tell words or descriptions of "what life was like in the Garden of Eden before the sin of Adam and Eve."

Review Lesson #5.

3) Teach the Lesson

Prepare a bulls eye target. Form teams of 5 to 7 from your class. Ask them to throw a soft object at the bulls eye target. Have each team stand right in front of the target when they throw the soft object at the target. Then, repeat the same process from ten feet from the target. Then, repeat the same process from twenty feet. Whoever misses the target has to sit down. By now, the entire class should be sitting down.

Explain to the class that sin is missing the mark. None of us are able to hit the mark every time. Sometimes, all of us miss the mark. That is how the Bible defines sin; it is missing the mark of God's perfection or holiness.

Teachers can use a target like this one to illustrate "missing the mark."

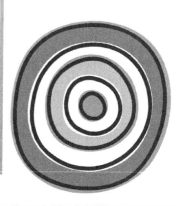

Tell the Story

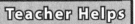

Imagine this ... it really happened! God had just finished talking to Satan about his future. One day, a Person would come who would deliver a death blow to the tempter, Satan himself. Satan had to know that God would one day defeat and crush him.

But, right after that, God spoke to Adam and Eve. Satan had tempted them and Satan would be ultimately punished with death. Adam and Eve would also have to bear the burden of their sin. God had some punishments for them also. He spoke first to the woman about her punishment. Then, He spoke directly to the man and told him about His punishment. So, God was not afraid to tell Satan, the woman, or the man that He would punish their sin. Each punishment was different but each one would surely happen. God always punishes sin.

Let's look at the woman's punishment first. God disciplined Eve in two separate ways. First, He told her that she would have pain when she gave birth to children. What God originally wanted was for women to have pain free child birth. Children would always be a gift from God. Having children was not the discipline. Having pain in child birth was the punishment. The second discipline was totally different. It had to do with her relationship with her husband, Adam. The painful consequence of her sin was that she would now respect the man's leadership in the home. Before her sin, there was mutual leadership in the home between the man and the woman but not now.

For the man, his work would now be difficult and hard. Before the sin of the Adam, it was easy and enjoyable, like playing your favorite game, but not now. God also told him that he would return to the ground or that Adam would die. Before Adam sinned, he would not have died and he would have lived forever, but not now. The painful consequence of his sin was that he and everyone who lived after him would return to the ground or die as a punishment for sin. When God says that we will return to the ground or die, it does not mean just going down into the ground after we die, like in a cemetery. It means that all who sin will be punished with eternal separation from God.

We will talk more about sin and God's punishment for sin. But for right now, we should remember that God always punishes sin. We determine when or if we will sin, God determines the consequences of our sin which is eternal separation from Him in a very bad place.

Marriage Conflict Activity

At this point in the lesson, bring in an adult couple who are arguing in front of the kids. Let them argue with each other for a few minutes. Then point out to your class that this is one of the negative effects of sin. It should not be this way. In marriage, by God's design, a husband and a wife should be loving and kind.

Memory Verse

Romans 8:20 (ESV) - For the creation was subjected to futility, not willingly, but because of him who subjected it, in hope.

Praise and Worship

Praise and Worship styles vary greatly around the world. It is the intent of this curriculum that praise and worship songs be selected that best fit the content of this lesson. Recommendations for praise and worship are given and this music can generally be located at www.itunes.com. However, the teacher can feel free to select a similar praise and worship song.

"He Is Good" by Steve Green is recommended for this lesson.

Bible Activity

One Bad Apple

You will need a ping pong ball or other small ball, slips of paper, a pencil, and yarn or masking tape. Write "A" or "B" on a slip of paper for each child. Fold the slips of paper and place them in a cup or other container. Use the yarn or masking tape to create two equal sized circles on the floor. Circles should be about the size of a dinner plate. The goal of this game is to blow the ball into the circle matching the letter that you just drew. You've got to work with your partner to blow the ball into your circle. Work in teams of two and see if you can hit the mark every time or see if you miss the mark. The teacher should give the two person team about one minute to blow the ball into the circle.

Sin is missing the mark like when we miss the circle with our ping pong ball.

Teacher Helps

Memory Verse Activity: Bean Bag Toss

With masking tape, mark off a large square on the floor, about 36 inches. Connect the opposite corners inside the square with tape to form an "X." If you have space and many students, make a second square. Give each section a number value (1,2,3,4). A bit of a distance away, put a line of tape to mark where the student will throw from. Divide into two teams. Each student takes a turn throwing a bean bag into one of the sections. (You may make a bean bag by putting beans in a sock and closing it tight with a rubber band. Take the long part of the sock and fold it over the bean section.) If they can say the verse correctly, their team scores the amount of the section where the bean bag was thrown.

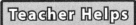

4) Review the Lesson

In one minute, name all the bad things you can list about this world and life in it.

Then, have children cross out the bad things that did not exist in God's paradise garden prior to Adam and the woman's sin.

Review the Lesson Activity: One Minute List

The teacher should write the list down on the board where every child can see the list. Let all kids suggest something, if possible.

5) Apply the Lesson

Understanding consequences is the application for this lesson. You do not choose the consequences for sin, God does. You make the choice to obey Him or disobey Him. As a righteous Judge, He will allow the right consequence for your actions ... besides the judgment He might bring.

In your home, what are some consequences that your parents give when you make the right choice?

In your home, what are some consequences that your parents give when you make the wrong choice?

When anyone sins, there are bad consequences for this choice.

> **Story Line: Sin affected God's creation in many negative ways.**

Adventure Number 11
Genesis 3:7, 21

Story Line: God killed an innocent animal to give clothes to Adam and Eve.

1) Study the Lesson (before class)

- After Adam and the woman rebelled against God, they felt guilt and shame.

- Their guilty feelings made them try to hide from God.

- Adam and the woman tried to cover themselves with fig leaves. They were sure that God knew everything but they still tried to hide their guilt.

- When Adam and the woman tried to cover themselves with fig leaves, they wrongly assumed that this would ease their feelings of guilt.

- The serpent promised that their eyes would be opened but what did they see? Not what the serpent had promised.

- The promise of divine enlightenment that the serpent had promised did not happen.

- Wisdom is never achieved by disobeying God.

- When God made clothes for Adam and the woman, He was showing them that He still loved and cared for them even though they had rebelled against what He wanted them to do.

- Biblical narratives seldom announce what conclusions we are supposed to draw from them, leaving us to draw lessons from the way thoughts are posed. It seems reasonable to conclude that God's response to Adam's faith was to deliberately cover their shame in a way that pleased Him more than Adam's effort to cover it.[1]

- This passage is a perfect case study on temptation. Sin cannot be blamed on environment or heredity.[2]

Footnotes - Adventure 11

1. David Brooks, *The Roots of Faith Old Testament Commentary* (Harrisburg: Good Soil Publications, 2013), COM-39.

2. John Walvoord and Roy Zuck, *Bible Knowledge Commentary: Old Testament*, 32.

2) Begin the Lesson

Have the children list all of the bad news that Adam and the woman had just experienced

- Pain in child bearing
- Conflicts in marriage
- Pain and hard labor for Adam's earth tilling job
- Adam and the woman would die physically
- Earth's perfect balance was now upset

How would many people react to such bad news?

- Shock
- Anger
- Despair
- Rebellion

The teacher should tell the class, **"Now let's see in today's lesson how Adam and the woman responded to such bad news."**

3) Teach the Lesson

Why do you think God did not accept the fig leaves that Adam and the woman made to clothe themselves? What do you think happened to those leaves after a few days?

Describe what you will say to God when He wants you to give an account of your life.

Tell the Story

What a tremendous success Satan was. He tempted Adam and the woman to sin and they sinned. All of Satan's followers must have been clapping and loving the temptation of somebody else. And Satan's success went even further. Adam and the woman tried to clothe themselves with fig leaves. Have you ever tried to wear leaves for clothes? Well, it is not fun and it certainly is not comfortable. Those leaves had to scratch and hurt but it was all that Adam and the woman could think of to do. Satan's followers must have been laughing now. They must have thought Adam and Eve were doing something very ridiculous.

Then, God pronounced His judgments on Satan, the woman, and Adam. Nobody was laughing then. There was not anything funny about that. In fact, Satan must have felt doomed. His followers must have felt defeated also. Even Adam and the woman had to feel awful. When God brought judgment on Satan, Satan knew that the party of tempting people and getting away with it would one day be over.

Then, God went even further to help the man and his wife. He made comfortable clothes for them. No more fig leaves that hurt and itched. These clothes were the best of clothes. An animal had to die for this to happen. It was the first time that an animal ever died, but it made Adam and Eve very happy to have clothes that fit and clothes that were comfortable.

But, even more important than comfortable clothes, they learned something very important about God. They learned that God was merciful and forgiving. They learned that even though they would be punished for their sin, that God still loved them and would provide for them. This gave them hope ... great hope! God was trying to show them that Satan was doomed and would one be crushed. But, that was not their destiny. God loved them and provided for them.

At about the same time, Adam named his wife. She would be called Eve. Her name means "life-giver." Adam knew that she would be the mother of all living. Adam had named all the animals but not his own wife. Now, he had hope in God and so much hope that he named his wife a very special name. They must have argued a lot after they sinned. They must have told each other who was at fault for the sin; in fact, Adam even told God that it was the woman that He gave him that caused him to sin. Now, he was not accusing Eve or even blaming her. He was blessing her and they were happy.

Teacher Helps

The Faith Journey of Adam

Adam named his wife, Eve. Up to this point, she was just called "woman." The name "Eve" means "life-giver." This was an act of faith on the part of Adam. If he had responded in despair or even doubt, he might have named the woman one of these names:

- Hopeless
- Bitter
- Failure
- Pain
- Problem

But he didn't. He called her "life-giver."

Memory Verse

Genesis 3:21 – Also for Adam and his wife the Lord God made tunics of skin, and clothed them.

Praise and Worship

Praise and Worship styles vary greatly around the world. It is the intent of this curriculum that praise and worship songs be selected that best fit the content of this lesson. Recommendations for praise and worship are given and this music can generally be located at www.itunes.com. However, the teacher can feel free to select a similar praise and worship song.

"He Is Good" by Steve Green is recommended for this lesson.

Bible Activity

1. Bring 2 kinds of leaves: nice & fresh, green, and also old & dried up, brittle.

2. Next, show a piece of leather or animal fur. Ask: "Would this make a better pair of pants than the leaves? (or dress or shirt, whatever your class can relate to) Why? Where did this come from? Talk about how an animal had to give its life to provide a proper covering for Adam and Eve. This is called a sacrifice. All through the Old Testament God required that an animal be killed as a sacrifice to cover the sins of people. If Adam and Eve had not sinned, the animal would not have died. Sin always has bad consequences.

Missing Words

On a chalk or white board write the verse to be learned, leaving blanks for words you have left out. Along the side list all the words omitted from the verse to give them choices. Ask one student at a time to write a word in the proper blank. Repeat until the verse is completed. Repeat several times until all children have the verse memorized.

Teacher Helps

Bible Memory Activity: Word Scramble

Put each word on a piece of paper and scramble all the words or pieces of paper. Have children unscramble the words by putting them in the correct order.

4) Review the Lesson

This is the first time in the Bible that an animal had to die to make provision for people. In the future, we will talk about other animals that had to die for people.

In their shame and guilt, Adam and Eve tried to cover themselves with fig leaves, but God provided better clothes, clothes that were made from animals.

5) Apply the Lesson

Since God is such a great Provider, name 2 or 3 ways that He has provided for you or someone you know.

Now, pick one of those ways and tell a friend or family member how God has provided for you. Practice by telling someone in your class or your teacher how God has provided for you.

When the class comes together next time, tell others what the response of your friends or family members was when you told them how God has provided for you.

Teacher Helps

Comparison Activity

Ask children to compare what they can do really well with what God can do really well. Make two lists.

The conclusion that the teacher wants to make here is that God is able to provide for people much better than people are able to provide for people. Like Adam, we must trust God.

Adventure Number 12
Genesis 3:22-24

> **Story Line:** God hates sin. God expelled Adam and Eve from the garden because of sin.

 ## 1) Study the Lesson (before class)

- Living in the garden of Eden was like living in heaven. It was perfect. If Adam and Eve had not disobeyed, they could have continued to live in the garden of Eden. Adam and Eve were expelled from the garden as the punishment for their sin.
- To make sure they stayed out of the garden, God put armed guards at the gate of the entrance.
- The reason why God expelled Adam and Eve from the garden of Eden was because of their sin.
- Adam and Eve were sent to a place of toil, not a place of torment.
- Eve either loosely quoted or misquoted what God told her. Jesus quoted the words of Scripture with reliability (Matt. 4:4, 7, 10).[1]
- The punishment was actually meant for man's good. Although he would be exposed to temporal death, he would not necessarily have to live eternally in his sin.
- God was displeased with Adam but God had mercy on Adam.
- The skin which God gave to Adam and Eve always reminded them of God's provision for them.
- Everything that was once so good was turned on its head. As we read on in the book of Genesis we find that murder, rape, disease, drunkenness, and death were further results of the sin of Adam and Eve.[2]

<u>Footnotes - Adventure 12</u>

1. John Walvoord and Roy Zuck, *Bible Knowledge Commentary: Old Testament*, 32.

2. Kurt Strassner, *Opening up Genesis: Opening Up Commentary* (Leominster: Day One Publications, 2009), Genesis 3.

2) Begin the Lesson

Teacher Helps

Lay out a game board for review that looks something like this:

Time Line	Story Line	Songs	Memory Verses
100 points	200 points	300 points	400 points
100 points	200 points	300 points	400 points
100 points	200 points	300 points	400 points
100 points	200 points	300 points	400 points
100 points	200 points	300 points	400 points

Begin the Lesson Activity: Bible Jeopardy

Divide the class evenly into two teams. The teams could be:

1) whoever has larger hands

2) whoever has smaller hands

This game will be continued with the review at end of the lesson.

Go back for each of the first 11 lessons and let the children name the time line for each lesson (100 points), the story line for each lesson (200 points), the song for each lesson (300 points), and the memory verse for each lesson (400 points).

A prize should be given to the winning team. Usually, competition is a fun thing for the children. So, keep them all involved. Depending on the size of your class, you may want to limit each child to only 1 or 2 answers. The reason for this is that a few children will answer all the questions, if you let them.

There will be a total of 11,000 points, 1000 points for each lesson.

3) Teach the Lesson

What have you done that needed punished? A loving father and mother will punish a child for doing something wrong but they will not kick you out of the family. That is exactly what God did. He removed His children from the garden as punishment but He did not remove His love from them.

Tell the Story

Adam had just named his wife. Her name was to be Eve for she would be the mother of all living people. This was an act of faith on Adam's part. Up to this point, Eve did not have a name; she was just called woman. Now, with God's provision of clothes, Adam named his wife, by faith. Remember, they had no children at this time.

Our story today takes place in three different scenes. The first scene occurs in heaven where God talks about how to punish sin. The second scene describes how God would punish sin. And the third scene shows us an amazing sword that was used by God's special angels, the cherubim.

Let's look at the first scene in heaven. God had to punish sin. In heaven, the Godhead discussed what would happen with Adam and Eve now. Their conclusion: it was not possible for them to continue with sin in the garden of Eden. They must be expelled. This discussion is amazing because we see that God wanted Adam and Eve to live forever but He also had to punish them for their disobedience.

Next, let's look at the scene on earth, outside the garden. The Lord God sent Adam and Eve out of the garden of Eden. They were banished from the land that they were to cultivate and develop. It was a beautiful garden and there was great peace, joy, and comfort in the garden. But now they were not allowed to live there anymore. Imagine having a beautiful home where there is love, joy, and peace. Then you have to leave this home forever. That would not feel good, would it? That must be how Adam and Eve felt. The garden was kind of like their sanctuary. It was where they worshipped God and served Him. They would still be able to do that but not like they had done so in the past.

Finally, let's look at the scene outside the garden at the entrance to it. At the end of the story, the special messengers from God, the cherubim guarded the entrance to the garden with a flaming sword that flashed back and forth. It would not be possible for Adam and Eve to reenter the garden. The cherubim with their flaming swords would not allow this to happen. The cherubim did what God told them to do.

God provided forgiveness for Adam and Eve but He also punished them for their disobedience by removing them from the garden.

Tell the Story Activity: Three Scenes

This story has three distinct different locations. To communicate this to your class, create three different locations in your classroom; and move the class to each scene.

If you have a large class, the teacher may want to move around to create three different locations instead of having the class move to different locations.

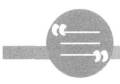
Memory Verse

Leviticus 19:2b – You shall be holy, for I the Lord your God am holy.

Praise and Worship

Praise and Worship styles vary greatly around the world. It is the intent of this curriculum that praise and worship songs be selected that best fit the content of this lesson. Recommendations for praise and worship are given and this music can generally be located at www.itunes.com. However, the teacher can feel free to select a similar praise and worship song.

"He Is Good" by Steve Green is recommended for this lesson.

Bible Activity

Ask: "**Have you ever seen a frog like this? The poison of this frog comes through its skin, much like a person would sweat. If you touch this frog, you WILL die! The amount of poison it takes to kill a person of about 150 pounds is equal to 2-3 grains of salt. That's not much!** Show salt and a glass of water. Explain: **this salt is not poison, but it only takes as much poison as this salt weighs to kill an adult, even less for a child. If I put this salt into a glass and stirred it up, could you even see it?**" (no) Demonstrate. "**You might not even be able to taste it, since it is such a small amount. Could someone lie to you and tell you that this water is perfectly pure?**" (yes) If you have a willing volunteer, let him/her drink some of the water; if not, the teacher should do this.

Lesson point : That's exactly what sin is like, it looks harmless, even beautiful like this dart frog. But hiding behind the part that shows is deadly poison! Not poison that will kill you physically every time, but that will separate you from God, your loving Creator. The devil is like the person who lies to you and tells you that it is perfectly all right to do this wrong thing; after all, everyone else is doing it! IT'S A LIE!!!! Don't listen to the enemy of your soul! Believe what God's word teaches about sin. It always has bad consequences!

Teacher Helps

Bible Memory Activity: Group Stand

After reviewing the verse, announce groups that are to stand and say the verse together. Say:

•All those wearing something green stand up and say this verse.

•All those who play soccer stand and say this verse.

•All those who are older than 2 …

Include opposites such as: All those who aren't wearing something green.

Bible Activity

If possible, show a picture of a poison dart frog called "Phyllobates Terribilis." This highly poisonous frog is found in Colombia, South America.

4) Review the Lesson

Continue your review game for points that you began at the start of the lesson.

- For 100 points, where does the first scene take place? (heaven)

- For 200 points, where does the second scene take place? (outside the garden)

- For 300 points, where does the third scene take place? (at the entrance outside the garden)

- For 400 points, what type of angels guarded the garden of Eden? (cherubim)

- Bonus question worth 500 points: What is the theme of this lesson? (God hates sin. God expelled Adam and Eve from the garden because of sin.)

Review the Lesson Activity: Bible Jeopardy

This review activity is a continuation of the review game at the beginning of the lesson.

5) Apply the Lesson

Eight essential truths emerge from the Bible's Story of Hope. From this story in the Bible, we learn that Adam and Eve broke their relationship with God and God expelled them from the garden because of that.

Adam and Eve broke their relationship with God and God expelled them from the Garden of Eden because of that. If you have broken your relationship with God in any way, you should begin to restore your relationship with God by acknowledging your disobedience to Him.

> **Story Line: God hates sin. God expelled Adam and Eve from the garden because of sin.**

Adventure Number 13
Genesis 4:1-12

> **Story Line: Cain and Abel responded to God in two very different ways.**

1) Study the Lesson (before class)

- Now, Eve has become the first human mother of all creation.

- Genesis chapter 4 is the story of a society without God.

- Adam and Eve had been promised a Person who would crush Satan in Genesis 3:15. In Genesis 4:1, Eve proclaims that she got a man from the Lord when she gave birth to her first son, Cain. Eve probably thought that Cain would be the one to crush Satan. Her anticipation was correct, her identification of the Satan crusher was wrong.[1]

- This chapter records the event which contrasts Abel, who offered an acceptable offering to God, with Cain, whose offering was unacceptable.

- Cain was a hard working farmer who brought an offering from his crops. Abel was a shepherd who brought an offering to the Lord from his flock. Both offerings seemed to be acceptable.

- Abel, the shepherd, offered to God what was the best offering that he could bring to God. It was the firstborn animal.

- The Scripture is silent when it comes to the quality of Cain's offering. Obviously, he did not bring his best offering. He brought an offering. But, unlike his younger brother, he did not bring the very best of what he had to offer.[2]

Footnotes - Adventure 13

1. David Brooks, *The Roots of Faith Old Testament Commentary*, COM-45.

2. Ibid., COM-45.

2) Begin the Lesson

Teacher Helps

The Bible's Top Ten

Do not let the kids go beyond where you are in telling the Bible's big story.

Possible suggestions might include:

10. Eve was the mother of all living people.

9. God promised to send a person who would crush Satan.

8. God's name (Elohim) means He is very powerful.

7. Adam and Eve tried to cover themselves with fig leaves after they sinned. But God clothed them with an animal's skin. An animal had to die.

6. God expelled Adam and Eve from the garden. He placed cherubim at the east entrance to guard the garden and a sword in the middle of the garden.

5. The angels were created to worship and serve God.

4. Satan started a rebellion in heaven and is continuing that rebellion on earth.

3. One third of the angels followed Satan in his rebellion.

2. Life in the garden of Eden was full of peace and pleasure.

1. God made all of creation.

Begin the Lesson Activity: The Bible's Top Ten

In this activity, the teacher will have kids review important ideas from previous lessons. There are no right and wrong answers. The teacher should ask the question, **"What are the top ten things you remember from the Bible up to this point?"**

3) Teach the Lesson

Introduction to Lesson 13: Cain and Abel

Ask children if they have ever had a time when they did not feel accepted by their friends. Have a few kids tell about a time when they did not feel accepted by their friends.

Ask the class if they have ever felt not accepted by God. The teacher could ask them, **"What does it take to be accepted by God?"**

Tell the Story

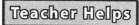

It was a wonderful day. Eve was going to be the first mom ever in all of history. God had told Adam to have children and now the day was coming when Adam and Eve would have their first child. They must have been so excited.

When the time came for Eve to give birth to her first child, a boy, she named him Cain which means "with the Lord's help, I have been given a man." Just a little while before, Adam and Eve were given the promise of a Person who would come to crush Satan. Because of the name they gave their first son, it appears that their anticipation was that Cain would crush Satan. As they would find out later, that would not be so. Later, Adam and Eve had another son. They named him Abel. We don't know why they named him Abel but they must have loved him also.

The boys grew up together. They probably enjoyed laughing and playing. They each had their own interests and strengths. The strength of Cain was that he was a good farmer. He knew how to till the ground and grow good vegetables and food to eat for the whole family. Abel grew up as a shepherd and was good at watching animals like sheep. God allowed each of them to have certain strengths, just like He has allowed you to have certain strengths.

The day came for Cain and Abel to bring an offering to God. There was a great difference in the offering that Cain brought and the offering that Abel brought. Cain brought some of his vegetables. It was an ordinary offering, not the best that Cain could bring. However, Abel brought the best of his flock to offer to the Lord. It was the firstborn and that was always considered the best or most important.

God was pleased with Abel because he brought an offering that was his best. God was not pleased with Cain because his offering was not the best that he could bring. Because God did not accept the offering from Cain, Cain got angry and killed his brother Abel. This made God very sad. God never likes it when we hurt other people. So, God had to punish Cain for this murder. He punished him by making him a wanderer. He would no longer be a farmer which was the thing he was so good at doing. God took this away from him. Cain did not like his punishment and thought that God was too harsh. Cain spent the rest of his life wandering around. He must have felt very sorry that he hurt his brother.

Tell the Story Activity: Contrast of Two Offerings

Bring two items with you to class today.

1) Bring one thing that is very valuable to you.

2) Bring one thing with you that is not very valuable.

After describing each item, have the class tell you which one would be a better offering to God.

Memory Verse

Genesis 4:7 (ESV) - If you do well, will you not be accepted? And if you do not do well, sin is crouching at the door. Its desire is for you, but you must rule over it.

Praise and Worship

Praise and Worship styles vary greatly around the world. It is the intent of this curriculum that praise and worship songs be selected that best fit the content of this lesson. Recommendations for praise and worship are given and this music can generally be located at www.itunes.com. However, the teacher can feel free to select a similar praise and worship song.

"He Is Good" by Steve Green is recommended for this lesson.

Bible Activity

Two Hearts Activity

Abel had a good heart and wanted to give God his best offering. Cain did not have a good heart and was willing to give God just any offering. This activity will show the kids how Cain and Abel had two different hearts.

1) Get two glasses. Fill one half full with water and fill the other glass half full with white vinegar. Tell the kids that these two glasses represent the hearts of Cain and Abel.

2) Put two or three drops of green food coloring in the white vinegar and stir it up. This glass represents Cain who was jealous of his brother and did not give God his best offering.

3) In the glass that is half full with water, put a teaspoon of baking soda. Nothing will happen.

4) Put a teaspoon of baking soda in the green vinegar glass. Watch the water as it bubbles over the edge of the class. Cain's heart did the same thing, only with jealousy because he did not bring his best offering to God.

Teacher Helps

Bible Memory Activity

Divide kids up into groups of 4-5 to work on memorizing the verse. You may choose to have teams by color (anybody wearing something green, red, or any other color). No more than 5 to a team.

Bible Activity: Two Hearts

The teacher will need to also bring cleaning supplies to take care of this potential mess.

4) Review the Lesson

The teacher should make two lists.

- The heading for the first list should read: Good Things To Do
- The heading for the second list should read: Best Things To Do

Let the kids discuss what are good things that we can do. Cain brought an offering to the Lord, but his heart was not right with God.

Then, let the kids discuss what are the best things that we can do. Abel brought an offering to the Lord; it was the best offering that he could bring.

Review the Lesson Activity: Good Things To Do (Possibilities)

- Go to church
- Don't cheat at school
- Don't lie to parents
- Talk about God

5) Apply the Lesson

- From the list of "Best Things To Do," select two or three of these and tell kids that you will ask them next week if they did them.
- "Best Things To Do" should be specific and achievable.
- Accountability to do what we learn is the key to any lesson. If the class knows that you are going to ask them about their response to your lesson, they are more likely to act on it.

Apply the Lesson Activity: Best Things To Do (Possibilities)

- Worship God on Sunday (and everyday)
- Be a godly friend at school
- Honor your parents all the time
- Witness for God

Story Line: Cain and Abel responded to God in two very different ways.

Adventure Number 14
Genesis 4:25-5:8

> **Story Line: Seth became the leader of a very godly family.**

 ## 1) Study the Lesson (before class)

- According to what Eve said, Seth was a provision from God. In other words, God provided a son for Adam and Eve whom God would use.

- Later, Seth also had a son. The name of this son was Enosh. It was at this time that men began to proclaim the name of the Lord.[1]

- Critics of the Bible say that the Bible is just a bunch of mythical stories. However, the genealogy of Genesis 5 and other genealogies in the Bible reveal that these are real people in real time living life in real places. They are not made up or fictional.

- Some people may ask why people lived so long in this era. It is probable that the effects of sin shortened the average lifespan of humans. Because there was a relatively short period of time for sin and its effects to become apparent, people lived longer.

- The name "Seth" actually means "substitute." The godly line of Seth was a substitute for the godliness of Abel, his older brother.

- There are two types of genealogies in Genesis, vertical (or linear) and horizontal (or branched). This genealogy is vertical, it shows that the last generation is related to the first generation.

- In Genesis 3, God condemned Adam to die. In Genesis 5, we read that Adam and his descendants died. God could be trusted: sin brought judgment.

- In the midst of judgment, there was grace. Enoch, the seventh man in the genealogy, did not die.[2]

Footnotes - Adventure 14

1. John Walvoord and Roy Zuck, *Bible Knowledge Commentary: Old Testament*, 35.

2. David Brooks, *The Roots of Faith Old Testament Commentary*, COM-50.

2) Begin the Lesson

Let's review the story lines from the previous adventures.

Adventure	Story Line
1	God is very strong.
2	God created angels.
3	God made everything.
4:	God made man and woman to be His special friends.
5	Life in the garden was full of pleasure.
6	Satan is God's enemy. Satan was proud. God threw Satan out of heaven.
7	Satan tempted Adam and the woman. Adam and his wife disobeyed God.
8	Sin separated Adam and the woman from God.
9	God promised to send a special Person who would crush Satan.
10	Sin affected God's creation in negative ways.
11	God killed an innocent animal to give clothes to Adam and his wife.
12	God hates sin. God expelled Adam and Eve from the garden because of sin.
13	Cain and Abel responded to God in two very different ways.

3) Teach the Lesson

Introduction to Lesson 14: Seth and His Family

Seth started a family that was godly and lived for the Lord. Can you name anybody in your family like that? Why?

Teacher Helps

Begin the Lesson Activity: Review by Themes

In this activity, the teacher will see how well the children remember previous lessons by telling the children the lesson number and the lesson title. Have children guess what the theme of each lesson was. The teacher should be flexible. Kids do not have to get the themes exactly right.

The purpose for this activity is that all kids will understand the one big story of the Bible. When they remember the themes, they will be more likely to see how the whole Bible fits together.

Optional Activity: Write the themes on a board for the students to choose from.

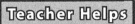

Tell the Story

Adam and Eve must have felt awful. Abel, who pleased the Lord with his offering, was now dead. Cain, the son who killed Abel, became a wanderer. They probably rarely if ever saw him. So, Adam and Eve lost two sons; not just Abel, but also Cain. Most parents don't like it when their kids get hurt. Also, most parents don't like it very much when they don't get to see their kids often.

But, God was merciful to Adam and Eve. Eve gave birth to another baby. His name was Seth. Eve knew that Seth would be the one who carried on a godly life. There was much evil in the world. Lamech killed somebody and probably even boasted about it. So, the world was getting worse and worse even though there were very few people.

Seth became a replacement for Abel. Abel was a godly man and so was Seth. In fact, many godly people were born into this family. Seth had sons and one of the son's name was Enosh. In the lifetime of Enosh, people began to call on the name of the Lord. Perhaps by his godly influence, people began to worship, pray, proclaim, and tell others about God. Later in time, two special men, Enoch and Noah came from this family.

It was said of Enoch that he lived in *"close fellowship with God."* For 300 years he lived as a friend with God. Enoch sought God and lived for Him for a long period of time. He lived 365 years and most of those were in close fellowship with God. One day, God decided just to bring Enoch home to heaven. He never died!

Another godly person from this family was Noah. We will learn more about Noah later but for now you should remember that he was called "righteous" by God. Seth, Enosh, Enoch, and Noah all lived for God. Enoch lived in close fellowship with God, Noah was righteous, Enosh led people to call on the name of the Lord. In spite of the wickedness of the day, God raised up people who would love Him and serve Him.

When wickedness was on the rise and most people forgot about God, the Lord raised up some people for Himself who sought to be close to God, proclaim His name, worship Him, pray to Him, and live a righteous life. It was a time when godly people stood up to be counted for the Lord. If Adam and Eve would have seen this, they would have been very happy. Now, other people were loving the same God that Adam and Eve loved.

Tell the Story Activity: Who Wants To Be in the "Proclaim God Family?"

The teacher could ask kids to line up in one of two lines: 1) "The Proclaim God" line and 2) the "Live for Self" line.

Ask: **"What do you think each group has to do to be in the line that they chose?"**

Memory Verse

Genesis 5:1 (ESV) - When God created man, he made him in the likeness of God.

Praise and Worship

Praise and Worship styles vary greatly around the world. It is the intent of this curriculum that praise and worship songs be selected that best fit the content of this lesson. Recommendations for praise and worship are given and this music can generally be located at www.itunes.com. However, the teacher can feel free to select a similar praise and worship song.

"He Is Good" by Steve Green is recommended for this lesson.

Bible Activity

The teacher should draw or find pictures of two trees, one is very beautiful and one is not. The teacher could use these pictures of two contrasting trees. Now, have the children draw a beautiful tree and a tree that is ugly. What made the difference between these two trees? What made one tree grow and the other tree to not grow?

Teacher Helps

Memory Verse Activity: Log Your Review

In this activity, the teacher will show children how to make a log or journal of their review times for their memory verses. Each day, the child should write down when and how long he or she reviewed the verse this week. The key to memory is review. If the teachers stresses reviewing this verse and others, then the student will retain the memory verses for a much longer period of time.

Bible Activity: Two Trees

The teacher should draw a contrast between what made a healthy or beautiful tree and what made an unhealthy or ugly tree.

The teacher should relate Seth to the godly line which experienced good growth.

4) Review the Lesson

Have children simplify the lesson into 10 words or less using their own words. What are their answers? When children simplify the story of the lesson into ten words or less, they will probably say something like these possibilities:

- Seth became a godly leader.
- Seth was a substitute.
- Seth had many people in his family who worshipped God.
- Seth was a provision from God.
- Seth replaced Abel as a godly son.
- Genealogies teach us a lot of important things.

Review the Lesson Activity: Simplify

Simplify can even become a game for the children. The teacher can give each team of 2 or 3 kids about 1-2 minutes to come up with the most significant 10 words of this lesson.

5) Apply the Lesson

Name 5 things you could do to start godly habits in your family. Things like:
- Read the Bible as a family.
- Tell your family about your Bible lesson.
- Read your Bible and pray every day.
- Don't fight or hurt people.
- Don't make fun of people.

Now, pick one of those and try to do that every day this week.

Apply the Lesson Activity: 5 Things

5 Things can help children focus in on one main thing to do this week that will help them to be more like Seth, a very good example for us.

Adventure Number 15
Genesis 6:5-8:22

Story Line: The people were evil. God sent a flood. Noah trusted and obeyed God.

1) Study the Lesson (before class)

- "Some people have thought that the 'sons of God' were fallen angels. But the 'sons of God' were probably not angels, because angels do not marry or reproduce (Matthew 22:30; Mark 12:25). Some scholars believe this phrase refers to the descendants of Seth who intermarried with Cain's evil descendants. This would have weakened the good influence of the faithful and increased moral depravity in the world, resulting in an explosion of evil."[1]

- The Bible says that Noah was "righteous" and "blameless" but that does not mean that Noah never sinned. In fact, one of his sins is recorded in Genesis 9:20. Noah was a man who loved God and obeyed Him.[2]

- Noah built a big boat which was six times longer than it was wide, exactly what modern day shipbuilders do today. This big boat was as tall as a four-story building.

- Pairs of every animal joined Noah in the boat; seven pairs were taken of those animals used for sacrifice. Some people have estimated that over 125,000 animals could have fit into the boat.

- The rains from heaven poured on the earth for 40 days and the springs of water from under the earth came up creating a massive universal flood that covered the whole earth for 5 months.

- For about another 5 months, the waters on the earth ebbed away.

Footnotes - Adventure 15

1. James Galvin, *Life Application Bible Notes*, 16.

2. Ibid., 17.

2) Begin the Lesson

The teacher should gather all the songs that have been used in the Adventures in the Bible's Big Story and play several of them.

The class should be able to sing along with the teacher the songs that they have previously learned in this curriculum.

After the teacher has played several songs and the class and sung them, play the game, "Name That Tune." "Name That Tune" is a game in which the students will attempt to match the song with the Bible adventure that best matches the song. The teacher should use extreme graciousness to encourage the class when an answer is given.

The purpose of this activity is for kids to associate music they have learned with events in the Bible. The teacher should stay focused on this primary purpose.

Teacher Helps

Review Activity: Name That Tune

The teacher should play songs that the class has learned for the previous Bible adventures. Children should guess which adventures in the Bible's big story best match the song that is being played or sung.

If time permits, the teacher could also ask if there are phrases or words in any of the songs that the children do not understand.

3) Teach the Lesson

Ask, **"Have you ever seen a situation where it rained so much that there was a flood?"** Let the children explain their stories.

Tell the Story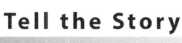

Teacher Helps

People became very destructive and they all were very evil. They enjoyed doing bad things and hurting people. God did not like this at all and it made Him very sorry that He had ever created people. God does not like it when people cause other people to be hurt. Everyone was like that, well, almost everyone was like that.

One person was not like that. What was his name? Yes, you guessed it. It was Noah. Noah was a righteous man. That means he did the right thing most of the time. He did not like to hurt other people like his neighbors did. Noah was also blameless. You could not accuse him of doing anything bad. He also walked in close fellowship with God. God noticed Noah and preserved the earth because of this one man. Noah was married and had three sons: Shem, Ham, and Japheth.

When Noah was 600 years old, God told him that everything on the earth was going to die from a flood that would cover the whole earth. Noah would have to build a big boat from gopher wood and get pairs of all the animals to come on this big boat. Noah also had to get all the food for his family and all the animals. So, Noah built this big boat. It was 525 feet long, longer than a football or soccer field. It had 4 levels of floors. It could hold 40,000 cubic meters or at least 525 railroad cars. It was massive! If the average size of an animal getting on the boat was a sheep, then the boat could hold over 125,000 animals. This big boat had only one door.

Well, it rained for 40 days and 40 nights. It was a massive torrential downpour. By the end of the rain, all the world was covered with water. In fact, the tallest mountain was under water by 22 feet. But God protected Noah, his family, and all the animals in the boat. After five months on the boat, Noah released a raven and a dove to see if they would come back, both of them came back to the boat. Seven days later, Noah released a dove. This time, the dove came back with an olive branch. Seven days later, Noah released a dove and the dove didn't come back. Then, God told Noah that it was time to get off the boat. So, Noah and all the animals got off the boat.

God made a special promise to Noah and really to everyone. He promised that He would never again flood the entire earth. To guarantee this promise, He told Noah that there would be a rainbow in the sky whenever it rained. So, God honored His promise, as He always does, and the earth has never completely flooded again. Noah was on the ark for about one year. In everything that happened, Noah completely obeyed God. Noah even built an altar of sacrifice to God after he got off the boat. God was pleased.

Tell the Story Activity: Name That Fact

As the teacher is telling the story, have children divide into two teams and have the teams write down as many facts about Noah and the flood as they can. They will need this list later in the lesson. If the children are unable to write, have them remember as much as possible.

Memory Verse

Genesis 6:8 (ESV) - But Noah found favor in the eyes of the LORD.

Praise and Worship

Praise and Worship styles vary greatly around the world. It is the intent of this curriculum that praise and worship songs be selected that best fit the content of this lesson. Recommendations for praise and worship are given and this music can generally be located at www.itunes.com. However, the teacher can feel free to select a similar praise and worship song.

"He Is Good" by Steve Green is recommended for this lesson.

Bible Activity

This is a great story for the children to act out. Every child should have a role to play. How this is set up depends on the size of your class. These are the characters needed:

- Noah
- Noah's wife
- Hecklers (a few or many, depending on class size)
- Animals, choose as many as you would like, again based on the size of the class. (2 of each kind)
- If you have enough children, assign the 3 sons of Noah and their wives.
- Voice of God - best played by the teacher or assistant

Read through the story from the Bible as you instruct the children in their parts. Help them see how Noah built the ark. Walk off the size of the area that will be considered "safe." Encourage Noah and his sons to make saw and hammer sounds as they "build" the ark. Here come the animals! Let the children ad-lib a little, but be ready to jump in and redirect them if needed to keep moving forward.

Lesson point: It's always best to trust God, even if we can't possibly see a way out.

Teacher Helps

Memory Verse Activity: Response Teams

Memorize this verse by dividing the class in half. Those on the teacher's right side will say the first, third, fifth, seventh, and ninth words. Those kids on the teacher's left side will say the second, fourth, sixth, eighth, and tenth words.

Bible Activity: Role Play - Noah's Ark

Read Genesis 6:5-8:22 before you begin. Divide the children up to their various parts. Children may use their Bibles to read their assigned parts, when relevant. Encourage the kids to read and act with lots of feelings as if they were really there.

4) Review the Lesson

1. The ark measured 525 feet in length.

2. The ark held 40,000 cubic meters which is about 500 standard railroad cars.

3. The ark was made of gopher wood. We do not know what gopher wood is but it had to be highly resistant to water and water rot.

4. The ark had floors filled with rooms but it had only one door.

5. If the average sized animal was the size of a sheep it means the ark could hold over 125,000 animals.

6. God put a rainbow in the sky as a covenant and promise to remind His people that He would never destroy all mankind by water again.

7. It rained 40 days and 40 nights.

8. Noah had three sons named Shem, Ham, and Japheth.

9. Noah was 600 years old when he went into the ark. Noah built the ark for 125 years.

Teacher Helps

Review Activity: Name The Facts

Divide the class up into two or three teams. Have the teams list as many facts about Noah's ark as they possibly can. Give them 5 minutes. Depending on the ages of your class, the teacher may need to assist the class in writing down the facts. Here are 9 facts about Noah's ark.

5) Apply the Lesson

Noah was probably mocked and belittled but he had a close relationship with God. In what ways will a close relationship with God make it possible for you to endure it when other kids make fun of you?

> **Story Line: The people were evil. God sent a flood. Noah trusted and obeyed God.**

Adventure Number 16
Genesis 11:1-9

Story Line: God confused the language of the people.

1) Study the Lesson (before class)

- Babel means "gate of the gods" in the Babylonian dialect but the word sound like the word for "confusion" in the Hebrew language.

- Genesis 11:10-26 contains the genealogies of Shem. It is likely that the construction of the tower of Babel took place during the lifetime of Peleg. Peleg means "division."

- The descendants of Noah could have followed the faith habits of Adam and Eve, Abel, Seth, Enoch, and Noah. Instead, they chose pagan religious habits and devised their own "way to God."

- The tower of Babel, most likely a ziggurat, was a tower built to support a stairway that reached high into the sky. The top was thought to be a gateway to the gods. The door at the top was supposed to be the entrance to heaven. The door at the bottom was the entrance to a temple where their so called "gods" worshipped.[1]

- This generation chose to establish their own view of God in an attempt to satisfy their own self-centered habits. They did not choose the God that Noah obeyed.

- This tower was a monument to people not a monument to God, even though it was a "gateway to the gods."[2]

- "The LORD came down to see the city and the tower, which the children of man had built." The result was that God confused their languages and dispersed the people.

- The people were supposed to spread out and fill the earth. They were not supposed to all locate in one place.[3]

Footnotes - Adventure 16

1. David Brooks, *The Roots of Faith Old Testament Commentary*, COM-58.

2. James Galvin, *Life Application Bible Notes*, 22.

3. John Walvoord and Roy Zuck, *Bible Knowledge Commentary: Old Testament*, 44.

2) Begin the Lesson

There are eight basic concepts that are emphasized throughout all of the Bible. We have studied these truths in previous lessons. Ask the children if they can name them and tell a little bit about each one. They are:

1. <u>God</u>. In the beginning, there was a very powerful God. (Lesson 1: The Eternal God)

2. <u>Man</u>. God created many things. He created man and woman to be His special friends. (Lessons 3: Creation of the Universe and 4: Creation of People)

3. <u>Sin</u>. Man and woman disobeyed God. They did not do what He told them to do. (Lesson 7: Beginning of Human Sin)

4. <u>Death</u>. God punished man and woman for their disobedience. Death, in the Bible, refers to separation. (Lesson 8: The Origin of Death)

5. <u>Christ</u>. God sent His one and only Son, His unique Son, who lived a perfect life. (Lesson 9: Promise of a Victor Over Satan)

6. <u>Cross</u>. Jesus died on the cross for the sins of the world. (Lesson 11: Provision of Coverings)

7. <u>Faith</u>. If anyone places their faith in Christ, God welcomes them. (Lesson 13: Cain and Abel)

8. <u>Life</u>. God gives eternal life to those who put their faith in Him. (Lesson 5: Life in Paradise)

Ask the children if they can think of how these eight gospel principles are emphasized in the first 15 lessons that we have studied.

Teacher Helps

Review Activity: Eight Basic Gospel Concepts - One Story

The teacher should emphasize these eight gospel concepts throughout Scripture. They are foundational to telling children the one story of redemption found in the Bible. We will emphasize these eight truths regularly.

3) Teach the Lesson

Tell children there are two ways men seek to find God. One of those ways God accepts and one He does not accept. One is my own way to God and the other is God's way to Himself. How do we try to create our own way to God? Why is this right or wrong?

Tell the Story

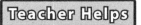

Everybody got together in the big city. The big city had so much to offer. All the friends you ever wanted and all the fun you could ask for was in the big city. Big cities are the place to be if you want to do some really entertaining stuff.

In the big city, some people decided that they wanted to build their own tower to God. Also, they wanted to make a name for themselves. At the base of the tower would be the temple entrance and at the very top there would be the entrance to the "gods" in heaven. The people in the big city thought they could determine how to get to God and they paid little or no attention to their ancestors, like Noah, Seth, and Adam. Instead, they tried to make God like one of them. They wanted to tell the gods that they were in control and that they were in charge. The people in the big city all worked together to make this magnificent structure. It had to be very beautiful!

This was their side of the story: they chose to be dependent on themselves and not on God. They chose to not listen to God and His spoken word. They chose to disobey. They did not remember the stories of how Eve listened to the tempter, Satan himself. They did not remember that an offering to God is made by faith not by building a tower to heaven. Yes, they decided to reach the heavens on their own without God.

God's side of the story was much different. When He saw that the people of the large city were building this tower, He came down from heaven and looked at it. As He always does, He had to punish disobedience. He was not worried about people building a tall tower. As Cain was punished for his disobedience, so the people of this large city would have to be punished. God chose to confuse their languages so that they would not be able to work together on this tower. When He confused their languages, they did not finish the tower. They became spread out and moved around on the face of the earth. That is really what God wanted. A long time ago, God told Adam and Eve to be fruitful and multiply on the earth.

In the end, the people did not get the tower they wanted and they lost many of their friends. They could not speak the same language so they dispersed and went other places. God did not allow them to build a gateway to heaven.

Tell the Story Activity: Story Chairs

This activity is kind of like the game "musical chairs" only the teacher uses the story instead. Give each of the kids, except one, a word in the story that is used often. When you tell the story, have all the children move to the empty seat when someone hears their word. Only each child knows what word he or she has.

Words to give to children could include:
- tower
- cities
- beautiful
- languages
- confused
- God
- story
- listen
- obey
- Noah
- Cain
- Adam
- Eve
- faith

Memory Verse

Genesis 11:9 (ESV) - Therefore its name was called Babel, because there the Lord confused the language of all the earth.

Praise and Worship

Praise and Worship styles vary greatly around the world. It is the intent of this curriculum that praise and worship songs be selected that best fit the content of this lesson. Recommendations for praise and worship are given and this music can generally be located at www.itunes.com. However, the teacher can feel free to select a similar praise and worship song.

"He Is Good" by Steve Green is recommended for this lesson.

Bible Activity

Ask someone who speaks a different language to come to class and give the children simple instructions on how to do something (example: "children, take a pencil and paper and write your name on the paper" or "open your Bible to Genesis chapter 11"). Discuss how difficult it would be to build a tower when everyone spoke different languages.

Activity: "To build or not to build, that is the question!" Divide your class up into groups of 6-10 children per group. Give each group a bag of building supplies (blocks, rocks, cans, disposable cups, or whatever you can find, making sure that the groups have the same number of supplies). They will compete to see which team can build the highest tower in a specified amount of time. After 4 minutes, call a "time out" and announce this: "For the rest of the time, you may continue to build, but you can't talk at all." Let them experience how difficult it is to build something together if there is no communication. The people of Babel thought they were so great, but God has a way of humbling the proud. He knew just what they needed to cure them of their prideful hearts. He also knows what we need if we let pride get in the way of our worship of God. They had begun to crave glory for their accomplishments, forgetting that it is God who gives everyone the abilities they have. All the glory belongs to Him, and He will not share it with anyone!

Teacher Helps

Memory Verse Activity: Around the Class

Have the children sit in a circle while music is playing. Pass around a phrase of the memory verse. When the music stops, whoever is holding the phrase of the memory verse should try to quote the verse. Do this until all phrases are memorized. Then, do the same thing for the whole memory verse.

Bible Activity: Around the Class

List some of the things that we might want to take the credit for, such as:

- Being smart or strong
- Helping a friend at school
- How much we give
- Making good grades
- How good we are at something
- Athletics

4) Review the Lesson

"Who" Questions:

1. Who built this tower?

2. Who did not like this idea?

"What" Questions:

1. What was the tower made of?

2. What did God do at the end of this story?

"When" Questions:

1. When did these people live?

2. When did God confuse their language?

"Where" Questions:

1. Where did these people live?

2. Where was God when these people were building the tower?

"Why" Questions:

1. Why did they build this tower?

2. Why did God confuse their language?

Teacher Helps

Review Activity: The Investigative Cube

Divide the class up into two teams. Make a cube with these labels on each side of the cube: who, what, when, where, why. When the cube is rolled to one team, they will answer the type of question that is face up on the cube. For instance, if the "why" is face up on the cube, then that team will answer a "why" question. Teachers can make up their own questions from the lesson, only they must pertain to the tower of Babel.

5) Apply the Lesson

God does not bless those who work their way to Him. He blesses those who put their faith in Him. Look for one way this week to put your faith in Him. Then, come to class next prepared to share how you put your faith in Him.

Adventure Number 17
Genesis 11:31-12:7

Story Line: God called Abraham to be a great nation and a blessing to all people.

1) Study the Lesson (before class)

- It had been more than 300 years since the universal flood in the time of Noah. It was the last recorded instance of God speaking to mankind.[1]

- Terah, Abraham's father, left Ur to go to Canaan but settled instead in Haran. Terah was a moon-worshipper living in a land where many people worshipped the moon as a god. God promised to bless Abraham but this promise had one condition, Abraham had to obey God.

- Abraham, by faith, obeyed and left everything to follow God's plan.

- Three promises were based on God's call for Abraham to leave his land. The first promise to Abraham was land. The second promise offered to Abraham was offspring, and the third promise offered to Abraham was that he would be a blessing.[2]

- God's promises were to bless those who blessed Abraham, curse those who treated Abraham with dishonor or contempt, and bless all the families of the earth through Abraham.

- Abraham was told to leave several things: his country, his people, and his father's household but he was told nothing about the land to which he would go. To leave and obey God not knowing where he was going would be difficult.

- We see evidences of Abraham's obedience in two different ways. First, he left. Second, he was a blessing.

- Abraham's descendants eventually owned the land of Canaan but Abraham owned only a cave when he died (Genesis 23:17-20).

Footnotes - Adventure 17

1. Kurt Strassner, *Opening up Genesis: Opening Up Commentary*, Genesis 12.

2. David Brooks, *The Roots of Faith Old Testament Commentary*, COM-62.

2) Begin the Lesson

Have your class name the main characters that we have studied so far and something that we know about them. Possibilities could include:

- God - is very strong. He created heaven and earth.

- Lucifer - rebelled against God and was expelled from heaven.

- Adam - was the first person that God created.

- Eve - was deceived by Satan.

- Cain - brought an unacceptable offering to God. Cain killed his brother, Abel.

- Abel - brought an acceptable offering to God. He was killed by his brother, Cain.

- Seth - was the third son that Adam and Eve had and he was thought to be a substitute for Abel.

- Noah - obeyed God and built a large boat.

- Builders of Tower of Babel - These builders tried to build a temple to God on their own terms, not God's terms.

3) Teach the Lesson

Abram grew up in a home that worshipped the moon. Satan had spread his rebellion to Terah, Abram's father. You may not worship the moon like Abram's family did but what are some things that people around you worship other than God?

Also, in this story we will learn about promises that God made to Abram who would later be called Abraham. Do you think God is able to keep His promises? If so, why? If not, why not?

Teacher Helps

Begin the Lesson Activity: Who They Are and What They Did

Create two stacks or lists. One list is the "who" list and the other is the "what they did list." Have the children match the two lists. For instance: God (from the "who" list) would be matched with very strong from the "what they did list."

Divide children up into teams and have them work together to put these two lists together. Time them. See who can do this the quickest.

Tell the Story

Abram grew up in Ur with his two brothers, Nahor and Haran. They probably did what most boys do in their day. It would be normal for boys to help their father do whatever he needed done. So, Abram, Nahor, and Haran in all likelihood helped their father, Terah. Terah was a moon-worshipper. The boys grew up worshipping the moon. It was the type of religion that was popular where they lived.

As the boys grew up, they became men and got married. Abram married Sarai but they could not have children. Haran got married and had a son named Lot. But a very bad thing happened. Haran died. The rest of the family helped take care of Lot, especially Abram.

One day, Terah decided to move from Ur to Haran. It was a long journey but all of Terah's family joined him and moved north. They loaded up all their belongings and all their animals. They did not leave anything behind. It must have been a sight to see all those animals and all those possessions travelling on a long journey. When Terah's family got to Haran, Terah lived there for a while and then he died.

After Abram's father died, God spoke to Abram and told him to go to live in another place. God made special promises to Abram which became very important to Abram and many other people. God said, *"I will make of you a great nation, and I will bless you and make your name great, so that you will be a blessing. I will bless those who bless you, and him who dishonors you I will curse, and in you all the families of the earth shall be blessed."*

So, Abram, Sarai, Lot, and other people moved again. This time, they went south to Shechem. When Abram arrived in Shechem, God spoke to Abram again, *"To your children I will give this land."* This was the second time that God appeared to Abram and made a special promise to him. Abram stayed in the same area but moved to Bethel where he built an altar to God and worshipped this God that had made promises to him. He would no longer be a moon worshipper, He worshipped the God that made these promises to him.

Abram began his faith journey. His family was not God-worshippers but now Abram would lead his family to worship a God that could not be seen. We know that Abram began to trust this God and he put his confidence in this God. When this God spoke, Abram trusted Him and obeyed what He said.

Teacher Helps

Tell the Story Activity: Let's Move Again!

Abram moved at least 3 times. The first place he lived was in modern day southern Iraq. That was Ur. Then, they moved to Haran or somewhere near modern day Syria. Then Abram moved to Israel, first to Shechem and then to Bethel.

Have your children move their chairs to designated places in your room so that they can get the feel of what happened and where it happened.

The teacher can sum up what happened in each location.

- Ur - where Abram grew up with his two brothers.

- Haran - where Terah took his family and then died.

- Shechem & Bethel - where God made special promises to Abram.

Memory Verse

Genesis 12:3 - I will bless those who bless you, and I will curse him who curses you; And in you all the families of the earth shall be blessed.

Praise and Worship

Praise and Worship styles vary greatly around the world. It is the intent of this curriculum that praise and worship songs be selected that best fit the content of this lesson. Recommendations for praise and worship are given and this music can generally be located at www.itunes.com. However, the teacher can feel free to select a similar praise and worship song.

"He Is Good" by Steve Green is recommended for this lesson.

Bible Activity

Materials: Crayons, scissors, and tape or glue

Play a game called "Hurry up and wait" - Show children a special treat you have prepared. It can be a snack, toy, whatever you want to choose, but make sure it is something they will be very excited about. Before the story of God's amazing promise to Abraham and Sarah, Ask: "Have you ever been promised something very special and then you had to wait for it?" Today I have brought _____ (fill in the blank with the treat you have prepared, for example, let's say it is cookies) Who would like a cookie?" Show treat, let them see and smell it, but not touch or eat. "You will have to wait until later for the treat." Ask them: "Do you believe I will keep my promise?"

Tell the story about Abraham and Sarah, and God's special promise to them.

Bring out the treat 2-3 more times during class, each time, ask "Do you believe I will keep my promise?" Talk about having faith in a person that is trustworthy. At the end of class, give out the treats. Remind them that God ALWAYS keeps His promises, because He is true and all-powerful. He has both the character and ability to promise anything, and always comes through.

Teacher Helps

Bible Memory Activity: Phrases

Phrases. Say Genesis 12:3 in three phrases. Designate each part of the class to learn just one phrase. After they have learned one phrase, rotate until all kids have learned all three phrases.

Teacher Helps

4) Review the Lesson

The teacher should locate three areas in the classroom where the story took place. Designate each place and let a volunteer tell you what happened in each place.

Ur
- Abram's birthplace and childhood
- Where Abram grew up in a moon-worshipping family

Haran
- Where Terah took his family
- Terah died there

Shechem and Bethel
- Where God made special promises to Abram
- Where Abram built an altar to God
- Where Abram began a special personal relationship with God

Review Activity: 3 Stations in Your Classroom

Let volunteers in your class tell you what happened in each of the areas where Abram lived. Have them go to the place in the classroom that you designated earlier when you were telling the story.

5) Apply the Lesson

God made special promises to Abraham. What are one or two special promises that God has made in His Word to you?
- Assurance of salvation - 1 John 5:13
- Assurance of guidance - Proverbs 3:5-6
- Assurance of forgiveness - 1 John 1:9
- Assurance of victory over sin - 1 Corinthians 10:13
- Assurance of answered prayer - John 16:24

Story Line: God called Abraham to be a great nation and a blessing to all people.

Adventure Number 18
Genesis 13:13; 19:1-26

Story Line: God destroyed Sodom because the people were very wicked.

1) Study the Lesson (before class)

- Lot had an important job in the city of Sodom; perhaps he was a judge. As he sat at the entrance to the gates, he discussed with other leaders the important issues that faced the city.[1]

- God executed judgment on the people that lived in the same time as Noah. It was because of their wickedness that they were judged. God sent a global flood then and He promised that He would never again flood the earth. However, He did not promise to never again judge the people living on the earth.

- In the same way, God showed Abraham that He would judge people for their wicked living. He would also rescue the righteous.

- God also demonstrated that He was a merciful God. The people of Noah's day had 120 years to repent and turn from their violence. Adam, Eve, and Enoch also experienced the amazing mercies of God. None of these individuals were perfect or sinless. Yet, they all understood that God was gracious.

- Most scholars place the twin cities of Sodom and Gomorrah at the southern end of the Dead Sea.

- As judge, God descended and investigated the crimes of wickedness. He rendered a verdict and pronounced a judgment. So, God presented Himself as the fair and just judge that He is. Sodom's judgment was justified.

- There are limits to the patience and mercy of a holy and just God.[2]

Footnotes - Adventure 18

1. John Walvoord and Roy Zuck, *Bible Knowledge Commentary: Old Testament*, 60.

2. David Brooks, *The Roots of Faith Old Testament Commentary*, COM-66.

2) Begin the Lesson

- A simple timeline has been developed to help us understand what happened in Scripture and when it happened. It is very difficult to put dates on Biblical events so we have not done that. However, we will learn periods of time.

- What was the first period of time that we studied? (Beginnings; specifically - creation) What were some of the lessons that we learned about the period of time we call creation? (God is strong. God made all things. God made people to be His special friends.)

- What other period of time have we discussed? (fall) What are some of the lessons that we learned from the period of time we call the fall? (Satan was thrown out of heaven because of his sin, Adam and Eve sinned, and Satan tempted Adam and Eve.)

- What other period of time have we discussed? (flood) What are some of the lessons we learned from the period of time we call the flood? (God judges sin.)

- What other period of time have we discussed? (Babel) What are some of the lessons we learned from this period of time? (Man cannot establish his own method of worshipping God. It must be God's way of worshipping Him.)

3) Teach the Lesson

Teach the Lesson Activity: Towel Tug-Of-War

Put two children of similar strength on each side of the towel and put a line on the floor in the middle. Have children pull until one is pulled across the line. Do this several times with different kids.

Towel Tug-Of-War. Have kids pull a towel toward them much like they would a rope tug-of-war. The purpose of this activity is to have one side represent the godly line of Abraham and the other side to be the godless side of Sodom. It was a struggle for Lot to decide which side to choose. Even though he was a believer, he had to struggle mightily to show that he was truly a follower of God.

There is a battle inside each of us. Two different sides are pulling against us and they each want us to follow. Which side will win?

Tell the Story

Because of a famine, the family of Lot and the family of Abraham went to Egypt where both families prospered greatly. God added a lot of animals to each of them. When it came time to leave Egypt, they all moved to southern Israel. In southern Israel, the shepherds of Abraham and the shepherds of Lot began to argue. It became such a big thing that Abraham and Lot decided that this would be the time to go different ways.

Abraham gave his nephew Lot his choice. Whichever land looked best to him was his to keep. So, Lot went East with all his family, all his workers, all his possessions, and all his animals. Abraham went the other way. Lot ended up just south of the Dead Sea. It looked like a better place to be but it really was not. Lot liked what he saw but he did not take into account the kind of people that lived there. Abraham, on the other hand, was able to go back to Bethel, where he had built an altar.

Lot moved his family to Sodom. Lot was very rich and became a leader in the city. He sat at the gates of the city and decided very important matters for the city. He may have even been a judge. But, the people of Sodom were very wicked and the ultimate Judge, God, had indicted them for their wickedness. God decided to destroy the entire city because of the great sin. But, the ultimate Judge is also the ultimate Grace-Giver. He allowed Lot and his family to leave the city of Sodom before He destroyed it. Lot, his wife, and their two daughters left the city and right after that God rained down fire from heaven. Normally, we think of rain as cool and wet. But, this was hot and burning. God caused the entire city to burn and everyone in the city. It caused total destruction.

Lot was told to go to the mountains with his family and not look back. Unfortunately, Lot's wife looked back. God had warned the family and she disobeyed. So, she became a pillar of salt and died also. Lot and his two daughters made the rest of the journey without Lot's wife.

Abraham woke up the next morning and saw the smoke coming from this region. It was like a burning furnace. He could probably even feel the heat from this incredible fire. God had demonstrated His justice by destroying wickedness but He also demonstrated His mercy by sparing Lot and his two daughters.

Teacher Helps

Tell the Story Activity: Justice Line and Mercy Line

- Put several pieces of string across the floor where you are teaching. Make the string look like lines on a soccer field or a football field.

- At the one end, place a card with "Justice Line" written on it and on the other write "Mercy Line."

- Ask children about their view of God. Is He more of a Judge or more a Mercy-Giver? Or, is He somewhere in between?

- Have the children locate themselves somewhere on the field and be prepared to answer why they are standing there.

- Now, tell the story.

Memory Verse

Genesis 19:29 (ESV) - When God destroyed the cities of the valley, God remembered Abraham.

Praise and Worship

Praise and Worship styles vary greatly around the world. It is the intent of this curriculum that praise and worship songs be selected that best fit the content of this lesson. Recommendations for praise and worship are given and this music can generally be located at www.itunes.com. However, the teacher can feel free to select a similar praise and worship song.

"He Is Good" by Steve Green is recommended for this lesson.

Bible Activity

Usually children can choose any colors you wish for coloring, but this time have kids try to color the page exactly as the teacher. Here is the catch: The teacher should only show them his or her paper for 5 seconds, and then let's see how much the class can remember to match their pictures to yours. After they have finished, bring out the original example and compare their pictures to yours.

Question: "What would have made it easier to color your picture exactly like mine?" Obvious answer: "We needed to be able to look at and study the original." The point is this: Following God and pleasing Him is a lot like what we just did. If we want our lives to "match" what God expects, we need to compare ourselves to what He has given us in His Word. The problem in Sodom and Gomorrah, just like in _____ (your city or country) is that they, and we are comparing ourselves to the wrong standard. We look at what our friends are doing, and we think 'This must be alright, everyone is doing it.' Sometimes we look at famous people, or people in movies or on TV, and we make our decisions about what we will do by their example. This is so dangerous!! Think about the people in the Bible that pleased God like Abraham, Noah, Seth, Abel. They were not perfect, but they had one thing in common: They looked to God for their instructions, not the world around them. God's ways will not be easy to follow if you don't spend time looking at Him through His Word, the Bible. Let's make our lives good copies of God!!

Teacher Helps

Bible Memory Activity: Relay Race

Form two teams. Put the memory verse in large letters about ten yards away from the teams. Have children take turns to run to the memory verse and read the next word of the verse out loud so that everyone can hear. When each child has read his one word, go back to the team, touch the next person in line, and repeat the process until all words of the verse have been read. Repeat this until everyone has memorized the verse.

Bible Activity: Color and Compare

"Let's compare" – Print copies of the Bible coloring page for each child in the class. Ahead of time, color one picture as the "example" picture. Before passing out the coloring pages to the children, say: **"We are going to have a little game with the coloring sheets today."**

4) Review the Lesson

Scenarios:
- Abraham and Lot went to Italy because of famine in the land. (false)
- After the famine, Abraham and Lot moved to southern Israel. (true)
- Abraham wanted to take a vacation in Italy. (not in story)
- Lot was Abraham's nephew. (true)
- Lot had three daughters. (false)
- Lot and Abraham were very rich men. (true)
- Lot might have been a judge. (true)
- Lot was a very good soccer player. (not in story)
- Abraham wanted the best land and did not let Lot choose. (false)
- Lot's wife turned into a pillar of stone. (false)
- Lot's wife enjoyed baking cookies. (not in story)
- Lot must have been a fast runner (not in story)
- Abraham's shepherds and Lot's shepherds got into arguments. (true)
- God always judges sin. (true)
- God likes to destroy people. (false)

Teacher Helps

Review Activity: True, False, or Not in Story

Have the children remain in their "relay race" teams. Read the following scenarios to the children and have them answer: true, false, or not in story. In large letters, put true, false, or not in story about ten yards away from the teams. When the scenario is read, the person at the head of the "relay race" team has to run and tap the correct answer: true, false, or not in story.

5) Apply the Lesson

Sodom was a terrible, no good, very bad place. If you have ever been to or in a place like this, describe how it made you feel.

Tell how you will resist temptation when you are in a terrible, no good, very bad place. Be specific.

Story Line: God destroyed Sodom because the people were very wicked.

Adventure Number 19

Genesis 15:1-4; 16:1-16; and 17:20

Story Line: Sarai did not respond in faith to the promise of God. Abram did.

1) Study the Lesson (before class)

- The king of Sodom offered Abram the spoils of the city. Abram declined his offer but may have feared retaliation by this king. However, God made a special promise to Abram, "I am your shield; your reward shall be very great" (Genesis 15:1).

- Abram immediately turned the conversation. There was a problem. The problem was that Abram had no children and he was 75 years old. Humanly speaking, it was most likely that he would not have children since Sarai was unable to bear children.[1]

- God reminded Abram of his promise, "your own son shall be your heir" (Genesis 15:4). To make the point even further, God told Abram to step outside and try to count the stars. If he was able to do that, then he would know the number of descendants he would have. It was an amazing promise and a visual reminder that Abram would have children and their descendants would be many. Abram believed God and it was counted to him as righteousness; simple faith.

- Sarai's response was different. Probably, Abram and Sarai had been married for over 50 years yet they were unable to have children. Sarai reasoned that if she couldn't have children in the first 50 years, she and Abram weren't going to have children now. So she devised a plan to help God. Abram would sleep with Sarai's servant, Hagar. Together, Abram and Hagar conceived Ishmael.

- God did not use Ishmael as the son of promise. However, Abram loved this son and God promised to look after him. God would keep His other promise and provide a son of His original promise.[2]

Footnotes - Adventure 19

1. Ibid., 69.

2. Ibid., 71.

2) Begin the Lesson

- Genesis 1:1 - In the beginning, God created the heavens and the earth.

- Colossians 1:16 - For by him all things were created, in heaven and on earth, visible and invisible, whether thrones or dominions or rulers or authorities—all things were created through him and for him.

- Genesis 2:2 - And on the seventh day God finished his work that he had done, and he rested on the seventh day from all his work that he had done.

- Genesis 2:8 - And the LORD God planted a garden in Eden, in the east, and there he put the man whom he had formed.

- Isaiah 14:12 - How you are fallen from heaven, O Day Star, son of Dawn! How you are cut down to the ground, you who laid the nations low!

- Genesis 3:6 - She took of its fruit and ate, and she also gave some to her husband who was with her, and he ate.

- Genesis 3:15 - I will put enmity between you and the woman, and between your offspring and her offspring; he shall bruise your head, and you shall bruise his heel.

- Romans 8:20 - For the creation was subjected to futility, not willingly, but because of him who subjected it, in hope.

- Genesis 12:3 - I will bless those who bless you, and I will curse him who curses you; And in you all the families of the earth shall be blessed.

3) Teach the Lesson

- Angel (reporter) to Abram: "When God told you that He was going to be your shield and your reward, what did you think He meant?"

- Angel (reporter) to Sarai: "Why did you laugh when God told you that you were going to have a baby?"

- Angel (reporter) to Abram: "You grew up in a home of people who worshipped the moon. What was it like to quit worshipping the moon and start worshipping God?"

Teacher Helps

Review Activity: Review Previous Memory Verses

The teacher should ask children to recall previous memory verses. Not all verses are listed on this page, but the teacher could ask for all 18 memory verses to be recited, if time permits. Ask for volunteers and maybe give them a few helps.

Divide up into teams and recognize the team that remembers more memory verses.

Teach the Lesson Activity: Angel Interview

Have one child be an angel, one child be Abram, and one child be Sarai. The angel should interview Abram and Sarai with these questions. Let the kids answer as if Abram and Sarai were answering. Maybe the teacher could think of more questions for the angel to ask.

Tell the Story

The king of Sodom wanted to make a pact with Abram. King Bera wanted to have Abram on his side as an ally. Because Abram was a powerful man and had great influence, Bera thought they should become friends and partners. Abram wasn't a king but he had a lot of power and he was a righteous man.

Abram wanted nothing to do with King Bera of Sodom. He totally rejected the pact that Bera was making. Abram knew the history of Sodom … they were very wicked men and Abram stayed away from those kind. His nephew, Lot, chose to live in that city, but not Abram. Abram must have been concerned when he rejected this pact with King Bera. But God spoke to Abram and told him that He would be his shield and very great reward. To Abram, that meant that God was going to protect him in every way. That had to mean a lot to Abram because he trusted God. When God spoke, Abram listened and obeyed. This was his regular habit.

One day, God reminded Abram of his promise of a son that would be an heir to everything. God even took him outside and told him to count the stars; if Abram could do that, that is how many descendants he would have. Well, Abram believed God and it was credited to him as righteousness, even though it would be ten more years before this special son was born.

Sarai took a different view. Through a lack of faith, she thought she would help God with this plan by telling Abram and Hagar, her servant, to have a child. They did that and named this child Ishmael. The problem was that Ishmael was not going to be the child of promise. Hagar made life for Sarai miserable. The two of them were upset at each other and Sarai even blamed Abram for this problem. Sarai's lack of faith caused a big problem for Abram. Now, he had to decide what to do with Ishmael. Sarai's lack of faith caused a big problem for Hagar. Now, she would have no friendship with Sarai. Sarai's lack of faith was a big problem for Sarai herself. And Sarai's lack of faith caused a big problem for Ishmael. He would be loved but would have to leave the house of Abram.

God kept His promise to take care of Ishmael. Later, Ishmael had one small difference with his brother but there is no record of any other problems between the two of them. God watched over Ishmael through the good times and the bad times. Abram knew God would honor anything that He said. That is why Abram trusted God.

Tell the Story Activity: From My Point of View

Ask the kids how Sarai's lack of faith affected these people:

- Abram
- Sarai
- Hagar
- Ishmael

From these four people's point of view, how were they affected by someone's lack of faith?

Possible answers:

- Abram: hated to see his own son leave
- Sarai: bitterness toward Hagar
- Hagar: bitterness toward Sarai
- Ishmael: no dad to raise him

Memory Verse

Genesis 15:6 (ESV) - And he (Abram) believed the LORD, and he counted it to him as righteousness.

Praise and Worship

Praise and Worship styles vary greatly around the world. It is the intent of this curriculum that praise and worship songs be selected that best fit the content of this lesson. Recommendations for praise and worship are given and this music can generally be located at www.itunes.com. However, the teacher can feel free to select a similar praise and worship song.

"He Is Good" by Steve Green is recommended for this lesson.

Bible Activity

The statements will come from today's Bible story involving Abram, Sarai, Hagar, and Ishmael. When the children answer "know for sure," invite someone to tell why they know that for sure what God had said about that promise.

1. Abram and Sarah would have a child (know for sure); Genesis 18:10.

2. When would be the exact time the child would come? (by faith)

3. Abraham would be the father of many people (know for sure); Gen. 15:5.

4. The "son of promise" would come through Sarai and Abram (know for sure); Genesis 18:14.

5. How God would do this with 2 very old people that were too old to have children? (by faith)

6. Even though Ishmael was not the son of promise, God still loved him (know for sure).

7. How would God care for Hagar & Ishmael when they had no power in the family? (by faith)

Now, we have looked at the Bible story where people were called on to trust God by faith in certain areas, but this is also something that we should do

Teacher Helps

Bible Memory Activity

Review the verse a few times then divide the children into two or more teams. Have the teams form lines across from a chalk or white board or piece of paper on a chair. Place something to write with at the board in front of each team. Have the first child of each team run to the board and write the first word of the verse, then run back to the line. The next child of the team will write the next word and it will continue until the verse is completed. Allow all teams to finish before playing again.

Bible Activity

Ahead of time, make 2 sets of cards or papers for each child in your class. Some of the cards will have the words "We know for sure," and some will say "by faith."

today. Let's talk about things in your life that you know for sure, and things that you need to trust God for by faith. This section should be prepared with the needs and situations that your children face. Some possible examples are:

1. God loves me and cares very much about my life (know for sure); Matthew 10:29-31.

2. How will God provide for my needs? (by faith)

3. God expects me to live a life that is obedient to Him (know for sure); 1 Samuel 15:22.

4. How will God reward me for standing up for doing the right thing when I am all alone? (by faith)

Teacher Helps

Bible Activity (continued)

Give these instructions to the children: I will read a statement and you decide which category it fits into, either it is something "we know for sure," or something the person needs to trust God "by faith." When you have decided which card to choose, hold it up and say the words on the card. After we have completed each statement, the "know for sure" cards you will keep in one stack by your feet, and the "by faith" cards we will put in a separate stack.

4) Review the Lesson

This lesson revolves around two main facts:

1. Abram responded by faith.

2. Sarai did not respond by faith.

5) Apply the Lesson

Faith Response's are crucial to understanding the Bible's big story. A person responds by faith to what God has said. That is a faith response. This faith response is from any person (man, woman, boy, or girl) to what God has said. Will you respond by faith to what God has said? What would that look like in your life this week?

Story Line: Sarai did not respond in faith to the promise of God. Abram did.

Review Activity

Tell children to write down one main thing that they learned from this lesson. Then, have them share with one person in the class what they learned. They should write down each new thing they add to what somebody learned in the class. Repeat this process several times. Then, form a master list of what the kids learned from the lesson.

99 Adventures in the Bible's Big Story

Timeline: Beginnings of a Nation

Adventure Number 20
Genesis 22:1-18

> **Story Line: God tested Abraham to sacrifice Isaac. God provided a ram instead.**

 ## 1) Study the Lesson (before class)

- God gave Abram a new name, Abraham. God tested Abraham to see if his faith was real. Abraham fully expected his son to live.

- Moriah means 'foreseen of Jehovah.' God was not taken by surprise by Adam's fall or by the long, stark tragedy of human sin. It was all foreseen by the Lord.[1]

- The command by God for Abraham to sacrifice his son seemed very unreasonable. However, Abraham instantly obeyed God.

- Abraham never expected that God would take his son away from him. If Isaac died, God would raise him to life again. Abraham, without question, knew this and was sure that God would protect Isaac from danger or permanent harm.

- Abraham's answer to Isaac's question, *"Where is the lamb?"* reveals that Abraham had confidence that God would take care of Isaac. Abraham said, *"God will provide the lamb."* (Genesis 22:8, 14)

- "On the mountain of the Lord, it will be provided" ("Jehovah Jireh," verse 14), means that God provided a sacrifice in the form of a ram, not a child. God does not hurt children.

- Abraham was the obedient servant who worshipped God at great sacrifice. All throughout the three day trip and especially at the end of the trip, God provided.

- The distance from Beersheba to Mount Moriah was about 50 miles, a three-day journey.[2]

Footnotes - Adventure 20

1. John Phillips, *Exploring Genesis: An Expository Commentary*, 179.

2. James Galvin, *Life Application Bible Notes*, 40.

2) Begin the Lesson

Teacher Helps

Adventure Number 17: Promises to Abraham

   1. Where did God make special promises to Abram?

   2. Read Genesis 12:3.

   3. Shechem and Bethel.

   4. Praise God for His promises.

Adventure Number 18: Sodom and Gomorrah

   1. Why did God put so many people to death in Sodom and Gomorrah?

   2. Read Genesis 19:29.

   3. Men were very wicked.

   4. Pray that we would turn from wickedness.

Adventure Number 19: Abram's Son Ishmael

   1. How did Abram respond in faith to what God said?

   2. Read Genesis 15:6.

   3. Abram trusted the promises of God.

   4. Praise God that we can trust what He says.

Begin the Lesson Activity: Ask, Read, Talk, Speak

A good review strategy from previous lessons will focus on four main elements.

1) Ask a question.

2) Read the Bible.

3) Talk about it.

4) Speak to God.

3) Teach the Lesson

Ask your class, "Have you ever made a long trip?" If anyone has, then ask them what they would bring on a long trip. If they haven't made a long trip, ask them what they might bring and what they might do on this very long trip. Abram is going to make a long trip for a very important reason.

# Tell the Story

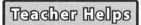

Abraham loved both of his sons, Isaac and Ishmael, but he really loved Isaac. God promised great things for Isaac. God was really going to use Isaac and Abraham knew this. Abraham was also very old so he probably wanted to protect Isaac, as a good father would want to do.

One day, God told Abraham to get Isaac and take him to Mount Moriah where Abraham would offer Isaac as a sacrifice. Sacrifices were not new but sacrificing your son was. God would never want a good father to physically hurt his son but God was testing Abraham's faith.

So, the next morning ... early the next morning, Abraham got wood for the sacrifice, told two servants to get prepared for the trip, get the donkeys ready, and of course he told Isaac that they were going on a long trip to make a sacrifice. They were all ready to go but it would be a long journey, three whole days of travelling. They travelled one day; then the second day; and on the third day, Abraham saw the place where they were to worship. It was Mount Moriah, not too far from Jerusalem. He told the two servants to stay behind while Isaac and he went to worship.

When Abraham and Isaac got to the place of worship, Abraham tied up his son and laid him on the altar. Isaac wanted to know where the sheep was for the sacrifice because that is what he was expecting. Isaac knew that sheep were to be used for offerings, not a son. When Abraham raised his knife up to kill Isaac, an angel told him to stop. It must have been a great relief for Abraham to hear those words from the angel. When he looked up, he saw a ram caught in some brush. Abraham untied his son and got the ram that was stuck. Then, he tied up the ram and offered that animal as a sacrifice to God. Together, they both worshipped God just like Abraham had told his servants earlier that day. They would worship God and that is just what they did.

Abraham decided to name that place with a very special name. He called it, "The Lord will provide." This place had to mean a lot to Abraham and Isaac because the Lord provided an animal as a sacrifice and not his own son. Later, we will learn of another choice God made as a sacrifice, only this time God would offer His own Son. We will talk more about that later. But, for right now, Mount Moriah had a new name because God provided just what Abraham needed and just when Abraham needed it.

Tell the Story Activity: Drama

This will be a great lesson to act out with the kids. We call it drama. As you tell the story, let the kids reenact the actual events. You will need kids to act these parts:

1) Abraham

2) Isaac

3) 2 servants

4) Several donkeys

5) Ram

Abraham should load up the wood (maybe a couple of sticks) on the back of the donkeys.

The whole group should walk around the class for each day travelled and be weary at the end of each day.

Abraham should pretend to tie up Isaac and place him on the altar of sacrifice.

Memory Verse

Genesis 22:14 (ESV) - And Abraham called the name of the place, The-Lord-Will-Provide; as it is said to this day, "In the Mount of The Lord it shall be provided."

Praise and Worship

Praise and Worship styles vary greatly around the world. It is the intent of this curriculum that praise and worship songs be selected that best fit the content of this lesson. Recommendations for praise and worship are given and this music can generally be located at www.itunes.com. However, the teacher can feel free to select a similar praise and worship song.

"Speak, O Lord" by Keith and Kristyn Getty is recommended for this lesson.

Bible Activity

Explain that we are going to go on a walk, but not just a regular walk, this will be a "trust walk." Each person will have a partner, and one of you will wear a blindfold, so you can't see where you are going. Your partner will lead you around, making sure that you do not bump into anything and get hurt. It is very important that you are a trustworthy friend to your partner. If you are wearing the blindfold, you need to trust your friend. After a few minutes, we will switch the blindfold to the other person, and do another short walk. Have the children pair up in groups of two. Give each pair of children a blindfold, and help them put the blindfold on their friend. Encourage children to be a trustworthy friend.

After the activity, talk about how it felt to trust someone else when you can't see what is ahead. Talk about how both Abraham and Isaac had to trust God in this difficult situation. God is always good, always true, always right, even if we can't see it at the moment. We trust a friend to lead us around when we can't see, how much more should we trust God to lead us through life. He is our Creator, and the Master of the universe. He can always be trusted!!

Teacher Helps

Memory Verse Activity: Hop It

In large letters, write phrases of the verse on sheets of paper. On the floor, tape the papers in a mixed up fashion, but close enough for succeeding words to be reached in a step. Children should step on one word at a time in the proper order to quote the verse. Let each child have a turn of hopping on the verse.

Bible Activity: Trust Walk

Materials needed: enough blindfolds for 1/2 the number of children expected in class (bring extras just to be safe)

4) Review the Lesson

Agree/Disagree Statements (If you disagree, why do you disagree?)

1. Abraham and Isaac travelled three days to Mount Moriah. (Agree)

2. Abraham did not have confidence that God would spare his son Isaac. (Disagree. He did have confidence in God.)

3. Abraham named this mountain and called it "Mount Moriah." (Disagree. He named it "The Lord will provide.")

4. Sarah did not think this was such a great idea. (Disagree. The Bible does not tell us if Sarah knew about this trip to Mount Moriah.)

5. This is the first time in the Bible that an animal was used as a sacrifice. (Disagree. God made clothes from an animal's skin for Adam and Eve.)

5) Apply the Lesson

Eight essential concepts are found in the Bible's big story. They are: 1. God, 2. Man, 3. Sin, 4. Death, 5. Christ, 6. Cross, 7. Faith, and 8. Life.

Abraham trusted God for many years. Now, when faced with a crisis, he trusted Him again. Name one or two ways that you will trust God for what He can and will provide for you. This lesson emphasizes trust or faith.

> **Story Line: God tested Abraham to sacrifice Isaac. God provided a ram instead.**

Teacher Helps

Review Activity: Agree and Disagree Statements

Kids will have fun disagreeing or agreeing with these seven statements. You may want to make up some statements of your own for them to agree or disagree with. They could move to one side of the room or the other.

Adventure Number 21
Genesis 32:24-29

Story Line: Jacob won a new name in a wrestling match with an angel.

1) Study the Lesson (before class)

- After Isaac's experience on Mt. Moriah, he grew up in southern Canaan. God gave him a wife from Mesopotamia, probably modern day Iraq. Her name was Rebekah. Rebekah, like Sarah, was unable to have children, but unlike his father, Isaac prayed and God gave him and Rebekah twins, Jacob and Esau.[1]

- God chose the second son, Jacob, to be the carrier of His blessings. Jacob was known to be a deceiver and his name even means "grasping the heel."

- Esau was cheated out of his birthright and his blessing by Jacob. Jacob had to flee from Esau who was very angry when this all happened.

- In Genesis 28:4, we learn that Isaac blessed Jacob again. This time his choice was clear. The older would serve the younger. Esau would serve Jacob just as Ishmael served Isaac.

- Jacob moved to Mesopotamia where he married two of Laban's daughters, Leah and Rachel. He loved Rachel much more than Leah. Things became very tense between Jacob and his father-in-law, Laban. So, Jacob had to move again, this time back to his homeland. When Esau heard that Jacob was coming back, he went out to meet him.

- We come now to a spiritual crisis in Jacob's life. At Bethel he saw the ladder, at the Jabbok he saw the Lord; at Bethel he became a believing man, here he became a broken man; at Bethel he became a son of God, here he became a saint of God.[2]

Footnotes - Adventure 21

1. David Brooks, The Roots of Faith Old Testament Commentary, COM-77.

2. John Phillips, Exploring Genesis: An Expository Commentary, 261.

2) Begin the Lesson

Bad News Reporters

- Lucifer rebelled against God.
- Lucifer persuaded Adam and Eve to sin against God.
- Cain killed Abel.
- The people of Noah's day were very wicked.
- Some people tried to build a tower to the "gods."
- Sarah did not have faith in God, at first.

Good News Reporters

- God is very strong.
- God created the earth.
- God provided clothes for Adam and Eve.
- Seth was a godly substitute for Abel.
- Noah was a righteous man.
- Abraham believed God.

Ask children to give as much detail in their reports as possible. Do not label children as good or bad. Instead, they are reporting good news and bad news.

Teacher Helps

Begin the Lesson Activity: Bad News and Good News Reporter

Have one group of children list as many bad things as they can remember thus far in the Bible stories. These are your bad news reporters.

Have another group of children list as many good things that have happened in the Bible stories. These are your good news reporters.

3) Teach the Lesson

Ask children if they have ever been lied to or deceived. The main character in the story for today, Jacob, had a history of deception and manipulation. In fact, his name even means "deceiver." Let children tell a few of their experiences of when they have been lied to or deceived.

Tell the Story

Isaac ... his name literally means "laughter." Perhaps, Abraham and Sarah both laughed at the thought of having a child in their old age. Now, Isaac had just become a dad as his wife, Rebekah, gave birth to twins, Esau and Jacob. Esau was born first which usually means that he would receive special blessings and an inheritance. When Jacob was born second, his parents named him "deceiver." That was very unusual and it proved to be true that Jacob would deceive even his own family, even his own father and brother. As the boys grew up, Esau became a hunter and Jacob stayed more at home. Esau was Isaac's favorite son while Jacob was Rebekah's favorite son. When Isaac was very old, he wanted some food that Esau would have to kill and prepare. While Esau was out hunting, Rebekah and Jacob devised a plan to deceive Isaac who could not see very well. Before Esau returned, Jacob deceived his own father and told him that he was Esau and had some good food ready for him. The plan worked ... Isaac gave him a special blessing and Esau came too late. Esau was furious. Another time, Esau came in from hunting and was very hungry. Jacob tricked him into trading his inheritance for a good dinner. Again, Jacob's deception worked. Esau was so upset that he wanted to take his own brother's life.

So, Jacob travelled 400 miles north to Uncle Laban in Haran. There, he met and married two of Uncle Laban's daughters, Leah and Rachel. Interestingly, Laban deceived "the deceiver," Jacob, by tricking him into marrying Leah first. Then, Jacob tricked Laban with goats and sheep. Jacob had to leave Haran and this time he decided to go back home. He had one big problem though: Esau. What would Esau think or even do?

The night before the two brothers were to reunite, an angel of the Lord appeared and wrestled with Jacob, the deceiver. Jacob came face-to-face with his own sinfulness and asked the angel to bless him which the angel did. The angel gave him a new name. Jacob would no longer be "the deceiver," he would be called Israel or "struggles with God." Now, God would fight for Jacob because Jacob had come face-to-face with his own mortality. He must have been very scared about what Esau would do to him and his family. When God appeared to him and even wrestled with him, Jacob (or Israel) now knew that God could not be manipulated like his family members. Jacob would have to deal truthfully and God would fight for him.

When Jacob and Esau reunited, it was a wonderful sight. Everybody was happy. God made it possible for Esau to forgive his brother. God also made it possible for Jacob to carry on the family blessing that God had promised.

Teacher Helps

Tell the Story Activity: Jacob's Deception and God's Intervention

As you tell the story, have the children count how many times Jacob deceived somebody. And say, "This is just the times that we know about; there were probably other times also."

The teacher should also have them list the people that Jacob deceived. There were a number of people that he deceived.

Jacob's Deceptions: many times ... many people.

God's Intervention: Jacob would no longer live a life of deception. What happened to change the life of Jacob?

Memory Verse

Genesis 32:30 (ESV) - So Jacob called the name of the place Peniel, saying, "For I have seen God face to face, and yet my life has been delivered."

Praise and Worship

Praise and Worship styles vary greatly around the world. It is the intent of this curriculum that praise and worship songs be selected that best fit the content of this lesson. Recommendations for praise and worship are given and this music can generally be located at www.itunes.com. However, the teacher can feel free to select a similar praise and worship song.

"Speak, O Lord" by Keith and Kristyn Getty is recommended for this lesson.

Bible Activity

Teacher Helps

Bible Memory Activity: Word Scramble

Put each word on a piece of paper and scramble all the words or pieces of paper. Have children unscramble the words by putting them in the correct order.

Write the word "truthful" in big letters down one side of a chalkboard, white board, or large piece of paper so all the kids in your class can see it.

Jacob had always been known as "the deceiver" both to his family, himself, and God. Now that his name was changed to "Israel," his character was changed as well. Let's see how many blessings we can list that match the letters of the word "truthful".

As the teacher, you must have some words in mind to get your kids started.

Example:

T- Trust (when you are truthful, people can trust you)

R – Right (being truthful is the right thing to do, and pleases God)

U - Unreserved (not restricted)

T - Truth-Telling (out of your mouth comes the truth, not lies)

H - Habitually (telling the truth to be a regular habit)

F - Factual (truth based on the facts)

U - Unreserved (the full and entire truth)

L - Like It Is (what really happened)

4) Review the Lesson

Jacob's Deceptions:

1) Jacob deceived Esau to get his blessing.

2) Jacob deceived Esau and Isaac to get the inheritance.

3) Jacob deceived Laban.

4) Laban deceived Jacob.

Review Activity: Charades

Kids will have fun trying to figure out which deception of Jacob you are reenacting. Don't use any words.

5) Apply the Lesson

- <u>Deception</u>: List 2 or 3 ways that you have deceived someone.

- <u>Truthfulness</u>: Now, tell what you should have done in each of those situations to demonstrate truthfulness.

- <u>Choice</u>: Jacob chose to be truthful after he met God (the angel of God). After a life full of lies and deception, Jacob's life changed. There is hope found in the Bible that God can change anyone. Will you let Him change you?

Story Line: Jacob won a new name in a wrestling match with an angel.

Adventure Number 22

Genesis 37:3-4; 23-28; 39:1-4; 45:4-13; 47:5-6

Story Line: Good can happen even when people do bad things.

1) Study the Lesson (before class)

- One fourth of the book of Genesis is devoted to the life of Joseph. God related the creation of the universe in five words, "He made the stars also." The Lord devotes chapter after chapter to the story of a man who was not even in the Messianic line.[1]

- Jacob had twelve sons by four different wives. The promise of God to Abraham and his descendants was that they would be a blessing to all nations. However, Jacob's sons did not look like they should be part of that.

- Jacob had a favorite son of the twelve, his eleventh son, Joseph, firstborn of his favorite wife, Rachel. Jacob showed his favoritism to Joseph in many ways. Most notably, Jacob gave Joseph a special tunic that should have been for the firstborn son.[2]

- The ten older brothers became jealous of Joseph. Led by Judah, they decided to sell him. The other brothers actually wanted to kill Joseph. But God used Judah to spare Joseph's life. Joseph was bought by slave traders who took him to Egypt.

- In Egypt, Joseph became a leader. But Pharaoh's wife made sexual advances to Joseph. She even accused him of rape. Potiphar put Joseph in jail for this accusation. In jail, Joseph also became a leader and an interpreter of dreams. He became the foreman of the other prisoners.

- There was a famine and Jacob's family heard that there was food in Egypt. Jacob's sons went to get food which they eventually received from Joseph himself. Joseph did not hold a grudge and forgave his brothers.

- The family of Jacob stayed in Egypt for about 400 years after this.

Footnotes - Adventure 22

1. David Brooks, *The Roots of Faith Old Testament Commentary*, COM-77.

2. John Phillips, *Exploring Genesis: An Expository Commentary*, 261.

2) Begin the Lesson

Remind your class that you are learning the one big story of the Bible. While there are many stories in the Bible, they are linked to one major theme or story in the Bible. It is a story of hope. So, to help your class know that story and be able to put all the lessons together, we are going to review the lessons from the past. Ask, **"What are the main events that we have studied in the Bible?"**

- God always existed and He is very powerful.
- God created the earth and everything in it.
- God created people to be His special friends.
- Lucifer led a rebellion against God and one third of the angels followed him.
- Lucifer, or Satan, deceived Eve. They sinned by disobeying God.
- God clothed Adam and Eve with the skin from an animal.
- Cain killed Abel.
- God sent a worldwide flood that killed almost everyone on the earth. God spared Noah and his family because Noah was a righteous man.
- God confused the language of the people because of their disobedience and worship of false gods.
- God made special promises to Abraham.
- Abraham offered a ram on Mount Moriah instead of his son, Isaac.
- Jacob wrestled with the angel of God and got a new name, Israel.

Teacher Helps

Begin the Lesson Activity: The Main Events

Review is a significant part of learning. Twelve events are listed here. Write each event on a slip of paper or poster board and have children put them in chronological order. Let them work together in small teams (2 or 3). Time how long it takes each team to put these events in the right order. Winner gets a prize.

3) Teach the Lesson

Living in a foreign land is sometimes difficult. That is what the Israelites had to do. They lived in Egypt for over 400 years. What are some of the difficulties that you think the Israelites faced as they lived in a different culture for a long period of time?

Tell the Story

My name is Joseph and I want to tell you my story. I grew up in Canaan with 11 brothers. I was the next to the youngest of the twelve of us. My mother was Rachel and I was her favorite son. So, some of the times, I got special treatment from my parents that my brothers did not get. My brothers were quite jealous of me. Some of them even hated me. One day, they developed a plot to get rid of me. Their jealousy was so strong that while we were in the fields, they put me in a deep hole and took my coat. They were going to tell my father that an animal had come and devoured me. That was a lie but they all agreed to it. Then, my brothers saw some slave traders and sold me into slavery. They thought they would never see me again.

Eventually, I ended up in Egypt and I was a slave to the chief of the palace guards. God enabled me to do my job well. In fact, He enabled me to do my job so well, even as a slave, that Potiphar put me in charge of everything. He really trusted me. However, his wife was really strange and she tried to take advantage of me. I resisted her but she screamed and claimed that I did something bad to her. For some reason, Potiphar listened to her and I was put in jail. In jail, God gave me favor with everybody and I became a leader in the jail. God used the following dreams and my interpretation of them.

One night, the king of Egypt had two dreams which meant the same thing. I was the only one the king knew who could interpret the dreams. These dreams were from God and they showed that there would be a severe famine for seven years. The king listened to my interpretation and then put me in charge of everything underneath him. I stored up grain during seven prosperous years. But when the seven years of famine happened, everyone came to me, including my brothers. They wanted food but they did not recognize me now.

When my brothers realized who I was, they feared that I would retaliate against them. They knew I was very powerful. But, even though my brothers hated me at one time, I still loved them and wanted to help them. It was a wonderful reunion when we all got together, with my father, in Egypt. My father lived 17 years in Egypt and then died. Our families all stayed in Egypt. In fact, our descendants stayed in Egypt for another 400 years.

God was using me to bless the other nations. That was the promise of God to Abraham and his family, which I am part of. God used me to be a blessing to my brothers, my family, my countrymen, and all the nations.

Tell the Story Activity: The Story of Joseph

The teacher should find a guest speaker who will tell the story of Joseph. Have Joseph dress up in costume, if possible. Introduce your guest speaker as one who has lived a long time ago but has a very important message for all of us.

This story is told from the life of Joseph and those closest to him. But, in another sense, it tells the story of the one big story in the Bible.

Memory Verse

Genesis 39:2 (ESV) - The Lord was with Joseph, and he became a successful man, and he was in the house of his Egyptian master.

Praise and Worship

Praise and Worship styles vary greatly around the world. It is the intent of this curriculum that praise and worship songs be selected that best fit the content of this lesson. Recommendations for praise and worship are given and this music can generally be located at www.itunes.com. However, the teacher can feel free to select a similar praise and worship song.

"Speak, O Lord" by Keith and Kristyn Getty is recommended for this lesson.

Bible Activity

Divide the class into 2 groups. One group will name all the people or circumstances that disappointed or hurt Joseph. The other group will respond to them by saying "But God was faithful to Joseph."

Write on pieces of paper these situations or people that hurt, disappointed, or forgot Joseph:

1. His brothers

2. Being a slave

3. Being in a foreign land all alone

4. Potiphar's wife

5. Potiphar

6. Being thrown in prison, even though he did no wrong.

Choose one child or a group of children to read each card. After each card is read, the other group will say "But God was faithful to Joseph." This is the fun part: Each time they say that phrase, they must do so a little bit louder. After the last card is read, have the entire group say it together one more time: "God was faithful to Joseph." Emphasize that God will always be faithful to us too, even if we can't see how it could possibly happen. Our job is to keep our eyes on God and His faithfulness, no matter what our circumstances are. Joseph is a great example of this principle!

Teacher Helps

Memory Verse Activity: Bean Bag Toss

With masking tape, mark off a large square on the floor, about 36 inches. Connect the opposite corners inside the square with tape to form an "X." If you have space and many students, make a second square. Give each section a number value (1,2,3,4). A bit of a distance away, put a line of tape to mark where the student will throw from. Divide into two teams. Each student takes a turn throwing a bean bag into one of the sections. (You may make a bean bag by putting beans in a sock and closing it tight with a rubber band. Take the long part of the sock and fold it over the bean section.) If they can say the verse correctly, their team scores the amount of the section where the bean bag was thrown.

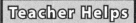

4) Review the Lesson

Divide the class into two teams. Give the teams one minute to write down as many statements as they can remember about Joseph, his family, and their time in Egypt.

- 11 brothers
- 400 years in Egypt
- Prosperity for 7 years and famine for 7 years
- the Lord was with Joseph
- Joseph's father lived 17 years in Egypt

Review the Lesson Activity: One Minute List

The teacher should give two teams one minute each to list as many facts as they can about the lesson.

After the one minute has passed, compare lists and see who has more facts. Be sure that children remember that you are looking for facts.

5) Apply the Lesson

Write down on a piece of paper all the people that have hurt you with words or actions. Now write down on the other side of that paper all the people that you have hurt with words or actions.

Like Joseph, are you willing to forgive them? If you have hurt someone else, you must go to them and ask for their forgiveness. Your choice is bitterness or forgiveness. Forgiveness is a loving action that God does all the time.

Bitterness is an unloving action. Satan wants us to be bitter and not forgive those who have hurt us.

Story Line: Jacob won a new name in a wrestling match with an angel.

Adventure Number 23

Exodus 1:1-14

> **Story Line: In spite of great oppression, God blessed the Israelites greatly.**

 ## 1) Study the Lesson (before class)

- When Joseph welcomed his father and family to Egypt in about 1876 B.C., there were 70 men. About 100 years passed between the time of Joseph and Exodus 1[1]. So, the male population of Israel increased from 70 to 600,000 in this time period.

- The people of Israel left Egypt about 430 years after they came to Egypt.

- At this time, there were about 2 million Israelites living in the land of Goshen in Egypt. God was keeping His promise to Abraham (Genesis 12:1-3). Yet, the Israelites still had no land of their own.[2]

- The cultures of Israel and Egypt were quite different. Israel worshipped one God (monotheistic). Egypt worshipped many gods (polytheistic). The Israelites had been a nomadic people and moved around but the Egyptians were deeply rooted. The Israelites were shepherds while the Egyptians were builders.[3]

- Ancient Egyptian culture was polytheistic with as many as 1,500 gods or goddesses. Ra, Amon, and Ptah were elevated above the other gods.

- The Bible reasons that there is one Deity and He is eternal. The Egyptian deities were not eternal and could even die.

- In the Egyptian culture, magic also played an important part in their religion. Theoretically, their gods responded to curses and chanting of words that had magical power.

- Up to this point, the biblical God did not insist that there were no other gods beside Himself. However, He would not remain silent much longer about this.[4]

Footnotes - Adventure 23

1. David Brooks, *The Roots of Faith Old Testament Commentary*, COM-85.

2. John Walvoord and Roy Zuck, *Bible Knowledge Commentary: Old Testament*, 108.

3. James Galvin, *Life Application Bible Notes*, 98.

4. David Brooks, *The Roots of Faith Old Testament Commentary*, COM-87.

2) Begin the Lesson

Lay out a game board for review that looks something like this:

Time Line	Story Line	Songs	Memory Verses
100 points	200 points	300 points	400 points
100 points	200 points	300 points	400 points
100 points	200 points	300 points	400 points
100 points	200 points	300 points	400 points

Go back for each of the last 10 lessons and let the children name the timeline for each lesson (100 points), the story line for each lesson (200 points), the song for each lesson (300 points), and the memory verse for each lesson (400 points).

A prize should be given to the winning team. Usually, competition is a fun thing for the children. Keep them all involved. Depending on the size of your class, you may want to limit each child to only 1 or 2 answers. The reason for this is that a few children will answer all the questions, if you let them.

There will be a total of 10,000 points, 1000 points for each lesson.

Teacher Helps

Begin the Lesson Activity: Bible Jeopardy

Divide the class evenly into two teams. The teams could be:

- whoever has birthdays in January through June
- whoever has birthdays in July through December

This game will be continued with the review at end of the lesson.

3) Teach the Lesson

One boy who was going to live in a different culture, said he did not want to learn a new language, he did not want to make new friends, he did not want to go to a new school, he did not want to eat new foods, and things like that.

Now, imagine living in that new culture with people who did not like you and treated you like you were a nobody. How would you feel? How would you react? What would you tell your parents?

Tell the Story

When Jacob came to Egypt, there were only 70 other men. But, about a hundred years later, there were 600,000 men. Most of the Israelite families lived in the northeast part of Egypt. God had promised to Abraham that his descendants would be as numerous as the sand grains on the seashore. There were lots of Israelites, perhaps 2 million of them.

This worried the new king of Egypt. The new king did not know Joseph. Joseph had been dead for some time now. Even though Joseph was very powerful in Egypt when he was alive, that was a long time ago. The king of Egypt was not only worried about the Israelites, he wanted to put a heavy load of work on them so they would not multiply so quickly. What the king did not realize was that God had promised to make Abraham's descendants as numerous as the sand on the seashore. The king was totally ignorant of the promise of God. Had he paid more attention to what God had promised, things might have been different.

Something interesting happened after the king declared more work for the Israelites. The more the king tried to work them, the more people were born to the Israelites. They became even more numerous. This must have really frustrated the king. What was he going to do? He was making life for the Israelites as miserable as possible so they would not have as many people. Just the opposite of what he planned was happening. The Israelites were treated like slaves now. Only one hundred years ago, they were treated like royalty. But not now. Not only were they not treated like royalty, the Egyptians dreaded the Israelites. They loathed and despised the Israelites. It was cruel what the king of Egypt was doing to the people of Israel.

God saw all that was happening to His people. It makes God very sad when people are treating other people harshly. But just as God saw Sarai when she could have no children, so God saw the people of Israel when they were treated so badly. God saw them and was about to do something very special for the Israelites. God would not be silent about the pain and suffering of His people. He would hear their pleas and He would respond. God's promises were coming true; there were many Israelites in a very short time. But, they still needed a land of their own and it wasn't clear at this point how they would be a blessing to the nations. So, the Israelites worked hard for the Egyptians. They worked just like slaves work. And in spite of their hard work, they kept having more and more babies. God was blessing them, even in their hardships.

Tell the Story Activity: Cheering for the Israelites

Have children listen to the story. As you tell the story, have the children clap or cheer when they hear the words "Israelites," "God," and "blessing."

Focus on cheering for these three words: God was going to bless the Israelites, even in their hardship.

Memory Verse

Exodus 1:12 (ESV) - But the more they were oppressed, the more they multiplied and the more they spread abroad.

Praise and Worship

Praise and Worship styles vary greatly around the world. It is the intent of this curriculum that praise and worship songs be selected that best fit the content of this lesson. Recommendations for praise and worship are given and this music can generally be located at www.itunes.com. However, the teacher can feel free to select a similar praise and worship song.

"Speak, O Lord" by Keith and Kristyn Getty is recommended for this lesson.

Bible Activity

As you make the chains, talk about the hardships of being a slave. Did God want His people to be in slavery? NO!! He had a plan to deliver them, but at this time life was very difficult for them. Remind the children of last week's lesson and how God was faithful to Joseph, even though he didn't know how it would all end.

Tell the children: There will always be some things in our lives that we don't understand, but there are other things that we know FOR SURE! Those are the things we learn about God in the Bible. Let's see how many things we can name about God that we know for sure:

- LOVE
- FAITHFUL
- JUST
- KIND
- HOLY
- RIGHTEOUS

Teacher Helps

Memory Verse Activity: The Telephone Game

Memorize this verse using The Telephone Game. Have your class form one line, then whisper into the first person in line a phrase of this verse, have that person repeat the phrase to the next person. Do this until all have quoted the first phrase. Then do the same thing with the second phrase, the third phrase, and so on until you have memorized the verse.

4) Review the Lesson

Continue your review game for points that you began at the start of the lesson.

- For 100 points, how many years were the Israelites in Egypt? (430)

- For 200 points, how many men originally went to Egypt with Jacob? (70)

- For 300 points, how many years had Joseph been dead when this story took place? (about 100)

- For 400 points, did the Egyptians believe in one God or many gods? (many gods)

- Bonus question worth 500 points: What is the theme of this lesson? (In spite of great oppression, God blessed the Israelites greatly.)

Review the Lesson Activity: Bible Jeopardy

This review activity is a continuation of the review game started during the beginning of the lesson.

5) Apply the Lesson

God gave the oppressed Israelites many babies against all odds. This was fulfilling His promise to Abraham in Genesis 12:1-3 that made this happen.

What are two or three promises in the Bible that you know to be true and that you can thank God for?

- Assurance of forgiveness
  I John 1:9

- Assurance of answered prayer
  John 15:7

- Assurance of guidance
  Proverbs 3:5-6

Story Line: In spite of great oppression, God blessed the Israelites greatly.

Adventure Number 24
Exodus 1:1-14 and Exodus 3:1-17

Story Line: God called Moses in a special way. Moses obeyed God.

1) Study the Lesson (before class)

- Moses had been a shepherd in the Midian wilderness for 40 years, but now God was calling him to lead Abraham's descendants out of Egypt.

- As a shepherd, Moses was to doing everything for himself. Now, he would have to lean heavily on God.

- God first spoke to Moses on Mt. Sinai when He spoke to Moses out of a burning bush. This same mountain is also where God would give Moses the Ten Commandments (Exodus 19:1-20:21).

- God spoke to Moses from an unexpected place and Moses listened.

- When Moses took off his shoes, that was an act of worship. It was showing respect for God. Moses was showing God that he was unworthy, and that God was worthy of his worship and reverence.

- Moses made excuses to God because he felt he was not able to do the job God had for him. Moses felt like he would have to work alone, but God had many other resources available to help Moses such as miracles and Moses' brother, Aaron. When Moses used the resources of God, he was quite effective as a leader. When Moses did not use the resources of God, he was quite ineffective as a leader.

- Moses immediately objected to the command of God because of his own lack of ability (Exodus 3:11) and his own lack of authority (Exodus 3:13). God responded with two promises: the promise of His presence (Exodus 3:14) and the promise of his return to Mt. Horeb.[1]

- The battle between the gods and Yahweh was about to begin, a story which has been told for the last 3000 years.[2]

Footnotes - Adventure 24

1. John Walvoord and Roy Zuck, *Bible Knowledge Commentary: Old Testament*, 112.

2. David Brooks, *The Roots of Faith Old Testament Commentary*, COM-91.

2) Begin the Lesson

One of the goals for review is for children to see the Bible's one big story. Today, we want to ask children to give us some of the recurring themes we saw so far in that story. For instance, let children volunteer their answers, but you might use the following examples as recurring themes in the Bible's one big story:

God's Amazing Power:

- Creation
- Worldwide Flood

Animal Substitution:

- Adam and Eve
- Abel
- Abraham and Isaac on Mount Moriah

Faith that Pleases God:

- Abel
- Noah
- Abraham

God Punishes Sin:

- Adam and Eve
- Cain
- Sodom and Gomorrah
- Babel

Teacher Helps

Begin the Lesson Activity: One Big Story

The teacher may want to give the class the topics such as: God's Amazing Power, Animal Substitution, Faith that Pleases God, and God Punishes Sin. Then, let the children tell Biblical examples of those stories that we have previously studied.

The purpose of this activity is for children to see recurring themes in the Bible's one big story.

3) Teach the Lesson

It is not very often that a bush catches on fire and then speaks to you. But, if that happened to you, what would you want to know from this burning bush that was speaking to you? (Maybe, who are You? and why are You speaking to me?)

Tell the Story

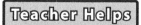

The Israelites were still treated like slaves and they still had no land they could call their own country. It must have been very discouraging for the Israelites. They had no place to go and the only place they could live was a place where they were treated very harshly. To make matters even worse, the king of Egypt ordered all Israelite baby boys to be thrown into the Nile River.

Jochebed, Moses' mother, positioned baby Moses in a waterproof basket in just the right spot in the Nile River. Jochebed knew the place where Pharaoh's daughter would bathe. Sure enough, Pharaoh's daughter found the baby and drew him out of the water. She named him Moses, a fairly common Egyptian name. Pharaoh's daughter permitted Jochebed to care for Moses for awhile. Then, Pharaoh's daughter raised Moses in the palace. Moses never forgot his true heritage. About 40 years later, Moses saw an Egyptian beating an Israelite. So, Moses killed the Egyptian. The very next day, Moses learned that somebody else had seen this and he fled to the wilderness. He met and married a young lady there and they lived in the wilderness for another 40 years.

While Moses was living in the wilderness, he was near a bush that was burning but it was not being consumed or burned up. When he noticed the bush burning but not being burned up, a voice spoke to him from that bush. That had to be a really weird feeling for Moses. Moses had a conversation with that voice which was an angel from God. The angel clearly told Moses that "I AM" had sent him. Moses believed this. Then, the angel told Moses that he would be the one to lead Israel out of Egypt. Moses balked ... he hesitated. He did not think he was the right guy for the job. He must have thought that someone else could do a better job, maybe his brother, Aaron; maybe someone else.

Moses was concerned that the Israelites would not believe that God had commissioned him to lead the Israelites out of Egypt. God understood Moses' concerns and was patient with him. To verify his leadership, God asked Moses what was in his hand ... it was a rod. When he picked up a snake, God told Moses to stick his hand in his side, which he did. When he pulled his hand out, it was full of a disease called leprosy. The Israelites believed Moses and worshipped the living God. Armed with God's presence, understanding God's commission, and with the help of Aaron, Moses chose to lead the people of Israel out of Egypt. The God of Abraham would do war against the gods of Egypt.

Tell the Story Activity: Excuses

If God asked you to do a big job for Him, what excuses would you possibly make:

- too young
- don't know anything
- don't know anybody
- don't know what to do
- not smart enough
- not strong enough
- not a good leader

Let the kids volunteer their answers and discuss their reasons or excuses with them. Are any of their excuses similar to those of Moses?

Memory Verse

Exodus 3:14 (ESV) - God said to Moses, "I AM WHO I AM." And He said, "Say this to the people of Israel, 'I AM has sent me to you.'"

Praise and Worship

Praise and Worship styles vary greatly around the world. It is the intent of this curriculum that praise and worship songs be selected that best fit the content of this lesson. Recommendations for praise and worship are given and this music can generally be located at www.itunes.com. However, the teacher can feel free to select a similar praise and worship song.

"Speak, O Lord" by Keith and Kristyn Getty is recommended for this lesson.

Bible Activity

Read Exodus 3:1-17 two times. Moses argues with God about God's special job He asked Moses to do. What did Moses say? How does God answer?

#1 - (Hint: look at verse 11) - Moses protested and said, "Who am I?" What was God's answer? (Hint - verse 12) - "I will be with You."

#2 - (Verse 13) - Moses: If I say the God of my fathers has sent me, they will ask "What is His name?" God's answer: (Verse 14) "Tell them 'I AM' has sent you."

What can we learn from this conversation about how God deals with His children? (Patient, firm, encouraging) What are some excuses we might make? Make a list of the reasons your class comes up with. What does God think of excuses and arguing with Him?

Teacher Helps

Memory Verse Activity: Graffiti

Graffiti can also be used to help children memorize this verse. Write each word of this verse on a separate piece of paper. Then have children put the words in order in groups of 2 or 3. When each group can put the verse together in order, they will probably have this verse memorized.

Bible Activity: A Discussion with God

Extra credit assignment (for older kids). Read Exodus 4:1-17 at home, and find 3 more times Moses argued with God about this job, and also find God's answers to Moses. You will be able to explain these to the class next week. You can offer a prize as incentive, if you wish.

4) Review the Lesson

This lesson revolves around three main facts:

1. God saw that the Israelites were treated as slaves. He had compassion on them.

2. God spoke to Moses. God told Moses who He was and what He wanted him to do.

3. Moses initially hesitated to obey God. But, eventually Moses obeyed and led the people of Israel out of Egypt.

Teacher Helps

Review the Lesson Activity: 3 Main Facts

Tell children to write down one main thing they learned from this lesson. Then, have them share with one person in the class what they learned. They should write down each new thing they add to what somebody learned in the class. Repeat this process several times. Then, form a master list of what the kids learned from the lesson.

5) Apply the Lesson

Join the Obedience Club. Moses is in the Obedience Club. Abraham is in the Obedience Club. So are Abel and Noah. Why not you? All you have to do is listen to God and do what He says. Then you will be in the Obedience Club.

Sign up today!

- Obedience in being a kind person
- Obedience in saying truthful statements
- Obedience in putting others first
- Obedience in listening to God
- Obedience in obeying parents

Story Line: God called Moses in a special way. Moses obeyed God.

99 Adventures in the Bible's Big Story

Timeline: Beginnings of a Nation

*Adventure Number 24
Page 124*

Adventure Number 25
Exodus 7:20 - 9:22

Story Line: God sent plagues in Egypt to free the Israelites.

 ## 1) Study the Lesson (before class)

- God wanted to release His people from slavery so He sent 10 plagues to demonstrate who He was and what He was like. None of the gods of Egypt were able to stand up against the God of the Bible.[1]

- Plague #1: Nile to Blood (Exodus 7). The god of the Egyptians, Khnum was defeated. Khnum was the Egyptian god of the Nile.

- Plague #2: Frogs (Exodus 8). This was defeat for Khnum's wife, Heket, who symbolized resurrection and help for women in childbirth.

- Plague #3: Gnats (Exodus 8). This was a humiliating defeat for Geb, the Egyptian god of the ground.

- Plague #4: Flies (Exodus 8). Kheper, the Egyptian god of flies, was defeated.

- Plague #5: Livestock (Exodus 9). Calf worship was popular in Egypt. This was a severe defeat for Hathor, the goddess of love represented by a cow.

- Plague #6: Boils (Exodus 9). The Egyptian gods (Serapsis, Isis, and Imhotep) were clearly helpless.

- Plague #7: Hail (Exodus 9). Osiris, the Egyptian god of vegetation, could not help.

- Plague #8: Locusts (Exodus 10). Again, Osiris was defeated.

- Plague #9: Darkness (Exodus 10). Ra, the Egyptian sun god, was defeated.

Footnote - Adventure 25

1. Ibid., COM-94, 95.

2) Begin the Lesson

Ask children to help you with previous memory verses. Maybe say something like, **"Who remembers what (verse) says?"**

- Adventure 1: Genesis: 1:1
- Adventure 2: Colossians 1:16
- Adventure 3: Genesis 2:2
- Adventure 4: Genesis 1:27
- Adventure 5: Genesis 2:8
- Adventure 6: Isaiah 14:12
- Adventure 7: Genesis 3:6
- Adventure 8: Romans 5:12
- Adventure 9: Genesis 3:15
- Adventure 10: Romans 8:20
- Adventure 11: Genesis 3:21
- Adventure 12: Leviticus 19:2
- Adventure 13: Genesis 4:7
- Adventure 14: Genesis 5:1
- Adventure 15: Genesis 16:8
- Adventure 16: Genesis 11:9
- Adventure 17: Genesis 12:3
- Adventure 18: Genesis 19:29
- Adventure 19: Genesis 15:6
- Adventure 20: Genesis 22:14
- Adventure 21: Genesis 32:30
- Adventure 22: Genesis 39:2
- Adventure 23: Exodus 1:12
- Adventure 24: Exodus 3:14

Teacher Helps

Begin the Lesson Activity: Memory Verse Review

Probably, most children will need help with at least some of these verses. If a child needs help, give him the first three words of the verse to help him get started. Emphasize to your class that if they can get the first three words of the verse, they will have a good start and will find the rest of the verse much easier to remember.

3) Teach the Lesson

The Center for Disease Control (CDC) is a worldwide organization that monitors diseases and plagues. The CDC defines a "plague" as "a disease that affects humans and other mammals." The Center for Disease Control was not available when this Bible story took place, but imagine what it would be like for the CDC to receive phone calls from Egypt about 10 different plagues. What do you think they would have done?

Tell the Story

Teacher Helps

Our last story ended like this: *"The God of Abraham would do war against the gods of Egypt."* The battle was about to begin. Would the gods of Egypt win over the God of the Bible? Would neither side win? What if some battles were won by each side? Well, the battle lines were drawn. Egypt, with its many gods would face the God of the Bible because the God of the Bible wanted His people freed from slavery.

The first battle was the defeat of the Egyptian god, Khnum, who guarded the Nile River. When the Nile River turned to blood, God was victorious over Khnum.

The second battle featured Heket vs. God. Heket was the Egyptian god of the resurrection. But when the frogs surrounded the Nile River, Heket went down in defeat. Score, God-2 and Egyptian gods-0.

The third battle was a battle between Geb, the god of the soil, and God. Geb was totally humiliated when swarms of gnats surrounded man and beast. Again, another victory for God and another loss for the Egyptian gods.

The fourth battle saw Kheper, the Egyptian god of flies, go down in defeat.

The fifth battle saw all the Egyptian livestock die. Again, the God of the Bible was victorious over the Egyptian gods.

The sixth skirmish saw boils break out all over humans and animals. The Egyptian gods could not do anything when the God of the Bible initiated the boils. Score: God-6 and the Egyptian gods-0.

The seventh (hail), eighth (locusts), and ninth (darkness) plagues all resulted in the same outcome. God was completely victorious over the Egyptian gods. In spite of all these powerful plagues, Pharaoh would not let the people of Israel go and offer sacrifices.

The Egyptian people must have been very weary of yet another plague. But, God wanted His people to be free and the leader of the Egyptian nation would not let God's people go free. For some, this might look like a battle between Moses and Pharaoh. But, really, it was a battle between the God of the Bible and the main Egyptian gods. God's power was decisive over the gods of the Egyptians. We still have one more plague to look at, but we will talk about that the next time we are together.

Tell the Story Activity: Scoreboard

Make a scoreboard similar to one that you would find in a soccer match. On one side, put "God" and leave a blank for the current score. On the other side, put "Egyptian gods" and leave a blank for the current score.

As you tell the story of the nine plagues in this lesson, let kids keep score. When the score changes, let a different child come up and change the score.

Make sure the children know who the contestants are: God and the Egyptian gods, not Moses and Pharaoh.

Timeline: Beginnings of a Nation

Memory Verse

Exodus 12:12 (ESV) - On all the gods of Egypt I will execute judgments: I am the Lord.

Memory Verse Activity: Pictures

Have children memorize this verse using pictures for any word in the verse. For instance, the teacher could simply put a map of Egypt up to represent Egypt. Judgment might be represented by a throne or a gavel.

Praise and Worship

Praise and Worship styles vary greatly around the world. It is the intent of this curriculum that praise and worship songs be selected that best fit the content of this lesson. Recommendations for praise and worship are given and this music can generally be located at www.itunes.com. However, the teacher can feel free to select a similar praise and worship song.

"Speak, O Lord" by Keith and Kristyn Getty is recommended for this lesson.

Bible Activity

Make a card with the name of each plague written on each card. Make a second set of cards with the name of the Egyptian god that corresponds to each plague. If possible, use one color of paper for the plagues, and a different color for the false gods. Let the kids match up the plague with the false god, and see who can do it the fastest. You can let them work in teams or individually, depending on the size of your class. Emphasize that the one true God is more powerful than any other power in the world.

4) Review the Lesson

Have children simplify the lesson into 10 words or less using their own words. What are their answers? When children simplify the story of the lesson into ten words or less, they will probably say something like these possibilities:

- The God of the Bible defeated gods of the Egyptians.
- God wanted His people to be free from slavery.
- God showed His power in the plagues.
- Pharaoh was very stubborn.
- God is very strong.

Review the Lesson Activity: Simplify

Simplify can be a useful game for the children. The teacher can give each team of 2 or 3 kids about 1-2 minutes to come up with the most significant 10 words of this lesson.

5) Apply the Lesson

Join the Power Club. Last week, we joined the Obedience club. Today, the Power Club belongs to those who let God do the work and we merely submit to Him. Don't resist Him like Pharaoh did. Submit to Him like Moses did.

Sign up today!

- Power for daily Christian living
- Power to resist the temptations of Satan
- Power for sharing the Good News
- Power to obey God

Story Line: God sent plagues in Egypt to free the Israelites.

Adventure Number 26
Exodus 12:1-32

Story Line: God protected people who put their faith in Him.

1) Study the Lesson (before class)

- God sent ten plagues while the Israelites were living in Egypt but Pharaoh did not let the people of Israel leave Egypt to sacrifice to their God.

- God is the one who rescued His people from helpless and hopeless bondage.[1]

- The final plague involved the death of firstborn children and animals.

- The last plague on Egypt was the death of the firstborn in each home. Since pharaoh was thought to be divine, his son was "a son of a god."

- The community of believers were to slaughter a lamb at twilight and spread the blood of the slain animal on the sides and top of the doorposts of the house.

- God wanted the firstborn dedicated to Him because in those days the firstborn was the most valuable and most dear to each family. When they dedicated their firstborn to Him, they were giving Him their best.

- The lamb was a sacrifice. Its innocent blood was shed.

- The people of God knew that if they were to be spared from death, an innocent life had to be sacrificed in their place.

- In killing the lamb, the Israelites shed innocent blood. The lamb was a sacrifice, a substitute for the person who would have died in the plague. From this point on, the Hebrew people would clearly understand that for them to be spared from death, an innocent life had to be sacrificed in their place.[2]

<u>Footnotes - Adventure 26</u>

1. Roy B. Zuck, *A Biblical Theology of the Old Testament* (Chicago: Moody Press, 1991), 34.

2. David Brooks, *The Roots of Faith Old Testament Commentary*, COM-97.

3. James Galvin, *Life Application Bible Notes*, 112.

2) Begin the Lesson

Let's think back over the last 25 adventures that we have studied and see if we can put the adventures in order. Here are the themes for the first 25 adventures:

1) God is very strong.

2) God created angels.

3) God made everything.

4) God made man and woman to be His special friends.

5) Life in the garden was full of pleasure.

6) Satan is God's enemy. Satan was proud. God threw Satan out of heaven.

7) Satan tempted Adam and his wife. Adam and Eve disobeyed God.

8) Sin separated Adam and the woman from God.

9) God promised to send a special Person who would crush Satan.

10) Sin affected God's creation in many negative ways.

11) God killed an innocent animal to give clothes to Adam and his wife.

12) God hates sin. God expelled Adam and Eve from the garden because of sin.

13) Cain and Abel responded to God in two very different ways.

14) Seth became the leader of a very godly family.

15) The people were evil. God sent a flood. Noah trusted and obeyed God.

16) God confused the language of the people.

17) God called Abram to be a great nation and a blessing to all people.

18) God destroyed Sodom because the people were very wicked.

19) Sarah did not respond in faith to the promise of God. Abraham did.

20) God told Abraham to sacrifice Isaac. God provided a ram.

21) Jacob won a new name in a wrestling match with an angel.

22) Good can happen even when people do bad things.

23) In spite of great opposition, God blessed the Israelites greatly.

24) God called Moses in a special way. Moses obeyed God.

25) God sent plagues in Egypt to free the Israelites.

Teacher Helps

Begin the Lesson Activity: Theme Review

The teacher should write these statements on pieces of paper and then mix them up. Do not put the number of the lesson on the piece of paper. Divide the children into 2 or 3 teams, depending on the size of the class. Time how long it takes each team to put the statements in the correct order. Remember, do not number the slips of paper so the children will think through the chronological order.

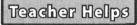

3) Teach the Lesson

What do these three events have in common?

- God provided clothes for Adam and Eve.

- God provided Abraham with a substitute sacrifice for Isaac.

- God provided protection when the Israelites oldest sons were spared.

Answer: God provided for each of them.

Tell the Story

Nine plagues had passed and Pharaoh was exceptionally angry. After the ninth plague, he banned Moses and Aaron from his presence. Little did he know that the tenth plague would be even worse for him than the first nine.

The last plague was the death of the firstborn male, a person or an animal. All firstborns were to die. God told the Israelites and Egyptians who feared the Lord to take the blood of a lamb and wipe it on the entrance of the door of the house. A promise was made between God and anyone who feared Him. The promise was this: the death angel would pass over any house that had the blood of a lamb on the entrance to the house. No one would die if they listened and obeyed the God who made this announcement. God had already proved to all how powerful He was. Now, it would be up to them to obey His instructions.

It happened at night. The death angel went throughout the land of Egypt looking at the entrance of every house. Those who had faith in Yahweh expressed that faith by putting the blood of the lamb on the doorposts of their house. Those who followed Yahweh's instructions were to stay inside their house so that they would not be blamed for the deaths of the firstborn. Also, they would not celebrate the death of any of God's creation. They waited in their homes until the morning. When they realized that even the Pharaoh's son was put to death by the death angel, they knew that God would keep His promise and provide for their salvation. Pharaoh immediately told Moses and Aaron to leave the country. They were to take all their people and all their animals. They were to pray to Yahweh and serve Him.

Tell the Story Activity: The Importance of the Lamb

The teacher should have the children listen to the story of the Passover and remember previous stories that a lamb had to be slain for the good of someone. What examples can the class think of?

Possible answers:
- Adam and Eve
- Cain and Abel
- Abraham and Isaac
- The Passover

The Bible's big story reminds us of the importance of the lamb.

Memory Verse

Exodus 12:13 (ESV) - The blood shall be a sign for you, on the houses where you are. And when I see the blood, I will pass over you, and no plague will befall you to destroy you, when I strike the land of Egypt.

Praise and Worship

Praise and Worship styles vary greatly around the world. It is the intent of this curriculum that praise and worship songs be selected that best fit the content of this lesson. Recommendations for praise and worship are given and this music can generally be located at www.itunes.com. However, the teacher can feel free to select a similar praise and worship song.

"Speak, O Lord" by Keith and Kristyn Getty is recommended for this lesson.

Bible Activity

Plagues and Passover

If possible, have unleavened bread as a snack in class today.

Sift the flour, sugar and salt. Cut in shortening. Add a little bit of milk at a time, and only enough to form into dough. Knead gently until elastic. Roll dough using floured rolling pin into a rectangle 1/4 inch thick. Cut dough into squares about 1/2 inch in size. Pierce the dough all over with a fork. Bake at 375 degrees for 15-20 minutes until lightly browned.

It can be purchased in some grocery stores, or you can make your own using this simple recipe. Explain to the children that the bread was to be unleavened for two reasons:

1. They could not take the time to add yeast and let the bread rise, since they would be making a hasty departure from Egypt.

2. Yeast, or "leaven" represents sin in a person's life. They were not to be stained with sin, but be in a right relationship with God.

Teacher Helps

Memory Verse Activity: Around the Class

Have the children sit in a circle while music is playing. Pass around a phrase of the memory verse. When the music stops, whoever is holding the phrase of the memory verse should try to quote the verse. Do this until all phrases are memorized. Then, do the same thing for the whole memory verse.

Bible Activity: Unleavened Bread Recipe

1 cup flour

3 tablespoons sugar

1/3 teaspoon salt

1/3 cup shortening

2 - 2 1/2 tablespoons milk

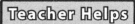

4) Review the Lesson

Two major themes emerge from the Bible's big story of hope. They are "God's provision" and "man's required faith response." In the story of the Passover, we see both of these themes very clearly. In what stories in the Bible do you see these two major themes?

- God's provision for the needs of man (Adam and Eve)
- Eve became the mother of all mankind
- Noah and the ark that he built
- Abraham and Isaac
- The Passover plague

Review the Lesson Activity: Two Major Themes

Have children name and describe as many Bible events as possible that show these two major themes: God's provision and man's required faith response.

5) Apply the Lesson

Responding by faith to God's provision is seen throughout the Bible. We will see it more in lessons to come.

What are some ways that God has provided for you and He expects your faith response?

- He has provided salvation through what Jesus Christ did on the cross and He expects a faith response from you.

- Will you respond by faith to what Jesus Christ did on the cross for you?

Story Line: God protected people who put their faith in Him.

Adventure Number 27

Exodus 14:1-31

Story Line: God is mighty to save. God parted the Red Sea.

 ### 1) Study the Lesson (before class)

- 600 chariots were bearing down on the Israelites. Each chariot had two soldiers in it, one to drive and the other to fight.[1]

- The Israelites were discouraged because they thought they were trapped. In front of them was the Red Sea and behind them was the Egyptian army who were in pursuit of the Israelites. They even complained to Moses and to the Lord about their desperate circumstances.

- This is the first time that we hear of the Israelites complaining on the journey to the promised land. It was a problem they did not forsake.

- The Israelites had at least 600,000 men. Pharaoh brought 600 chariots, charioteers, and troops. Yet, the superior military strength of the Egyptians caused the Israelites to complain.[2]

- The Lord told Moses to quit crying out to Him and get moving. Prayer was important but so was action.

- With no apparent place for the Israelites to go, God dried up the Red Sea for the Israelites to cross.

- When the Israelites had crossed the Red Sea, the Egyptian chariots tried to cross also. As the sun began to rise, Moses raised his hand and the Red Sea waters drowned the Egyptian chariots and their riders.

- When the Israelites saw the crushing defeat of the Egyptian army, they stood in awe and praised God. They also put their faith in God and His servant Moses.

Footnotes - Adventure 27

1. Ibid., 118.

2. John Walvoord and Roy Zuck, *Bible Knowledge Commentary: Old Testament*, 131.

2) Begin the Lesson

Teacher Helps

- Name That Timeline has the class putting in order each of the previous events on a timeline. If a board is available, use a board. If the teacher can put the events of the timeline on a wall so that it is visible to all, that would work the best.
- Timeline Events and People
    - Beginning of Angels
    - Beginning of the World
    - Beginning of People
    - Beginning of Satan's Fall
    - Beginning of People's Sin
    - Promise of a Satan Crusher
    - Expelled from the Garden
    - Cain and Abel
    - Seth
    - Noah and the Flood
    - Sodom and Gomorrah
    - Abraham
    - Isaac
    - Jacob

Review Activity: Name That Event

The teacher could scramble all the events and people and ask for volunteers to put the events and people in order on the wall.

Teams could be created by letting groups of 2 or 3 work together to create the correct order of events on the timeline.

3) Teach the Lesson

What are the three most important events in your nation's history?

1)

2)

3)

Teach the Lesson Activity: 3 Most Important Events

In the history of the nation of Israel, this event is one of the most important events.

 # Tell the Story

The Israelites were now on their way to their own land which God had promised to them. What an exciting time that had to be ... a land of their own and no more slavery. To make it even better, God was on their side visibly now. They had seen His powerful working over the Egyptian gods and they realized how mighty their God was.

After they hit the road, some problems developed. First, the king of Egypt realized he had made a mistake. He let his slave labor go without a payment and without any kind of promise. So, the king decided with his best army to go after the Israelites who were unarmed. It should have been an easy match. Six hundred of Egypt's best charioteers, who were like the armored vehicles of the day, against the helpless Israelites. Add on to that, Egypt had their best foot soldiers. This would be an easy victory for the Egyptians.

And that is exactly what the Israelites thought. When they saw this massive army coming after them, they complained to Moses. They told him that it would have been better for them to die as slaves in Egypt than to die in the wilderness. Apparently, they forgot about the mighty God who had just won ten major victories by sending the plagues against the Egyptian gods.

God told Moses to quit praying and get moving. There was a time to pray but now it was time to travel. God led the Israelites with a bright light in front of them and protected their back side from the Egyptians with a cloud. God had this thing entirely under control. It was night time now and neither side moved. God made sure that the Egyptians didn't attack. In the morning, after a strong wind from the east, Moses held up his rod; the sea parted, and millions of Israelites crossed the Red Sea on dry ground. God showed His mighty power again to the Israelites.

The Egyptian army thought they could cross over on dry ground also. What a big mistake they made. They assumed that the two walls of water on each side of the Red Sea that protected the Israelites would protect them also. They did not realize that it was God who was holding up the water and the entire Egyptian army drowned when God released the waters of the Red Sea. Not one of the Egyptians survived. It was one incredible sight!

Moses wrote a song about this deliverance and the Israelites praised God. They learned to trust Moses and Moses' God, at least for right now.

Tell the Story Activity: Complaining or Praising?

This is the first time that we know that the Israelites complained. After such recent great victories by their God, one would think that complaining against God would be the furthest thing from them. Yet, complaining became a regular part of their daily lives.

After you tell this story, divide your class up into two groups: complainers and praisers. Ask them to do the best job they can to convince the other group that they should join them.

Wrap up this part of the lesson by encouraging kids to look for what God is doing and praise Him for that. Also, encourage them to resist the temptation to join the complainers.

Memory Verse

Exodus 14:29 (ESV) - But the people of Israel walked on dry ground through the sea, the waters being a wall to them on their right hand and on their left.

Praise and Worship

Praise and Worship styles vary greatly around the world. It is the intent of this curriculum that praise and worship songs be selected that best fit the content of this lesson. Recommendations for praise and worship are given and this music can generally be located at www.itunes.com. However, the teacher can feel free to select a similar praise and worship song.

"Speak, O Lord" by Keith and Kristyn Getty is recommended for this lesson.

Bible Activity

"In our Bible lesson today, we learned that the people crossed the Red Sea. We're going to pretend to go across the Red Sea, too."

- Line the children up at one end of the classroom.

- You will need 4 children or 4 teachers to hold the ends of the ropes.

- Stretch the ropes out with a gap of about one foot in between them. Have the children jump over both ropes.

- Once all of the children have jumped across the ropes, move the ropes a little further apart. Let them jump again.

- Continue moving the ropes further apart until the distance is too great for any of the children to successfully jump across.

Teacher Helps

Bible Memory Activity: Phrases

Phrases. Say Exodus 14:29 in three phrases. Designate each part of the class to learn just one phrase. After they have learned one phrase, rotate until all kids have learned all three phrases.

Bible Activity: Crossing the Red Sea

The teacher will need two ropes for this activity.

This activity is divided into two parts. The first part is when the ropes are close enough together so that everyone can "cross the Red Sea."

The second part is when the ropes are very far apart so that no one (the Egyptian army) can "cross the Red Sea" successfully.

Teacher Helps

4) Review the Lesson

"Who" Questions:

1. Who held out the rod of God and the sea parted?

2. Who changed His mind?

"What" Questions:

1. What led the Israelites?

2. What followed up behind the Israelites?

"When" Questions:

1. When did the Israelites cross the Red Sea?

2. When did Pharaoh come after the Israelites?

"Where" Questions:

1. Where is the Red Sea?

2. Where did the Israelites tell Moses that they wanted to go?

"How" Questions:

1. How did the Israelites show their faith in God?

2. How did God dry up the sea bed?

"Why" Questions:

1. Why did the Israelites complain?

2. Why did the Israelites praise God?

Review Activity: The Investigative Cube

Divide the class up into two teams. Make a cube with these labels on each side of the cube: who, what, when, where, how, why. When the cube is rolled to one team, they will answer the type of question that is face up on the cube. For instance, if the "why" is face up on the cube, then that team will answer a "why" question. Teachers can make up their own questions from the lesson.

5) Apply the Lesson

Name 3 things that you should stop complaining about.

Name 3 things that you should praise God for.

Story Line: God is mighty to save. God parted the Red Sea.

Adventure Number 28
Exodus 20:1-17

Story Line: God is holy. God gave the Ten Commandments. Disobedience to His commands is sin.

1) Study the Lesson (before class)

- The Ten Commandments were given to Moses by God on two stone tablets on Mount Sinai which is located on the Sinai Peninsula across the Gulf of Suez from the larger part of Egypt.
- The Israelites had just come from Egypt where they lived for 430 years where the Egyptians had many gods.[1]
- God is worthy of the greatest reverence, and anything else was forbidden. Regardless of how creative they might be, any image would be unworthy of worshipping Yahweh.[2] The Israelites had lived among a people that had many idols. Now, they were to have no idols. This was forbidden by God.
- God told the Israelites that they should not use the name of God in a careless way. He is holy and His name is holy.
- God expected the Israelites to worship and rest on one particular day. It was called the Sabbath.
- The Israelite children were expected to honor their parents. This is the first commandment that attached a promise to it.
- The Israelites were expected not to take the life of another innocent human being; they were expected to not commit murder.
- The Israelites were not to commit adultery. That is, a man could have only one wife to live with and sleep with.
- They were not to steal or take anything that did not belong to them.
- They were not to give false witness. That is, if they went to court and testified, they were supposed to tell the whole truth.

Footnotes - Adventure 28

1. David Brooks, *The Roots of Faith Old Testament Commentary*, COM-106.

2. Ibid., COM-106.

2) Begin the Lesson

- What was the first adventure that we learned about? (creation) What did we learn in the period of time we call creation? (God is strong. God made all things. God made people to be His special friends.)

- What other adventures have we discussed? (fall) What are some of the themes that we learned from the period of time we call the fall? (Satan was thrown out of heaven because of his sin, Adam and Eve sinned, and Satan tempted Adam and Eve.)

- What is another adventure we discussed? (flood) What are some of the themes that we learned from the period of time we call the flood? (God judges sin.)

- What is another adventure we discussed? (Babel) What are some of the themes that we learned from this period of time? (Man cannot establish his own method of worshipping God. It must be God's way of worshipping Him.)

- What is another adventure we discussed? (Beginnings of a Nation) What are some of the themes that we learned from this period of time? (God called Abraham to be a great nation and a blessing to all people.)

- What is another adventure we discussed? (Moses) What are some of the themes that we learned from this period of time? (God called Moses in a special way and Moses obeyed.)

3) Teach the Lesson

What kind of laws are important in the place where you live?

Up to this point in time, the nation of Israel did not have a set of laws that they had to obey. Now, God was going to give them a very specific moral code that we call the Ten Commandments. The nation was to follow closely this moral code by obeying what God said to do and also what He said not to do.

Tell the Story

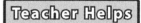

The Israelites had been travelling for two months now. They left Egypt and were on their way to their promised land. They came to Mount Sinai, a familiar place to Moses. This is where Moses heard God speak from the burning bush. It was here that Moses knew that God was calling him to lead the people of Israel out of Egypt. It was a holy place for Moses and now it would be a holy place for the rest of Israel.

Israel had lived without a moral code of obedience to their God. Living among the Egyptians, who have many gods, did not help them. Certainly, they adopted some of the religion of the Egyptians. Now, God wanted to separate Himself and enter into a new covenant with the nation of Israel. Covenants were not new to these people. They knew of the covenant with Noah. They knew of the covenant with Abraham. Now, they would receive their own covenant with God through Moses.

The people of Israel waited for Moses, who had gone to the top of the mountain to meet with God and receive this moral code of obedience. We call this code the Ten Commandments. Here is what they say and briefly what they mean.

1) "You must not have any other god but me." God expected loyalty to Him.

2) "You must not make for yourself an idol." No creative image of Him would come close to representing the glory of Yahweh.

3) "You must not misuse the name of the Lord your God." The name of the Lord was to be treated with the highest reverence and honor.

4) "Remember to observe the Sabbath day by keeping it holy." God's people were to be people who worshipped Him. Their Creator rested and so should they.

5) "Honor your father and mother." Children and adults were to give special support and respect to their parents.

6) "You must not murder." The taking of innocent life was forbidden.

7) "You must not commit adultery." The marriage relationship was to be special for one man and one woman only.

Tell the Story Activity: Most Accepted and Least Accepted Commandments

Tell children to listen to all Ten Commandments. The teacher may even want to give them a copy of the Ten Commandments.

As you tell them the Ten Commandments, have the children put a circle around the commandment that is most accepted in the place where they live.

Also, have the children put an "x" beside the commandment that is least accepted in the place where they live.

When you have finished telling them this story, ask them what they thought was the most accepted and the least accepted commandments in their culture.

8) "You must not steal." Keep, or give away, what is your property but don't take what belongs to someone else.

9) "You must not testify falsely against your neighbor." Don't tell a lie.

10) "You must not covet." Not only were they to not take what belongs to someone else, they were to be content with what they had and not want what someone else had.

Memory Verse

Exodus 20:3 (ESV) - You shall have no other gods before me.

Praise and Worship

Praise and Worship styles vary greatly around the world. It is the intent of this curriculum that praise and worship songs be selected that best fit the content of this lesson. Recommendations for praise and worship are given and this music can generally be located at www.itunes.com. However, the teacher can feel free to select a similar praise and worship song.

"Speak, O Lord" by Keith and Kristyn Getty is recommended for this lesson.

Bible Activity

Make a big poster. On the left side, list each of the Ten Commandments. On the right side, show what each commandment tells us about God.

1. God is exclusive - God alone.

2. God will not share His glory - it is His alone.

3. God's name is very special - respect it.

4. God's day is special.

5. God set up the family - honor that.

6. God shows respect for life, so should we.

7. God is pure and self-controlled.

8. God is just.

9. God is truth.

10. God is satisfied, not wanting more.

Teacher Helps

Bible Memory Activity: Build A Verse

Divide into two groups. Repeat the verse as follows, each side adding one word to what the other group said.

Group 1: Exodus

Group 2: Exodus 20

Group 1: Exodus 20:3

Group 2: Exodus 20:3, "You

Group 1: Exodus 20:3, "You shall . . ."

Bible Activity: Parchment Commandments

Here are some examples of statements that could go on the right side of the poster. God's laws are not made up to spoil all the fun in life! They reflect God's nature and character. God's laws protect us from harm in so many ways! If you have time, help the children think of how each commandment protects us.

4) Review the Lesson

Take the top three vote getters for the "least accepted" commandment that you discussed earlier in the lesson. Discuss with your class:

- Why are these commandments not accepted in our culture?

- What does God expect from us when He gives us commandments that are not part of the moral code of the place where we live?

- Is it more important to obey God or is it more important to follow what everybody else does? Why?

- Does God expect us to obey Him all the time? Does He expect us to obey Him even when many others around us don't obey Him?

Teacher Helps

Review Activity: Question and Answer

These four questions are to be used in conjunction with the "tell the story" part of the lesson. The teacher should note the "least accepted" commandments in the place where you live and encourage kids to live in God's culture and in obedience to Him.

5) Apply the Lesson

1. <u>God</u>. In the beginning, there was a very powerful God.
2. <u>Man</u>. God created people to be His special friends.
3. <u>Sin</u>. Man and woman disobeyed God.
4. <u>Death</u>. God punished man and woman for their disobedience. Death, in the Bible, refers to separation.
5. <u>Christ</u>. God sent His one and only Son who lived a perfect life.
6. <u>Cross</u>. Jesus died on the cross for the sins of the world.
7. <u>Faith</u>. If anyone places their faith in Christ, God welcomes them.
8. <u>Life</u>. God gives eternal life to those who put their faith in Him.

Apply the Lesson Activity

The eight essential truths of the Bible's big story are very important. Which truth does the Ten Commandments emphasize and what will you do to follow the moral code that God has given?

Story Line: God is holy.
God gave the Ten Commandments.
Disobedience to His commands is sin.

99 Adventures in the Bible's Big Story

Timeline: Beginnings of a Nation

Adventure Number 28
Page 144

Adventure Number 29
Exodus 32:1-35

Story Line: The Israelites rebelled against God.

1) Study the Lesson (before class)

- The Israelites expressed concern that Moses might not return from his trip to the mountain top to meet with God. They ordered Aaron to make "gods" for them that would lead them on their journey. So, Aaron gathered gold and fashioned a golden calf.[1]

- Two popular Egyptian gods, Hapi and Hathor, were represented as a bull and a heifer. The Canaanites worshipped Baal, thought of as a bull. In so doing, the Israelites were adopting the religions that were around them and ignoring the second commandment that God had just given them. They were to make no idols or images of Him, of any kind.

- Moses broke the tablets that God had given to him when he saw the idolatry of the Israelites.[2]

- Aaron's compromise to please the people and yet follow God, or gods, resulted in complete failure. However, at the very same time as this compromise, Yahweh designated Aaron and his sons as priests for the Most High God.

- Yahweh communicated to Moses what was happening in the camp. Angrily, Moses left the mountain and came down to rebuke the people of Israel. When Aaron was confronted by Moses, he blamed the people.

- Moses returned to the mountain where he sought forgiveness from God. He even offered himself as a sacrifice for the people's sins. However, as we will learn later, God does not like human sacrifices.[3]

Footnotes - Adventure 29

1. Ibid., 109.

2. James Galvin, *Life Application Bible Notes*, 143.

3. David Brooks, *The Roots of Faith Old Testament Commentary*, COM-110.

2) Begin the Lesson

- Genesis 1:1 - In the beginning, God created the heavens and the earth.

- Colossians 1:16 - For by him all things were created, in heaven and on earth, visible and invisible, whether thrones or dominions or rulers or authorities—all things were created through him and for him.

- Genesis 2:2 - And on the seventh day God finished his work that he had done, and he rested on the seventh day from all his work that he had done.

- Genesis 2:8 - And the LORD God planted a garden in Eden, in the east, and there he put the man whom he had formed.

- Genesis 3:15 - I will put enmity between you and the woman, and between your offspring and her offspring; he shall bruise your head, and you shall bruise his heel.

- Romans 8:20 - For the creation was subjected to futility, not willingly, but because of him who subjected it, in hope.

- Genesis 12:3 - I will bless those who bless you, and I will curse him who curses you; And in you all the families of the earth shall be blessed.

- Exodus 12:13 - The blood shall be a sign for you, on the houses where you are. And when I see the blood, I will pass over you, and no plague will befall you to destroy you, when I strike the land of Egypt.

- Exodus 14:29 - But the people of Israel walked on dry ground through the sea, the waters being a wall to them on their right hand and on their left.

- Exodus 20:3 - You shall have no other gods before me.

Teacher Helps

Review Activity: Review Previous Memory Verses

The teacher should ask children to recall previous memory verses. Not all verses are listed on this page, but the teacher could ask for all 28 previous memory verses to be recited, if time permits. Ask for volunteers and maybe give them a few helps or prompts.

3) Teach the Lesson

When was the last time you saw somebody get really upset? Maybe they even got mad. What were the circumstances that led them to get so bothered about something?

Today's lesson is about Moses who was quite angry at the Israelites because of something they did. It even affected his own brother and sister.

Tell the Story

Moses and Joshua set out for a long journey, a journey that only Moses could make to the top of the mountain. Moses went all the way to the top of the mountain to talk to God while Joshua only went part way up. Joshua waited patiently for Moses. The Israelites did exactly the opposite.

They thought Moses wasn't coming back and they got restless. They got the idea that Aaron would be the next best choice for a leader and they told him to just do something. It didn't matter what ... just do something!

What was Aaron thinking? He told the people to bring their gold to him and they would make a bull out of the gold earrings. Then, they began to worship the golden calf and throw a big party. They proclaimed this golden calf as their deliverer from Egypt.

WOW! God was really upset! He had just told them not to make an image of Him but they went ahead and did it anyway. And, Aaron was their leader! God could see everything and he told Moses what was going on. God was so upset that He threatened to destroy all of the people. Moses came down the mountain and was rejoined by Joshua. Joshua heard the noise from the Israelites and thought they must be at war but Moses knew better. He knew because God told him that the Israelites were having one big party and it wasn't one that honored God. When Moses saw what was going on, he threw the two tablets with the Ten Commandments down and broke them. Now, Moses was really upset also, especially at his brother, Aaron.

Moses rebuked the people. He told them they had sinned and that he would pray for them. He would go back to God, on the mountain, and make atonement for their sin. They were all in big trouble for making this golden calf, worshipping it, and partying around it.

God forgave the people for doing such a wrong thing. He told Moses that no one would be blotted out of the God's book who wanted forgiveness. God gave Moses this assurance and He also gave him another set of tablets with the Ten Commandments on them. God's grace was very evident as He forgave the people. However, He did send a plague on them for doing such a wicked thing. It was similar to when Adam and Eve sinned. God forgave them and gave them a new set of clothes. However, He also punished them by expelling them from the garden. That is how God works. He is gracious but He always punishes sin.

Tell the Story Activity: Listening Locations

Ask children to listen to the story from various locations.

1) Listen from the top of the mountain where Moses was. What did he see? What did he hear? What did he feel?

2) Listen from the middle of the mountain where Joshua was. What did he see? What did he hear? What did he feel?

3) Listen from the bottom of the mountain where Aaron and the Israelites were. What did they see? What did they hear? What did they feel?

Compare locations. What was it like at each of the three locations?

Timeline: Beginnings of a Nation

Memory Verse

Exodus 20:4 (ESV) - You shall not make for yourself a carved image.

Praise and Worship

Praise and Worship styles vary greatly around the world. It is the intent of this curriculum that praise and worship songs be selected that best fit the content of this lesson. Recommendations for praise and worship are given and this music can generally be located at www.itunes.com. However, the teacher can feel free to select a similar praise and worship song.

"Speak, O Lord" by Keith and Kristyn Getty is recommended for this lesson.

Bible Activity

The goal of this activity is to illustrate the things that are idols in our lives today. Ask the kids this question: "If there was a cow made of gold here in our classroom today, would you be tempted to bow down and worship it?" (NO! That would be wrong, like we learned in the lesson today) OK, lets say this together: "NO IDOLS!!" (Do this with the children, several times in a row) Now, let's think about the things we have as idols today. You might be thinking, I don't have any cows made of gold, I don't have any idols. But what is an idol? It is anything that takes the place of God in our lives. Is there anything that takes more of your time and attention than God does? (Be prepared ahead of time and bring in objects that could be idols to your group of kids) What about video games? TV? Sports? Bring a picture or an actual object to represent each idol that could be relevant to your class. Are you willing to look at this _____ and say "NO IDOLS?" Let's say it again, only this time I will hold up each object that could be an idol to us today. Do this together. Pray, and ask God to keep us from idols!

Teacher Helps

Bible Memory Activity

Review the verse a few times then divide the children into two or more teams. Have the teams form lines across from a chalk or white board or piece of paper on a chair. Place something to write with at the board in front of each team. Have the first child of each team run to the board and write the first word of the verse, then run back to the line. The next child of the team will write the next word. This continues until the verse is completed. Allow all teams to finish before playing again.

4) Review the Lesson

This lesson revolves around two main facts:

1. Moses worshipped God at the top of the mountain.

2. The Israelites worshipped the golden calf at the bottom of the mountain.

5) Apply the Lesson

Choosing who or what you worship is the application for this lesson. Israel chose to worship a false god and party around it. God judged them with a plague.

As a righteous Judge, He will choose the right consequence for your actions.

What are some good choices you can make to worship God? (pray, read Bible, go to church, and obey Him)

What can you do to NOT worship God?

When anyone chooses to not worship God, there are bad consequences for this choice.

Review Activity

Tell children to write down one main thing that they learned from this lesson. Then, have them share with one person in the class what they learned. They should write down each new thing someone share with them. Repeat this process several times. Then, form a master list of what the kids learned from the lesson.

Story Line: The Israelites rebelled against God.

Adventure Number 30
Exodus 40:17-35

> **Story Line:** God told the Israelites to build a tent where they could meet Him and offer sacrifices for forgiveness.

 ## 1) Study the Lesson (before class)

- The tabernacle was first built near Mount Sinai about one year after the Israelites left Egypt.
- The Israelites stayed in this same basic location for about eight and a half months. For at least 80 days, Moses was on Mount Sinai. So, for about 6 months, Israel was collecting materials needed for the tabernacle.
- Seven times in Exodus 40, Moses is said to have built the tabernacle exactly as the Lord directed.
- The two tablets of stone containing the Ten Commandments that Moses received from God were placed in the ark.
- The promise of God, "I will dwell among the Israelites and be their God" (Exodus 29:45) was fulfilled as the glory of the Lord filled the tabernacle (Exodus 40:34).
- The tabernacle was God's home on earth. It is where He showed His glory, where sacrifices could be made, and where sins were forgiven.
- When the lamp stands were ready, they were lit so that the place of worship would not remain in darkness (v. 25).
- The construction of the tabernacle suggest a pattern to follow. First, believers must understand God's instruction clearly. Second, carry them out exactly.[1]
- The tabernacle taught two fundamental principles. First, God dwelt among His people. Second, He was inaccessible to them because of His holiness and their sinfulness.[2]

Footnotes - Adventure 30

1. Lawrence O. Richards, *The Bible Reader's Companion: Your Guide to Every Chapter of the Bible* (Wheaton, IL: Victor Books, 1991), 74.

2. David Brooks, *The Roots of Faith Old Testament Commentary*, COM-116.

2) Begin the Lesson

Adventure Number 27: The Exodus

   1. How did God lead the Israelites to the Red Sea?

   2. Read Exodus 14:19-20.

   3. The cloud and the fire.

   4. Praise God for His clear leading.

Adventure Number 28: The Ten Commandments

   1. How many of the Ten Commandments can you name?

   2. Read Exodus 20:1-17.

   3. God's moral code for living.

   4. Pray that we would follow God's commandments for living.

Adventure Number 29: The Golden Calf Rebellion

   1. How could Aaron lead such a rebellion against God?

   2. Read Exodus 32:1-6.

   3. Following God with all of our heart is not an easy thing to do.

   4. Pray that none of us would cause others to rebel against God.

> **Teacher Helps**
>
> **Begin the Lesson Activity: Ask, Read, Talk, Pray**
>
> A good review strategy from 3 previous adventures will focus on four main elements.
>
> 1) Ask a question.
>
> 2) Read the Bible.
>
> 3) Talk about it.
>
> 4) Pray to God.

3) Teach the Lesson

Have you ever seen a place where people worship? What are some different things that you have noticed about places where different religions worship?

What are some things that you would expect to see at a place where Christians worship?

Tell the Story

Welcome to the Tabernacle Tour located in beautiful southern Israel. I want to show you the Tabernacle or tent area where God dwelled among His people. I am glad that so many of you could come today for the tour. Please feel free to ask any questions.

As we stand outside the Tabernacle, you will notice heavy curtains that are surrounding the entire Tabernacle area. With a height of over seven feet, the length of the Tabernacle is about 150 feet and the width of the Tabernacle is about 75 feet. As you can see, it is not a permanent building. That is because God wanted to dwell among His people as they travelled. So, it took many workers to load and unload the Tabernacle gear and equipment.

As we enter the Tabernacle, the first thing that we see is the bronze altar. The bronze altar is where both animal and grain sacrifices were made for the people. Because many animals died here, the priests had to be very careful to clean up all the messes.

As we proceed further into the Tabernacle, we see the bronze basin. That is where the priests cleansed their hands and feet. Before they could go any further, God expected them to be clean. Their sins were taken care of at the altar and their bodies were also clean now.

As we face the front of the Tabernacle, we see two rooms. The first room was called the Holy Place and there are three pieces of furniture. On the right side, you will see a low table. On top of this table, you will notice 12 loaves of bread. These symbolized the fellowship among the 12 tribes of Israel. Across from the table, you will notice a gold lamp stand. It looks like a stylized tree and it reminds us of the Tree of Life in the Garden of Eden. The last item in this first room is a gold-plated hardwood altar on which incense was offered. The incense that was burned was a form of worship; only the priests could do this.

The second room was called the Holiest Place. This very special place contained the Ark, a hardwood chest that was overlaid with gold. It contained a copy of the Law that God gave to Moses. Notice the golden cherubs or angels that are on the lid. This Ark was the main symbol of the presence of God. This was a restricted access area. Only the chief priest could enter this room and he could only do that once every year. So, the Tabernacle shows us that God dwelt among His people. It also shows us that He is holy and how we can deal with our sin.

Tell the Story Activity: Tour Guide

The teacher should act as a tour guide for the telling of this lesson. As the "tour guide" goes through the tent or tabernacle, the teacher will describe what he or she sees and why it is there.

Let the children ask questions at the end about your tour. You may even want to print "Tabernacle Tour Tickets" for each "customer."

The teacher may even want to lay out a replica of the items in the Tabernacle. As you give your tour, have items similar to those in the Tabernacle for your class to see. Let them ask questions.

Memory Verse

Exodus 40:34 (ESV) - Then the cloud covered the tent of meeting, and the glory of the LORD filled the tabernacle.

Praise and Worship

Praise and Worship styles vary greatly around the world. It is the intent of this curriculum that praise and worship songs be selected that best fit the content of this lesson. Recommendations for praise and worship are given and this music can generally be located at www.itunes.com. However, the teacher can feel free to select a similar praise and worship song.

"Speak, O Lord" by Keith and Kristyn Getty is recommended for this lesson.

Bible Activity

Give each child a piece of construction paper, Bible verse, craft sticks and glue. Let the children glue their Bible Verse on their paper. While the children are gluing, go around and write each child's name on his/her paper. Demonstrate to the children how to glue the craft sticks onto their paper in the shape of a building (each child's building will look different – encourage their creativity). Demonstrate to the children how to tear the scraps of construction paper and glue them onto their building.

Teacher Helps

Memory Verse Activity: Hop It

In large letters, write phrases of the verse on sheets of paper. On the floor, tape the papers in a mixed up fashion, but close enough for succeeding words to be reached in a step. Children should step on one word at a time in the proper order to quote the verse. Let each child have a turn of hopping on the verse.

Bible Activity

In our Bible story today, the people of Israel built a tabernacle (a place to meet God) so that they had a place to worship God. Let's build our own.

Story Line: God told the Israelites to build a tent where they could meet Him and offer sacrifices for forgiveness.

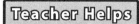

4) Review the Lesson

Agree/Disagree Statements (If you disagree, why do you disagree?)

1. The Tabernacle was over 75 feet tall (Disagree. It is 7.5 feet tall)

2. The basin in the Tabernacle was made out of gold. (Disagree. It was made out of bronze.)

3. The Tabernacle was located in the center of the Israelites camp because God wanted to dwell among His people. (Agree.)

4. The twelve loaves of bread symbolized twelve different soccer teams. (Disagree. The twelve loaves symbolized fellowship among the twelve tribes of Israel.)

5. The first thing you see when you enter the Tabernacle is the Holy of Holies or the Holiest Place (Disagree. The first thing you see when you enter the Tabernacle is the bronze altar.)

6. There were lots of rooms inside the Tabernacle. (Disagree. There were two rooms inside the Tabernacle; the Holy Place and the Holiest Place.)

Review Activity: Agree and Disagree Statements

Kids will have fun disagreeing or agreeing with these statements. You may want to make up some statements of your own for them to agree or disagree with.

5) Apply the Lesson

The Tabernacle was a great place to be because it represented God's presence. You could not come to the Tabernacle (God's presence) though without an offering.

If you truly wanted to be in God's presence, name an offering that you could bring to God that you think He would accept. What are some things that people bring to God as offerings that you are sure He won't accept?

Don't bring an offering to God that is your favorite thing or idea. Only bring an offering to God that you think He will accept. What is that offering?

Adventure Number 31

Leviticus 1:1-9

Story Line: A sacrifice was needed to worship a holy God.

1) Study the Lesson (before class)

- Now that Israel had a Tabernacle to worship God, they needed to learn how to worship this holy God who lived in their midst.

- The book of Leviticus gave the Israelites instructions in how to live in the presence of a holy God. Leviticus 1-7 tells about the five offerings the Israelites should make to the Lord.[1]

- The first offering is called the burnt offering and is found in Leviticus 1. It expresses both commitment to Yahweh and cleansing from sin. Both were necessary for holy people to worship a holy God.[2]

- The animal for the burnt offering could be a bull, sheep, goat, turtledove, or pigeon. The turtledove and pigeon were for people who could not afford a larger animal.

- The offerer put his hand on the head of the animal. This indicated that this was his offering. The priests made sure there was fire on the altar with wood arranged as it should be. The animal pieces were consumed by the fire on the altar.[3]

- Giving the whole burnt offering was an act which symbolized giving oneself completely to Yahweh.

- In contrast to the other offerings, every part of the animal was burnt as an aroma to God.

- Abraham used this to express the supremacy of God.

- Moses used this to worship God.

Footnotes - Adventure 31

1. Ibid., COM-117.

2. Ibid., COM-117.

3. Ibid., COM-117.

2) Begin the Lesson

Teacher Helps

Let's review the eras and time periods that we have studied over the last couple of months.

- Put these time periods in order? (Beginnings and Beginnings of a Nation)

- Who are some of the people that we met in each era?
    1) Beginnings: Adam and Eve
    2) Beginnings: Lucifer, Cain, and Abel
    3) Beginnings: Noah
    4) Beginnings: worshippers of false gods
    5) Beginnings of a Nation: Abraham, Sarah, Isaac, Rebekah, Jacob, and Joseph
    6) Beginnings of a Nation: Moses and Pharaoh

- What are some of the things that these individuals had in common?
    1) Adam, Abel, Noah, Abraham, and Moses all had moments when they placed their faith exclusively in God.
    2) An offering that required a sacrifice. (Adam, Abel, Abraham, and Moses)
    3) They faced Satan's temptations and attacks. (Adam, Eve, Cain, the people of Noah's day, worshippers of false gods, Abraham, Sarah, Moses, and Pharaoh)

- What are some of the ways that God provided for these people? (God gave Adam and Eve clothes, God gave Noah a special boat for protection from the flood, God gave Abraham a ram to offer on Mount Moriah, and God provided protection from Pharaoh's army for Moses.)

Begin the Lesson Activity: Ball Toss

Gather your class of children in a circle with a small ball. Have children take turns rolling the ball gently to each other. When a child catches the ball, have each child answer one part of the question. At this point, do not correct children if they give a wrong answer. Let each child that wants to participate and then roll the ball to another person in the class for the next question.

3) Teach the Lesson

Suppose that you have committed a crime: you stole something. And suppose there was a penalty for that crime ... you would have to go to jail for the rest of your life! Now, suppose that someone else said they would take your place in jail and you could go free. How would you feel? Why?

Tell the Story

I came from a poor family. We did not have very much. I did not know that we were poor. I liked to play with my friends who lived near me. All of us were always on the move in the wilderness. It was hot and we had to help our parents get everything ready to move. We even had to carry some of our own clothes until we got to the next place. We did not know where we were going. We just followed our parents.

After we left Egypt, I learned that God wanted to dwell or live in the middle of all of us. There were millions of people but God chose to live right in the center of our camp. Certain people even built a special place to worship God; they called it a Tabernacle. I couldn't go into the Tabernacle but my parents could. Really, they couldn't go all the way into the Holiest Place, they could just go into the courtyard. The priest was the only one who could go into the Holiest Place and he could only do that once a year.

Because my family was poor, we could not sacrifice a bull like some families could. You see, a bull was expensive and my family could never afford a bull. It didn't matter to me that we weren't able to afford some of the things that my friends' parents could afford. But I found out something really exciting about our family's offering to God and I want to tell you about it.

God told our leaders that all of us could offer a turtledove or a pigeon as a sacrifice to God. We didn't have to offer an expensive offering, like a bull, a sheep, or a goat. I found out that God just wants us to bring our best offering. If we couldn't afford a more costly offering, we could bring an offering that didn't cost as much. We just had to bring our best offering. That is all that God required.

I learned this about God. He loved me so much that I didn't have to be rich or famous to be in His presence. He liked me just the way I am. He only had one requirement: bring the best offering that you can bring. And that is what my parents did ... they brought the best offering that they could bring.

That will make me sleep better tonight because I know that God really likes my family. I know He is holy, that is why He wants us to bring an offering to Him. But, I also know that He is kind. So, whether you are rich like some of my friends and can bring a bull, a sheep, or a goat for an offering or whether you are poor like us and can only afford a pigeon, God expects a sacrifice from us to worship Him. I learned from the Tabernacle that He loves everybody and wants to forgive our sins if we ask for forgiveness.

Tell the Story Activity: First Person Kid in the Wilderness

This story is designed to be told as a child would tell the story as if he or she was a kid in the wilderness wanderings. The teacher could tell the story or you could have one of the children tell the story, as if they were there in the wilderness.

Memory Verse

Leviticus 17:11 (ESV) - For the life of the flesh is in the blood, and I have given it for you on the altar to make atonement for your souls, for it is the blood that makes atonement by the life.

Praise and Worship

Praise and Worship styles vary greatly around the world. It is the intent of this curriculum that praise and worship songs be selected that best fit the content of this lesson. Recommendations for praise and worship are given and this music can generally be located at www.itunes.com. However, the teacher can feel free to select a similar praise and worship song.

"Salvation Belongs to Our God" by Eric Quiram is recommended for this lesson.

Bible Activity

Together, we will see how many examples of this decision we can think of. Give the first group a paper with these names written on it: Cain and Abel, Adam and Eve, Lucifer. Give the second group these names: Noah, Abraham, Moses. The children should work together to come up with 2 choices each person or people had to decide. For example, Cain and Abel each had an offering, Cain's was vegetables (man's way), and Abel's was a lamb (God's way). They should have 2 answers for each person on their list. When they have finished, group 1 will ask group 2 to say either "God's way" or "man's way" as the group leader reads the list. For example, the leader for group 1 would say, Adam and Eve – "Eat from any tree they wanted to" Group 2 would respond by saying, "Man's way!" Group 1 leader would then say: "Eat from any tree in the garden except the tree of the knowledge of good and evil." Group 2 would say "God's way!" Emphasize that the people in the Bible stories didn't always understand God's commands, but they were still expected to obey, and do things God's way. They either chose to trust God, and obey Him, or they chose to follow their own ideas, even if it meant disobeying God. God can always be trusted! He is loving and good, and His commandments are for our protection and will always bring blessing.

Teacher Helps

Bible Memory Activity: Word Scramble

Put each word on a piece of paper and scramble all the words or pieces of paper. Have children unscramble the words by putting them in the correct order.

Bible Activity

Divide your class into 2 groups. Appoint a leader for each group. Today we are going play a game called "God's way, or man's way." Say this: We have learned about many different people in the Bible that had to make a choice. Were they going to do things God's way, or man's way?

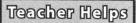

4) Review the Lesson

The theme of this lesson is this: a substitutionary sacrifice was needed to worship God. Because we are telling the Bible's one big story, what other examples from the Bible tell this same story of substitutionary sacrifice?

1. Adam and Eve. An animal had to die so that Adam and Eve could have clothes to cover their shame.

2. Cain and Abel. An animal had to die so that Abel could bring an acceptable offering to God.

3. Abraham and Isaac. An animal had to die so that Isaac would not die on Mount Moriah.

4. The Tabernacle in the Wilderness. An animal had to die for the people to receive forgiveness from God.

Review Activity: The Big Story

Up to this point, we have studied at least four examples of substitutionary sacrifice found in Scripture. Can you name them?

After you name all four examples, have children tell you what happened in each story for substitutionary sacrifice to take place.

5) Apply the Lesson

To worship God, we must be right with Him and with others also. Is there anything that you have done that needs forgiveness from God or forgiveness from people? True worship involves recognizing a holy God and our sinfulness. Sinful people need forgiveness. If you need to be forgiven by God, what will you do? If you need to be forgiven by people, what will you do? True worshippers of God will seek forgiveness.

Story Line: A sacrifice was needed to worship a holy God.

Adventure Number 32
Leviticus 16:6-34

Story Line: The sins of God's people could be removed from them.

1) Study the Lesson (before class)

- People sin naturally and they sin often. They need forgiveness and cleansing from their sin. Blood sacrifices were needed to accomplish both cleansing and forgiveness.

- Leviticus 1-7 gives details for atonement, forgiveness, fellowship, restoration, commitment, and worship.

- Leviticus 8-10 describe how priests would be commissioned.

- Leviticus 11-15 tells us what situations make people unclean.

- Leviticus 16 describes the annual Day of Atonement for cleansing and forgiveness.

- Leviticus 17 explains why blood was necessary for atonement and forgiveness.[1]

- The annual Day of Atonement occurs in late September or early October and is known as Yom Kippur.

- The Day of Atonement was the only day the high priest could enter the Most Holy Place. No one else was ever allowed inside.

- The high priest would offer a bull for his own sins first. Then, he would take some of the blood and incense with hot coals into the Tabernacle. After this, he would set the coals on the golden incense altar and add incense to make a cloud of smoke between him and the Ark of the Covenant. While the cloud was in front of him, he would enter the most Holy Place and sprinkle the bull's blood on the cover, also known as the mercy seat. After this, he cleansed the sin of his family.[2]

Footnotes - Adventure 32

1. Ibid., COM-123.

2. Ibid., COM-123.

2) Begin the Lesson

Remind your class that you are learning the one Big Story of the Bible. While there are many stories in the Bible, they are linked to one major theme or story in the Bible. It is a story of hope. Help your class know that story and be able to put all the lessons together, we are going to review the lessons from the past. Ask, **"What are the main events that we have studied in the Bible?"**

- God always existed and He is very powerful.
- God created the earth and everything in it.
- God created people to be His special friends.
- Lucifer led a rebellion against God and one third of the angels followed him.
- Lucifer, or Satan, deceived Eve. She and Adam sinned by disobeying God.
- God sent a worldwide flood that killed everybody on the earth. God chose to spare Noah and his family because Noah was a righteous man.
- God made special promises to Abraham.
- Abraham offered a ram on Mount Moriah instead of his son, Isaac.
- Jacob wrested with the angel of God and got a new name, Israel.
- The Israelites lived in Egypt for 430 years.
- Through special plagues and deliverance, God led the Israelites out of Egypt.
- God established a moral code called the Ten Commandments that the Israelites were to obey.

Teacher Helps

Begin the Lesson Activity: The Main Events

Review is a significant part of learning. Twelve events are listed here. Write each event on a slip of paper or poster board and have children put them in chronological order. Let them work together in small teams of 2 or 3. Time how long it takes each team to put these events in the right order. Winner gets a prize.

3) Teach the Lesson

Contamination makes something harmful or unusable. This happens regularly. When a food source gets contaminated with a disease, it becomes unusable. When a water source gets contaminated with chemicals, it becomes harmful.

God does not want us to live a contaminated life. A sinful life is a contaminated life. What has God done to prevent this?

Tell the Story

It was a special day. There would be no other day in the year like this day. It would be a day that would be celebrated for years to come by many families. It was the Day of Atonement. To tell you why this day is so extraordinary will require a little bit of background information.

The Israelites had just been given a special moral code to live by, it was called the Ten Commandments. Now, they also had a place of worship, the Tabernacle. Between those two, God established that He is holy and that people are unholy or sinful. God showed He is a personal God by conveying the Ten Commandments to Moses directly and by dwelling in the midst of the Israelites. He was not an impersonal God as some supposed Him to be. He was personal to the Israelites.

Because God was up close and personal, He required that everyone's sin be atoned for, even the priests. To have a place of worship was not enough. To have a code of conduct was not enough. They needed to be forgiven and cleansed from sin. The code of conduct, the Ten Commandments, established what needed to be forgiven when one of the commandments was violated. The Tabernacle established where and how repentance and forgiveness were to take place.

So, once a year, around late September or early October, the Israelites honored God on that day. The priest entered the Most Holy Place on this special day. It was the only day that he could enter. On this particular day, the priest offered a bull that made atonement for his sins and for the sins of his family. He had to do this every year on this special day. He and the Israelites received forgiveness from God when they brought the right sacrifice to the right place with the right reasons, because they had violated God's moral code of living.

On this great day, the Israelites expressed sorrow for sin gratitude because God had chosen to be merciful and forgiving. The people of Israel learned a lot about God's character from the Day of Atonement. They learned that He is kind, loving, and wants to forgive all those who call on His name with the right offering. Those who had violated His moral code of living were not completely wiped out or destroyed. They were forgiven, if they wanted to be forgiven. On this day, the Day of Atonement, sins were removed. It was temporary removal, good until the next year. But, still, sins were removed and for that the Israelites were thankful.

Tell the Story Activity: Special Day

After telling this story, see if children can tell you the following about the Day of Atonement:

- Where? (Tabernacle)

- Who? (the high priest could go into the Holiest Place)

- What? (forgiveness and cleansing)

- When? (late September or early October)

- Why? (the people were sinful and needed to be forgiven by God)

Memory Verse

Leviticus 16:30 (ESV) - For on this day shall atonement be made for you to cleanse you. You shall be clean before the LORD from all your sins.

Praise and Worship

Praise and Worship styles vary greatly around the world. It is the intent of this curriculum that praise and worship songs be selected that best fit the content of this lesson. Recommendations for praise and worship are given and this music can generally be located at www.itunes.com. However, the teacher can feel free to select a similar praise and worship song.

"Salvation Belongs to Our God" by Eric Quiram is recommended for this lesson.

Bible Activity

The purpose of this activity is to help kids understand the complete forgiveness of sin. If possible, bring a globe in to class for this lesson. If no globe is available, use a ball to represent the earth. Let's pretend we wanted to go as far north as we could from where we live. Point out the approximate location of your town, and use your finger to travel north on the globe, until you get to the North Pole. Now let's go as far south as we can. (again, trace your finger southward until you reach the south pole). Can you go any further north? (No) Can you go any further south? (No). When God forgives our sin, He doesn't even remember it anymore. That's hard to understand, because it's very hard for us to forget when someone wrongs or hurts us. We might try really hard to forgive them, but it would be even harder for us to forget it forever, like God does. Have a volunteer read Psalm 103:12 "As far as the east is from the west, So far has He removed our transgressions from us." OK, now lets see how far to the east we can travel from our church! Move your finger east, and even when you get all the way around to the starting point, you can still keep going east. God didn't say as far the north is from the south, because then there would be a stopping place. You can never go far enough east to start going west, and never go far enough west to start going east. God's forgiveness goes on forever!

Teacher Helps

Memory Verse Activity: Bean Bag Toss

With masking tape, mark off a large square on the floor, about 36 inches. Connect the opposite corners inside the square with tape to form an "X." If you have space and many students, make a second square. Give each section a number value (1,2,3,4). A bit of a distance away, put a line of tape to mark the throw line. Divide into two teams. Each student takes a turn throwing a bean bag into one of the sections. (You may make a bean bag by putting beans in a sock and closing it tight with a rubber band. Take the long part of the sock and fold it over the bean section.) If they can say the verse correctly, their team scores the amount of the section where the bean bag was thrown.

4) Review the Lesson

Divide the class into two teams. Give the teams one minute to write down as many statements as they can about the Day of Atonement.

- The Holiest Place could only be entered once a year.

- The priest is the only one who could go into the Holiest Place.

- Everyone needed to have their sins forgiven, even the priest.

- The Day of Atonement occurred in late September or early October.

- The blood of a bull was the only source of satisfaction to God or substitution.

- The Tabernacle was the location for the Day of Atonement activities.

Review the Lesson Activity: One Minute List

The teacher should give two teams one minute each to list as many facts as they can about the lesson.

After the one minute has passed, compare lists and see who has more facts. Be sure that children remember that you are looking for facts.

5) Apply the Lesson

God can and does forgive all sin, regardless of how bad that sin is. Perhaps, someone in your class needs forgiveness from God. The sacrifice of Jesus Christ on the cross is our only hope of forgiveness. Without the shedding of His blood, there is no forgiveness of sin. This special day reminds all of us that we are unholy and God has a remedy for our unholiness, the blood of Jesus Christ which cleanses us from all sin.

Story Line: The sins of God's people could be removed from them.

Adventure Number 33
Number 13:26 - 14:4

Story Line: God's people chose to believe that God could not give them the land.

1) Study the Lesson (before class)

- The Israelites spent nearly a year at Mount Sinai. There, they received the Law. They had left Egypt about two years earlier. Now, they were headed northeast to the promised land. All seemed to be going well. Anticipation of arrival in the land that God promised to Abraham 650 years earlier must have been high.

- The Promised Land was indeed bountiful, as the 12 scouts discovered. The Bible often calls it a land flowing with milk and honey. Although the land was relatively small, 150 miles (241 kilometers) long and 60 miles (97 kilometers) wide, its lush hillsides were covered with fig, date, and nut trees. It was the land God had promised to Abraham, Isaac, and Jacob.[1]

- The twelve scouts were sent to evaluate the number of people in the land, their strengths, and whether the land was rich or poor. God was giving them information that might weigh against their confidence in God.[2]

- Some of the walled cities had walls as high as 60 feet. Three major groups of people occupied the land: the Amorites, the Jebusites, and the Hittites. Except for Joshua and Caleb, the scouts communicated their fear to the rest of the nation, which caused a national revolt.

- Only two of the spies believed Yahweh. The rest of Israel followed the ten spies. They complained about Yahweh, they forgot their misery in Egypt, and they predicted their wives and children would be exploited.

- This lack of faith resulted in 38 more years in the wilderness.[3]

Footnotes - Adventure 33

1. James Galvin, *Life Application Bible Notes*, 222.

2. Lawrence O. Richards, *The Teacher's Commentary* (Wheaton: Scripture Press, 1983), 127.

3. David Brooks, *The Roots of Faith Old Testament Commentary*, COM-129.

2) Begin the Lesson

Lay out a game board for review that looks something like this:

Time Line	Story Line	Songs	Memory Verses
100 points	200 points	300 points	400 points
100 points	200 points	300 points	400 points
100 points	200 points	300 points	400 points
100 points	200 points	300 points	400 points
100 points	200 points	300 points	400 points

Go back for each of the last 10 lessons and let the children name the time line for each lesson (100 points), the story line for each lesson (200 points), the song for each lesson (300 points), and the memory verse for each lesson (400 points).

A prize should be given to the winning team. Usually, competition is a fun thing for the children. So, keep them all involved. Depending on the size of your class, you may want to limit each child to only 1 or 2 answers.

There will be a total of 11,000 points, 1000 points for each lesson (100 for the time line, 200 for the story line, 300 for the song, and 400 for the memory verse).

Teacher Helps

Begin the Lesson Activity: Bible Jeopardy

Divide the class evenly into two teams. The teams could be:

1) whoever has birthdays in January through June

2) whoever has birthdays in July through December

This game will be continued with the review at end of the lesson.

3) Teach the Lesson

All computers have a basic operating system. The operating system for Apple computer is ios. The operating system for PC computers is Windows. It is the language that the computer "speaks" to make it work properly.

God has an operating system for people also. It is for people to put their faith in what He said He would do; believing that what He said He would, that is what He will do. This lesson is about people who put their "operating system" in their fears, not in the promises of God.

Tell the Story

We left Egypt two years ago through God's miraculous intervention. We have spent about the last year at Mount Sinai where Moses received the Ten Commandments. Now, we were ready to move into the promised land that God had promised to Abraham over 600 years earlier. Twelve of us were selected to scout out our new land.

My name is Joshua and I was one of the twelve scouts that were selected to go into the land of Canaan. Things were going very well. All of us saw the miraculous crossing of the Red Sea. We now had a moral code of behavior from God Himself; it was called the Ten Commandments. It told us how to live. Now, for the first time, we had a written set of beliefs and behaviors we were to follow. Anticipation to enter the promised land was high.

So, twelve of us, one from each tribe, set out to search out the land. We spent 40 days in the land of Canaan. Caleb and I saw things much differently than the other ten scouts.

All of us saw that the land was very fruitful and productive. The grapes that grew in Canaan were huge. We had been living in the wilderness so when we saw how great the land was for growing crops, we were all delighted.

But, a major difference arose between the other ten scouts and us. We, Caleb and I, saw this problem coming but we believed God could and would overcome our fears. The people of the land were protected very well in their cities and some of the people were quite strong. The other ten scouts thought this should stop us; they thought there was no way that we could overcome their well fortified cities. Caleb and I disagreed. We knew God would help us overcome the people that lived in the promised land just like He helped us overcome the Egyptians. We knew that God would give it to us. The other ten scouts convinced the rest of the Israelites that taking the land would be impossible. Their report resulted in a huge revolt against our God and against Moses.

We ended up spending another 38 years in the wilderness because of our unbelief at Kadesh Barnea. Had we trusted God, we would have entered the promised land much sooner. Caleb and I, and everyone under the age of 20 were the only ones who would ever see the promised land. If the others had just believed God, they would have seen and lived in the promised land.

Tell the Story Activity: Joshua Tells the Story of Faith or Consequences

The teacher should tell this story as if he or she was Joshua. The teacher may want to dress up as Joshua. As Joshua tells the story, your class should listen for:

1) What is the truth about what God had promised Abraham?

2) What are the consequences of not believing that truth?

Memory Verse

Numbers 13:31 (ESV) - Then the men who had gone up with him said, "We are not able to go up against the people, for they are stronger than we are."

Bible Activity

Teach the song/poem called "12 men went to spy on Canaan." The words to the song are in black, motions are in red. Tune is in blue, key of G major.

G G   G   G G D B D   E   E   D   D   E F# G

12 men went to spy on Canaan, 10 were bad and 2 were good.

Shield eyes and look around.   Hold up 10 fingers, thumbs down for bad, hold up pointer on each hand for "2" and then thumbs up for "good".

G G   G   G G G G   D B   D   E E   D   D E F# G

What do you think they saw in Canaan, 10 were bad and 2 were good.

Palms up, questioning look on your face, Hold up 10 fingers, thumbs down for bad, hold up pointer on each hand for "2" and then thumbs up for "good."

G   G G D E E   D   A   A   A   G F# E   D

Some saw giants big and strong. Some saw grapes on clusters long.

Flex muscles in arms, then hold up imaginary grapevine with left hand, trace imaginary cluster of grapes from the vine, all the way down to the floor.

G   G G D E E D   E E   D D E F# G

Some saw God was in it all, 10 were bad and 2 were good.

Point up to heaven for "God," Hold up 10 fingers, thumbs down for bad, hold up pointer on each hand for "2" and then thumbs up for "good."

Teacher Helps

Memory Verse Activity: The Telephone Game

Memorize this verse using The Telephone Game. Have your class form one line, then whisper into the ear of the first person in line a phrase of this verse, have that person repeat the phrase to the next person. Do this until all have quoted the first phrase. Then do the same thing with the second phrase, the third phrase, and so on until you have memorized the verse.

4) Review the Lesson

Continue your review game for points that you began at the start of the lesson.

- For 100 points, how many scouts were sent out? (12)
- For 200 points, how many days did they scout out the land? (40)
- For 300 points, where did they leave from and return? (Kadesh Barnea)
- For 400 points, who were the two scouts who brought back a good report? (Joshua and Caleb)
- Bonus question worth 500 points: What is the theme of this lesson? (God's people chose to believe that God would not give them the land.)

Teacher Helps

Review the Lesson Activity: Bible Jeopardy

This review activity is a continuation of the review game at the beginning of the lesson.

5) Apply the Lesson

Lack of faith in God affected the whole nation. How can you be a "faith scout" and not an "unbelief scout?"

- Complain about circumstances or praise God for circumstances?
- Remember what God said and obey or disregard what God said?
- Tell others what God can do or tell others that God is unable?

Story Line: God's people chose to believe that God could not give them the land.

Adventure Number 34

Numbers 21:4-9

Story Line: People were healed if they believed God and looked at the bronze snake.

1) Study the Lesson (before class)

- From Psalm 78, we learn that Israel was complaining because they were not faithful to God, they did not obey God, and forgot the great miracles God had done for them.

- In Numbers 21, a new chapter begins in the history of redemption.[1]

- They had bread enough to eat, but they complained that they had no bread. They were disgusted with the bread God gave them.

- That part of the desert where the Israelites now were, near the gulf of Akaba, is infested with venomous reptiles, particularly lizards, which raise themselves in the air and swing themselves from branches; and scorpions, which, being in the habit of lying in long grass, are particularly dangerous to the barelegged, sandaled people of the East.[2]

- Moses was told to put a bronze snake on a pole. When the Israelites just looked at the bronze snake, they would be healed.

- It was not the bronze snake that healed them but looking at the bronze snake that healed them, which represented their belief in God's word.

- If they refused to look at the snake, then they would die from the bite of the poisonous snake.

- Israel realized their sin and confessed their sin to God.

- Those who had quarreled about God did not want Him as their best friend.

- God made provision for the people so they would have relief from His judgment.

Footnotes - Adventure 34

1. Lawrence O. Richards, *The Teacher's Commentary*, 130.

2. Robert Jamieson, A.R. Fausset, and David Brown, *Jamieson-Fausset-Brown Bible Commentary*, Numbers 21.

2) Begin the Lesson

One of the goals for review is for children to see the Bible's big story. Today, we want to ask children to give us some of the recurring themes we see so far in that story. For instance, let children volunteer their answers, but you might use the following examples as recurring themes in the Bible's one big story:

God's Amazing Power:
- Creation
- Worldwide Flood
- Red Sea Crossing

Animal Substitution:
- Adam and Eve
- Abraham and Isaac on Mount Moriah

Faith that Pleases God:
- Noah
- Abraham
- The Passover

God Punishes Sin:
- Adam and Eve
- Unbelief at Kadesh Barnea

Begin the Lesson Activity: One Big Story

The teacher may want to give the class the topics such as: God's Amazing Power, Animal Substitution, Faith that Pleases God, and God Punishes Sin. Then, let the children tell Biblical examples of those stories we have previously studied.

The purpose of this activity is for children to see recurring themes in the Bible's one big story.

3) Teach the Lesson

Complaining and arguing are two things God really doesn't like at all. Many people have a tendency to complain about their circumstances. If any thing at all happens different than what they hoped for, they complain.

This lesson is about a bunch of complainers. They found fault with three different things. What are some things that you are most likely to complain about?

Tell the Story

Teacher Helps

It was another change of plans. Moses decided to enter the Promised Land from the East, not from the South. The Israelites were already upset at all the delays at getting into their new homeland. Now, Moses' new plans were all it took to get them complaining, bickering, and arguing. Instead of following their leader who was following God, they developed another national rebellion. This time the rebellion looked like this: they didn't like the water … they didn't like the food … and they didn't like the wilderness wandering. The complaining caught on and soon almost everyone was caught up in the "bad food, bad water, and bad land mentality."

Now, it was time for the Lord to punish sin, again! This time, He sent poisonous snakes. The bites of these poisonous snakes were deadly. Many people died because of these snake bites. When people started dying, there was a feeling among the living that they had done the wrong thing, they had sinned. So, they went to Moses and asked him to pray for them, which he did. Moses prayed for them and God sent a special answer for their problem.

The remedy for their sin of complaining came in a much different form than anyone expected. The Lord told Moses to get a bronze snake and put it on a tall pole. Anyone who looked at the bronze snake on the pole would be healed of their deadly snake bite. It just required faith, that was all. Of course, Moses obeyed God. He put the bronze snake on the pole. Who else would obey? Now, would they listen to what God said to do and then do it?

We don't know how many people would listen to the voice of God and obey it. But, we do know that Moses listened and obeyed the voice of God. It was a reminder that God expects faith in Him even when circumstances don't look as promising as what we may like sometimes. The Israelites had circled around Kadesh for 38 years. They were tired of the wilderness, they were tired of the food, and they were tired of the lack of water. When Moses changed their plans to enter their new homeland, they complained. That was not a good idea and of course, God punished them for their complaining.

Now, perhaps many people learned a vital lesson … maybe they learned a couple of vital lessons. They learned that God doesn't like complaining. They learned that God does like faith; not just any kind of faith. He likes the kind of faith that people put in Him that looks like this: what He said is what He will do! God always honors His own word and He expected the Israelites to do the same.

Tell the Story Activity: Complaining

Before telling the story, tell your class to find as many things to complain about as possible. Then, have your class tell others what to complain about.

If it is possible to bring in a tall pole and an imitation of a snake on a pole, use that when Moses lifts up the pole with the bronze snake. Something as simple as a scarf or piece of fabric, twisted tightly, could be used to represent the bronze snake.

Children are very good at using their imagination.

Memory Verse

John 3:14 (ESV) - And as Moses lifted up the serpent in the wilderness, so must the Son of Man be lifted up.

Praise and Worship

Praise and Worship styles vary greatly around the world. It is the intent of this curriculum that praise and worship songs be selected that best fit the content of this lesson. Recommendations for praise and worship are given and this music can generally be located at www.itunes.com. However, the teacher can feel free to select a similar praise and worship song.

"Salvation Belongs to Our God" by Eric Quiram is recommended for this lesson.

Bible Activity

Give each child a card or piece of paper, and have them write down as many things as they can think of to be thankful for. Give children about 5 minutes to work on this. At the end of 5 minutes, let each child share a few of the things on their list. Ask: **"Can you think of anything in the whole world that you would like to have that you don't have? Of course! There are always things we would like to have, but we can choose to be content by thinking of and thanking God for the blessings He has given us."**

The Israelites were short on contentment and thankfulness! What did they have to be thankful for? (water from the rock, deliverance from the Egyptians, manna from heaven) How did they feel when they complained to Moses? (Grumpy, mad)

How did they feel when the snakes started biting people and killing them? (scared, sorry, ashamed)

Did God give all of them what they deserved? (no, He offered a way of escape from the consequences of their sin)

Were all of them forgiven? (no, just the ones who turned from their sin and obeyed God by looking up to the bronze snake)

Teacher Helps

Memory Verse Activity: Graffiti

Graffiti can be used to help children memorize this verse. Write each word of this verse on a separate piece of paper. Then have children put the words in order in groups of 2 or 3. When each group can put the verse together in order, they will probably have this verse memorized.

Bible Activity: Thankfulness

Thankfulness activity - Start by asking the question: "Have you ever been around a person who complained all the time? Do you enjoy spending time with a person like that? Are those people usually the ones who have nothing to be thankful for, and that's why they complain?" NO!! So ... let's see how many blessings we can count today!

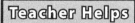

4) Review the Lesson

Review the lesson and see which of these you can find.

- Sin of unbelief and rebellion
- Judgment from the Lord
- Confession
- Prayer for deliverance
- God's provision
- Faith
- Life

Review the Lesson Activity: Scripture Search

The teacher should have the class break up into groups of 2 or 3. Have them find each of the 7 main ideas in the lesson which are listed to your left. For younger children, or non-readers, the teacher should help them by looking up verses.

5) Apply the Lesson

Complain or Be Thankful - You Choose! It is God's will for us to be thankful. It is also God's will for us not to complain. Of the following areas: what will you do? It is a choice that you need to make. Will you choose to be thankful or will you choose to complain?

- School
- Parents
- Friends
- Your brother or sister
- Something else

Story Line: People were healed if they believed God and looked at the bronze snake.

Adventure Number 35
Deuteronomy 6:1-10

Story Line: People who followed God were to be completely loyal and obedient to Him.

 ## 1) Study the Lesson (before class)

- After travelling for almost 40 years, the Israelites were now ready to enter the land promised to Abraham. All those who were 20 years old or older in Kadesh were now dead with the exception of Moses, Caleb, and Joshua.

- Before Moses died, he wanted to prepare the next generation to enter this special place. Since none of them remembered Mt. Sinai, Moses refreshed this new generation with instructions on how to follow the Lord their God.[1]

- The book of Deuteronomy is a set of sermons from Moses to this new generation. Moses began by giving a historical background of what Yahweh had done (Deuteronomy 1-4). He followed that by repeating the Ten Commandments that were issued nearly 40 years ago on Mount Sinai (Deuteronomy 5). Then, Moses emphasized the impact of the Ten Commandments on the Israelites (Deuteronomy 6-11).[2]

- The nation of Israel was now ready for a land that was flowing with milk and honey. They had missed their chance 40 years earlier. Now, Moses warned them how to prepare to enter the land. Numbers 13 and 14 explained where they went wrong.[3]

- They should also know that He is the only Deity in the world. No other deity would ever successfully challenge Him.

- The response of every Israelite to this truth was simple: love the Lord your God with everything that you have and everything that you are. Complete loyalty to Yahweh was expected.

Footnotes - Adventure 35

1. David Brooks, *The Roots of Faith Old Testament Commentary*, COM-135.

2. Ibid., COM-135.

3. James Galvin, *Life Application Bible Notes*, 273.

2) Begin the Lesson

Ask children to help you with previous memory verses. Maybe say something like, **"Who remembers what (verse) says?"**

- Adventure 5: Genesis 2:8
- Adventure 6: Isaiah 14:12
- Adventure 7: Genesis 3:6
- Adventure 8: Romans 5:12
- Adventure 9: Genesis 3:15
- Adventure 10: Romans 8:20
- Adventure 11: Genesis 3:21
- Adventure 12: Leviticus 19:2
- Adventure 13: Genesis 4:7
- Adventure 14: Genesis 5:1
- Adventure 15: Genesis 16:8
- Adventure 16: Genesis 11:9
- Adventure 17: Genesis 12:3
- Adventure 18: Genesis 19:29
- Adventure 19: Genesis 15:6
- Adventure 20: Genesis 22:14
- Adventure 21: Genesis 32:30
- Adventure 22: Genesis 39:2
- Adventure 23: Exodus 1:12
- Adventure 24: Exodus 3:14
- Adventure 25: Exodus 12:12
- Adventure 26: Exodus 12:13
- Adventure 27: Exodus 14:29
- Adventure 28: Exodus 20:3
- Adventure 29: Exodus 20:4
- Adventure 30: Exodus 40:34
- Adventure 31: Leviticus 17:11
- Adventure 32: Leviticus 16:30
- Adventure 33: Numbers 13:31
- Adventure 34: John 3:14

Teacher Helps

Begin the Lesson Activity: Memory Verse Review

The last 30 memory verses are given here. Divide the children up into two teams and see which team can tell you the most memory verses. Give the teams five minutes and they must work together.

The teacher can provide a few helps.

3) Teach the Lesson

What are the most important things these people have ever told you?

- Your mom
- Your dad
- One of your teachers
- One of your friends
- A family member

Today's lesson will summarize the most important thing that God has ever told us.

Tell the Story

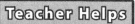

The journey was almost over. The Israelites had wandered in the wilderness for almost 40 years. Most of the people who started the journey were dead now, buried somewhere in the wilderness. Moses was getting up in years but he still had a lot of strength. To prepare the Israelites for their new land, Moses delivered a series of sermons. It was helpful because he wanted the next generation to be better prepared to know and obey God. The last generation had failed miserably.

Moses knew that the nation was at a crossroads. The last generation was a bunch of complainers that focused less on Yahweh and more on circumstances. God had to punish all the adults over 20 years old for that. These people never got to enter the land promised to Abraham. It was their choice to complain that hurt them the most. Now, the next generation was ready to enter the land. But, they had not seen the great miracles of the past. Miracles like the ten plagues, the crossing of the Red Sea, and the miraculous provisions that God had made for the nation. Their shoes did not even wear out. Think of that ... they wandered for 40 years in the desert and they used the same pair of shoes.

The next generation needed to know about all this. The next generation needed to know who God is and what He is like. They didn't learn this from their parents like they should have. So, Moses delivered a sermon series to the nation. This sermon series was to help the Israelites worship Yahweh. You see, they were surrounded by nations that believed in many gods but not the true and unique God. They came from Egypt where there were many false gods. They were going to Canaan ... same thing, a lot of false gods. Because their parents did not instruct them about the one true God, Moses would have to do that.

It was like new marching orders for the new generation. The new marching orders were for everybody, kids and adults. Adults were instructed to tell their kids about this great God. They were supposed to talk about this great God all the time. Like at dinner time, when they travelled, in the morning and in the evening ... almost every time was to be used. This great God wanted adults and children to know who He was and what He had done. So, when they entered the new land, the Israelites would know Who got them there and what they were supposed to do when they got there. One last thing, God provided another great leader. His name was Joshua and he would lead this nation into their new land with their new marching orders for this next generation.

Tell the Story Activity: The Last Words of Moses

Moses gives a glimpse as he ends his time as leader of the great nation of Israel. These are his last words. What does he say in this last address to the nation that is most significant to you? Write it down and share it with a friend in class at the end of the lesson.

Memory Verse

Deuteronomy 6:5 (ESV) - You shall love the Lord your God with all your heart and with all your soul and with all your might.

Praise and Worship

Praise and Worship styles vary greatly around the world. It is the intent of this curriculum that praise and worship songs be selected that best fit the content of this lesson. Recommendations for praise and worship are given and this music can generally be located at www.itunes.com. However, the teacher can feel free to select a similar praise and worship song.

"Salvation Belongs to Our God" by Eric Quiram is recommended for this lesson.

Bible Activity

Craft – Making Phylacteries

Cut strips of paper, about 1 inch wide by about 12 inches long. You will need 3 or 4 strips for each child. Paper that is colored or has a pattern printed on one side is nice, but not necessary. If you are using white paper, it would be fun to let the children color one side of the paper, if you have time. On the other side, have the children write Bible verses. Today's memory verse should be one, and the others can be whatever you choose. Some suggestions: Joshua 1:8 (this is next week's memory verse), and 2 other verses you would like to use from previous lessons. After the verses have been copied onto the papers, wrap each paper around a pencil to form a cylinder shape. Tape the end to keep it rolled up, then thread the rolls onto the yarn to form a necklace. Tell the children that the Israelites were instructed to keep God's Word close to them at all times. They wore special jewelry with Bible verses to help them remember God's commands. They were to talk about God's Word all the time! God especially wanted them to teach their children God's ways. Living a life that is pleasing to God is not easy! We need to keep God's Word in our minds all the time. Let's say our verse together one more time.

Teacher Helps

Memory Verse Activity: Pictures

Have children memorize this verse using pictures for any word in the verse. For instance, the teacher may use a triangle for "the LORD God" or a red heart for the "love." "Soul" could be a picture of a person and "might" could be visualized with a picture of a strong right arm.

Bible Activity: Making Phylacteries

Supplies needed for each child:

- 4 strips of paper
- pencil
- 1 piece of yarn or string 24" long
- tape

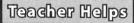

4) Review the Lesson

Have children simplify the lesson into 10 words or less using their own words. What are their answers? When children simplify the story of the lesson into ten words or less, they will probably say something like these possibilities:

- The Lord our God is one Lord.
- Love the Lord with all your heart.
- God wants us to be totally obedient to Him.
- Teach children who God is.
- Talk about God all the time.
- Don't worship other gods.

Review the Lesson Activity: Simplify

Simplify can be a useful game for the children. The teacher can give each team of 2 or 3 kids about 1-2 minutes to come up with the most significant 10 words of this lesson.

5) Apply the Lesson

The Lord wants us to have an intimate personal relationship with Him and obey Him.

Obedience is emphasized regularly in Deuteronomy. Encourage daily obedience. Talk about practical ways that children can obey God.

- With all your heart (what you desire)
- With all your soul (what you think about)
- With all your strength (what you do)

Story Line: People who followed God were to be completely loyal and obedient to Him.

Adventure Number 36
Joshua 1:1-7 and 2:8-11

Story Line: With God's help, the people entered the Promised Land.

1) Study the Lesson (before class)

- Yahweh first made the promise of land to Abraham when he was about 75 years old. Now, 700 years later, the Lord directed Joshua to lead the Israelites into this land.

- In Joshua 2, we are told that the inhabitants of Jericho were terrified of the people of Israel. The people of Jericho knew that Yahweh had given Israel this land.

- Yahweh urged Joshua to be courageous, not for the battles that lie ahead, but for Joshua to be careful to obey the Lord. The success of the battles was up to God. Joshua was to trust and obey.

- Joshua sent two scouts to spy out the land. These scouts encountered Rahab who converted from polytheism to the worship of Yahweh. Her speech to the spies reveals the errors of the ten scouts 38 years ago. If the Canaanites still feared Yahweh 40 years after Israel's deliverance from Egypt, then surely they had feared Him 2 years after their exodus.

- The first five chapters of Joshua detail the entering of the land of Canaan by the Israelites. Yahweh was with them and would give them the land. Chapters 6-12 tell how Israel conquered the land. God was with them when they fought for the land. That is why they conquered the land.

- The book of Joshua ends with two speeches by Joshua. To encourage the Israelites to be faithful to Yahweh, Joshua told of their history and its most notable leader, Abraham, who had been an idolater. In His grace, creator God revealed Himself to Abraham. Joshua told of the plagues, the Israelites deliverance from slavery, the Red Sea and other acts. Yahweh expected the people to be loyal and obedient to Himself.[1]

Footnotes - Adventure 36

1. David Brooks, *The Roots of Faith Old Testament Commentary*, COM 141-143.

2. Lynn Solem and Bob Pike, *50 Creative Training Closers* (San Francisco: Jossey-Bass Pfeiffer, 1997), 70.

3. Lawrence O. Richards, *The Bible Reader's Companion: Your Guide to Every Chapter of the Bible*, 74.

2) Begin the Lesson

Let's think back over the all of our lessons that we have studied and see if we can put the lessons in order. Here are the story lines for some of the first 35 lessons:

1) God is very strong.

3) God made everything.

5) Life in the garden was full of pleasure.

7) Satan tempted Adam and Eve. Adam and Eve disobeyed God.

9) God promised to send a special Person who would crush Satan.

11) God killed an innocent animal to give clothes to Adam and Eve.

13) Cain and Abel responded to God in two very different ways.

15) The people were evil. God sent a flood. Noah trusted and obeyed God.

17) God called Abraham to be a great nation and a blessing to all.

19) Sarah did not respond in faith to the promise of God. Abraham did.

21) Jacob won a new name in a wrestling match with an angel.

23) In spite of great opposition, God blessed the Israelites greatly.

25) God sent plagues in Egypt to free the Israelites.

27) God is mighty to save. God parted the Red Sea. God drowned His enemies.

29) The Israelites rebelled against God.

31) A substitutionary sacrifice was needed to worship a holy God.

33) God's people chose to believe that God could not give them the land.

35) People who followed God were to be completely loyal and obedient to Him.

> **Begin the Lesson Activity: Story Line Review**
>
> The teacher should write these statements on pieces of paper and then mix them up. Do not put the number of the lesson on the piece of paper. Divide the children into 2 or 3 teams, depending on the size of the class. Time how long it takes each team to put the statements in the correct order. Do not number the slips of paper.

3) Teach the Lesson

Describe something new that you have tried in the last year. What was it like? Who helped you? Were you afraid? Did you know that you could do it? Today's lesson is about a brand new experience, with new marching orders, and a new leader. How would they do?

Tell the Story

Teacher Helps

It was a new day for a new leader with new marching orders for a new nation entering a new land. It was a thrilling day for the nation to enter the land that had been promised 700 years earlier to their highly respected leader, Abraham. This would be the group that would realize the great promise made by Yahweh so many generations ago.

Moses, the previous leader, was dead now. Everyone assumed that Moses would lead the nation into the promised land. But, because of his anger, God allowed Moses to see the land but not enter the land. The nation mourned the death of Moses.

Yahweh had specific instructions for the new leader, Joshua. Joshua would need to be careful to obey the Lord and lead the nation in obedience. In fact, God would give them the land, that was His responsibility. The responsibility of the leader and the people was obedience ... specifically, obedience to the Word of God. So, when the nation entered the land, they would see tall walls and tall people, but they should not be afraid. Yahweh repeated several times that they should be very courageous. It was a reminder that was remembered by Joshua at the end of his life when he spoke to the nation. It made a lasting impact on him and many other people.

The new leader sent in 2 scouts and they quickly found a new convert. Her name was Rahab. She had a rough life but now she found faith in Yahweh and was a big help to the 2 scouts. In fact, when the Israelites attacked her city, Jericho, her life was spared. Later in the Bible, she is named as one of the heroes of the nation. She was courageous and God rewarded her for her faith.

The 10 scouts of 38 years ago were wrong. These Canaanites were afraid of the Israelites. The Israelites could have been here 38 years ago had the 10 scouts not brought back a negative report. Now, Joshua and Caleb were rewarded for their faith and they not only got to see the Promised Land, they got to enter it. What the Lord had promised 700 years earlier to Abraham was now fulfilled. As He always does, God kept His Word.

God was faithful to His people and He expected the same loyalty from them. That is why Joshua, at the end of his life, talked to the people about Whom they should serve. It was a clear choice for Joshua: he and his family would not serve the gods of the surrounding nations, they would serve Yahweh.

Tell the Story Activity: The First and Last Words of Joshua

Joshua gives a glimpse of us as he begins his tenure as leader of the great nation of Israel. These are his first words. What does he say in this first address to the nation that is most significant to you? Write it down and share it with a friend in class at the end of the lesson.

Timeline: Possessing the Land

Memory Verse

Joshua 1:8 (ESV) - This Book of the Law shall not depart from your mouth, but you shall meditate on it day and night, so that you may be careful to do according to all that is written in it.

Praise and Worship

Praise and Worship styles vary greatly around the world. It is the intent of this curriculum that praise and worship songs be selected that best fit the content of this lesson.

"Salvation Belongs to Our God" by Eric Quiram is recommended for this lesson.

Bible Activity

The children of Israel were told to follow God closely by following the leaders He had given to them. Joshua told them EXACTLY what they were to do as they entered the promised land. At the very end of his life, many years later, he gave them the same instructions to keep on following God all their lives. We should follow that wise advice today. Start by reading Joshua 3:3-4 (the instructions going into the land) and Joshua 23:1-16 (the end of Joshua's life) Line up and let's follow the leader wherever the path may go. Let's remember the instructions:

Joshua 3:3-4 – "When you see the Levitical priests carrying the Ark of the Covenant of The Lord your God, move out from your positions and follow them. Since you have never traveled this way before, they will guide you." As you walk along, following your leader, some bad voices will call out to you, to try to get you off the path that God has shown you. Don't listen to them! Listen only to the voice of TRUTH. Whenever someone tries to get your attention, you will all say this together: "We will follow The Lord our God!" As you walk along, remind them of what the Bible said: don't turn to the right or the left! Then the children should "act out" your words – everyone would lean to the right, then lean to the left. Point to each of the distractions when you want them to read the card, and lead the group that is following the Ark of the Covenant to say together: "We will follow The Lord our God!"

Teacher Helps

Memory Verse Activity: Pray

Encourage children to pray this verse. Pray something like: "Lord, help me to meditate on Your Word day and night so that I may be careful to do all it says."

Bible Activity: Stay On the Right Path!

Choose one child to be the "Leader" who will carry the Ark of the Covenant. Choose 4 children to be "distractors," 2 on the right and 2 on the left. Give each distractor a card to read. Some suggested temptations:

1. Come watch this bad movie with me, everyone else is going.

2. Don't listen to your mom and dad, they are old-fashioned.

3. Skip church today, we are all going to the park for a picnic and games.

4. Don't waste your time reading your Bible, you should sleep a little longer.

4) Review the Lesson

The teacher should have the class think of the main ideas of the lesson that they want them to take home. Then they should number off 1 through 5. Child number 1 should tell the main thing that he or she learned from the lesson. All five groups should get an opportunity to share the main thing they learned from this lesson.

Ideas might include:
- Obedience to God's Word
- Memorize God's Word
- Faithful to obey God
- Serve God with my family

Review the Lesson Activity: Repetition[2]

The teacher should allow about 5 minutes for children to share the main thing that they learned. If more than 5 children are in the class, allow for each of the groups to share with each other.

5) Apply the Lesson

We prepare for spiritual warfare by making sure of our personal relationship with God.[3]

God's Word promotes faith and obedience to God's Word is expected. In which of the following areas do you need to obey God's Word?

- Kindness to other kids who are mean to you.

- Saying the truth when you are thinking about lying.

- Meditating on God's Word so that you can obey it.

- Something else

Story Line: With God's help, the people entered the Promised Land.

Timeline: Possessing the Land

Adventure Number 37
Judges 2:1-23

Story Line: Israel failed to be loyal to God. God punished them for this.

1) Study the Lesson (before class)

- Near the end of Joshua's life, he was not convinced that the Israelites would remain faithful to Yahweh. Instead of expelling the Canaanites, Amorites, and others, they mingled with them and even intermarried with them.

- The lifestyle of these nations was quite immoral. The more the Israelites intermarried with them, the more the Israelites withdrew their loyalty from Yahweh.

- Yahweh directed people groups in the area to oppress the Israelites so that they would call on Him for help. Repeatedly, in these situations, God raised up a military leader which was called a judge. Only one judge was not a military leader, that was Deborah who settled disputes.

- When the Israelites fell away from God, they adopted the gods of the Canaanites. Since this land was the land *"flowing with milk and honey,"* it was generally assumed that the gods of the Canaanites caused the land to be so productive. Even the Israelites believed this.

- When the Israelites went away from Yahweh, a messenger from God confronted them regarding their apostasy. Then he announced their judgment. Israel entered sinful periods of time, they would cry out to God, He would send a deliverer or judge, they would have rest or peace until that judge died, and then they would turn away from Yahweh.

- There were 9 judges, 7 of which were primary and 2 of which were secondary. Gideon is the best known, despite his objections. Samson was also well known; however, Samson was never serious about his loyalty to Yahweh and he is the first judge to not lead anyone.[1]

Footnotes - Adventure 37

1. David Brooks, *The Roots of Faith Old Testament Commentary*, COM 145-148.

2. Dave Arch and Sue Arch, *Moving Beyond Lecture* (Omaha: Dave Arch and Associates, Inc., 2014), 105.

3. Susan Lingo, *Written on Our Hearts* (Grand Rapids: Zondervan Publishing House, 1995), 92.

2) Begin the Lesson

Let's name the eras or periods of time that we have learned and some of the special people and events that happened in each era.

1. <u>Creation</u>. God created the heavens and the earth. He created Adam and Eve to be His special friends.

2. <u>Fall</u>. Lucifer decided he wanted to be like the Most High God and led a rebellion of angels against God. He was expelled from heaven. After that, he tempted Adam and Eve to disobey God and they sinned. Adam and Eve were expelled from the Garden of Eden. God gave them special clothes.

3. <u>Flood</u>. Because there was so much violence on the earth, God decided to flood the entire earth. But Noah found grace in God's sight. God spared Noah and his family as well as two of all the different kinds of animals.

4. <u>Babel</u>. The people wanted to build a tower to God so that they could have a gateway to the gods. Because of this, God confused their languages and the building of this tower stopped.

5. <u>Patriarchs</u>. Abraham is the best known patriarch. Great promises were made to Abraham by Yahweh. God's promises gave Abraham's descendants a certain land and anyone who was a blessing to Abraham's descendants would receive a blessing.

6. <u>Moses</u>. Moses received a special call from God to do a special work. Moses was given the task of leading the Israelites out of slavery. He also received the Ten Commandments on Mount Sinai and led the Israelites for 40 years in the wilderness. Because of his anger, he was not able to enter the Promised Land.

Teacher Helps

Begin the Lesson Activity: Mix and Match Time Line Review

The teacher should put one era on a piece of paper.

Then the teacher should put names on another piece of paper for each period of time. For example, Adam and Eve could be listed twice; once for creation and once for fall.

Then, on separate sheets of paper, the teacher should put events that happened in each time period.

Mix up all the sheets of paper and have teams of students (3-4 on each team) match the era with the people and events of that time period.

3) Teach the Lesson

Did you ever do the wrong thing over and over again? You wish you could stop but you just don't. Israel had the same problem. Over and over again, they kept doing the wrong thing; they kept turning away from God. Today, we will learn about a dark period in the history of the Israelites.

Tell the Story

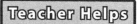

God had given the nation so many wonderful leaders. Moses was followed by Joshua. Perhaps, everyone in Israel just assumed that Joshua would have a successor to lead Israel just like Moses had a successor. That did not happen. After the death of Joshua, something mysterious happened. There were no leaders in Israel that knew God or what He had done.

In Moses' day, the parents died in the wilderness because of their complaining. No one taught their children about God. So, at the end of Moses' life, he taught the nation mighty lessons about God. Joshua picked up on that. His first and last words encouraged the people to listen to God and to serve Him. God Almighty was worthy of their worship and service. Joshua told the nation that his whole family would serve the Lord. But, now Joshua was gone and there was nobody to take his place.

The nation of Israel now occupied the land that God had promised to Abraham. The nation of Israel had their marching orders that God had given to Moses. The nation of Israel had the courageous leadership that God had given to Joshua. They had everything to look forward to; it was all theirs. But, something went wrong.

After Joshua, there was a lack of leadership that followed Yahweh, a lack of leadership that worshipped Yahweh, and a lack of leadership that served Yahweh. Everyone did what was right in his or her own eyes. It was a time of great spiritual darkness. The Israelites began to accept the gods of the Canaanites. Because the Israelites did not drive out the other nations from the land, they lived with each other. Eventually, they married with each other. They weren't supposed to do this. The Israelites lost their love for God and gave it to the gods of the Canaanites. Over and over again, God punished them for this and then God provided miraculous deliverers. These deliverers were called judges. There were 9 judges that delivered Israel from their oppressors. Most of them were military leaders and most of them had a deep personal commitment to Yahweh. When God provided a judge, the people followed God and the land had rest. When the judge died, the nation went back to their old ways. They adopted the gods of the nations around them. This happened every time!

This was a very troubling time for the nation of Israel because they had it all. God was with them and the other nations were afraid of them. But, they gave it all away and did that which was right in their own eyes, not the eyes of Yahweh.

Tell the Story Activity: Skits[2]

There are 9 judges in the book of Judges. Pick out one or two of the judges and have some of the children in your class perform a skit or two. Let the other kids guess which judge they are trying to demonstrate.

Perhaps the teacher could assign Gideon or Samson as skits to perform. These are probably the most well known and easiest to reenact in a skit.

Memory Verse

Judges 21:25 (ESV) - Everyone did what was right in his own eyes.

Praise and Worship

Praise and Worship styles vary greatly around the world. It is the intent of this curriculum that praise and worship songs be selected that best fit the content of this lesson. Recommendations for praise and worship are given and this music can generally be located at www.itunes.com. However, the teacher can feel free to select a similar praise and worship song.

"Salvation Belongs to Our God" by Eric Quiram is recommended for this lesson.

Bible Activity

Let's think about one of God's rules:

- *"Thou shalt not lie."* Where is this found? (In the Bible, Ten Commandments) We know that God is truth, He can never lie. When we lie, we might get ourselves out of a sticky situation, but we have gone against God's rule. What are some bad consequences of lying? (We will be disciplined by God, we will start a habit of lying, we could lose the respect of the person we lied to, etc.).

- What about another one of God's rules: *"Thou shalt not steal."* What do we hope to gain by stealing? (we get what we want without working for it, we get rich by stealing money, etc.) What are some bad consequences of stealing? (someone will come after us that we stole from, get a bad reputation, have a guilty conscience, etc.)

- You see, we need to remember that God puts rules in the Bible for our good, to protect us from bad things, just like this umbrella. Don't be like the people of Israel long ago! If you worship and obey the one true God, you will NEVER be sorry!

Teacher Helps

Memory Verse Activity: Scripture Card Battle[3]

Divide your class up into groups of 2 or 3. Give each group a set of cards. On each card is one word from the memory verse. Groups should try to put the words of the memory verse in the right order.

Bible Activity: The Umbrella

Hold up the umbrella. Ask: Who knows what this is? (of course, an umbrella!) What is the purpose of an umbrella? (To keep you dry in the rain, or to keep the sun off your head on a really hot day). That's right, it is to protect you from something. Do you HAVE to carry an umbrella in the rain? (No, but you will get wet). God's rules are something like an umbrella. They are not forced on us, but when we use them as our guide to live by, we are protected from many bad consequences.

4) Review the Lesson

"Who" Questions:

1. Who were the Canaanites?

2. Who was one of the judges?

"What" Questions:

1. What did the Israelites do wrong?

2. What happened when Joshua died?

"When" Questions:

1. When did God send a judge?

2. When did the people cry out to God?

"Where" Questions:

1. Where did the Israelites live now?

2. Where did the Canaanities live?

"Why" Questions:

1. Why did the Israelites adopt the gods of other nations?

2. Why did the Israelites do that which was right in their own eyes?

Teacher Helps

Review Activity: The Investigative Cube

Divide the class up into two teams. Make a cube with these labels on each side of the cube: who, what, when, where, why. When the cube is rolled to one team, they will answer the type of question that is face up on the cube. For instance, if the "why" is face up on the cube, then that team will answer a "why" question. Teachers can make up their own questions from the lesson, only they must pertain to this lesson.

5) Apply the Lesson

What is one sin that you should turn your back on (repent)? Make a confession to God and tell Him that you want to have a change of mind about this sin. Don't continue in darkness like the Israelites did.

> **Story Line: Israel failed to be loyal to God. God punished them for this.**

Timeline: Possessing the Land

Adventure Number 38
1 Samuel 3:19 - 4:1 and Ruth 1-2

Story Line: The darker the night, the brighter the stars.

 1) Study the Lesson (before class)

- Ruth and Samuel were two amazing people who lived in the period of the judges.

- Ruth, from the country of Moab, was not an Israelite but had married an Israelite. When Ruth's husband died at an early age, Ruth chose to live with her mother-in-law, Naomi. Ruth could have gone back to her own people and remarried as a young widow. However, she chose to stay with Naomi.

- Ruth converted to the worship of Yahweh and became a committed believer. Ruth renounced her homeland gods in Moab.

- Ruth married again, this time to Boaz. Ruth was known for her faithfulness, her kindness, her integrity, and her protection of her mother-in-law. God blessed Ruth and she became the great grandmother of King David.[1]

- We know very little about the childhood of most of the Bible's heroes. One exception to that is Samuel. Samuel was given to Hannah and Elkanah as a result of fervent prayer.

- God shaped the heart of young Samuel. Hannah delivered her son to be given to the Lord which meant Samuel would live with Eli, the priest. Eli, however, was not a good parenting example. Eli's sons, Hophni and Phineas, were quite wicked. Yet, Samuel grew up in the fear of the Lord and became a shining light in a very dark time.[2]

- All of Israel recognized Samuel as their leader, something which was not true of most judges during this same time period.

Footnotes - Adventure 38

1. James Galvin, *Life Application Bible Notes*, 397.

2. Ibid., 413.

3. David Brooks, *The Roots of Faith Old Testament Commentary*, COM-151.

4. Susan Lingo, *Written on Our Hearts*, 99.

Timeline: Possessing the Land

2) Begin the Lesson

The teacher should gather all the songs that have been used in the Adventures in the Bible's Big Story and play several of them.

The class should be able to sing along with the teacher the songs that they have previously learned in this curriculum.

After the teacher has played several songs and the class and sung them, play the game, "Name That Tune." "Name That Tune" is a game in which the students will attempt to match the song with the Bible adventure that best matches the song. The teacher should use extreme graciousness to encourage the class when an answer is given.

The purpose of this activity is for kids to associate music they have learned with events in the Bible. The teacher should stay focused on this primary purpose.

Review Activity: Name That Tune

The teacher should play songs that the class has learned for the previous Bible adventures. Children should guess which adventures in the Bible's big story best match the song that is being played or sung.

If time permits, the teacher could also ask if there are phrases or words in any of the songs that the children do not understand.

3) Teach the Lesson

One Russian proverb says, "The darker the night, the brighter the stars." Have children tell you national or international heroes who have stood out in your nation's history or international history.[3]

1.

2.

Timeline: Possessing the Land

Tell the Story

Teacher Helps

Samuel was a judge for the nation of Israel. He did not write a diary, but we do know a lot about his life. If he did keep a diary, this is what it might have said:

- Today, my mom and dad took me to live with Mr. Eli, the priest. A long time ago, my mom could not have children and she begged the Lord for a child. As a result of her fervent prayers, I was born. Mom promised the Lord that if He gave her a child, then she would give that child back to the Lord. I will certainly miss my mom and dad. They gave me a firm foundation for a godly life.

- When I went to bed tonight, I heard this voice calling me by name. I thought it must have been Mr. Eli. When I asked him about it, Mr. Eli said it wasn't. The same thing happened again and then again. The third time that it happened, Mr. Eli told me that it was the voice of the Lord and that I should tell Him that I was listening. So, that is what I did. I made a decision to listen to the voice of God and obey it. The words of God have been so precious to me. I want to spend the rest of my life obeying God.

- I have been assisting Mr. Eli in the work of the Tabernacle. I really like it and I think this is what God wants me to do for the rest of my life. The whole nation of Israel is recognizing me as a prophet of God.

- Mr. Eli has two sons, Hophni and Phineas. They are also priests like Mr. Eli. However, they are wicked. They take the Lord's offering and use it for themselves. They also have some bad relationships with women. I don't know how they can talk about God and live the way that they do.

- The people of Israel want a king to be over them. I talked to the Lord about it. The Lord told me that it wasn't me they were rejecting; it was Him they were rejecting. He told me to anoint Saul as king over Israel and Saul would be the leader of Israel now.

- God wanted me to find the sons of Jesse and establish one of them as the second king. Saul had messed up as king so bad that God wanted a new king to lead the Israelites. I went through all the sons of Jesse until there were none left and the Lord didn't pick any of them. Finally, I asked Jesse if there were any other sons and he told me that the youngest was still out in the field. It was David, and that is who God wanted to be king.

Tell the Story Activity: Samuel's Diary

Six different scenes or posts from Samuel's diary are given here. The teacher should have the children listen to the posts on Samuel's diary, pick one of those posts, then explain to the class why this post from Samuel's diary stood out to them.

Memory Verse

1 Samuel 3:19 (ESV) - And Samuel grew, and the Lord was with him and let none of his words fall to the ground.

Praise and Worship

Praise and Worship styles vary greatly around the world. It is the intent of this curriculum that praise and worship songs be selected that best fit the content of this lesson. Recommendations for praise and worship are given and this music can generally be located at www.itunes.com. However, the teacher can feel free to select a similar praise and worship song.

"Salvation Belongs to Our God" by Eric Quiram is recommended for this lesson.

Bible Activity

Ruth's Journal – We have learned about Samuel, a person who stood for God in a dark time. There was another person who was a light in the darkness. It was a young woman named Ruth. (Set up the story by reading and explaining Ruth 1:1-5). Our job today is to work together to make a journal of what Ruth might have written down as she left her homeland of Moab. Each passage listed will be one journal entry by Ruth. If your children are old enough to read independently, they can be assigned a passage each, or in small groups. If they are too young for this method, read or summarize the passages together, and let them help decide what should be written, and the teacher will write it down. After the entries are complete, read them together as a class.

1. Ruth 1:6-18
2. Ruth 1:19-22
3. Ruth 2:1-23
4. Ruth 3:1-18
5. Ruth 4:1-12
6. Ruth 4:13-22

When Ruth heard about the one true God, she decided to follow Him, not to go back to the gods of Moab. God honored her faith, and she became the great-grandmother of king David, who was in the genealogy of Christ!

Teacher Helps

Memory Verse Activity: Scripture Scrambler[4]

Write the words to this verse on the top of a paper. Then number down the paper, one number for each word in the verse. Beside the numbers, write a scrambled word to the verse. Challenge your children to unscramble each word to the verse in its correct order.

Example:

1 dna	and
2 maules	Samuel
3 werg	grew
4 dan	and
5 het	the
6 drol	Lord
7 asw	was
8 thiw	with
9 mih	him

Timeline: Possessing the Land

4) Review the Lesson

Based on the lives of Samuel and Ruth, rate yourself on this grid:

- Listening to God skills   1 2 3 4 5 6
- Obedient to parents   1 2 3 4 5 6
- Fervent in prayer   1 2 3 4 5 6
- Serving God   1 2 3 4 5 6
- Speak out for God   1 2 3 4 5 6
- Stay away from bad relationships 1 2 3 4 5 6
- Respond to God's leading   1 2 3 4 5 6
- Overall commitment to God   1 2 3 4 5 6

Teacher Helps

Review Activity: Grid for Growth

The teacher should teach the class of children that the examples of Samuel and Ruth should help us evaluate our own lives.

Children should fill out this chart (1= low; 6 = high).

5) Apply the Lesson

Pick one of the eight skills above and determine in prayer and accountability to improve only one of these skills. Make it a matter of daily work and daily prayer to improve one of these "shining lights" skills.

> **Story Line: The darker the night, the brighter the stars.**

Adventure Number 39
1 Samuel 13 and 15

Story Line: The Israelites asked for a king and God gave them Saul.

1) Study the Lesson (before class)

- God did not want Israel to be like the other nations. But Israel wanted to be like the other nations and have a king as their leader. Up to this point, Israel was a theocracy, a government under the leadership of God. When Israel needed a military leader, God would raise up a military leader like Gideon or Othniel.

- Previous rebellions that we have studied: the golden calf rebellion, the rebellion at Kadesh Barnea, and the rebellion that caused the poisonous snakes. Israel's desire to have a king over them was also a rebellion against God.

- God told Samuel, the last judge, to anoint Saul as the nation's first king. A private ceremony was held first and then a public coronation followed.

- Saul relied on the Lord at first. But, soon afterwards, he violated the sanctity of the priesthood (1 Samuel 13:9-13). Samuel rebuked Saul for this. Instead of repentance, Saul's rebellion was followed by more rebellion. He refused to remove all Amalekites as the Lord directed. After this, God determined that Saul would no longer be fit to lead Israel. Saul became a troubled man. Although Saul would continue to rule over Israel, David would be the next king of Israel.[1]

- At first, Saul was known for his courage and generosity. He was also tall and handsome. Later, he became impulsive, jealous, and rebellious toward the desires of the Lord.

- God was looking for someone who would lead Israel with a right heart attitude toward Yahweh. For much of his reign, Saul did not have this but merely wanted to be respected by the people of Israel.[2]

Footnotes - Adventure 39

1. David Brooks, *The Roots of Faith Old Testament Commentary*, COM-155-157.

2. James Galvin, *Life Application Bible Notes*, 413.

3. Susan Lingo, *Written on Our Hearts*, 79.

4. Lynn Solem and Bob Pike, *50 Creative Training Closers*, 94.

2) Begin the Lesson

There are eight basic concepts that are emphasized throughout all of the Bible. We have studied these truths in previous lessons. Ask the children if they can name them and tell a little bit about each one. They are:

1. God. In the beginning, there was a very powerful God. (Lesson 1: The Eternal God; Lesson 27: The Exodus)

2. Man. God created many things. He created man and woman to be His special friends. (Lessons 3: Creation of the Universe; 4: Creation of People; Lesson 24: Moses Leads His People)

3. Sin. Man and woman disobeyed God. They did not do what He told them to do. (Lesson 7: Beginning of Human Sin; Lesson 33: Unbelief at Kadesh)

4. Death. God punished man and woman for their disobedience. Death, in the Bible, refers to separation. (Lesson 8: The Origin of Death; Lesson 16: The Tower of Babel)

5. Christ. God sent His one and only Son, His unique Son, who lived a perfect life. (Lesson 9: Promise of a Victor Over Satan)

6. Cross. Jesus died on the cross for the sins of the world. (Lesson 11: Provision of Coverings; Lesson 32: The Day of Atonement)

7. Faith. If anyone places their faith in Christ, God welcomes them. (Lesson 13: Cain and Abel; Lesson 34: The Bronze Serpent)

8. Life. God gives eternal life to those who put their faith in Him. (Lesson 5: Life in Paradise; Lesson 38: Bright Lights in an Era of Darkness)

Teacher Helps

Review Activity: Eight Basic Gospel Truths - One Complete Story

The teacher should emphasize these eight gospel concepts throughout Scripture. They are foundational to telling children the one story of redemption found in the Bible. We will emphasize these eight truths regularly.

Ask the children if they can think of how these eight gospel principles are emphasized in the first 38 lessons that we have studied.

3) Teach the Lesson

Some people look at other people and think that it must be nice to be them. They have all the good things. Israel looked at the other nations around them who had kings. Israel decided they wanted to be like the other nations and not have God as their king. What are some ways that you understand why Israel would feel this way?

Timeline: A United Kingdom

Tell the Story

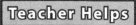

The people of Israel had a tendency to look at the other nations around them. They adopted their ways, they married their women, and they liked their politics. God wanted Israel to be a distinct nation that worshipped Him but they regularly chose to be more like the nations around them than the God who delivered them.

Such was the case of wanting a leader. Most of the other countries around them had a king. So, naturally, Israel saw that and thought that would be good for them. Even though they had a great national leader in Samuel and even though God was really their king, they wanted a human to be their king, like the other nations.

This grieved God and it also grieved Samuel. When God discussed this matter with Samuel, He told Samuel that they were rejecting Him. Samuel was to establish a kingship and God chose Saul to be the first king of Israel.

At first, Saul got off to a good start. He was tall, handsome, humble, and he feared God. But, soon after that, he became impulsive and tried to take the place of the priest even though he was not a priest. Samuel rebuked Saul for this but it didn't seem to change anything Saul did. He certainly did not have a change of heart. Later, Saul and his troops were supposed to eliminate the Amalekites, who had disturbed Israel for 300 years but Saul did not completely obey. It was at this point that God determined that Saul did not have what it took to be a king of this great country. His kingship would not be passed on to his family. Instead, a young boy named David would be the next king.

It took some time for David to become king. Saul ruled Israel for 40 years. For much of that time, he was a bitter man who never really repented of anything he did wrong by disobeying God. He tried to have the next king, David, killed on at least two occasions.

Saul's life ended sadly on a battlefield with his three sons. It was an embarrassing battle loss to the Philistines. Eventually, David became the king of Israel. He had a heart for God and even though David made mistakes, he repented of his sin, something that Saul never did. When God wants someone to lead His people, He wants that person to have a humble and repentant heart.

Tell the Story Activity: Provides Line and Discipline Line

- Put several pieces of string across the floor where you are teaching. Make the string look like lines on a soccer field or a football field.

- At the one end, have the "Provides Line" and on the other have "Discipline Line."

- Ask children about their view of God. Is He more of a Judge (discipline) or more a Provider? Or, is He somewhere in between?

- Have the children locate themselves somewhere on the field and be prepared to answer why they are standing there.

- Now, tell the story.

Memory Verse

1 Samuel 16:7 (ESV) - For the Lord sees not as man sees: man looks on the outward appearance, but the Lord looks on the heart."

Praise and Worship

Praise and Worship styles vary greatly around the world. It is the intent of this curriculum that praise and worship songs be selected that best fit the content of this lesson. Recommendations for praise and worship are given and this music can generally be located at www.itunes.com. However, the teacher can feel free to select a similar praise and worship song.

"Salvation Belongs to Our God" by Eric Quiram is recommended for this lesson.

Bible Activity

Let's pick a great team! Bring pictures to class of 10 different sports figures that your children would be familiar with. Tell them: Let's pretend that these famous people came to your school to play a game of _____. Choose a game your students might play at school, such as soccer, or kick ball. If you were the captain of your team, who would you pick first? Let a few students answer, and ask them why they would choose the ones they name. For example, they might say that their player was the best runner, or the best goalie, or most skillful at scoring. Then ask: **"If God was picking a team of people to do a special job for Him, how would He decide who to pick? Would He look for the biggest, fastest, or best-looking people? No, God does not care what a person looks like on the outside, or even how talented they might be. He cares about a person's heart, and how they love and obey Him. He is also very interested in the willingness of a person to repent when they have done something wrong. When God chose David as the next king of Israel, no one else thought he was a good choice."**

"He's just a shepherd boy!" is what David's own father said. But God saw past the outside and knew that David had a heart that was strong and true. Let's take a few minutes to look at our own hearts and see if we are the kind of people that God would choose.

Teacher Helps

Memory Verse Activity: Scripture Log[3]

Make a page for children to take home with labels down the left column: Sunday, Monday, Tuesday, Wednesday, Thursday, Friday, and Saturday.

Across the top, put practice times and review times.

Children should work on this memory verse each day and mark on their log when they practiced this verse and when they review this verse. Bring this log to class with you next week.

This type of activity will encourage Scripture memory and obedience throughout the week, not just as part of the lesson.

4) Review the Lesson

The teacher should divide the class up into two teams.

- One team could be the "red" team and receive red cards or pieces of paper. The other team could be the "yellow" team and receive yellow cards or pieces of paper.

- Each team has the responsibility of writing out 3 to 5 questions that they want the other team to answer.

- Each question has to pertain to the lesson today.

- After questions are written out, the other team has five to seven minutes to answer the questions. The "yellow" team will answer the questions from the "red" team and the "red" team will answer questions from the "yellow" team.

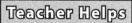

Review Activity: Two Team Review[4]

After an appropriate time, the teacher will gather up the cards or pieces of paper and reward points to the best questions and best answers from each team.

It is highly advisable to have 2 adult teachers in every classroom for kids. If there are 2 adults, then one adult should be the leader of each team.

5) Apply the Lesson

King Saul had early successes but later he failed to obey God. When he failed to obey God, God rejected him as a king of Israel.

What are ways that you used to obey God but now you are not obeying God? List only one or two and make it an effort of prayer and devotion to obey God in these areas.

> **Story Line:** The Israelites asked for a king and God gave them Saul.

Adventure Number 40
2 Samuel 7:1-16

Story Line: God chose David to be a king. God will one day send a Man to be King forever.

 ## 1) Study the Lesson (before class)

- David returned to Jerusalem and enjoyed a time of peace. He had fought many wars. During that time of peace, he thought it would be a good idea for the Lord to have a more permanent place to be worshipped. The portable tent was no longer suitable.

- This is the first time that the prophet Nathan appears on the scene. David learned from Nathan that his intentions of building a place of worship for God were premature.[1]

- Since the Israelites left Egypt, the Lord had made His residence in a portable tent and there was no need to change that.

- However, David learned that he would not build a house for God but that God would build a "house" for him. It would originate with David and it would never end.

- The kingdom and its throne would be a place over which the Son of David would rule forever.

- David was aware that a Messiah would follow after him who would one day be an Eternal King.

- As for a literal temple of worship, David would not be allowed to build it. However, his son, Solomon, would build it.

- David's response to God is one of praise as he describes the incomparable majesty of God.

- He also describes himself as a servant, a term which he uses ten times in verses 19-29.

Footnotes - Adventure 40

1. James Galvin, *Life Application Bible Notes*, 473.

2. Lynn Solem and Bob Pike, *50 Creative Training Closers*, 86.

2) Begin the Lesson

Adventure Number 37

   1. When Israel failed to be loyal to God, what did God do?

   2. Read Judges 2:1-23.

   3. God always punishes disobedience.

   4. Pray to be faithful to God and confess all sin to Him.

Adventure Number 38

   1. Who were two shining heroes during the time of the judges?

   2. Read 1 Samuel 3 and Ruth 1.

   3. Ruth and Samuel.

   4. Pray that we would shine for Jesus in a wicked world.

Adventure Number 39

   1. Saul got off to a good start as king. What went wrong?

   2. Read 1 Samuel 13 and 15.

   3. Saul did not have a heart to obey God.

   4. Pray that God would give us a heart that is loyal and obedient to Him.

Teacher Helps

Begin the Lesson Activity: Ask, Read, Talk, Pray

A good review strategy from 3 previous lessons will focus on four main elements.

1) Ask a question.

2) Read the Bible.

3) Talk about it.

4) Pray to God.

3) Teach the Lesson

There are lots of people who think they are nobody, they have nothing, and they are not able to do anything. They have limited abilities, limited resources, and they don't know anybody important.

Such is the case of our hero for this lesson. He was the youngest son of a relatively obscure family. Do you see any hope for yourself from this?

Tell the Story

David rose to prominence in Israel as a teenager. When the entire army of Israel was afraid of Goliath, the giant, David knew that he could defeat Goliath because of his previous experiences as a shepherd. He had killed lions and bears. With God's help, he could also kill the giant. David not only rose to prominence among the people of Israel, He was chosen by God to lead the nation. That was much more important to David. In a private ceremony, Samuel anointed David with oil, preparing him to be the next king of Israel. However, David spent many years avoiding the wrath of Saul. David had at least two different opportunities to put Saul to death and he refused to do it because he did not want to kill the Lord's anointed king.

After Saul and his three sons died on the battlefield, eventually David became the king of Judah and then later over all of Israel. After the tribes of Israel anointed David as their king, David went to Jerusalem and defeated the Jebusites. Later, this city would be called the city of David. It was the most important city to David. It was so important that he wanted to have the Ark of God brought to Jerusalem. So, David made arrangements to have the Ark brought from the house of Obed-Edom to Jerusalem. When the ark arrived, there was great rejoicing!

Sometime after the ark arrived, David felt like it wasn't right for the Ark to dwell in a tent while he lived in a king's house. He decided to build a house for God that would be awesome. But David's friend, Nathan, told him that God wanted someone else to build the house, not David. That someone else would be his son, Solomon. So, David made all the preparations for the temple so that Solomon would have everything he needed to build the house.

But, God was interested in building a different kind of house. David and later Solomon wanted to build a physical house for the Ark. God wanted to build a dynasty or a legacy of people who followed Him and obeyed Him. God was more interested in David's family being loyal to God than to have a nice and fancy house for the Ark. God was looking for men and women who followed David's example and had a heart for Him.

When God made this covenant with David, it related back to his promise to Abraham. About 1000 years earlier, God had promised to Abraham a land, many descendants, and a blessing to all people. Now, the land and offspring promises were fulfilled through David. Once again, God honored His promise.

Tell the Story Activity: 40 Chapters of the Life of David

- Forty chapters in the Bible are devoted to the life of David.

- As children listen to the teacher tell the story, have them write down or tell you about significant events in the life of David. Some will be in this lesson, some may not be in this lesson.

- Discuss with your class the significant events of David's life. What made him a man of God? How did God raise up a nobody to be king?

Memory Verse

2 Samuel 7:16 (ESV) - And your house and your kingdom shall be made sure forever before me. Your throne shall be established forever.

Praise and Worship

Praise and Worship styles vary greatly around the world. It is the intent of this curriculum that praise and worship songs be selected that best fit the content of this lesson. Recommendations for praise and worship are given and this music can generally be located at www.itunes.com. However, the teacher can feel free to select a similar praise and worship song.

"Salvation Belongs to Our God" by Eric Quiram is recommended for this lesson.

Bible Activity

Make harps like David played made from cardboard, adding string or yarn, and pretend to strum them as you sing "Sing of the King".

"Sing of the King" is a festive song that begins with the Israelites singing in response to Samuel's first announcement of a king, moves through the monarchy, then turns mournful as they await God's promise of a forever king from David's line, but finally ends exultant in the realization that Jesus is that promised king.

Teacher Helps

Memory Verse Activity: Hop It

In large letters, write phrases of the verse on sheets of paper. On the floor, tape the papers in a mixed up fashion, but close enough for succeeding words to be reached in a step. Children should step on one word at a time in the proper order to quote the verse. Let each child have a turn of hopping on the verse.

4) Review the Lesson

Agree/Disagree Statements (If you disagree, why do you disagree?)

1. David knew he could kill Goliath because he killed other giants before. (Disagree. He killed a lion and a bear.)

2. Moses privately commissioned David as the next king of Israel. (Disagree. Samuel commissioned David.)

3. The city of Jerusalem is sometimes called the city of David. (Agree.)

4. Nathan told David that Absalom should build the temple for God. (Disagree. Nathan told David that Solomon should build it.)

5. God's promises to Abraham were partially fulfilled through David. (Agree.)

Teacher Helps

Review Activity: Agree and Disagree Statements

Kids will have fun disagreeing or agreeing with these statements. You may want to make up some statements of your own for them to agree or disagree with.

5) Apply the Lesson

King David had a heart to obey God and serve God. He made some mistakes but for most of his life, he chose to love and honor God.

Who is one person that you know who reminds you of this?

How would you tell another person that they could be like this?

Apply the Lesson Activity: See It, Do It, Tell It[2]

Kids will learn more about the kind of heart that David had if they tell others who has a heart like David and how they can be like this.

> **Story Line: God chose David to be a king. God will one day send a Man to be King forever.**

Adventure Number 41
Psalm 2 and 22

Story Line: David wrote of a future leader Who would rule the earth.

1) Study the Lesson (before class)

- The concept of a future Satan conqueror was not new. Adam and Eve learned of this future ruler thousands of years before David.

- The promise of God to Abraham was that all nations would be blessed through his descendants. Later, we learn that *"the scepter would not depart from Judah"* (Genesis 49:10). That is, a ruler would come from the descendants of Judah.

- Before and during his reign over Israel, David wrote many psalms which have been used for worship throughout the centuries by God's people. Over 70 psalms are attributed to David.

- At least two of those psalms talk about the Lord's covenant that would come with suffering.

- Psalms that describe Yahweh's deliverance for David from his enemies are not surprising. Psalms that talk about what Yahweh did for David are not surprising. A new fact comes from David in these psalms that a future descendant of his would be afflicted and need Yahweh's help.[1]

- Psalms are considered Messianic because they speak of Christ's life, death, resurrection, and future reign. Psalm 2 describes the rebellion of the nations and the coming of Jesus Christ to establish His eternal reign. Psalm 2 is referred to quite often in the New Testament (Acts 4 and 13, Hebrews 1, and Revelation 2, 12, and 19).[2]

- The details of Psalm 22 describe an execution, not an illness. No known event would fit this description in the life of David. Rather, this Psalm depicts the death of one of David's future descendants, Jesus Christ.[3]

Footnotes - Adventure 41

1. David Brooks, *The Roots of Faith Old Testament Commentary*, COM-163-165.

2. James Galvin, *Life Application Bible Notes*, 844.

3. John Walvoord and Roy Zuck, *Bible Knowledge Commentary: Old Testament*, 809.

4. Lynn Solem and Bob Pike, *50 Creative Training Closers*, 52.

2) Begin the Lesson

Let's review the time periods that we have studied over the last couple of months.

- In order, what are these time periods? (Beginnings of the World, Beginnings of a Nation, Possessing the Land, and United Kingdom)

- Who are some of the people that we met in each time period?
    1) Beginnings of the World: Adam and Eve, Lucifer, Cain, Noah and pagan worshippers
    2) Beginnings of a Nation: Abraham, Sarah, Isaac, Rebekah, Jacob, Joseph, Moses and Pharaoh
    3) Possessing the Land: Joshua, Gideon, and Samuel
    4) United Kingdom: Saul and David

- What are some of the main themes from each of these time periods?
    1) Beginnings of the World: God is powerful. People are to be His special friends. Sin entered the world. God punished sin. God punished sin.
    2) Beginnings of a Nation: God made special promises. God delivered His people from slavery.
    3) Possessing the Land: God fulfilled His promise to enter the land. God punished sin.
    4) United Kingdom: God gave special rulers for His people.

Begin the Lesson Activity: Ball Toss

Gather your class of children in a circle with a small ball. Have children take turns rolling the ball gently to each other. When a child catches the ball, have each child answer one part of the question. At this point, do not correct children if they give a wrong answer. Let each child roll the ball to another person in the class for the next question.

3) Teach the Lesson

David was a warrior, a leader, a king, and a song writer. He was enabled by God to do all of these. God gave David special abilities to do special tasks.

When you think of the life of David, what are some of the special abilities and special tasks involving him?

Timeline: A United Kingdom

Tell the Story

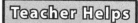

The harp was always a special musical instrument for David. As a young boy, he learned to play the harp. His brothers were warriors and soldiers who went to war to defend Israel. But, David played the harp and watched sheep. Doesn't seem very important, does it? Shepherds were not considered to be leaders. It was just a common job for a common person. Playing the harp was nice but had no real value. At least, that is what everyone thought when David was young.

As David grew up, the men around King Saul wanted David to play his harp for the king. Now, maybe David's musical abilities would really be used by God. David's music really encouraged King Saul and brought him out of bad moods. Probably, David began to see that God was going to use his musical skills. You could say that God anointed David with a special ability to do this special job. It was not the last time that we would see David anointed by God to do a special job with a special ability.

Before David became king, he started writing music for worship. We call them psalms. After he became king, he wrote even more psalms. As far as we know, David wrote over 70 psalms. Some of them praised God for Who He is. Some of the psalms lamented the failure of Israel to please God. Some of David's psalms told of his sin and God's forgiveness. David wrote about many things. His love for God was expressed through the Psalms.

One of the topics that he wrote about in the psalms was a coming leader. It was maybe surprising to the people of Israel that this future leader would suffer but that is what several of David's psalms revealed. These psalms are called messianic psalms because they talk about the coming Messiah's life, death, resurrection, and future reign. They are prophecies about the Messiah. The people of Israel expected a ruling Messiah. They did not expect a suffering Messiah. Two hundred years later, Isaiah also wrote about a suffering Messiah.

The messianic psalms are important because they reveal God's one big story. That story revolves around the person of the Messiah. The Messiah, as He was known as in the Old Testament, would come and suffer. New Testament writers referred back to these psalms regularly. The Messiah would come from the family of Judah. The Messiah would be someone who suffers. The Messiah would enable believers to rule the world. This worship music that David wrote about the Messiah lets us know that there is a future Leader who will reign over all the earth.

Tell the Story Activity: Favorite Psalms

- Over 70 Psalms are attributed to David. Other than Psalm 23, can you name any of David's psalms?

- Have children talk about their favorite verse in the Psalms and why it is their favorite.

Memory Verse

Psalms 22:1 (ESV) - My God, my God, why have you forsaken me?

Praise and Worship

Praise and Worship styles vary greatly around the world. It is the intent of this curriculum that praise and worship songs be selected that best fit the content of this lesson. Recommendations for praise and worship are given and this music can generally be located at www.itunes.com. However, the teacher can feel free to select a similar praise and worship song.

"Salvation Belongs to Our God" by Eric Quiram is recommended for this lesson.

Bible Activity

Choose one of David's Psalms, and help your children come up with a tune for the words. Psalm 23 would be a good choice. Read the Psalm together, and play around with tunes that could be used. Idea: Use a familiar folk tune that your class would know. As you look through the book of Psalms in preparation for this activity, you will realize that many songs have already been written that take some or all their words from the book of Psalms. Make a note of the ones you already know a tune for, and point these out during this time. Have a tune in mind to get the creative juices flowing with your class, and be encouraging of any efforts they give. It can be intimidating to try this at first, but lots of fun once you get started!

Teacher Helps

Memory Verse Activity: Around the Class

Have the children sit in a circle while music is playing. Pass around a phrase of the memory verse. When the music stops, whoever is holding the phrase of the memory verse should try to quote the verse. Do this until all phrases are memorized. Then, do the same thing for the whole memory verse.

4) Review the Lesson

Volunteers from the class should list on a board or big piece of paper that everyone can see, the 5 Most Important Things To Know from this lesson.

For instance:

1. David wrote over 70 Psalms.

2. Some psalms predicted a suffering Messiah.

3. The New Testament refers to these messianic psalms.

4. Jesus quoted from the Old Testament when He died on the cross.

5. David was anointed. God gave him special abilities to do a special job.

5) Apply the Lesson

God anointed King David with the special abilities to do a special job that God gave him to do.

What are some special jobs that God may have for you to do? How has God prepared you to do these jobs?

Story Line: David wrote of a future leader Who would rule the earth.

Teacher Helps

Review Activity: 5 Scribes[4]

Have five different volunteers come to the front of the class to write one of the five most important things to know from this lesson. Ask the class why these are important.

Adventure Number 42
1 Kings 6

Story Line: Solomon built the temple for the Lord.

 ## 1) Study the Lesson (before class)

- Solomon was the third king of Israel and was the wisest man who ever lived. Though he had asked the Lord for wisdom, he had begun a practice that would make his rule over Israel ineffective. He began to marry foreign wives, hundreds of them. In doing so, Solomon went against his father's last words to him. These wives would turn his heart away from the Lord his God.

- Not very much is recorded about the last ten years of Solomon's reign. He did not repent of sin until the very end. His personal life had compromised his public life.

- Like his father, Solomon was a great author and wrote about 3000 proverbs found in the book of Proverbs. He wrote over 1000 songs. He also wrote Song of Solomon at the beginning of his reign and Ecclesiastes at the end of his reign.[1]

- Solomon's greatest accomplishment was his building of the temple for the Lord. He began construction of the temple in his fourth year of ruling over Israel. It took 7 and a half years to build this marvelous structure.[2]

- Like King Saul, Solomon's commitment to the Lord began to change as he supported the worship of false gods.

- God promised to establish the throne of David forever through Solomon if Solomon would remain faithful to the Lord. However, Solomon's turning away from the Lord caused the Lord to not give complete safety and protection to the nation. God honored His promise but Solomon did not remain faithful.[3]

Footnotes - Adventure 42

1. James Galvin, *Life Application Bible Notes*, 521.

2. John Walvoord and Roy Zuck, *Bible Knowledge Commentary: Old Testament*, 499.

3. Wayne Haston, *Old Testament Chronological Bible Cards* (Harrisburg: Good Soil Evangelism and Discipleship, 2013), OT-42.

2) Begin the Lesson

Tell your class that you are learning the one story of the Bible. While there are many stories in the Bible, they are linked to one major theme or story in the Bible. It is a story of hope. So, to help your class know that story and be able to put all the lessons together, we are going to review the lessons from the past. Ask, **"What are the main events that we have studied in the Bible?"**

- God always existed and He is very powerful.
- God created the earth and everything in it.
- God created people to be His special friends.
- Lucifer, or Satan, deceived Adam and Eve. They sinned by disobeying God.
- God sent a worldwide flood that killed everybody on the earth. God spared Noah and his family because Noah was a righteous man.
- God made special promises to Abraham.
- Abraham offered a ram on Mount Moriah instead of his son, Isaac.
- Jacob wrestled with the angel of God and got a new name, Israel.
- Through special plagues and deliverance, God led the Israelites out of Egypt.
- God established a moral code called the Ten Commandments that the Israelites were to obey.
- With God's help, Israel entered the Promised Land.
- God chose David to be king. He will one day send someone to be King forever.

Teacher Helps

Begin the Lesson Activity: The Main Events

Review is a significant part of learning. Twelve events are listed here. Write each event on a slip of paper or poster board and have children put them in chronological order. Let them work together in small teams 2 or 3. Time how long it takes each team to put these events in the right order. Winner gets a prize.

3) Teach the Lesson

Think of your own "Wish List." If you could have anything that you wanted, what would you put on this "Wish List."

Now, if you were going to ask God for something, would you name anything on this "Wish List" or something else? If something else, what would you ask God for?

99 Adventures in the Bible's Big Story

Timeline: A United Kingdom

Adventure Number 42
Page 211

Tell the Story

It was a title no other human being would ever have: Wisest Man in the Whole Earth. It was a position no one else would ever have: Son of the Greatest King. It was a job no one else could do: build the temple for the Lord. What a great beginning and what incredible resources! Solomon truly had the makings of being a great king. On top of that, God let him ask for anything and he made an extremely good choice when he chose wisdom as the gift he wanted from God. Solomon: a wise king with great parents and prepared to do a great job. Exciting times lay ahead for Solomon and for the nation of Israel.

Solomon began building the Lord's temple four years after he became king. It was a magnificent structure that took over seven years to build. Exact specifications were given by God. The highest quality of materials was used. When the temple was completed, Solomon had a bronze platform built in the middle of the outer court where he prayed and dedicated the new temple to Yahweh. Solomon knew that a man-made building, no matter how beautiful, could not contain the God of the universe. Solomon had built the temple that his father, David, wanted to build. And now, almost twelve years into his kingship, it was completed.

Maybe that is where things started to go wrong for Solomon. He began making foreign treaties and political alliances that were not pleasing to Yahweh. He married a lot of women who were not Yahweh worshippers. In fact, these foreign women even turned his heart away from God. These foreign women worshipped pagan gods, not Yahweh. But, that did not seem to matter to Solomon.

Solomon had written thousands of proverbs and a thousand songs that proclaimed Yahweh as the only true God. He had written a book about love in marriage. But, all of that was gone at the end of his life and his heart did not remain loyal all of his life, like his father's heart did. Yes, David had a loyal heart to God nearly all of his life. But, Solomon grew very weak in his commitment to Yahweh at the end of his life.

In fact, at the end of his life, he even wrote a book about how meaningless life was. His heart had grown cold. He did not love Yahweh any more. Such exciting times at the beginning of his reign as king and such misery at the end. The love of God for Solomon remained steadfast but the love of Solomon for God did not remain steadfast.

Tell the Story Activity: Good Start and Poor Finish

Ask children to think of other Bible people who started well and finished poorly. Some suggestions might include:

- Cain
- Lot
- Satan
- Israelites in the wilderness

Why did these and Solomon not love God all their life?

Memory Verse

2 Chronicles 7:14 (ESV) - If my people who are called by my name humble themselves, and pray and seek my face and turn from their wicked ways, then I will hear from heaven and will forgive their sin and heal their land.

Praise and Worship

Praise and Worship styles vary greatly around the world. It is the intent of this curriculum that praise and worship songs be selected that best fit the content of this lesson. Recommendations for praise and worship are given and this music can generally be located at www.itunes.com. However, the teacher can feel free to select a similar praise and worship song.

"Salvation Belongs to Our God" by Eric Quiram is recommended for this lesson.

Bible Activity

"Building up or tearing down?" Ask your children this question: "What is easier, to build something, or to tear something down?" (Tearing down) Why is this true? (You have to have skill to build, and a plan, and patience to do it just right.) Why is it so easy to tear down? (You don't have to be careful, or skilled, or patient! Just brute force is all it takes.)

If possible, bring in some blocks or material that could represent the building of the Temple. Let the kids build a structure as you read parts of I Kings 6, describing the Temple Solomon built. You might bring brightly colored fabric, a necklace to represent the gold chains in v. 21, spices to represent the incense, etc. Once you have completed the building, have someone read Proverbs 4:23 - "Guard you heart above all else, for it determines the course of your life."

This was the big mistake Solomon made, he didn't guard his heart, and as a result, he ended up on the wrong path, a path that led him away from God, and destroyed the nation of Israel. Do you think Solomon might have made better choices if he had read this verse? Guess what? Solomon WROTE that verse!! Yes! It's true. You see, just knowing the right thing isn't enough. We must OBEY the God of the Bible. Boys and girls, let's make a commitment right now to be obedient to God ALL of our lives! It begins by guarding your heart, one day at a time.

Teacher Helps

Bible Memory Activity: Relay Race

Form two teams. Put the memory verse in large letters about ten yards away from the teams. Have children run to the memory verse and read the next word of the verse out loud so that everyone can hear. When each child has read his one word, go back to the class, touch the next person in line, and repeat the process until all words of the verse have been read.

Repeat this until everyone has memorized the verse.

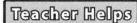

4) Review the Lesson

Divide the class into two teams. Give the teams one minute to write down as many statements as they can about the life of Solomon. Here are a few ideas:

- Solomon wrote 3000 proverbs.
- Solomon wrote over 1000 praise songs.
- Solomon married many foreign women who turned his heart away from God.
- Solomon began building the temple in his fourth year as king.
- It took Solomon seven and a half years to build the temple.

Review the Lesson Activity: One Minute List

The teacher should give two teams one minute each to list as many facts as they can about the lesson.

After the one minute has passed, compare lists and see who has more facts. Be sure that children remember that you are looking for facts.

5) Apply the Lesson

Have each child draw two pictures.

- Picture number 1: Draw one way you would like to be like Solomon.
- Picture number 2: Draw one picture which shows how you would like to not be like Solomon.

Pick one of these pictures and work hard this week on doing the right thing.

Story Line: Solomon built the temple for the Lord.

Adventure Number 43
1 Kings 11-14

> **Story Line:** The sins of Solomon led to the division of the nation.

1) Study the Lesson (before class)

- Besides a king being forbidden by God to increase the number of his horses (Deuteronomy 17:16), a king was also forbidden by God to marry many wives *"or his heart will be led astray"* (Deuteronomy 17:17). This is precisely what happened to Solomon. Solomon did not abandon Yahweh but he worshiped other gods as well. His heart was not fully devoted to the Lord; he compromised his affections.[1]

- Jeroboam was a skilled supervisor for building projects. A prophet named Ahijah came to Jeroboam to reveal God's word. Ahijah told Jeroboam that he was going to divide the nation of Israel. The northern kingdom would consist of ten tribes that were north and west of Benjamin and Judah, the most southern tribes.

- Ahijah acquired a garment and divided it into twelve different pieces. He handed ten of those garment pieces to Jeroboam to show that he would rule ten of the tribes. Rehoboam, son of Solomon, would rule the other two tribes. Ahijah assured Jeroboam that if he was faithful to Yahweh, then his reign would be secure for many generations. Jeroboam soon revealed that he was more concerned about political power than faithfulness to Yahweh. His faithless approach to Yahweh resulted in every king from the northern kingdom following his example or worse. Most people followed the leadership of these kings.

- In the southern kingdom, Rehoboam worshipped Yahweh for three years and then led the southern kingdom into idol worship. Under the leadership of Rehoboam, they built high places for worship, sometimes for Yahweh and sometimes for other gods. Rehoboam's reign lasted only 17 years.[2]

Footnotes - Adventure 43

1. John Walvoord and Roy Zuck, *Bible Knowledge Commentary: Old Testament*, 508.

2. David Brooks, *The Roots of Faith Old Testament Commentary*, COM-173.

2) Begin the Lesson

Lay out a game board for review that looks something like this:

Time Line	Story Line	Songs	Memory Verses
100 points	200 points	300 points	400 points
100 points	200 points	300 points	400 points
100 points	200 points	300 points	400 points
100 points	200 points	300 points	400 points
100 points	200 points	300 points	400 points

Go back for each of the last 10 lessons and let the children name the time line for each lesson (100 points), the story line for each lesson (200 points), the song for each lesson (300 points), and the memory verse for each lesson (400 points).

A prize should be given to the winning team. Usually, competition is a fun thing for the children. So, keep them all involved. Depending on the size of your class, you may want to limit each child to only 1 or 2 answers. The reason for this is that a few children will answer all the questions, if you let them.

There will be a total of 10,000 points, 1000 points for each lesson (100 for the time line, 200 for the story line, 300 for the song, and 400 for the memory verse).

Begin the Lesson Activity: Bible Jeopardy

Divide the class evenly into two teams. The teams could be:

1) whoever has the most brothers and sisters

2) whoever has the fewest brothers and sisters

This game will be continued with the review at end of the lesson.

3) Teach the Lesson

It is never fun to have something that you thought was yours taken from you. To have something taken from you does not mean you lost it, it means somebody else gets what should have been yours; at least, that is what you thought.

Today's lesson talks about something that was taken. What are one or two things that have been taken from you that you were not happy about when they were taken? Did you understand why they were taken? How did you respond?

Timeline:
A Divided Kingdom

Tell the Story

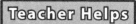

Solomon's life ended poorly and his conclusion to life was that everything under the sun was meaningless. Because of his turning away from God, Yahweh sent a punishment that resulted in two kingdoms.

Jeroboam was the son of a widow and was a talented construction supervisor. Ahijah, a prophet, brought the word of the Lord to Jeroboam with a visual aid that would be hard to forget. One would think that this visual aid would make a life long impression on Jeroboam. Ahijah showed Jeroboam a newly purchased garment or piece of clothing. Then, he tore it into twelve strips and told Jeroboam that ten of the strips of clothing would belong to him. The reference was clear: each strip of clothing represented the twelve tribes of Israel. Because of their unfaithfulness to Yahweh and their pursuit of other gods, the kingdom would become divided. Ten tribes would go with Jeroboam. A clear job was given to Jeroboam from Ahijah. Ahijah's instructions from Yahweh were very clear. Jeroboam was to lead the northern nation of Israel into worship of Yahweh. If he did so, then Jeroboam would be like David, his ancestor. All Jeroboam had to do was obey the commandments of Yahweh. When Solomon heard about this meeting, he threatened to kill Jeroboam. So, Jeroboam fled to Egypt until Solomon died. Jeroboam had plenty of time to think about the newly purchased garment that Ahijah tore into twelve pieces. He knew the significance of the ten pieces of clothing and he knew the significance of the two pieces of clothing. Obeying Yahweh had great reward but turning his back on Yahweh would have awful consequences.

After Solomon died, Rehoboam took charge and thought he would be the leader of the whole nation. His first decision was to make the taxes and forced labor even worse than Solomon had done at the end of his life. Meanwhile, Jeroboam returned from Egypt and the northern ten tribes voted him as their leader. They didn't want any more higher taxes or any more forced labor. Rehoboam, the leader of Judah, wanted to go to war against Jeroboam, the leader of Israel. He would have except for a clear word from God that warned him not to do so.

Israel's King Jeroboam got off to a good start but built idols of worship. He violated the first and second commands given by Yahweh to Moses. Judah's King Rehoboam also got off to a good start but built places for worship which were sometimes used for Yahweh and sometimes for other gods. He violated the first command given by Yahweh to Moses.

Tell the Story Activity: Good Start and Poor Finish

Add two more to the Bible people who started well and finished poorly. Why did Jeroboam and Rehoboam do this?

Others:

- Cain (jealousy)

- Lot (wealth)

- Satan (pride)

- Israelites in the wilderness (complaining)

- Rehoboam (idolatry)

- Jeroboam (other gods)

Memory Verse

1 Kings 11:38 (ESV) - And if you will listen to all that I command you, and will walk in my ways, and do what is right in my eyes by keeping my statutes and my commandments, as David my servant did, I will be with you and will build you a sure house, as I built for David, and I will give Israel to you.

Praise and Worship

Praise and Worship styles vary greatly around the world. It is the intent of this curriculum that praise and worship songs be selected that best fit the content of this lesson. Recommendations for praise and worship are given and this music can generally be located at www.itunes.com. However, the teacher can feel free to select a similar praise and worship song.

"Salvation Belongs to Our God" by Eric Quiram is recommended for this lesson.

Bible Activity

"Guess who I am" – Allow children to volunteer to "act out" one of the Bible people who started well and finished poorly from the list on the "Tell the Story" page. They should portray the person's life without speaking, just by actions. The class has to guess who they are.

For example, Cain could walk up with hands outstretched, as if presenting an offering. He would then look angry when his offering was not accepted. He might even pretend to hit Abel (Abel can be invisible, or two kids could act it out together). Depending on the time you have available, you could use all 6 examples. It might even be fun to give a small prize to whoever is able to guess the right answer first. If you offer a prize, make sure to have an organized system for guessing the answer! If your class is younger children, the teacher could be the one to act out the person, and let the kids try to figure it out.

Teacher Helps

Memory Verse Activity: The Telephone Game

Memorize this verse using The Telephone Game. Have your class form one line, then whisper into the first person in line a phrase of this verse, have that person repeat the phrase to the next person. Do this until all have quoted the first phrase. Then do the same thing with the second phrase, the third phrase, and so on until you have memorized the verse.

4) Review the Lesson

Continue your review game for points that you began at the start of the lesson.

- For 100 points, how many tribes of Israel were there? (12)
- For 200 points, who led the northern kingdom? (Jeroboam)
- For 300 points, who led the southern kingdom? (Rehoboam)
- For 400 points, what did the prophet Ahijah command Jeroboam to do? (obey the Lord God)
- Bonus question worth 500 points: What is the theme of this lesson? (The sins of Solomon led to the division of the nation.)

Review the Lesson Activity: Bible Jeopardy

This review activity is a continuation of the review game at the beginning of the lesson.

5) Apply the Lesson

The Bible is filled with people who were clearly commanded to do something and they did not do it. Selfishness, stubbornness, and pride often caused them to abandon God.

Today, if you were warned to follow God and there would be great reward, would you follow Him with all of your heart?

Today, if you were warned to not follow false gods because there would be tragic consequences, would you avoid those false gods?

> **Story Line: The sins of Solomon led to the division of the nation.**

Adventure Number 44
1 Kings 16-18

Story Line: Elijah and Elisha were bright lights in a time of darkness.

 ## 1) Study the Lesson (before class)

- The ministry of Elijah and Elisha was a very special ministry. Their task was formidable as they resisted the worship of Baal.[1]

- Elijah and Elisha performed the following miracles: stopping the rain and causing a drought, praying and bringing rain to end the drought, calling lightning from a clear sky repeatedly, raising the dead, making a small supply of food replenish for several years, multiplying oil from a jar, multiplying food, stopping the flow of a river and immediately drying the river bed, departing earth to be with God without dying, removing poison from food and water, healing incurable skin disease, blinding an enemy army until he had captured them, making an iron axe head resurface and float, and exposing a distant king's secret plans.[2]

- Baal was the god of rain and dew, the storm god who controlled the weather. Elijah challenged Ahab to a contest. It was reminiscent of Egypt's gods being defeated by Yahweh 600 years earlier when Moses confronted Pharaoh. Of course, Baal was powerless and Yahweh showed who was God.

- Yahweh directed Elijah to mentor a young understudy named Elisha. Elisha wanted to further the ministry of Elijah so he asked for a double portion of Elijah's spirit. Interestingly, it is recorded that Elisha did twice as many miracles as Elijah.

- From around 850 B.C. and for over 50 years, Elisha served Yahweh and Israel. However, the nation continued to rebel against Yahweh.[3]

Footnotes - Adventure 44

1. Roy B. Zuck, *A Biblical Theology of the Old Testament*, 133.

2. David Brooks, *The Roots of Faith Old Testament Commentary*, COM-176.

3. Ibid., 178.

2) Begin the Lesson

One of the goals for review is for children to see the Bible's big story. Today, we want to ask children to give us some of the recurring themes we see so far in that story. For instance, let children volunteer their answers, but you might use the following examples as recurring themes in the Bible's one big story:

God's Amazing Power:

- Creation
- Worldwide Flood
- Red Sea Crossing
- Entering the Promised Land

Animal Substitution:

- Adam and Eve
- Abraham and Isaac on Mount Moriah
- God's Provision for Forgiveness
- The Day of Atonement

Faith that Pleases God:

- Noah
- Abraham
- The Passover
- Ruth and Samuel
- King David

God Punishes Sin:

- Adam and Eve
- Unbelief at Kadesh Barnea
- Saul, Israel's First King
- King Solomon
- The Divided Kingdom

Begin the Lesson Activity: One Big Story

The teacher may want to give the class the topics such as: God's Amazing Power, Animal Substitution, Faith that Pleases God, and God Punishes Sin. Then, let the children tell Biblical examples of those stories that we have previously studied.

The purpose of this activity is for children to see recurring themes in the Bible's one big story.

3) Teach the Lesson

What is one of the greatest challenges you have ever seen? Was one person a great underdog and the other person a heavy favorite? Was one team supposed to win and the other team supposed to lose?

In today's lesson, we will learn about one of the greatest challenges ever. It came from one of the prophets of God as he faced 450 challengers. Do you know who this one prophet of God is and what he did?

 # Tell the Story

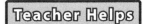

Jeroboam showed lots of potential. He worked very effectively as a construction supervisor for some of the work that Solomon had wanted done. He was so effective that Yahweh sent a prophet named Ahijah to declare him the next leader of the northern kingdom. Oh yes, the northern kingdom which never had one king that Yahweh described as good. The southern kingdom had eight of the "good" kings, but the north was different. There was a lack of spiritual leadership amongst the northern kingdom kings.

However, that does not mean God left the northern kingdom without a witness. To be specific, Yahweh raised up two very special witnesses for Himself. First, there was Elijah and he was succeeded by Elisha. They were known for their awesome miracles.

One of those awesome miracles featured a challenge by the man of God, Elijah. He challenged King Ahab's and Queen Jezebel's prophets. Ahab had 450 prophets of Baal and Jezebel had 400. There was a total of 850 prophets. For some reason, Jezebel did not let her 400 prophets participate in this duel. Elijah gave the rules for the duel. First, Ahab's prophets and Elijah would each butcher an animal and place it on separate altars. Then Ahab's prophets and Elijah would call down fire from their gods to consume the animal. Whichever god responded with fire must be the ultimate Deity. Baal's prophets went first. When nothing happened after several hours, Elijah began mocking Ahab's prophets. Maybe their god was asleep. Maybe he was busy. Maybe he was travelling or out on business. Nothing happened. Then, it was Elijah's turn. In an unusual move, Elijah dug a trench around the altar and poured water on the sacrifice, the altar, and the wood! Elijah made sure that there would be no doubt about who was the absolute Deity. Elijah prayed a 34 word prayer. Then, BOOM! No sooner had Elijah prayed and there was lightning from the sky that consumed the sacrifice, the altar, the wood, and even the water. The people were so impressed that they even said, "The LORD, He is God; the LORD, He is God." It was a spectacular sight.

Sometime after that, Yahweh directed Elijah to mentor another prophet who was younger. His name was Elisha. Elisha wanted to continue the good things that Elijah had begun and asked for a double portion of Elijah's spirit. He wanted to be just like his leader, Elijah. God enabled Elisha to continue the work that Elijah had begun. For over 50 years, Elisha did the work of prophet in a place where there was not much spiritual leadership in the land.

Tell the Story Activity: Contrast Two Kinds of Prophets

Bring two items with you to class today.

1) Bring one thing that is very reliable with you to class (maybe a solid chair).

2) Bring one thing with you that is not very reliable (something that looks broken down).

After describing each item, have the class tell you which one would you rather trust. Why?

Such was the case with the people choosing the prophet of God or the prophets of Baal.

Memory Verse

1 Kings 18:39 (ESV) - And when all the people saw it, they fell on their faces and said, "The Lord, he is God; the Lord, he is God."

Praise and Worship

Praise and Worship styles vary greatly around the world. It is the intent of this curriculum that praise and worship songs be selected that best fit the content of this lesson. Recommendations for praise and worship are given and this music can generally be located at www.itunes.com. However, the teacher can feel free to select a similar praise and worship song.

"Salvation Belongs to Our God" by Eric Quiram is recommended for this lesson.

Bible Activity

Dramatization – Let's pretend that we were there that day so long ago, when God proved Himself to the people of Israel through Elijah the prophet. The teacher will be the "narrator" and the students will have different roles. Choose one child to be Elijah, several to be the "Mockers" that make fun of the prophets of Baal, and the rest will shout "The Lord He is God!!" Ahead of time, print Elijah's prayer from I Kings 18:36-37 for Elijah to read at the appointed time. Give the mockers some ideas of what to say from I Kings 18:27 – "Shout louder!" "Maybe he is daydreaming!" "Maybe he had to go to the bathroom!" "He might be away on a trip!" "He is asleep and needs to be awakened!" Have the rest of the kids practice saying all together: "The LORD He is God; The LORD He is God!"

Tell the story again, this time act as a narrator to the story, and have the kids participate in their assigned roles. As you are reenacting the story, try to help the kids feel the emotion that would have been a part of this amazing scene. Emphasize the miraculous way that God showed His mighty power, and how He used the faithful prophet Elijah to accomplish His work.

Teacher Helps

Memory Verse Activity: Graffiti

Graffiti can also be used to help children memorize this verse. Write each word of this verse on a separate piece of paper. Then divide the children into groups of 2 or 3 and have them put the words in order. When each group can put the verse together in order, they will probably have this verse memorized.

4) Review the Lesson

Review the lesson and see which of these you can find.

- Name someone who showed lots of potential. (Jeroboam)
- Name one kingdom that had no good kings. (Israel)
- Name one kingdom that had eight good kings. (Judah)
- Name the two successful prophets of God (Elijah and Elisha)
- How many prophets did Baal have? (450)
- How many prophets did Jezebel have? (400)
- How many years did Elisha work for the Lord? (50 years)

Teacher Helps

Review the Lesson Activity: Scripture Search

The teacher should have the class break up into groups of 2 or 3. Have them find each of the 7 main ideas in the lesson which are listed to your left. For younger children, or non-readers, the teacher should help them.

5) Apply the Lesson

God used two ordinary people in a very special way at a very difficult time. Elijah and Elisha worked together to honor God when not a lot of other people did.

Find one friend who will encourage you to honor God. It may be one of your parents, it may be one of your friends at school, or it may be a grandma or a grandpa. Who is that person?

Now, ask the person to be a godly friend and serve the Lord together.

Story Line: Elijah and Elisha were bright lights in a time of darkness.

Adventure Number 45
Isaiah 7:14; 9:1-7; 53; and Micah 5:2

Story Line: Prophets told about Jesus 700 years before He came to earth.

1) Study the Lesson (before class)

- Although Ahaz did not want a sign, God gave him one anyway through the prophet Isaiah. The sign was that a boy would be born of a virgin (Isaiah 7:14), he would be raised in a time of national trouble (v. 15), and while he was still a boy, a two-king alliance would be broken (v. 16).[1]

- The Hebrew word speaks of a young unmarried woman. But the Greek of the New Testament and the rabbi's translation in the LXX uses a word which definitely means "virgin."[2]

- The coming Messiah would rule over God's people (*"the government shall be upon his shoulders"*).

- The coming Messiah would have names that describe His character or who He is. Names such as *"wonderful"* meaning He would be distinguished; *"counselor"* meaning He would be authoritative. He would also be *"mighty God"* meaning He would be a powerful God. He would also be the *"prince of peace"* meaning He would bring peace.

- In his book, Isaiah tells us that the Messiah would suffer for the sins of all people. Isaiah tell us of a lamb who would offer Himself as a sacrifice for sin.

- The prophet Micah tells us in Micah 5:2 that the birthplace of the Messiah would be in Bethlehem of Ephrathah. This was a tiny town not far from Jerusalem and very unlikely to have someone important born there. Ephrathah was the village in which Bethlehem was located.[3]

Footnotes - Adventure 45

1. John Walvoord and Roy Zuck, *Bible Knowledge Commentary: Old Testament*, 1047.

2. Lawrence O. Richards, *The Teacher's Commentary*, 371.

3. James Galvin, *Life Application Bible Notes*, 1471.

2) Begin the Lesson

Ask children to help you with previous memory verses. Maybe say something like, **"Who remembers what (verse) says?"**

- Adventure Number 31: Leviticus 17:11
- Adventure Number 32: Leviticus 16:30
- Adventure Number 33: Numbers 13:31
- Adventure Number 34: John 3:14
- Adventure Number 35: Deuteronomy 6:5
- Adventure Number 36: Joshua 1:8
- Adventure Number 37: Judges 21:25
- Adventure Number 38: 1 Samuel 3:19
- Adventure Number 39: 1 Samuel 16:7
- Adventure Number 40: 2 Samuel 7:16
- Adventure Number 41: Psalm 22:1
- Adventure Number 42: 2 Chronicles 7:14
- Adventure Number 43: 1 Kings 11:38
- Adventure Number 44: 1 Kings 18:39

3) Teach the Lesson

Have you ever met someone who knew a lot? Have you ever met someone who knew a lot that would happen in the future? He had the ability to predict the future? Well, the Old Testament has prophets and prophets of the true God had to be right one hundred percent of the time when they predicted the future.

Now, your friend may be right a lot but I doubt if he is right all the time. In this lesson, we will learn that several prophets told about the coming Messiah and they were all right.

Teacher Helps

Begin the Lesson Activity: Memory Verse Review

The last 14 memory verses are given here. Divide the children up into two teams and see which team can tell you the most memory verses. Bonus points should be given if they can recite more than the last 14 memory verses.

Give the teams five minutes and they must work together.

The teacher can provide a few helps.

Tell the Story

God's prophets were given the special ability to warn people about the times in which they lived. They were prophets like Elijah and Elisha who we just studied. Some prophets would tell about the future. The earliest of this kind of prophet from God were Isaiah and Micah. In all, there were 16 prophets who wrote about the future. Isaiah and Micah lived about 700 years before Jesus Christ was born, yet they both told about Him. They were the earliest of God's writing prophets.

Seven hundred years before Christ was born, Isaiah wrote about the special way in which Jesus Christ would be born. He told that one of the descendants of David would give birth to a son. The descendant of David would be a young lady who had never slept with a man. That was very unique because a lady would have to sleep with a man to have a baby. But Isaiah told about this unique birth a long time before it ever happened.

Isaiah also foretold that this future Messiah would bring great light to the people of Galilee who lived a long way north of Jerusalem. The people of Galilee were upset because a foreign nation, Assyria, had conquered that area.

Isaiah prophesied that this Messiah would be oppressed and afflicted. He would even be crushed. He would be wounded for the sins of the people and He would carry the iniquity of all of us. Yet in spite of this, the Lord God would prosper Him.

Isaiah also told about the Messiah's future kingdom. The government would be on His shoulders and there would be peace that would never end. His eternal throne would be established.

So, Isaiah wrote about the birth, life, purpose, death, and future life of the coming Messiah.

Micah also wrote about this Messiah at about the same time. Micah wrote about the place where Messiah would be born. It was a very small village just outside of Jerusalem called Bethlehem.

None of these prophets contradicted each other. They told about the coming Messiah as God showed them what to say. And everything they said about the Messiah would eventually come true.

Tell the Story Activity: Story Chairs

Give each of the kids, except one, a word in the story that is used often. With the kids seated in a circle, give each one a word in the story. As you tell the story, the children who hear "their" word must get up and find a new seat. This activity is kind of like the game "musical chairs" only the teacher will use this story instead.

Words to give to children could include:
- Messiah
- 700 years
- prophets
- prophecy
- Micah
- Isaiah

Memory Verse

Isaiah 53:6 (ESV) - All we like sheep have gone astray; we have turned—every one—to his own way; and the Lord has laid on him the iniquity of us all.

Praise and Worship

Praise and Worship styles vary greatly around the world. It is the intent of this curriculum that praise and worship songs be selected that best fit the content of this lesson. Recommendations for praise and worship are given and this music can generally be located at www.itunes.com. However, the teacher can feel free to select a similar praise and worship song.

"Salvation Belongs to Our God" by Eric Quiram is recommended for this lesson.

Bible Activity

"Prophecy match" Print the following verses on cards or pieces of paper to pass out to your class. Each Old Testament verse (prophecy) has a corresponding New Testament verse (fulfillment of the prophecy).

Old Testament Prophecy	New Testament Fulfillment
Genesis 12:3	Matthew 1:1
Isaiah 7:14	Matthew 1:18-23
Numbers 24:17	Matthew 1:2
Micah 5:2	Luke 2:1-7
Hosea 11:1	Matthew 2:13-15
Genesis 49:10	Luke 3:33
Malachi 3:1	Luke 2:25-27
Jeremiah 23:5	Matthew 1:6
Jeremiah 31:15	Matthew 2:16
Isaiah 53:10-11	Luke 23:33

Teacher Helps

Bible Memory Activity

Review the verse a few times then divide the children into two or more teams. Have the teams form lines across from a chalk or white board or piece of paper on a chair. Place something to write with at the board in front of each team. Have the first child of each team run to the board and write the first word of the verse, then run back to the line. The next child of the team will write the next word and it will continue until the verse is completed. Allow all teams to finish before playing again.

Bible Activity

For older children, you might only print the scripture reference on the card and they can look up the verse in their own Bible.

After the OT verses have all been read, the NT people should stand beside the one they think matches their card. They will have to work together to figure out which one best matches.

4) Review the Lesson

Have children simplify the lesson into 10 words or less using their own words. What are their answers? When children simplify the story of the lesson into ten words or less, they will probably say something like these possibilities:

- Two prophets told about the Messiah.
- Seven hundred years before Messiah came, Isaiah wrote.
- Seven hundred years before Messiah came, Micah wrote.
- The prophets told where Messiah would be born.
- The prophets told that Messiah would suffer.
- The prophets told that Messiah would have an eternal kingdom.

Teacher Helps

Review the Lesson Activity: Simplify

Simplify can be a useful game for the children. The teacher can give each team of 2 or 3 kids about 1-2 minutes to come up with the most significant 10 words of this lesson.

5) Apply the Lesson

Promise Seekers. From the following verses, find promises that the prophets wrote about that you think came true. Thank God that He is a faithful promise Giver.

- Isaiah 7:14
- Isaiah 9:6-7
- Isaiah 53:5-6
- Micah 5:2

Apply the Lesson Activity: Promise Seekers

The goal of "Promise Seekers" is to identify promises from God to the prophets about the coming Messiah. The class can work on this together or in groups of 3 or 4.

Story Line: Prophets told about Jesus 700 years before He came to earth.

Adventure Number 46
2 Kings 17 and 25

Story Line: God punished Israel and Judah for their disobedience.

1) Study the Lesson (before class)

- The Assyrian empire was very powerful in the middle of the 8th century. While Hosea the prophet was serving in Israel, the northern nation, Assyria invaded Israel in 725 B.C. and conquered the Israelites. Most of the Israelites were sent to northern Mesopotamia (northern Iraq and northern Iran).

- Amos had prophesied that the Israelites were more accountable to God since they were in covenant with Him; see Amos 3:2. Since the time of Jeroboam, Israel had abandoned their faith in Yahweh for about 200 years. Hence, God removed them from the land by using the Assyrian empire.

- While Israel was being exiled to Mesopotamia, the southern nation of Judah was responsive to the message of Micah and Isaiah under the leadership of King Hezekiah. Therefore, God let them remain in the land that He had promised to them.

- During the middle of the 7th century, Nahum (in the southern nation) prophesied against Nineveh because of their violence and idolatry.

- Also in the southern nation of Judah, Habakkuk foretold of the Babylonians coming to punish Judah. In 588 B.C., that is exactly what happened. After a 2-year battle, Jerusalem and Judah lost to the Babylonian empire. Most of the people of Judah were deported to Babylon. Only the poorest were allowed to remain in the land.

- The covenant that God had promised to David was never at risk.[1]

Footnotes - Adventure 46

1. David Brooks, *The Roots of Faith Old Testament Commentary*, COM-185-186.

2. Lynn Solem and Bob Pike, *50 Creative Training Closers*, 70.

2) Begin the Lesson

Let's think back over all of our lessons that we have studied and see if we can put the lessons in order. Here are the themes for some of the lessons:

1) God is very strong.

4) God made man and woman to be His special friends.

7) Satan tempted Adam and Eve. Adam and Eve disobeyed God.

12) God hates sin. God expelled Adam and Eve from the garden because of sin.

15) The people were evil. God sent a flood. Noah trusted and obeyed God.

18) God destroyed Sodom because the people were very wicked.

21) Jacob won a new name in a wrestling match with an angel.

24) God called Moses in a special way. Moses obeyed God.

27) God is mighty to save. God parted the Red Sea. God drowned His enemies.

30) God told the Israelites to build a tent where they could meet Him and offer sacrifices.

33) God's people chose to believe that God could not give them the land.

36) With God's help, the people entered the Promised Land.

39) The Israelites asked for a king and God gave them Saul.

42) Solomon built the temple for the Lord.

45) Prophets told about Jesus 700 years before He came to earth.

Begin the Lesson Activity: Story Line Review

The teacher should write these statements on pieces of paper and then mix them up. Do not put the number of the lesson on the piece of paper. Divide the children into 2 or 3 teams, depending on the size of the class. Time how long it takes each team to put the statements in the correct order.

3) Teach the Lesson

Is God fair? Is God just? Is God holy? Is God merciful? Is God patient? Is God loving? Is God kind?

The answer to all those questions is "yes." However, it may not seem like it at times. Today's lesson is about God's discipline of both nations (Israel and Judah) because of their desire to abandon Him.

Tell the Story

The nation of Israel had now lived in disobedience to God for almost 200 years. God was patient with them and He gave them plenty of time to turn from their idolatry and pagan worship. Some people look at these stories and think that God is not merciful and loving. Actually, the exact opposite is true.

God sent prophets to warn the nation. The prophets told the people not to abandon the Lord their God. Prophets like Micah and Isaiah in the south around 700 B.C. told the people of God's coming judgment. Amos, in the northern kingdom, told the people of Israel that they were more responsible to Yahweh since they were in a covenant with Him.

Because the northern nation of Israel did not listen to their prophets from God, God used the Assyrian nation to defeat Israel. Most of the people of Israel had to leave the land and live in a foreign land. They were exiled to a place called Mesopotamia (northern Iraq and northern Iran).

On the other hand, many of the people of Judah listened to the prophecies of Micah and Isaiah. God called Judah and eight of her kings "good." Two of those kings became king of Judah when they were kids. Josiah became king when he was only eight-years-old and Joash became king when he was only seven years old. Both of these were good kings in the eyes of the Lord Almighty.

However, Judah's commitment to Yahweh began to slip and God determined to punish them also. In the south, Habakkuk warned Judah that God was going to send the Babylonians to punish them for abandoning their commitment and faith in Yahweh. By this time, Babylon had conquered Assyria or Mesopotamia. Babylon was now a very powerful country. Babylon went to war with Judah and after a two year battle, Judah lost. Judah was now subject to whatever the leadership of the Babylonian empire wanted. So, about 136 years after Israel's exile to Mesopotamia, most of the people of Judah were sent to Babylon. They did not want to go but they had to go. Only the poorest were allowed to remain in Judah. They should have watched what happened to their northern neighbors, Israel, but they did not do that.

God had promised many good things to the people of Judah and Israel. But, because of the disobedience to Him, God had to punish them. Was He still loving? Yes. Was He still kind? Yes. Does He judge and punish sin? Yes.

Teacher Helps

Tell the Story Activity: Teaching with a Timeline

The teacher may want to develop a timeline of their own that shows the history of the one nation (Israel) which became two nations (Israel and Judah). These dates are estimates.

United Kingdom of Israel:
- Saul (1050 B.C.)
- David (1000 B.C.)
- Solomon (930 B.C.)

Divided Kingdom:
- Israel (northern) led by Jeroboam (930 B.C.). Exiled to Mesopotamia in 722 B.C.
- Judah (southern) led by Rehoboam (930 B.C.). Exiled to Babylon in 586 B.C.

When a prophet is mentioned, the teacher may want to place the prophet's name on the timeline. Was he in the north or south? In what time frame did he live and prophesy?

Memory Verse

2 Kings 17:19 (ESV) - Judah also did not keep the commandments of the Lord their God, but walked in the customs that Israel had introduced.

Praise and Worship

Praise and Worship styles vary greatly around the world. It is the intent of this curriculum that praise and worship songs be selected that best fit the content of this lesson. Recommendations for praise and worship are given and this music can generally be located at www.itunes.com. However, the teacher can feel free to select a similar praise and worship song.

"Salvation Belongs to Our God" by Eric Quiram is recommended for this lesson.

Bible Activity

Step 1: "Consider the choices" (hold out your hands on each side of your body, and move them up and down as if you are weighing 2 things on a scale, and instruct the children to do the same motion). Plain and simple, what are the 2 choices you have? (example: you could tell a lie and maybe not get in trouble for what you did wrong or you could tell the truth and be honest)

Step 2: "Compare it to God" (clasp both hands together in front of your chest and point up to heaven, kids do the same). What do you know about God that can help you decide what is the right thing to do? (God is truth, He cannot ever lie)

Step 3: "Commit to God's way" (give a "thumbs up" sign, or something similar). Decide right now that when you are faced with a choice, you will always do your best to obey God, and do what pleases Him, not put anyone else above Him.

Step 4: "Count on God's protection and provision." (Make an arc with both arms above your head, as if it were an umbrella, shielding you from the rain). When you choose to obey God, He has promised many blessings. That doesn't mean it is easy, but if God is for us, then who can ever stand against us?!? (No one!)

Teacher Helps

Memory Verse Activity: Pray

Encourage children to pray this verse. Pray something like: "Lord, I pray that I would keep your commandments and be faithful to You. Help me to not do things that do not honor You."

Bible Activity

Did the people of Israel make good or bad choices about their actions? Some made good choices, most made bad choices. How can we decide what is the right thing to do in a situation? This is especially hard when it seems like everyone around us is making bad choices. Today we will learn a 4-step process to help us make the right choice.

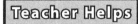

4) Review the Lesson

The teacher should have the class think of the main ideas of the lesson that they want to take home. Then the children should number off 1 through 5. Number 1 group should tell the main thing that he or she learned from the lesson. All five groups should get an opportunity to share the main thing they learned from this lesson.

Ideas might include:
- Commitment in daily habits
- Listen to what God says
- Faithful to obey God
- Praise God for His faithful lovingkindness

Review the Lesson Activity: Repetition[2]

The teacher should allow about 5 minutes for children to share the main thing that they learned. If more than 5 children are in the class, allow for each of the groups to share with each other.

5) Apply the Lesson

- Make an assignment for the children. Have them review all their memory verses from the first 46 lessons.

- Any child who can recite half of the memory verses should win a prize.

- Any child who can recite two thirds of the memory verses should get a better prize.

- Any child who can recite all the memory verses should be the teacher's helper.

Apply the Lesson Activity: Assignment

The teacher could ask the children to come early to recite their verses. Or, if parents will cooperate, the teacher can ask kids to bring in a signed note that the children have recited all memory verses.

Story Line: God punished Israel and Judah for their disobedience.

Adventure Number 47
Jeremiah 23, 25, 29 and 31

Story Line: God punished Judah for their disobedience.

1) Study the Lesson (before class)

- Jeremiah lived about 3 miles from Jerusalem in the city of Anathoth. He prophesied for about 40 years in Judah. He warned Judah to submit to the coming Babylonian invasion. If Judah submitted, they had a chance to survive.

- When the Babylonians invaded Judah and conquered Jerusalem in 586 B.C., King Nebuchadnezzar allowed Jeremiah to remain in Judah. However, most of the people of Judah were forced to leave their homes and move eastward to Babylon where they would become forced labor.

- Earlier, God used Moses (around 1406 B.C.) to warn Israel not to continue in their rebellion or else they would be exiled. Yahweh repeated the warning to Solomon (906 B.C.). In 597 B.C., Yahweh revealed that the exile would last 70 years (Jeremiah 29:10 and 25:12).

- The exile was because of their sin and rebellion, not because the Lord did not love them anymore.

- The prophet Habakkuk, a contemporary of Jeremiah, complained to the Lord that the Babylonians were in rebellion against Yahweh also. However, Yahweh explained to Habakkuk that the Babylonians would experience the discipline of Yahweh also, only after the exile ended. Yahweh also punished other nations, not just Babylon (Jeremiah 46-51). Isaiah also wrote of God punishing other nations (Isaiah 13-23).

- Jeremiah wrote of a new covenant that Yahweh would establish (Jeremiah 31). Instead of Yahweh's laws being written on stone, they would be written on hearts. This covenant would not replace the Abrahamic or Davidic covenants, but it would replace the Mosaic covenant.[1]

Footnotes - Adventure 47

1. David Brooks, *The Roots of Faith Old Testament Commentary*, COM-187-189.

2. Susan Lingo, *Written on Our Hearts*, 92.

2) Begin the Lesson

Let's name the time periods that we have learned and some of the special people and events that happened in each era.

1. <u>Beginnings of the World</u>. God created the heavens and the earth. He made Adam and Eve to be His special friends.

2. <u>Beginnings of the World</u>. Lucifer decided he wanted to be like the Most High God and led a rebellion of angels against God. He was expelled from heaven. After that, he tempted Adam and Eve to disobey God and they sinned.

3. <u>Beginnings of the World</u>. Because there was so much violence on the earth, God decided to flood the entire earth. But Noah found grace in God's sight.

4. <u>Beginnings of the World</u>. The people wanted to build a tower to God so that they could have a gateway to the gods. Because of this, God confused their languages and the building of this tower stopped.

5. <u>Beginnings of a Nation</u>. Great promises were made to Abraham by Yahweh.

6. <u>Beginnings of a Nation</u>. Moses received a special call from God to do a special work. He also received the Ten Commandments on Mount Sinai.

7. <u>Possessing the Land</u>. Joshua led the people of Israel into the Promised Land.

8. <u>Possessing the Land</u>. Israel failed to be loyal to God and He punished them for this.

9. <u>United Kingdom</u>. God gave the Israelites a king. David was the greatest of those kings.

10. <u>Divided Kingdom</u>. Because Solomon failed to be loyal to Yahweh like his father had been, Yahweh divided the kingdom.

11. <u>Exile</u>. After hundreds of years of rebellion, God sent the Israelites to Assyria and Babylon.

Teacher Helps

Begin the Lesson Activity: Mix and Match Time Line Review

The teacher should write each time period on a separate piece of paper.

Then the teacher should put names on other pieces of paper for each time period. For example, Adam and Eve could be listed twice: once for creation and once for the fall.

Then, on separate sheets of paper, the teacher should put events that happened in each time period.

Mix up all the sheets of paper and have teams of students (3-4 on each team) match the era with the people and events of that time period.

3) Teach the Lesson

Troubling messages from friends always tend to bother us. What are some troubling messages that some of your friends have told you?

Timeline: Taken from Home

Tell the Story

Warnings came to the people of Judah over and over again. They were warned that if they continued in their rebellion, they would be sent away. They would not live in the land that God had promised them, at least for a period of time. Moses had warned them hundreds of years before. The Lord warned Solomon and now Micah warned them. Yet, they kept pushing Yahweh out of their lives.

Since God always honors what He said He would do, He punished them by sending the Babylonians to conquer Judah and exile them to the east. The northern kingdom of Israel had already experienced deportation, perhaps about 136 years earlier. Judah should have learned from that, but they did not. They kept trying to rebel against God. Habakkuk and Jeremiah were contemporaries of each other; that is, they lived at about the same time. When Habakkuk learned of the coming Babylonian exile, he complained to God that the Babylonians were in rebellion against Yahweh also. Yahweh would punish the Babylonians too, but only after the punishment of Judah.

The Babylonians came to conquer Judah. It took them two years to do it, but they eventually defeated Judah. It was a very sad day when most of the people of Judah were forced to leave their homes and live in a different country. A few people were allowed to stay behind in Judah, but not many. One of those who was allowed to stay in Judah was the prophet Jeremiah. Jeremiah was quite sad and even wept over the rebellion of Judah and their exile to Babylon. He warned Judah not to continue in their rebellion, but they did not heed his advice.

But good news was coming from Yahweh. The exile would only last 70 years. Although their rebellion had lasted hundreds of years, their captivity would not be that long. More good news was coming: Yahweh would send a coming Descendant of David that would bring justice and righteousness. Earlier, Isaiah had referred to this Descendant of David as the suffering servant.

When God punished Adam and Eve, He also gave them hope when He gave them new clothes. When God punished the people of Noah's day, He also gave them hope when He promised the rainbow and that He would never flood the earth again. Now, just like then, God was punishing Judah for their rebellion, but He was also giving them hope. The people of Judah would be allowed to go back to the land; that gave them hope. God would sent a deliverer; that gave them hope.

Teacher Helps

Tell the Story Activity: Messages from God

As the teacher is telling this story, have the children indicate which part of the messages from God are troubling and which part of the messages bring hope. Perhaps they could hold up a craft stick with a happy face on one side and a sad face on the other side.

Memory Verse

Jeremiah 31:33 (ESV) - For this is the covenant that I will make with the house of Israel after those days, declares the Lord: I will put my law within them, and I will write it on their hearts. And I will be their God, and they shall be my people.

Praise and Worship

Praise and Worship styles vary greatly around the world. It is the intent of this curriculum that praise and worship songs be selected that best fit the content of this lesson. Recommendations for praise and worship are given and this music can generally be located at www.itunes.com. However, the teacher can feel free to select a similar praise and worship song.

"Salvation Belongs to Our God" by Eric Quiram is recommended for this lesson.

Bible Activity

"Good News, Bad News" – Divide your class in half. Choose one person to be the leader of each group. This should be an older, responsible child. Give one leader a sign that says "Good News," and the other leader a sign that says "Bad News." Tell the story again, but this time, every time you make a statement that is good news, the "Good News" group will cheer. Every time you make a statement that is bad news, the "Bad News" group will boo. The leader should listen especially closely, and hold up the sign to cue the rest of the group that it is their turn. The teacher may need to give a little help also, depending on the ages of the children.

Teacher Helps

Memory Verse Activity: Scripture Card Battle[2]

Divide your class up into groups of 2 or 3. Give each group a set of cards. On each card is one word from the memory verse. Groups should try to put the words of the memory verse in the right order.

4) Review the Lesson

"Who" Questions:

1. Who was Jeremiah?

2. Who was a contemporary of Jeremiah?

"What" Questions:

1. What did Jeremiah say would happen to Judah?

2. What warnings came to Judah?

"When" Questions:

1. When did Babylon invade Judah?

2. How long did the exile last?

"Where" Questions:

1. Where is Babylon?

2. Where is Judah?

"Why" Questions:

1. Why did God send His people to exile in Babylon?

2. Why did Judah ignore the warnings from the prophets?

Teacher Helps

Review Activity: The Investigative Cube

Divide the class up into two teams. Make a cube with these labels on each side of the cube: who, what, when, where, why. When the cube is rolled to one team, they will answer the type of question that is face up on the cube. For instance, if the "why" is face up on the cube, then that team will answer a "why" question. Teachers can make up their own questions from the lesson, only they must pertain to this lesson.

5) Apply the Lesson

God's words belong in our hearts. From the past Bible stories or memory verses, recall which stories from God have most affected the way you live.

Children should recall how their lives have changed from hearing the stories of God. Try to be specific.

Story Line: God punished Judah for their disobedience.

Timeline: Taken from Home

Adventure Number 48
Ezekiel 34-36 and Daniel 2

Story Line: Daniel and Ezekiel spoke faithfully for God in Babylon.

 1) Study the Lesson (before class)

- When King Nebuchadnezzar of Babylon conquered Jerusalem in 597 B.C., he deported 10,000 people. One of those was 25-year-old Ezekiel who came from a line of priests. He was from the tribe of Levi. Since he was not yet 30-years-old, he had not served in the temple.

- Ezekiel explained that Yahweh was just in His judgment. The first 24 chapters of the book explain this judgment. Ezekiel also described the judgment of God on Gentile nations (chapters 25-32) and the restoration of Judah and Jerusalem (chapters 33-48).

- Concerning the restoration of Judah and Jerusalem, Ezekiel wrote that God would give them a new heart and a new spirit. The inner change would make their hearts responsive to God, unlike the hard hearts that they currently had. The result is the same as Jeremiah's new covenant (Jeremiah 31:31-34).

- The Babylonians also took youths from their homes to educate them. While the Babylonians took many youths, we only know of four of them: Daniel, Hananiah, Mishael, and Azariah. Near the end of the three year education for the youth, God gave them a promotion when the king had a dream that no one else could interpret, except for Daniel.

- The dream was interpreted to the king: the head of gold symbolized King Nebuchadnezzar. He would be replaced by an inferior kingdom of silver (chest and arms), Persia. The third kingdom was symbolized by bronze (belly and thighs) and probably represented Greece. The fourth empire was symbolized by iron (legs) and clay (feet) and would crush the other kingdom. This was probably the Roman empire. The last empire was symbolized by stone and represented the kingdom of God that would never be smashed.[1]

Footnotes - Adventure 48

1. David Brooks, *The Roots of Faith Old Testament Commentary*, COM-191-192.

2. Susan Lingo, *Written on Our Hearts*, 99.

2) Begin the Lesson

- What was the first time period that our lessons studied? (Beginnings) What were some of the lessons that we learned about the period of time?

- What is the next period of time? (Beginnings of a Nation) What are some of the lessons that we learned from the period of time?

- What is the next period of time? (Possessing the Land) What are some of the lessons that we learned from the period of time?

- What is the next era or period of time? (United Kingdom) What are some of the lessons that we learned from this period of time?

- What is the next period of time? (Divided Kingdom) What are some of the lessons that we learned from this period of time?

Teacher Helps

Begin the Lesson Activity: Cards

The teacher can put on pieces of paper or 3 by 5 cards, the Time Period on one side of the card and the Story Line on the other side of the card or piece of paper.

The students can take a quiz with the teacher's help about matching the Story Lines on the Time Line.

3) Teach the Lesson

Today's lesson is about two young men who honored God in a foreign country. One of them was a teenager (Daniel) and one of them was a young adult (Ezekiel).

What challenges do you face in today's culture if you want to honor God?

Tell the Story

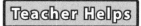

The statesman and the prophet, that is what they were. We are talking about Daniel (the statesman) and Ezekiel (the prophet). Both of them were young men and both of them honored God with what they said, how they lived, and the messages that they brought from God.

When Ezekiel was forced to leave Jerusalem because of the Babylonians conquering Jerusalem, he was a young man. Ezekiel was probably about 25-years-old. He came from a family of priests. So, when Ezekiel and thousands of others left home and traveled east to Babylon, they left everything behind. One thing that Ezekiel did not leave behind was his faith in God. In Jerusalem, he had faith in God. Now, in Babylon, he grew in that faith and in dependence on God alone.

Ezekiel was a writing prophet who told a lot about the nations and the judgment of God on them. He also wrote about the return of the exiles to Jerusalem and how God would write His laws on the hearts of His people. Most of Ezekiel's message dealt with the judgments of Yahweh because of the sins of people. However, Ezekiel provided hope also when he wrote of Yahweh placing His laws inside people. That would be incredible!

A contemporary of Ezekiel in Babylon was Daniel. Daniel was probably a teenager and was educated in the Babylonian school system. He, and his three godly friends, set out to worship and live for Yahweh in Babylon.

One day, the king of Babylon had a dream that no one could interpret. It made the king so mad that he wanted to put all his dream interpreters to death. God revealed the meaning of the dream to Daniel. It was a very unique dream.

The dream went like this: there was a statue of a body made up of many metals. The head was made of gold. It represented the king of Babylon. The chest and the arms were made of silver which was inferior to gold. The silver chest and arms represented the next ruling empire after Babylon which would be Persia. The next part of the body was the bronze belly and thighs. This bronze kingdom, probably Greece, would rule the entire world. The next part of the body was the iron legs and iron and clay feet. This fourth kingdom would be strong, so strong that it could crush all the others. We might assume this to be the Roman empire. Later, it would be divided. The last kingdom was a kingdom of stone. The stone kingdom was not made by human hands. It was the kingdom of God that would never be destroyed.

Tell the Story Activity: Messengers from God

Have half the class be a "Daniel reporter" and half the class be an "Ezekiel reporter."

The reporters should ask any question that they would like to ask the teacher about each of these two men. Encourage children to ask one question that they think of as the teacher tells the story.

The teacher should do his or her best to answer your reporters' questions from a Biblical perspective.

Memory Verse

Ezekiel 36:26 (ESV) - And I will give you a new heart, and a new spirit I will put within you.

Praise and Worship

Praise and Worship styles vary greatly around the world. It is the intent of this curriculum that praise and worship songs be selected that best fit the content of this lesson. Recommendations for praise and worship are given and this music can generally be located at www.itunes.com. However, the teacher can feel free to select a similar praise and worship song.

"Salvation Belongs to Our God" by Eric Quiram is recommended for this lesson.

Bible Activity

Ahead of time, list several choices Daniel would have been faced with in Babylon. (He had a commitment to eat certain foods, but not others such as some meat that the king served. He prayed every day to the one true God, no matter what the king commanded.)

Let's review the activity from 2 lessons ago – the 4-step process for making right choices. Let's apply this process to Daniel, and the choices he was faced with. As you do this, remind the kids that Daniel could have gotten in big trouble for doing things God's way instead of the king's way. Making the right choice is not easy most of the time. Many times it is easier to go the wrong way, but in the end, doing the right thing will always bring God's protection and provision. Now let's think about you. What is a situation that you might face where you have to make a choice that is not easy. Allow children to suggest a situation they face, but have something in mind that is appropriate for their situation if no one has an idea to share. Go through the 4-step process as it relates to their choices.

Teacher Helps

Memory Verse Activity: Scripture Scrambler[2]

Write the words to a verse on the top of a paper. Then number the paper, one number for each word in the verse. Beside the numbers, write a scrambled word to the verse. Challenge your children to unscramble each word to the verse in its correct order.

Example:

1	dna	and
2	lliw	will
3	vegi	give
4	oyu	you
5	trhae	heart
6	tpiirs	spirit
7	tpu	put
8	htniwi	within

4) Review the Lesson

Compare the last two memory verses and see what they have in common. List those things that these verses have in common.

- Ezekiel 36:26 (ESV) - And I will give you a new heart, and a new spirit I will put within you.

- Jeremiah 31:33 (ESV) - I will put my law within them, and I will write it on their hearts. And I will be their God, and they shall be my people.

Things in common:

- God will write it
- new heart
- gift or He puts it in
- His Word

Teacher Helps

Review Activity: Memory Verse Comparison

Compare these verses and remember that they are written by contemporaries from two different locations with no knowledge of what the other was writing. Jeremiah wrote from Judah and Ezekiel wrote from Babylon.

God's Word was given by inspiration to each of these men and they wrote down what God told them to write.

5) Apply the Lesson

Two courageous young men took their stand for God. They worshipped and obeyed God while living in a foreign land.

What are some specific ways you can honor God as a boy or as a girl? At home? At school? With family? With friends?

Story Line: Daniel and Ezekiel spoke faithfully for God in Babylon.

Adventure Number 49
Ezra 1-4 and Isaiah 44:28

Story Line: The Jews returned to Jerusalem to rebuild their temple.

1) Study the Lesson (before class)

- The Israelites were deported from Judah to Babylon from 605 B.C. to 586 B.C. After Jeremiah and Ezekiel had died, and when Daniel was about 80 years old, a prophecy of Isaiah came to be fulfilled.

- In Isaiah 40-48, Isaiah talked about a foreign king names Cyrus who would issue a decree to rebuild Jerusalem. Cyrus would not be a worshipper of Yahweh. This prophecy occurred around 700 B.C. Cyrus was born about a century after Isaiah wrote this prophecy.

- Jeremiah foretold that Judah would be exiled to Babylon for 70 years. The Israelites would pray and then God would restore them to the land that He had promised to them (Jeremiah 29:10-14).

- Sixty-seven years after the exile, Daniel read this prophecy and realized the exile was almost over. So, he did what Jeremiah said to do, he confessed the sins of Israel and begged God for His favor (Daniel 9:3-19). By 536 B.C., 50,000 Jews had decided to return to Jerusalem.

- The decree by Cyrus declared all the stolen temple items would be returned. Ezra 3 describes the construction of the second temple in Jerusalem. This happened around 536 B.C.

- In Ezra 4, the reader learns that the Samaritans wanted to join the rebuilding of the temple. The Samaritans worshipped Yahweh. However, they also worshipped other gods. The writer of 2 Kings 17 tells us that the Samaritans feared the Lord but they also served other gods. They were not allowed to be part of the building project.

- By 515 B.C., the building project had stopped. However, the prophets Haggai and Zechariah confronted the Jews about their priorities and the building efforts resumed.[1]

Footnotes - Adventure 49

1. David Brooks, *The Roots of Faith Old Testament Commentary*, COM-195-197.

2. Susan Lingo, *Written on Our Hearts*, 79.

3. Lynn Solem and Bob Pike, *50 Creative Training Closers*, 94.

2) Begin the Lesson

There are eight basic concepts that are emphasized throughout all of the Bible. We have studied these truths in previous lessons. Ask the children if they can name them and tell a little bit about each one. They are:

1. <u>God</u>. In the beginning, there was a very powerful God. (Lesson 1: The Eternal God; Lesson 27: The Exodus; Lesson 40: The Reign of David)

2. <u>Man</u>. God created many things. He created man and woman to be His special friends. (Lessons 3: Creation of the Universe; Lesson 4: Creation of People; Lesson 24: Moses Leads His People)

3. <u>Sin</u>. Man and woman disobeyed God. They did not do what He told them to do. (Lesson 7: Beginning of Human Sin; Lesson 33: Unbelief at Kadesh; Lesson 43: The Divided Kingdom)

4. <u>Death</u>. God punished man and woman for their disobedience. Death, in the Bible, refers to separation. (Lesson 8: The Origin of Death; Lesson 16: The Tower of Babel; Lesson 46: The Exiles of Israel and Judah)

5. <u>Christ</u>. God sent His one and only Son, His unique Son, who lived a perfect life. (Lesson 9: Promise of a Victor Over Satan; Lesson 45: Prophecies of a Coming Messiah)

6. <u>Cross</u>. Jesus died on the cross for the sins of the world. (Lesson 11: Provision of Coverings; Lesson 32: The Day of Atonement)

7. <u>Faith</u>. If anyone places their faith in Christ, God welcomes them. (Lesson 13: Cain and Abel; Lesson 34: The Bronze Serpent)

8. <u>Life</u>. God gives eternal life to those who put their faith in Him. (Lesson 5: Life in Paradise; Lesson 38: Bright Lights in an Era of Darkness)

Teacher Helps

Review Activity: Eight Basic Gospel Truths - One Complete Story

The teacher should emphasize these eight gospel concepts throughout Scripture. They are foundational to telling children the one story of redemption found in the Bible. We will emphasize these eight truths regularly.

Ask the children if they can think of how these eight gospel principles are emphasized in the first 48 lessons that we have studied.

3) Teach the Lesson

Coming home is a wonderful thing to do. Have you ever been away from home for a short period of time? Have you ever been away from home for a long period of time? How did it feel when you came home?

Today's lesson will tell us about 50,000 people who came home.

Tell the Story

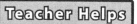

It was near the end of my life. As young teenage boys in Babylon, my three friends and I worshipped and served God. Even when the king issued a decree that we could not worship God, I still continued to pray. It almost cost me my life but God spared me. The king put me in a lions' den and they were hungry. God chose to let me live and that is why I am here today. The king also put my three friends in a fiery furnace because of their faith in Yahweh. Again, God spared them. Now, at the end of my life, God has allowed me to be a part of His great work in another way.

I was reading the prophet Jeremiah. While I was reading, I realized that my countrymen and I would be in captivity for 70 years. This was our sixty-seventh year of captivity. If Jeremiah was correct and I knew he was, then we would only have three more years of captivity in Babylon. Then, we could go home to Jerusalem. I earnestly confessed the sins of my countrymen and begged for the favor of God to be upon us. Yahweh graciously granted my request. Three years later, King Cyrus issued a decree that the Jews could return to Jerusalem and he would even give us all the stolen items from the temple. That amounted to 5,400 articles of gold and silver which had been stolen from the first temple that were returned to the temple that would be rebuilt.

Isaiah, the prophet of Yahweh, had written 170 years earlier about this decree by Cyrus. He even mentioned "Cyrus" by name. My great God revealed it to Isaiah and now it was coming true. God is a promise-giving God and He always keeps His promises.

My countrymen started building the temple in 536 B.C. They got off to a great start but because of some opposition, they slowed down and eventually stopped. They did not compete the job of rebuilding the temple. The opposition came from neighbors of ours, the Samaritans. The Samaritans worshipped Yahweh and served Him, but they also worshipped and served other gods. We could not tolerate that because God does not share His glory with other gods.

After a long delay, we continued rebuilding the temple in 515 B.C. The preaching of Haggai and Zechariah got the people going again. Finally, the temple was completed. There was great joy and celebration. We had returned to the land promised to Abraham. We were now living in the City of David, Jerusalem. It was all because of God's faithful love for His people. Praise be to Yahweh! May His name be honored!

Tell the Story Activity: A Monologue from Daniel

Tell this story as if you were Daniel. Dress up in costume, if possible. It is written in the first person as if Daniel was telling the story.

All the story comes from the Bible, especially the prophets Daniel, Isaiah, and Jeremiah.

Memory Verse

Ezra 6:16 (ESV) - And the people of Israel ... celebrated the dedication of this house of God with joy.

Praise and Worship

Praise and Worship styles vary greatly around the world. It is the intent of this curriculum that praise and worship songs be selected that best fit the content of this lesson. Recommendations for praise and worship are given and this music can generally be located at www.itunes.com. However, the teacher can feel free to select a similar praise and worship song.

"Salvation Belongs to Our God" by Eric Quiram is recommended for this lesson.

Bible Activity

Daniel's Faithful Life

"Daniel had a very exciting and sometimes scary life! Let's see how many things we can remember about Daniel's life, and then we will play a game." Lead the children to think of events from Daniel's life, and write each one on a different card. Some suggestions:

1. As a young teenager, taken from his home in Judah to Babylon
2. Thrown in a den of lions for praying to God
3. His 3 friends were thrown in a fiery furnace
4. Interpreted the king's dream at risk to his own life
5. Prophesied about God's judgement
6. Confessed the sins of his countrymen

Once the cards have been written, turn them over & mix them up. See who can put them in chronological order the fastest. Kids can work on this alone, or in teams.

Teacher Helps

Memory Verse Activity: Scripture Log[2]

Make a page for children to take home that shows down the left column: Sunday, Monday, Tuesday, Wednesday, Thursday, Friday, and Saturday.

Across the top, put practice times and review times.

Children should work on this memory verse each day and mark on their log when they practiced this verse and when they review this verse. Bring this log to class with you next week.

Bible Activity: Daniel's Faithful Life

Supplies needed: Cards, about 3x5 or 4x6, a pen or marker to write on the cards.

4) Review the Lesson

The teacher should divide the class up into two teams.

- One team could be the "red" team and receive red cards or pieces of paper. The other team could be the "yellow" team and receive yellow cards or pieces of paper.

- Each team has the responsibility of writing out 3 to 5 questions that they want the other team to answer.

- Each question has to pertain to the lesson today.

- After questions are written out, the other team has five to seven minutes to answer the questions. The "yellow" team will answer the questions from the "red" team and the "red" team will answer questions from the "yellow" team.

Teacher Helps

Review Activity: Two Team Review[3]

After an appropriate time, the teacher will gather up the cards or pieces of paper and reward points to the best questions and best answers from each team.

It is highly advisable to have 2 adult teachers in every classroom for kids. If there are 2 adults, then one adult should be the leader of each team.

5) Apply the Lesson

The Jews came home to Jerusalem with good intentions. They were going to rebuild the temple. But, the original group stopped and did not finish.

Describe one or two ways that you have begun your journey of faith but you have slowed down or stopped. What caused you to slow down or stop? What did you do about it? What will you do about it?

Story Line: The Jews returned to Jerusalem to rebuild their temple.

Adventure Number 50
Nehemiah 1-8

Story Line: The Jews returned to Jerusalem to rebuild the walls.

 ## 1) Study the Lesson (before class)

- The Jews' attempts to rebuild the temple and the walls of Jerusalem had opponents during the reign of Cyrus, around 530 B.C. In 515 B.C., the Jews completed the temple but not the walls.

- During the reign of Artaxerxes (465 B.C. - 424 B.C.), the Jews began to rebuild the walls, again with opposition. After much prayer, Nehemiah approached the king and asked the king to allow the rebuilding of the walls of Jerusalem. The king granted Nehemiah's request.

- Nehemiah and a small group of men went to Jerusalem and surveyed the damage of the walls. With much enthusiasm, they enlisted workers not only from Jerusalem, but also from Judah.

- Even with opposition, Nehemiah and his friends continued the work. In 52 days, they rebuilt the nine foot thick walls.

- Nehemiah and his contemporary, Ezra, taught the word of the Lord to the people and exhorted them to be faithful in obedience. They assembled the people of Jerusalem for five hours at the beginning of each morning at the city gates. The word of the Lord was read in Hebrew and explained in Aramaic, the current language of most of the people. Nehemiah urged people to rejoice in the Lord and to continue to live as holy people in His presence.

- Approximately 80 years earlier, Haggai had prophesied that other nations would bring valuable gifts for the temple. Zechariah, a contemporary of Haggai, told about the king who would enter Jerusalem in humility.

- The Old Testament ended with a message of hope from three prophets: Haggai, Zechariah, and Malachi. Each of these prophets declared something wonderful about promises by Yahweh for His people.[1]

Footnotes - Adventure 50

1. David Brooks, *The Roots of Faith Old Testament Commentary*, COM-199-202.

2) Begin the Lesson

Adventure Number 47: Prophecies from Judah

1. Where did God promise to write His promises?

2. Read Jeremiah 31:34.

3. God's promises are trustworthy.

4. Ask God to write His promises on your heart now.

Adventure Number 48: Prophecies from Babylon

1. Who were two prophets who spoke for God in Babylon?

2. Read Ezekiel 34 and Daniel 2.

3. Ezekiel and Daniel were young men who honored God.

4. Pray that we would honor God with our daily lives.

Adventure Number 49: Jews Return to Jerusalem

1. Where did the opposition to rebuild the temple come from?

2. Read Ezra 4.

3. Sometimes, opposition to live for God comes from our friends.

4. Pray to live for God even if there is opposition from friends.

Teacher Helps

Begin the Lesson Activity: Ask, Read, Talk, Pray

A good review strategy from 3 previous lessons will focus on four main elements.

1) Ask a question.

2) Read the Bible.

3) Talk about it.

4) Pray to God.

3) Teach the Lesson

Maybe you have experienced a spiritual revival and maybe you haven't experienced one. If you haven't, what do you think is necessary to have a spiritual revival? In today's lesson, we are going to learn how revival happened for the people of God.

Tell the Story

This was the last chapter of the Old Testament history, and it ended with a note of hope and optimism. It ended on a revival. God's people had come back to Jerusalem to rebuild the temple and the walls. With opposition, they rebuilt the temple but they did not rebuild the walls. This put the temple and the people of Jerusalem at great risk. In those days, walls around the city were for protection. With no protective walls, everyone was vulnerable to attack from outsiders.

At great risk to himself, Nehemiah approached King Artaxerxes of Persia. Nehemiah had prayed much about the city and its unbuilt walls. God answered the prayers of Nehemiah. Not only did the king give Nehemiah approval to rebuild the walls, he provided the materials necessary to make it happen.

So, Nehemiah and some of his friends went to see what needed to be done to get the walls rebuilt. When they looked over the task ahead of them, they were excited and started recruiting helpers to rebuild the walls. It was amazing to see how God was working and answering prayers.

But opposition came to the builders and it came from an unusual source. It came from the friends of the builders. Sanballat and Tobiah were friends of some of the builders, they might have even been related to some of the builders. Even with the opposition, the construction of the walls was completed in less than two months. There was great joy and celebration.

In the middle of the building, Nehemiah and Ezra began teaching the word of the Lord to the people of Jerusalem. Every morning, they read the word of the Lord for five hours. There was some explanation given and the people responded in faith and obedience. So, there were not only the walls being built, there were people being built.

The walls went up and the people grew up. The people grew up to learn about Yahweh and obey Him. Nehemiah encouraged the people to make the joy of the Lord their strength.

This last chapter of the Old Testament also saw hopeful messages from Haggai, Zechariah, and Malachi. Haggai wrote of the Lord giving peace in this place. Zechariah wrote about a coming king who would enter Jerusalem in humility. Malachi wrote about a great messenger who is coming. The promises made throughout the Old Testament would soon come to pass.

Teacher Helps

Tell the Story Activity: Cheering for the Israelites

Have children listen to the story. As you tell the story, have the children clap or cheer when they hear the words "Jerusalem," "temple," and "walls."

The reason for focus on cheering for these three words: God was going to bless the Israelites with joy and celebration as the walls and temple of Jerusalem were rebuilt.

Haggai 2:7-9
Zechariah 9:9
Malachi 3:1
Malachi 4:2-5

Memory Verse

Nehemiah 8:10 (ESV) - And do not be grieved, for the joy of the LORD is your strength.

Praise and Worship

Praise and Worship styles vary greatly around the world. It is the intent of this curriculum that praise and worship songs be selected that best fit the content of this lesson. Recommendations for praise and worship are given and this music can generally be located at www.itunes.com. However, the teacher can feel free to select a similar praise and worship song.

"Salvation Belongs to Our God" by Eric Quiram is recommended for this lesson.

Bible Activity

"Red Light/Green Light" Activity

Prepare 2 circles of paper, one solid green, and the other solid red. Tell the children, "**I will name an activity that pleases God (such as helping sweep the floor, pulling weeds in the garden, helping a friend who has fallen down, etc). When I hold up the green light and say 'go,' everyone should pretend to do the good activity. When I hold up the red light and say 'stop' everyone should stop doing the good thing.**"

After a few rounds, tell them: "**God wants us to do good things, but sometimes people try to stop us. It's like they are the red light.**" That's how it was for Nehemiah and the people of Israel. They wanted to do the right thing and obey God, but their enemies tried to stop them. What are some things you might try to do that are good, and how do others sometimes try to stop you? What can we learn from Nehemiah's example that can help us?

Teacher Helps

Memory Verse Activity: Hop It

In large letters, write phrases of the verse on sheets of paper. On the floor, tape the papers in a mixed up fashion, but close enough for succeeding words to be reached in a step. Children should step on one word at a time in the proper order to quote the verse. Let each child have a turn of hopping on the verse.

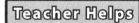

4) Review the Lesson

Agree/Disagree Statements (If you disagree, why do you disagree?)

1. Isaiah and Micah lived at the same time as Nehemiah. (Disagree. They lived about 170 years before Nehemiah).

2. Nehemiah and Ezra taught the word of God together to the people who lived in Jerusalem. (Agree.)

3. Nehemiah went to King Artaxerxes to have the walls of Jerusalem rebuilt. (Agree.)

4. Nehemiah did not pray about going to the king. (Disagree. He did pray.)

5. It took 6 months to rebuild the walls of Jerusalem. (Disagree. It took less than 2 months.)

Review Activity: Agree and Disagree Statements

Kids will have fun disagreeing or agreeing with these statements. You may want to make up some statements of your own for them to agree or disagree with.

5) Apply the Lesson

Revival came to the people when they read the Bible and followed its teachings. The joy of the Lord became their strength.

How often are you reading the Bible? Will you read it every day?

How well are you following the teachings of the Bible? Will you turn away from things that do not please the Lord?

Story Line: The Jews returned to Jerusalem to rebuild the walls.

Adventure Number 51
Daniel 2

Time Line: Between the Old and New Testaments, a lot changed.

1) Study the Lesson (before class)

- Between the Old and New Testaments, the role of the local synagogue greatly increased.

- Between the Old and New Testaments, the language changed. The Jewish people now spoke Aramaic which was similar to their old language, Hebrew.

- Between the Old and New Testaments, a Greek translation of the Old Testament was made. The Greek version is called the Septuagint.

- Between the Old and New Testaments, a very strict sect of the Jews resisted the influence of the Greek and Roman cultures. They were called Pharisees. They accepted the authority of the Old Testament Scriptures as well as their oral traditions.

- Between the Old and New Testaments, another group of Jews became popular. They accepted only the books of Moses as authoritative and were much less resistant to Greek and Roman cultures. They were called Sadducees.

- Between the Old and New Testaments, there arose of group of Jewish enthusiasts who refused to pay taxes to Rome. They were called Zealots. Many were violent and murdered Jews who were loyal to Rome.

- Between the Old and New Testaments, a council called the Sanhedrin, now ruled the Jews as much as non-Jewish authorities would allow.

- Between the Old and New Testaments, crucifixion as a form of execution became popular under the Roman government. Other nations had used crucifixion, but now it was heavily used in the Roman empire.[1]

Footnotes - Adventure 51

1. Wayne Haston, *The Roots of Faith New Testament Workbook* (Harrisburg, Good Soil Publications, 2013), 01-C.

2. Lynn Solem and Bob Pike, *50 Creative Training Closers*, 52.

2) Begin the Lesson

Let's review the time line of the Old Testament.

- In order, what are these eras or time periods? (Beginnings of the World, Beginnings of a Nation, Possessing the Land, United Kingdom, Divided Kingdom, Taken from Home, Return to Home)

- Who are some of the people that we met in each time period?

1) Beginnings of the World: Adam and Eve, Lucifer, Cain, and Abel, Noah, and pagan worshippers
2) Beginnings of a Nation: Abraham, Sarah, Isaac, Rebekah, Jacob, Joseph, Moses, and Pharaoh
3) Possessing the Land: Joshua, Gideon, and Samuel
4) United Kingdom: Saul and David
5) Divided Kingdom: Jeroboam, Elijah, and Elisha
6) Taken from Home: Jeremiah, Daniel, and Ezekiel
7) Return to Home: Ezra and Nehemiah

- What are some of the main themes from each of the eras?

1) Beginnings of the World: God is powerful. People are to be His special friends. Sin entered the world. God punished sin.
2) Beginnings of a Nation: God made special promises. God delivered His people from slavery.
3) Possessing the Land: With God's help, the Jews entered the Promised Land. Israel failed to be loyal to God and God punished them.
4) United Kingdom: God chose David to be a special king. God will one day appoint a man to be King forever.
5) Divided Kingdom: The sins of Solomon led to the division of the nation.
6) Taken from Home: God sent the Jews to Assyria and Babylon because of their disobedience.
7) Return to Home: The Jews were allowed to return to Jerusalem to build the temple and rebuild the walls.

Begin the Lesson Activity: Ball Toss

Gather your class of children in a circle with a small ball. Have children take turns rolling the ball gently to each other. When a child catches the ball, have each child answer one part of the question. At this point, do not correct children if they give a wrong answer. Let each child participate that wants to and then roll the ball to another person in the class for the next question.

3) Teach the Lesson

What are some of the changes that have happened in your country over the last 100 years?

What are some of the changes that have happened in your country over the last 400 years?

Tell the Story

The Jews were now back in their homeland. They were comfortable in their own homes. They did not have to live under the customs of other people from foreign countries anymore. The temple was rebuilt so that they could worship their Almighty God. The walls around Jerusalem were rebuilt and they had protection from intruders. There was anticipation that the promised King, the Messiah, would come. Many thought He would come as a victorious King, not a humble servant.

But 400 years went by and the King did not come. There were a lot of changes, but no King. So, over the course of this time, the language changed, the rulers changed, the method of worship in local synagogues changed, and the Jewish authorities changed. There was a new copy of the Scriptures that was translated in Egypt so that many people could read the Scriptures with their new language. Do not think that the Old Testament ended and immediately the New Testament began without any changes. Oh yes, there were lots of changes: politically, religiously, and even socially.

In the days of Daniel, he wrote about a vision of a kingdom. It was a dream that was given by God to King Nebuchadnezzar and Daniel was able to interpret that dream. The first kingdom was a gold head and represented the nation of Babylon. The second kingdom was represented by silver arms and chest and represented the Medo-Persian empire. The third kingdom was the Greek empire portrayed by a bronze belly and thighs. The last kingdom was the Roman empire shown by the iron legs and iron and clay feet.

All those empires had come and gone during this time, except for the Roman empire which was now ruling. God's promises to Daniel about 600 years earlier were coming true. The Babylonians ruled from 612 B.C. until 539 B.C. The Medo-Persians ruled after that from 539 B.C. until 332 B.C. After that came the Greek empire which ruled from 332 B.C. until 63 B.C. Last, the Roman empire succeeded the Greek empire in 63 B.C. and lasted until 476 A.D.

The dream that God had given King Nebuchadnezzar was a reality. God had kept His word, as He always does. The Roman empire was ruling over the Jews now as they looked for their King. They were not looking for a Roman king, they were looking for a Jewish King that would rule the world. Now, God would do another great thing. He would bring that King to the nation.

Teacher Helps

Tell the Story Activity: Facts About History

If history books are available to the teacher, they will verify the events of this story. Perhaps the teacher could bring a history book or two that would verify the order of these four kingdoms that were prophesied by Daniel six hundred years before the birth of Jesus Christ.

Memory Verse

Daniel 2:44 (ESV) - And in the days of those kings the God of heaven will set up a kingdom that shall never be destroyed.

Praise and Worship

Teacher Helps

Memory Verse Activity: Around the Class

Have the children sit in a circle while music is playing. Pass around a phrase of the memory verse. When the music stops, whoever is holding the phrase of the memory verse should try to quote the verse. Do this until all phrases are memorized. Then, do the same thing for the whole memory verse.

Praise and Worship styles vary greatly around the world. It is the intent of this curriculum that praise and worship songs be selected that best fit the content of this lesson. Recommendations for praise and worship are given and this music can generally be located at www.itunes.com. However, the teacher can feel free to select a similar praise and worship song.

"Give Me Jesus" by Fernando Ortega is recommended for this lesson.

Bible Activity

How Well Can You See?

Bring in a large poster with a picture on it that the kids have not seen before in your class. Have another piece of paper (or cloth) that is large enough to completely cover the poster. Show the covered picture to the class. Ask the kids, **"Who thinks they know what this picture is?"** Let them guess.

Then take a pair of scissors and cut a small hole in the cover paper, about 1 inch in diameter. Ask again, **"Who thinks they know what this picture is?"** Let them guess.

Cut another small hole in a different spot. Ask again, **"Who thinks they know what this picture is?"** Let them guess. Is it easy or hard to tell what the picture looks like when we can only see a small part of it? It is hard, of course. That is how it was for God's people during these 400 years, and even at the end; they could only see a very small part of the "big picture." That's when we have to rely on the things that we know for sure. How can we know for sure what God wants us to do, and what His plans for us are?

He has told us in His Word what He wants us to do and what His plans are.

4) Review the Lesson

Volunteers from the class should list on a board or big piece of paper that everyone can see, the 5 Most Important Things To Know from this lesson.

For instance:

1. Daniel interpreted King Nebuchadnezzar's dream about 600 years before Jesus Christ was born.

2. There were 400 years of silence between the last Old Testament prophet and the birth of Jesus Christ.

3. There were lots of political, religious, and social changes between the end of the Old Testament and the beginning of the New Testament.

4. God always keeps His promises.

5. The Jews were expecting a victorious king, not a humble Servant.

Teacher Helps

Review Activity: 5 Scribes[2]

Have five different volunteers come to the front of the class to write one of the five most important things to know from this lesson. Ask the class why these are important.

5) Apply the Lesson

Anticipation is like waiting for something you really want. Sometimes, you have to wait a long time. The Jews anticipated or waited a long time for a king. List two or three things that you should be doing while waiting for God to do something special for you.

Time Line: Between the Old and New Testaments, a lot changed.

Adventure Number 52
Luke 2:1-14; Matthew 1:1-2 and 18-25

Story Line: God's Son was born. His name was Jesus.

1) Study the Lesson (before class)

- Luke tells us the exact time of Jesus' birth. It was during the reign of Caesar Augustus. Roman emperors were thought to be gods so there is a great contrast between Caesar Augustus and Jesus, Who became a king.

- Jesus Christ is the main character in Matthew's presentation, and the opening verse connected Him back to two great covenants in Jewish history: the Davidic Covenant (2 Samuel 7) and the Abrahamic Covenant (Genesis 12 and 15).[1]

- Both Joseph and Mary were in the royal line of ancestors.

- Jesus was born and placed in a manger, or a place where livestock fed.

- Because there was no room for Mary and Joseph in the hotel, Jesus was most likely born in a cave or a place where animals live.

- The appearance of the angel terrified the shepherds. The angel responded with a very calming message and told them not to be afraid. This was good news of great joy, Christ the Lord was just born.

- Detailing the genealogy of Jesus Christ was one of the most interesting ways that Matthew could begin a book for a Jewish audience. Because a person's family line proved his or her standing as one of God's chosen people, Matthew began by showing that Jesus was a descendant of Abraham, the father of all Jews, and a direct descendant of David, fulfilling Old Testament prophecies about the Messiah's line. The facts of this ancestry were carefully preserved. This is the first of many proofs recorded by Matthew to show that Jesus is the true Messiah.[2]

Footnotes - Adventure 52

1. John Walvoord and Roy Zuck, *Bible Knowledge Commentary: New Testament*, 18.

2. James Galvin, *Life Application Bible Notes*, 1533.

2) Begin the Lesson

Remind the class that you are learning the one story of the Bible. While there are many stories in the Bible, they are linked to one major theme or story in the Bible. It is a story of hope. So, to help your class know that story and be able to put all the lessons together, we are going to review the lessons from the past. Ask, **"What are the main events that we have studied in the Bible?"**

- God always existed and He is very powerful.
- God created the earth and everything in it.
- Lucifer, or Satan, deceived Adam and Eve. They sinned by disobeying God.
- God sent a worldwide flood that killed everybody on the earth. God spared Noah and his family because Noah was a righteous man.
- God made special promises to Abraham.
- Jacob wrestled with the angel of God and got a new name, Israel.
- Through special plagues and deliverance, God led the Israelites out of Egypt.
- God established a moral code called the Ten Commandments that the Israelites were to obey.
- With God's help, Israel entered the Promised Land.
- God chose David to be king. He will one day send someone to be King forever.
- The kingdom was divided in two because of the sins of Solomon.
- Israel and Judah were exiled to Assyria and Babylon.
- The Jews returned from exile to rebuild the temple and the walls.

Teacher Helps

Begin the Lesson Activity: The Main Events

Review is a significant part of learning. Twelve events are listed here. Write each event on a slip of paper or poster board and have children put them in chronological order. Let them work together in small teams 2 or 3. Time how long it takes each team to put these events in the right order. Winner gets a prize.

3) Teach the Lesson

Jesus Christ was born in a very special way. What are some things that you think you already know about the birth of Jesus?

There may be some misinformation about the birth of Jesus that comes out.

Tell the Story

This is the story of the most miraculous birth in history. It all started when Mary's cousin, Elizabeth, became pregnant when she was very old. The angel of God told Mary about Elizabeth and the angel also told Mary that nothing was impossible with God. Mary travelled from Nazareth in the north to Judah in the south. It was a long journey but when she arrived, she found her cousin six months pregnant. At about this same time, the angel Gabriel appeared to Mary and told her that she would have a son and she should name Him, Jesus. They both praised God and were full of joy. Mary stayed for three months and then went back home.

Well, Mary was engaged to Joseph. Both of them were godly and had a virtuous relationship. When Joseph discovered that Mary was pregnant, Joseph did not want Mary to feel any disgrace so he thought of a plan that would protect Mary and yet he would not marry her since she was pregnant. But, an angel of God told Joseph that Mary was pregnant even though she never slept with any man. It was a very special way that Mary became pregnant. The angel told Joseph that God's Holy Spirit made Mary pregnant. He should name the child "Jesus" because He would save His people from their sins.

The time came for Mary to give birth to her baby. She must have felt very uncomfortable. Joseph and Mary had to make a long trip from Nazareth to Bethlehem. They had to register for a census in Bethlehem. When they got to Bethlehem, they discovered that there was no place for them to stay. All the hotels and hostels were full. That night, the time came for Mary to give birth to Jesus. It was a miraculous birth. Only the farm animals were there. God told some shepherds in nearby fields. A Savior had been born and it was good news for the whole world. A very large choir of angels sang praises to God. The shepherds were terrified but they went into the town of Bethlehem to find this Savior and sure enough, it was just like the angel told them. They found a baby wrapped in a swaddling clothes and lying in a box that cattle and horses ate from. They could not contain themselves. They told everybody about this special baby.

A long time later, scholars from the East came to bring gifts to this baby who was a king. A star led these scholars all the way from the east to this very special baby. They brought special gifts to Jesus as a symbol of their worship. The Messiah had been born. The angels knew it. Mary and Joseph knew it. The shepherds knew it. The scholars knew it. Soon, many people found out about this special baby. Truly, nothing was impossible for God.

Tell the Story Activity: Two Gospel Writers Tell the Story

Matthew and Luke tell the story of the birth of Jesus. Read both passages to your class. Discuss:

- What do these passages have in common?

- What is unique to each passage in the Bible?

Memory Verse

Luke 2:11 (ESV) - For unto you is born this day in the city of David a Savior, who is Christ the Lord.

Praise and Worship

Praise and Worship styles vary greatly around the world. It is the intent of this curriculum that praise and worship songs be selected that best fit the content of this lesson. Recommendations for praise and worship are given and this music can generally be located at www.itunes.com. However, the teacher can feel free to select a similar praise and worship song.

"Give Me Jesus" by Fernando Ortega is recommended for this lesson.

Bible Activity

A Very Special Announcement

Have you ever known a really big secret? A really happy secret? I remember one time being told that our family was going to have another baby! I was so excited, I could hardly wait to tell someone else the happy news! Well, what if you had just been told that a KING had been born!! And you had to decide who would be the very first people to hear about it! Who would you call? (let the children respond) Who do you think God decided to tell first about the birth of His very own Son, Jesus? Another king? The church leaders? The rulers of the government? No! He chose to tell a group of shepherds! Were they considered to be important, powerful people? Not in the eyes of the world. I often wonder if God told the shepherds first to help us understand that a person doesn't have to be rich or powerful in the eyes of this world to be important to Him.

Idea: have the children make signs and posters announcing the birth of Jesus.

Teacher Helps

Bible Memory Activity: Relay Race

Form two teams. Put the memory verse in large letters about ten yards away from the teams. Have children run to the memory verse and read the next word of the verse out loud so that everyone can hear. When each child has read his one word, go back to the team, touch the next person in line, and repeat the process until all words of the verse have been read.

Repeat this until everyone has memorized the verse.

4) Review the Lesson

Divide the class into two teams. Give the teams one minute to write down as many statements as they can about the birth of Jesus. Here are a few ideas:

- Jesus was born during the reign of Caesar Augustus.

- Matthew and Luke are the only two gospel writers that recorded the story of the birth of Jesus.

- Mary and Elizabeth were cousins.

- Joseph and Mary were godly.

- Joseph and Mary travelled to Bethlehem for a census.

- Jesus' first crib was a manger (a box from which horses or cattle ate).

Teacher Helps

Review the Lesson Activity: One Minute List

The teacher should give two teams one minute each to list as many facts as they can about the lesson.

After the one minute has passed, compare lists and see who has more facts. Be sure that children remember that you are looking for facts.

5) Apply the Lesson

The anticipation was over. The arrival of the Messiah was here. When the scholars from the East came, they brought special gifts for the Lord Jesus.

Name one or two special gifts that you could give to someone this week.

Story Line: God's Son was born. His name was Jesus.

Adventure Number 53
Matthew 1:1-16 and Luke 3:23-28

Story Line: The family history of Jesus includes Abraham and David.

1) Study the Lesson (before class)

- In Jewish family history, a linear genealogy shows the connection between a man and an important ancestor.

- An open linear genealogy shows the overall series of generational connections, but skips some generations. If all generations are presented, then the genealogy is closed.

- The word "father" sometimes means grandfather, great-grandfather, or another in-line descendant. The word "son" sometimes means just a descendant.[1]

- The Matthew record was possibly given to trace the lineage of Jesus through Joseph, as his legal son. Luke probably traces the lineage of Jesus through Mary, as her physical son.[2]

- The promises of God were given in the form of a covenant (a contract, or oath). They would be fulfilled through one Man, who must come from Abraham's line. The genealogy in Matthew proves that Jesus comes from the covenant line. The second significant genealogical element is the relationship to David. Later in Israel's history God promised to David that the Messiah would come through his family line.[3]

- *"Luke is very careful. He says that Jesus was 'supposed' to be the son of Joseph (3:23). He was nothing of the kind. He was the long-awaited 'seed of the woman' (Gen. 3:14-15: the first prophecy of Scripture). Joseph, the husband of Mary, seems to have had his adoption of Jesus formally registered in the temple archives. When Joseph married Mary, the regal line through Solomon and the natural line through Nathan were united."*[4]

Footnotes - Adventure 53

1. Wayne Haston, *The Roots of Faith New Testament Workbook*, 03-B.

2. Lawrence O. Richards, *The Teacher's Commentary*, 526.

3. Ibid., 526.

4. John Phillips, *Exploring the Gospel of Luke: An Expository Commentary*, 89.

2) Begin the Lesson

Lay out a game board for review that looks something like this:

Time Line	Story Line	Songs	Memory Verses
100 points	200 points	300 points	400 points
100 points	200 points	300 points	400 points
100 points	200 points	300 points	400 points
100 points	200 points	300 points	400 points
100 points	200 points	300 points	400 points

Go back for each of the last 10 lessons and let the children name the time line for each lesson (100 points), the story line for each lesson (200 points), the song for each lesson (300 points), and the memory verse for each lesson (400 points).

A prize should be given to the winning team. Usually, competition is a fun thing for the children. So, keep them all involved. Depending on the size of your class, you may want to limit each child to only 1 or 2 answers. The reason for this is that a few children will answer all the questions, if you let them.

There will be a total of 10,000 points, 1000 points for each lesson (100 for the time line, 200 for the story line, 300 for the song, and 400 for the memory verse).

Begin the Lesson Activity: Bible Jeopardy

Divide the class evenly into two teams. The teams could be:

1) whoever has the most brothers and sisters

2) whoever has the fewest brothers and sisters

This game will be continued with the review at end of the lesson.

3) Teach the Lesson

How many people can you name in your family genealogy?

How far back can you go?

What do you know about these people?

Jesus was a man born with a lot known about his family history. The records for Jesus' family history went back about 2000 years to Abraham. This lesson will give us some of the details about his family history and why it is so important.

Tell the Story

Teacher Helps

It all began about 4000 years before Jesus was born. Adam was created and was given the promise of a "Satan crusher." It was the Bible's first prophecy. Throughout the next 4000 years, many people were born and lots of generations came and went. However, one family line keenly stands out. It is the family history of Jesus which is tracked all the way back to Adam. Not only was the birth of Jesus Christ a miraculous event, it was a historical event of the greatest magnitude.

Two researchers detail the family history of Jesus Christ. They are Matthew and Luke. Matthew tracks the family history of Jesus through His legal heritage which went all the way back to Abraham. At the same time, the research of Luke led him all the way back to the human origin of Jesus's family history, Adam.

This tracking of the family history of Jesus shows us the uniqueness of this Jesus. He was tracked by Luke all the way back to Adam. This tracking by Luke included such well known men as Abraham and David. Matthew tracked the legal heritage of Jesus to be a king. He also included Abraham and David. Jesus was uniquely qualified to be the "God-Man." He was all God yet He was born of a woman. He was all Man yet God the Father was His true Father.

Throughout the years, no one else could make this claim. Jesus Christ had both legal rights to be the expected Messiah and He was also born with the humanity that enabled Him to identify with people like you and me. That is why He is called the "only begotten Son." He was and is the unique Son of God. There was no one else like Him and there will never be another person like Him. That is why He is unique ... there is no one else like Him! Both Matthew and Luke, through their extensive research, lead us to the conclusion that Jesus Christ is the only One who could be the Savior of the world!

Jesus was called the "son of David." This meant He was the One promised by God to be the Messiah. Being called the "son of David" meant He had the legal right to be the Messiah, or the Jewish King. His realm of authority was established by God the Father. Many would find fault with this "God-Man." However, the heavenly Father was well pleased with Him. He was the long awaited "Satan crusher" that was promised 4000 years before His birth. The family history of Jesus Christ is important because it tells us about His unique relatives of many years ago.

Tell the Story Activity: Comparison

Compare Matthew 1:16 with Luke 3:23. What do these verses tell us about the uniqueness of Jesus Christ?

- Matthew 1:16 (ESV) *"And Jacob the father of Joseph the husband of Mary, of whom Jesus was born, who is called Christ."*

- Luke 3:23 (ESV) *"Jesus, when he began his ministry, was about thirty years of age, being the son (as was supposed) of Joseph."*

Luke is very careful to say that Jesus was the "supposed" son of Joseph. Matthew calls Him the Christ.

Timeline:
The Early Life of Jesus Christ

Memory Verse

Matthew 1:16 (ESV) - And Jacob the father of Joseph the husband of Mary, of whom Jesus was born, who is called Christ.

Praise and Worship

Praise and Worship styles vary greatly around the world. It is the intent of this curriculum that praise and worship songs be selected that best fit the content of this lesson. Recommendations for praise and worship are given and this music can generally be located at www.itunes.com. However, the teacher can feel free to select a similar praise and worship song.

"Give Me Jesus" by Fernando Ortega is recommended for this lesson.

Bible Activity

The Family History of Jesus

Ahead of time, prepare 13 strips of paper about 1 inch wide and 8 inches long. Write these names on the strips (1 name per piece of paper). Adam, Abraham, Isaac, Jacob, Judah, David, Joseph. On 5 strips of paper, write names of people your children would recognize, such as political figures, sports stars, or celebrities of another kind. The last strip of paper will have the name "Jesus Christ." Tell the children: **"We are going to make a chain that links Jesus back to His ancestors who lived about 2,000 years earlier than him."**

The goal is for the children identify the names that are part of the lineage of Jesus, and put them in one group (yes), and the ones that are not in the lineage of Jesus in another group (no). Mix up the papers and pick them up one by one. Read the names and have the kids say either "yes" or "no" for each one. Once they have been separated, then help the kids put them in chronological order (see list above). Loop each strip of paper together to form a chain. Last of all, bring out the paper that says "Jesus Christ". Jesus is the final link of the chain. Tell about how Jesus is linked all the way back to Adam. You see, God had a plan from the very beginning to bring Jesus to the world to save them (us) from our sin.

Teacher Helps

Memory Verse Activity: The Telephone Game

Memorize this verse using The Telephone Game. Have your class form one line, then whisper into the ear of the first person in line a phrase of this verse, have that person repeat the phrase to the next person. Do this until all have quoted the first phrase. Then do the same thing with the second phrase, the third phrase, and so on until you have memorized the verse.

4) Review the Lesson

Continue your review game for points that you began at the start of the lesson.

- For 100 points, who were the two researchers of Jesus' family history? (Matthew and Luke)

- For 200 points, which writer tracks Jesus' legal right to be the Messiah? (Matthew)

- For 300 points, which writer tracks Jesus' human right to be the Messiah? (Luke)

- For 400 points, what two chapters of the Bible talk about the family history of Jesus? (Matthew 1 and Luke 3)

- Bonus question worth 500 points: What is the theme of this lesson? (The family history of Jesus includes Abraham and David.)

Review the Lesson Activity: Bible Jeopardy

This review activity is a continuation of the review game at the beginning of the lesson.

5) Apply the Lesson

Matthew and Luke were researchers. They researched the family history of Jesus. Give children the assignment of reading these verses. Then, after their research, let them decide who these verses are talking about.

- Micah 5:2 (written by Micah)
- Isaiah 53 (written by Isaiah)
- Psalm 22 (written by David)
- Genesis 3:15 (written by Moses)

Apply the Lesson Activity: Assignment

Give the children of your class this assignment. It will be the first thing the class does next time they meet.

Story Line: The family history of Jesus includes Abraham and David.

Adventure Number 54
Matthew 2:1-15 and Luke 2:22-38

Story Line: Early events in the life of Jesus marked Him as a very special Person.

1) Study the Lesson (before class)

- Simeon had been told by God that he would see the consolation of Israel. So, when Jesus was old enough, Mary and Joseph brought Him to the temple. When Simeon saw them, he took the baby Jesus in his arms and blessed Him. Simeon stated that he could now die in peace after this event.

- Anna was an elderly widow, 84-years-old. She had been a widow most of her life. She was called a prophet indicating that she was unusually close to God. She stayed at the temple regularly, worshipping, fasting, and praising God. Similar to Simeon, Anna knew that Jesus was the redemption of Israel. He was the promised Messiah.

- Because Anna and Simeon lived in a culture that valued older people, their prophecies carried even more significance.[1]

- "The Law commanded a young bull or a lamb for parents who could afford such an offering. But the poor were allowed to bring two young birds. Joseph and Mary offered only the sacrifice of the poor."[2]

- Later, when Jesus was 12-years-old, His mother and father went again to the temple to worship, along with other people. At the temple, He began a highly sophisticated conversation with the scholars of the day in the temple. When His parents left the temple, they did not realize Jesus was not with this large group. Generally, women and children travelled in the front of a large group and men brought up the rear. Jesus could have travelled with either group as a 12-year-old boy.[3]

Footnotes - Adventure 54

1. James Galvin, *Life Application Bible Notes*, 1677.

2. Lawrence O. Richards, *The Teacher's Commentary*, 646.

3. James Galvin, *Life Application Bible Notes*, 1677.

2) Begin the Lesson

One of the goals for review is for children to see the Bible's big story. Today, we want to ask children to give us some of the recurring themes we see so far in that story. For instance, let children volunteer their answers, but you might use the following examples as recurring themes in the Bible's one big story:

God's Amazing Power:
- Creation
- Worldwide Flood
- Red Sea Crossing
- Entering the Promised Land

Animal Substitution:
- Adam and Eve
- Abraham and Isaac on Mount Moriah
- God's Provision for Forgiveness
- The Day of Atonement

Faith that Pleases God:
- Noah
- Abraham
- The Passover
- Ruth and Samuel
- King David

God Punishes Sin:
- Adam and Eve
- Unbelief at Kadesh Barnea
- Saul, Israel's First King
- King Solomon
- The Divided Kingdom

The Unique Person - Jesus Christ
- Prophecies about Jesus
- The Birth of Jesus
- Early Events in the Life of Jesus

Begin the Lesson Activity: One Big Story

The teacher may want to give the class the topics such as: God's Amazing Power, Animal Substitution, Faith that Pleases God, God Punishes Sin, and the Unique Person - Jesus Christ. Then, let the children tell Biblical examples of those stories that we have previously studied.

The purpose of this activity is for children to see recurring themes in the Bible's one big story.

3) Teach the Lesson

Matthew and Luke were researchers. They researched the family history of Jesus. As a review from the last lesson, ask kids what they found out about their research into who Micah, Isaiah, David, and Moses were writing about.

- Micah 5:2 (written by Micah)
- Isaiah 53 (written by Isaiah)
- Psalm 22 (written by David)
- Genesis 3:15 (written by Moses)

Teach the Lesson Activity: Assignment

Be sure kids have an opportunity to talk about completing their assignment from last week.

Tell the Story

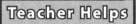

Thirty-three days after Jesus was born, some very exciting events happened. Mary and Joseph travelled a very short distance from Bethlehem to Jerusalem where they went to the temple and made an offering. Mary and Joseph could not afford a sheep for an offering so they brought a pair of doves or pigeons for their offering.

So, when they came into the temple complex with baby Jesus, they were met by an old man. His name was Simeon. Somehow, the Lord had promised him that he would see the consolation of Israel before he died. Everybody knew what that meant ... it meant that he would see the Messiah before he died. The religious leaders of the day were not looking for the Messiah, but Simeon was. When Mary and Joseph came into the temple, they were simply going to bring their offering ... that was it. But, when Simeon met them, everything changed. Simeon recognized that this one-month-old baby was the Messiah. He had to have direct guidance from God to know this. Once Simeon recognized the Messiah, he immediately began praising God. He wrote a psalm in recognition of this event and Simeon even acknowledged that the Messiah would be for all people, not just the Jews. Mary and Joseph were amazed. They had come to the temple to bring an offering and now a complete stranger was recognizing their baby as the long awaited Messiah. Mary and Joseph knew who Jesus was but they didn't know that other people knew this.

The day got even more exciting for Joseph and Mary when an elderly lady named Anna recognized who Jesus was, the Messiah, and she also praised God for this gift from God. The consolation for Israel, the Messiah, had come. After hundreds of years of waiting, the Messiah was now here.

Jesus moved several times in his early life. From Bethlehem, his family moved to Egypt for several years and then they moved back to Nazareth. We don't know anything else about Jesus until he turned twelve-years-old. When he was twelve, His parents returned to the temple. Evidently, there was a large group. When it came time to leave the temple, Joseph and Mary both assumed that Jesus was with them. In those days, when a large group travelled, it was customary for women to go first and then for the men to come at the last. As a twelve-year-old boy, Jesus could have been with either group. So, when Mary and Joseph both realized that their son was not with them, they went back to the temple and found Him reasoning with the scholars of the day. The scholars were quite impressed with this twelve year-old-boy. Mary thought a lot about those early days with her son.

Tell the Story Activity: Tell a Wordless Story

The teacher should tell the class that Simeon and Anna were old and probably had a difficult time moving around. Instead of saying "Simeon" or "Anna," as the teacher tells the story, the teacher should hunch over (maybe with a cane) and let the kids say the name of "Simeon" or "Anna."

Memory Verse

Luke 2:52 (ESV) - And Jesus increased in wisdom and in stature and in favor with God and man.

Praise and Worship

Praise and Worship styles vary greatly around the world. It is the intent of this curriculum that praise and worship songs be selected that best fit the content of this lesson. Recommendations for praise and worship are given and this music can generally be located at www.itunes.com. However, the teacher can feel free to select a similar praise and worship song.

"Give Me Jesus" by Fernando Ortega is recommended for this lesson.

Bible Activity

My Father's Business

Start this activity by asking: **"What is your Father's business?"** Explain that you want to know how many different careers are represented by our class. Ask for 3 or 4 volunteers to "act out" the career of their fathers. For example, a chef's child could pretend to be cooking something, a computer specialist could pretend to sit at a desk working on a computer. As the child portrays the career of their father, the other children may try to guess what the career is. When someone correctly identifies the job, ask the child a few questions about their father's career. Point out that they know more about this career because it is their family. Once all the jobs have been identified, ask this: Who was Jesus' Father? (God). What is His business? (Teaching others the Bible, healing, loving, etc.) Where would you go to work on God's business? (to church, or to people that don't know the truth about God). When Jesus was 12 years old, He went to the Temple to ask questions of the men there that studied the Bible. He was always interested in "His Father's business!" Let's think of some things that would please our Heavenly Father and allow for responses. Let's always be interested in doing our Heavenly Father's business!

Teacher Helps

Memory Verse Activity: Graffiti

Graffiti can also be used to help children memorize this verse. Write each word of this verse on a separate piece of paper. Then have children put the words in order in groups of 2 or 3. When each group can put the verse together in order, they will probably have this verse memorized.

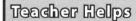

4) Review the Lesson

Review the lesson by groups and come up with 7 main ideas from this lesson.

- Joseph and Mary enter the temple.
- Joseph and Mary bring an offering of two doves or pigeons.
- Simeon recognizes the baby Jesus as the Messiah.
- Simeon praises God with a psalm.
- Anna recognizes the baby Jesus as the consolation of Israel.
- Jesus goes to the temple.
- Jesus remains at the temple to talk to the scholars of the day.

Review the Lesson Activity: Scripture Search

The teacher should have the class break up into groups of 2 or 3. Have each group of 2 or 3 write down or talk about the 7 main ideas in the lesson which are listed to your left. For younger children, or non-readers, the teacher should help them.

5) Apply the Lesson

The teacher should tell the class, "**Your family history is very important. You may not think that it is, but it is.** The family history of Jesus goes back over 4,000 years. What is most impressive about that to you?

Tell one or two people what you know about the family history of Jesus. One way to do that would be to ask a friend or family member how many relatives they can name. Then, ask them how many family members of Jesus they could name."

Story Line: Early events in the life of Jesus marked Him as a very special Person.

Adventure Number 55
Matthew 4:1-11

Story Line: Satan tempted Jesus. Jesus did not sin.

1) Study the Lesson (before class)

- After Jesus was baptized, Jesus was led by the Spirit of God into the wilderness where He fasted for 40 days.

- After Jesus fasted for 40 days, the devil tempted Him three different times.

- The three tests demonstrated that Jesus was without sin and could not sin.

- The first test, verses 3-4, was a test of His Sonship. He was hungry and the devil tried to convince Him that if He was the Son of God, He should turn the stones into bread. It was God's will for Him to be hungry at that time. Jesus answered with the Word of God by saying that man should live by every word of God (Deuteronomy 8:3). When Jesus quoted from Deuteronomy, He was recognizing the inerrancy of the Bible.

- In the second test, verses 5-7, Satan tempted Jesus with popularity. Satan incorrectly referred to Psalm 91:11-12 where it says that the angels would protect Him. However, Satan left out *"in all your ways."* That was a glaring error by Satan and Jesus again answered the temptation with Scripture, quoting from Deuteronomy 6:16 and telling Satan that it would not be right to try to test God.

- The third test, verses 8-11, was a test of the authority of Jesus. If Jesus bowed down to Satan, He would not have been the sinless Substitute on the cross. He would have submitted to Satan, but He did not. Once again, Jesus answered from Scripture (Deuteronomy 6:13 and 10:20) by saying that God alone should be worshipped and served.

Footnotes - Adventure 55

1. John Walvoord and Roy Zuck, *Bible Knowledge Commentary: New Testament*, 26.

2. Ibid., 26.

3. Ibid., 26.

2) Begin the Lesson

Ask children to help you with previous memory verses. Maybe say something like, **"Who remembers what (verse) says?"**

- Adventure Number 41: Psalm 22:1
- Adventure Number 42: 2 Chronicles 7:14
- Adventure Number 43: 1 Kings 11:38
- Adventure Number 44: 1 Kings 18:39
- Adventure Number 45: Isaiah 53:6
- Adventure Number 46: 2 Kings 17:19
- Adventure Number 47: Jeremiah 31:34
- Adventure Number 48: Ezekiel 36:26
- Adventure Number 49: Ezra 6:16
- Adventure Number 50: Nehemiah 8:10
- Adventure Number 51: Daniel 2:44
- Adventure Number 52: Luke 2:11
- Adventure Number 53: Matthew 1:16
- Adventure Number 54: Luke 2:52

Teacher Helps

Begin the Lesson Activity: Memory Verse Review

The last 14 memory verses are given here. Divide the children up into two teams and see which team can tell you the most memory verses. Bonus points should be given if each team can recite more than the last 14 memory verses.

Give the teams five minutes and they must work together.

The teacher can provide a few helps.

3) Teach the Lesson

Satan knows when we are weak. He will try to tempt us. Give some specific examples of people we have studied that have been tempted by Satan. These people gave in to Satan's temptations. We will learn of Someone who did not give in to Satan's temptations today.

- Adam and Eve (Genesis 2)
- Cain (Genesis 4)
- Noah's generation (Genesis 6)
- Unbelief in Kadesh Barnea (Numbers 21)

Timeline:
The Ministry of Jesus Christ

 ## Tell the Story

God the Father had expressed His great pleasure in Jesus Christ when Jesus got baptized. In a voice that could be heard, God the Father told everyone at the baptism of Jesus that God was pleased with Jesus Christ. Now, that moment was over. After making this phenomenal public announcement, the Holy Spirit led Jesus into the wilderness for a very special test. Jesus prepared for this test by praying and fasting for forty days.

After his forty-day fast, Jesus was tempted by the devil. And wouldn't you know it, the first thing Satan did was tempt Jesus with food. Satan told Jesus to turn stones into bread. That made sense. If Jesus had food, He would feel better. But, Jesus knew better. He was not going to listen to the voice of Satan. He knew that was wrong. Instead, He quoted something that Moses had written much earlier. Jesus told Satan that man does not live by bread alone. Jesus passed the first test by not submitting to Satan's temptation.

The next thing Satan did was this: he took Jesus to the top of the temple, quoted something that King David had written much earlier, and questioned the loving care of God the Father. Jesus knew Satan was only tricking him by misusing the words of God. Again, Jesus quoted from something Moses wrote much earlier when He told Satan that he should not put the Lord to the test. Again, Jesus successfully faced Satan's temptation when He resisted the temptation. Satan had now questioned the loving care of God and he had questioned the provision of food from God. Satan was attacking the character of God and Jesus knew it. That is exactly what Satan did when he tempted Eve in the garden. Satan is the great deceiver and liar. He tempted Eve, he tempted Jesus, and that is what he does all the time ... he tempts people.

The last temptation may have been the most difficult. Satan took Jesus to the top of a large mountain. Both of them could see a long way off. Satan offered Jesus all the kingdoms of the world if Jesus would fall down and worship Satan. Jesus told Satan to get lost. He told Satan that He would worship and serve God, that is, He would worship and serve God alone. Nobody else should be worshipped or served.

When Jesus passed all the tests of temptation, the angels came and ministered to Him. Satan left Him alone for awhile. But, he was coming back. Satan was going to wait for another time to test Jesus, just hoping that Jesus would give into his temptations.

Teacher Helps

Tell the Story Activity: Resisting Temptation

Jesus shows how to resist temptation. Write out these questions, hand them out to volunteers, and have the volunteers answer the questions after you have finished telling the story.

- Who led Jesus into the wilderness to be tempted?
- Why did Satan tempt Jesus at the end of Jesus' time of fasting?
- What did Satan tell Jesus to do in the first temptation. Why?
- What did Satan tempt Jesus with in the second temptation? Where did he tempt Him?
- What did Satan offer Jesus in the third temptation?
- Who cared for Jesus when the temptations were over?
- How is Jesus our example for resisting temptation?

Memory Verse

Matthew 4:4 (ESV) - But he (Jesus) answered, "It is written, "'Man shall not live by bread alone, but by every word that comes from the mouth of God.'"

Praise and Worship

Praise and Worship styles vary greatly around the world. It is the intent of this curriculum that praise and worship songs be selected that best fit the content of this lesson. Recommendations for praise and worship are given and this music can generally be located at www.itunes.com. However, the teacher can feel free to select a similar praise and worship song.

"Give Me Jesus" by Fernando Ortega is recommended for this lesson.

Bible Activity

Temptations by Satan. Start out by asking your children: **"Have you ever been really hungry?"** Explain that when Satan came to tempt Jesus, He had nothing to eat for 40 days! Encourage the children to imagine how very hungry and weak Jesus would have been at that point. Re-enact the scene, as Satan comes up to Jesus and says in a convincing voice: *"So, if you are really the Son of God, turn these stones into bread."* Pull out the first sword! Jesus was ready, and strong with the words of God. Have a child read the words on the sword if possible, or the teacher can read. Emphasize that Jesus fought Satan with the words of God from the Bible. Follow the same pattern with the other 2 temptations. Then ask the children: **"So what about you, what will you do when Satan comes to tempt you?"** Give a scenario that is appropriate for your class. For example, **"What if you have lost your pencil you need for school? You see someone else's pencil on their desk. No one is looking, and you will get in big trouble if you don't have a pencil. You are tempted to take it. I know, you can pull out your sword, and fight the temptation with the Word of God!"** Quickly pull out the blank sword. Look shocked when you realize it is blank. "What?!?! You don't know what the Bible says? Oh no!! You are not equipped to fight against Satan! You must learn what the Bible says so that like Jesus did, you can "fight" against Satan!

Teacher Helps

Bible Memory Activity

Review the verse a few times then divide the children into two or more teams. Have the teams form lines across from a chalk or white board or piece of paper on a chair. Place something to write with at the board in front of each team. Have the first child of each team run to the board and write the first word of the verse, then run back to the line. The next child of the team will write the next word and it will continue until the verse is completed. Allow all teams to finish before playing again.

Bible Activity

Ahead of time, prepare 4 "swords" made of heavy paper, or even cardboard if possible. Cut them out in the shape of a sword, with a handle at the top and a point at the end. On 3 of the swords, write the scripture verse Jesus quoted when confronting Satan; Deuteronomy 8:3, 6:16, and 10:20. The fourth sword should be left blank.

Teacher Helps

4) Review the Lesson

Have children simplify the lesson into 10 words or less using their own words. What are their answers? When children simplify the story of the lesson into ten words or less, they will probably say something like these possibilities:

- Jesus was tempted by Satan three times.
- Jesus resisted Satan's temptations with words from God.
- Satan took Jesus to different places to be tempted.
- Satan is a deceiver, a liar, and a tempter.
- Jesus is our example for facing temptation.
- God can help us in and after our temptation.
- Everyone should understand and use the Scriptures.

Review the Lesson Activity: Simplify

Simplify can be a useful game for the children. The teacher can give each team of 2 or 3 kids about 1-2 minutes to come up with the most significant 10 words of this lesson.

5) Apply the Lesson

Jesus faced temptation and overcame Satan's attack. Pose this situation to your class:

- You are in school and you are getting ready to take a test but you have not studied very much. The person sitting next to you is very smart. During the test, the smart person beside you shows you the right answers to the test you are taking. You did not know the right answers. No one else is looking. Only you and your friends will know. What will you do?

The Next Lesson Bible Activity

The teacher should look at next week's Bible lesson. There is a "show and tell" activity that children should prepare for when they come to the next lesson.

Story Line: Satan tempted Jesus. Jesus did not sin.

Adventure Number 56
John 1:29-34 and Hebrews 10:10, 14

Story Line: Jesus is the Lamb of God Who takes away all the sins of the world.

1) Study the Lesson (before class)

- John saw Jesus and said that He would take away the sin of the world. John was referring to Old Testament sacrifices such as those found in Leviticus 16 where a goat was the sin offering on the Day of Atonement.

- John may have been referring to the Passover Lamb from Exodus 12. Isaiah also made mention of this in Isaiah 53:7.

- John the Baptist saw Jesus Christ as the sacrifice for the sins of the world. John may have been thinking about Isaiah 53:12.

- The invisible Holy Spirit descended in a visible body as a dove who had come from heaven.

- John had been told by God that when this sign of the dove occurred, it would be the One who would baptize with the Holy Spirit. So when John saw Jesus again after the baptism, he declared ... "Behold the Lamb of God."

- It probably wasn't until the baptism of Jesus by John that John recognized Jesus as the Messiah Who was prophesied about in the Old Testament.

- From Luke 1:36, it is probable that John and Jesus were related. However, it was not until this event that John recognized Jesus as God.

- John's testimony was clear. This was the Son of God. The King Who had been prophesied in 2 Samuel 7:13 was now present.

- The Messianic King is uniquely the Son of God; Psalm 2:7.

Footnotes - Adventure 56

1. Lynn Solem and Bob Pike, *50 Creative Training Closers*, 70.

2) Begin the Lesson

Let's think back over all of our lessons that we have studied and see if we can put the lessons in order. Here are the story lines for some of the previous lessons:

1) God is very strong.

5) Life in the garden was full of pleasure.

10) Sin affected God's creation in many negative ways.

15) The people were evil. God sent a flood. Noah trusted and obeyed God.

20) God told Abraham to sacrifice Isaac. God provided a ram instead.

25) God sent plagues in Egypt to set free the Israelites.

30) God told the Israelites to build a tent where they could meet Him and offer sacrifices.

35) People who followed God were to be completely loyal and obedient to Him.

40) God chose David to be a king. God will one day appoint a Man to be King forever.

45) Prophets told about Jesus 700 years before He came to earth.

50) The Jews returned to Jerusalem to rebuild the walls.

55) Satan tempted Jesus. Jesus did not sin.

Teacher Helps

Begin the Lesson Activity: Story Line Review

The teacher should write these statements on pieces of paper and then mix them up. Do not put the number of the lesson on the piece of paper. Divide the children into 2 or 3 teams, depending on the size of the class. Time how long it takes each team to put the statements in the correct order.

3) Teach the Lesson

Some announcements can be very important. For instance, suppose the president in the country where you live just died. There would be a very important announcement by someone very prestigious. Some announcements are not as important. Discuss one important announcement that you have heard in your life.

Today's lesson is about an announcement by the most important person ever born of a woman other than Jesus Christ. It is a very special message that relates to many things that we have studied in the Old Testament.

Tell the Story

John the Baptist was known for baptizing people. A group of religious people called the Pharisees wondered why John the Baptist was baptizing people. They asked him if he was the Messiah, Elijah, or even a prophet. John the Baptist told them that he was none of these but that there was coming Someone after him Who was very important. In fact, that Person was so important that John the Baptist told the Pharisees that he was not even worthy enough to untie His sandal. Untying somebody's sandal was like the lowliest thing you could do for somebody very important.

Well, the very next day, that Person arrived at the place where John the Baptist was baptizing and where the religious men had questioned John the Baptist just the day before. That Person was Jesus Christ. When Jesus Christ came to John the Baptist, John declared, "Behold the Lamb of God Who takes away the sin of the world." To say that Jesus was the Lamb of God was like a picture for the people to see. He was not literally an animal and a human. He was like the lambs in previous years who took away sins. Jesus was a real person Who made a real sacrifice for all the sins of all people.

What John meant was that other lambs merely covered sins. In the Old Testament, animal sacrifice was common for people's sins to be removed. In fact, it was commanded by God. Now, there was Someone Who would take away all sins. No more animal sacrifices. Jesus would become the sacrifice for sins.

It was a tremendous announcement because it meant that Jesus Christ was the Messiah and the Sin Bearer for the sins of all people, even non-Jewish people. Just to make it even clearer, John included that this "Lamb of God" was the "Son of God." Now, everyone must have understood something very significant. Jesus was the Lamb of God ... that is, He would take away sins. He was also the Son of God ... that is, because He was God, He had the authority to take away sins. What a magnificent announcement!

Soon, the Son of God would become the Lamb of God Who would remove sins by His sacrifice. John's announcement revealed the identity of Jesus Christ. Jesus Christ would begin His public ministry soon. He would decide who would become His followers soon. He would do many special miracles soon. But, this special announcement by John the Baptist happened before any of those other special events took place. It was the announcement of the Sin Bearer of the world, the Lamb of God was here.

Teacher Helps

Tell the Story Activity: Lambs in the Old Testament

When John the Baptist announced Jesus Christ as the "Lamb of God," he was causing his listeners to think of other lambs in the Old Testament. The teacher should ask the class, **"What other lambs died as a substitute for somebody else in the Old Testament?"**

- Adam and Eve
- Abraham and Isaac on Mount Moriah
- God's Provision for Forgiveness
- The Day of Atonement

Memory Verse

John 1:29 (ESV) - The next day he saw Jesus coming toward him, and said, "Behold, the Lamb of God, who takes away the sin of the world!"

Praise and Worship

Praise and Worship styles vary greatly around the world. It is the intent of this curriculum that praise and worship songs be selected that best fit the content of this lesson. Recommendations for praise and worship are given and this music can generally be located at www.itunes.com. However, the teacher can feel free to select a similar praise and worship song.

"Worthy Is The Lamb" by Hillsong is recommended for this lesson.

Bible Activity

Plan ahead for this activity. On the previous lesson day, tell the children that next time we will be having a "show and tell" session. They are to bring in one special thing and they will have one minute to tell everyone about their special object. Depending on the size of the class, you may need to allow only a few students to bring something so this doesn't use up all your lesson time.

As the children tell about their chosen object, notice how excited they are to share with the class something that means a lot to them. At the end of the "show and tell" time, say: **"Today we are going to learn about a man who was very excited to tell everyone about a special person. That person was Jesus! The man who was introducing Jesus was called John, and this was his great job, to tell everyone about Jesus. Why were you so excited to share with the others when it was your turn? (because the object was very special to them). Is Jesus that special to you? Let's see what John had to say about this most special person."**

Teacher Helps

Memory Verse Activity: Bean Bag Toss

With masking tape, mark off a large square on the floor, about 36 inches. Connect the opposite corners inside the square with tape to form an "X." If you have space and many students, make a second square. Give each section a number value (1,2,3,4). A bit of a distance away, put a line of tape to mark where the student will throw from. Divide into two teams. Each student takes a turn throwing a bean bag into one of the sections. (You may make a bean bag by putting beans in a sock and closing it tight with a rubber band. Take the long part of the sock and fold it over the bean section.) If they can say the verse correctly, their team scores the amount of the section where the bean bag was thrown.

4) Review the Lesson

The teacher should have the class think of the main ideas of the lesson that they want to take home. Then they should number off 1 through 5. Number 1 should tell the main thing that he or she learned from the lesson. All five groups should get an opportunity to share the main thing they learned from this lesson.

Ideas might include:
- Jesus is the Lamb of God, according to John the Baptist.
- Jesus is the Son of God, according to John the Baptist.
- John the Baptist recognized that he was not the Messiah.
- Jesus Christ would become a sacrifice for sins.
- John the Baptist's announcement about Jesus came before His public ministry began, the calling of His disciples, and His miracles.

Teacher Helps

Review the Lesson Activity: Repetition[1]

The teacher should allow about 5 minutes for children to share the main thing that they learned. If more than 5 children are in the class, allow for each of the groups to share with each other.

5) Apply the Lesson

The Lamb of God Who takes away the sins of the world has come to take away your sins also. Perhaps you have been a religious kid. Perhaps you have gone to church a lot. Maybe you have been a very good kid. You help your parents and you make good grades in school. You may even try to help others.

But, have you ever asked the Lamb of God, Jesus Christ, to take away your sins? You can do that today. He is the only One who can do that.

Apply the Lesson Activity: Invitation

Today's lesson would be a good time to give an invitation for children to let Jesus take their sins away. With younger children, seek advice and counsel from their parents or guardians.

Story Line: Jesus is the Lamb of God Who takes away the sins of the world.

Adventure Number 57

Matthew 4:18-22; Luke 6: 12-16, 9:1-6

Story Line: Jesus chose twelve men to become His committed followers.

 ## 1) Study the Lesson (before class)

- John gives us a logical connection between John the Baptist's declaration of the *"Lamb of God Who takes away the sin of the world"* and how some became followers. It was the next day. Two of the witnesses heard this announcement and followed the Messiah; John 1:29-42.

- The first words these followers heard from Jesus was, *"What do you want?"* Jesus seemed to be asking them, "What are you seeking in life?" Jesus invited the disciples to come and see. In other words, a person must first come to Christ by faith and then he will see.[1]

- Matthew 4:18-22 records another interaction between Jesus and some of His followers. This was not their first meeting. Jesus now called these men to leave their profession of fishing and follow Him all the time.[2]

- Jesus did not rebuke Peter and Andrew for not leaving their fishing business. However, the time had come for them to make a life commitment to following the Messiah. The two men needed no further persuasion. They knew that Jesus was the Messiah.[3]

- The gospel writers note that Jesus spent a long time in prayer before He chose His disciples. They did not choose Him, He chose them after conferring with the Father (Luke 6:12).[4]

- These men were specifically called apostles. Disciples were followers but apostles were messengers with delegated authority. These disciples were now willing to be apostles. They were willing to be sent out full time.[5]

- The mission of these new full-time followers was to draw other people to Christ like a fisherman draws his nets filled with fish.

Footnotes - Adventure 57

1. John Walvoord and Roy Zuck, *Bible Knowledge Commentary: New Testament*, 275.

2. Ibid., 275.

3. John Phillips, *Exploring the Gospel of Luke: An Expository Commentary*, 81.

4. James Galvin, *Life Application Bible Notes*, 1690.

5. John Walvoord and Roy Zuck, *Bible Knowledge Commentary: New Testament*, 219.

6. Susan Lingo, *Written on Our Hearts*, 92.

2) Begin the Lesson

Let's name the periods of time that we have learned and some of the special people and events that happened in each era.

1. Beginnings. God created the heavens and the earth.

2. Beginnings. Lucifer was expelled from heaven. After that, he tempted Adam and Eve to disobey God and they sinned.

3. Beginnings. Because there was so much violence on the earth, God decided to flood the entire earth.

4. Beginnings of a Nation. Great promises were made to Abraham by Yahweh.

5. Beginnings of a Nation. Moses received a special call from God to do a special work. He also received the Ten Commandments on Mount Sinai.

6. Possessing the Land. Joshua led the people of Israel into the Promised Land.

7. Possessing the Land. Israel failed to be loyal to God and He punished them for this.

8. United Kingdom. God gave the Israelites a king. David was the greatest of those kings.

9. Divided Kingdom. Because Solomon failed to be loyal to Yahweh like his father had been, Yahweh divided the kingdom.

10. Taken from Home. After hundreds of years of rebellion, God sent the Israelites to Assyria and Babylon.

11. Return to Home. The Jews returned to Jerusalem to rebuild the walls and the temple.

12. The Early Life of Jesus. Jesus arrived on earth in a very special way.

Begin the Lesson Activity: Mix and Match Time Line Review

The teacher should write each time period on a separate piece of paper.

Then the teacher should put names on other pieces of paper for each time period. For example, Adam and Eve could be listed twice: once for creation and once for the fall.

Then, on separate sheets of paper, the teacher should put events that happened in each time period.

Mix up all the sheets of paper and have teams of students (3-4 on each team) match the era with the people and events of that time period.

3) Teach the Lesson

Some people are called to do very special jobs. They have the ability and skill to perform a task.

What are some skills and abilities that you would need to be an apostle?

99 Adventures in the Bible's Big Story Guide

Timeline: The Ministry of Jesus Christ

Tell the Story

The announcement by John the Baptist meant a new beginning. *"Behold, the Lamb of God Who takes away the sin of the world."* He was here, the long awaited Messiah. The Sin-Bearer was in their midst. The very next day, Jesus gained at least two followers. They were Andrew and Peter. Then, the next day after that, Philip and Nathanael became followers of Jesus.

Jesus asked them what they wanted. He seemed to be saying, "What do you want to get out of life?" Jesus was questioning their life direction. Did they really have faith in the Messiah and were they willing to let Him be their Lord or were they curiosity seekers? They wanted to become followers of Christ. Their relationship with Him began on that day. However, they went back to their occupation ... fishing. They were good fishermen and made their living from the Sea of Galilee.

Later, Jesus met up with these men. He told them to follow Him and they would become fishers of men. Now, they were already followers but Jesus was asking more of them. He was asking them to become full-time committed followers. If they would do so, they could do the very same kind of occupation that they were used to only with people instead of fish. They would catch men for the kingdom of God as their full time occupation.

At one point in time, Jesus went out to a mountain to pray all night. He was asking His heavenly Father Who His apostles should be. An apostle is a messenger with special authority. Jesus knew it was very important to pick the right men for the job. That is why He spent so much time in prayer.

The next day, he called His disciples together and from those people, He chose twelve men that would be called apostles. These were different from the disciples. These were twelve men who had a special mission with a special authority and they were certainly special messengers.

Jesus called the twelve apostles together and gave them authority over demons and diseases. The twelve: Peter, Andrew, James, John, Phillip, Bartholomew, Matthew, Thomas, James, Simon the Zealot, Judas the son of James, and Judas who betrayed Jesus. They were the apostles that Jesus selected. He chose them. They did not choose Him. The twelve apostles were to proclaim the kingdom of God and heal people. They were not to take money for their work. So, the twelve apostles departed and began doing their work. They preached the kingdom of God everywhere and they healed people.

Teacher Helps

Tell the Story Activity: Timeline

The teacher could develop a timeline for the class that shows how and when the disciples became apostles. The timeline might be very simple but it would look like this:

- The announcement by John the Baptist.
- Next day: Jesus meets Peter and Andrew. They meet the Messiah and put their trust in Him.
- Next day: Jesus meets Philip and Nathanael. They follow the Messiah also.
- Some time later: Jesus calls Peter and Andrew to follow Him and fish for men.
- Later: Jesus spends the evening in prayer on a mountain.
- Next day: Jesus calls the twelve apostles to be His special messengers.

Memory Verse

Matthew 4:19 (ESV) - And he said to them, "Follow me, and I will make you fishers of men."

Praise and Worship

Praise and Worship styles vary greatly around the world. It is the intent of this curriculum that praise and worship songs be selected that best fit the content of this lesson. Recommendations for praise and worship are given and this music can generally be located at www.itunes.com. However, the teacher can feel free to select a similar praise and worship song.

"Worthy Is The Lamb" by Hillsong is recommended for this lesson.

Bible Activity

Here are some examples:

- Matthew – "I will no longer be a tax collector."
- Peter – "I will now fish for men." (same for Andrew)
- James and John – "I will leave my home to follow Jesus."
- Others – "I will follow Jesus and work for His kingdom," or "I will spend my life telling others about Jesus." (You can use the same phrase for more than one disciple).

On their turn, a child will turn over one card, then one more, trying to find a "match." When they find a match, they should call out: "Peter, I call you to be a disciple!" The child who volunteered to be Peter will answer by saying the phrase written on their card, and join the person who called them. Talk about what it might have been like to be called by Jesus. What was scary about it? What was exciting? What was hard? What was the reward?

Ask for 12 volunteers to be the 12 disciples who will be "called," and give them the card bearing one disciple's name and statement. Start by having 4 of the children that are not disciples play a matching game with the 24 cards facing down on a table.

Teacher Helps

Memory Verse Activity: Scripture Card Battle[6]

Divide your class up into groups of 2 or 3. Give each group a set of cards. On each card is one word from the memory verse. Groups should try to put the words of the memory verse in the right order.

Bible Activity: Disciple Calling Game

Disciple calling game – ahead of time, prepare 24 papers or cards with the 12 disciple's names on each. There will be 2 cards for each disciple's name. These 24 cards will be used for a matching game. Next, prepare 1 more card for each disciple with the name of the disciple AND a statement about them.

4) Review the Lesson

Teacher Helps

"Who" Questions:

1. How many apostles can you name?

2. Who were they supposed to follow?

"What" Questions:

1. What did Jesus tell the apostles to do?

2. What did Jesus do before He called the twelve apostles?

"When" Questions:

1. When did Jesus call the apostles?

2. When did they leave their fishing nets?

"Where" Questions:

1. Where did Peter do most of his fishing?

2. Where is the Sea of Galilee?

"Why" Questions:

1. Why did John the Baptist make this special announcement about Jesus?

2. Why did the fishermen follow Jesus?

Review Activity: The Investigative Cube

Divide the class up into two teams. Make a cube with these labels on each side of the cube: who, what, when, where, why. When the cube is rolled to one team, they will answer the type of question that is face up on the cube. For instance, if the "why" is face up on the cube, then that team will answer a "why" question. Teachers can make up their own questions from the lesson, only they must pertain to this lesson.

5) Apply the Lesson

Jesus may be calling you to do a special job for Him. If He wants you to talk to other people about God, can He count on you to do the job? If so, how?

Story Line: Jesus chose twelve men to become His committed followers.

Adventure Number 58
John 3:1-18

Story Line: The religious man needs to be forgiven of his sin.

1) Study the Lesson (before class)

- Nicodemus represented the most respected people in the nation. He was a teacher, a Pharisee, and a member of the Sanhedrin (the Jewish ruling council). The Sanhedrin was responsible for religious decisions while under Roman law.

- Two Sanhedrin members who were spiritually sensitive are Joseph of Arimathea (John 19:38) and the Rabbi Gamaliel (Acts 5:34-39; 22:3).

- The Sanhedrin put Jesus on trial (Luke 22:66). Later, Nicodemus challenged the Pharisees for condemning Jesus without hearing Him (John 7:50-51), and he helped Joseph of Arimathea bury Jesus (19:39-40).

- John does not tell us why Nicodemus came to Jesus at night. But, we can probably assume that Nicodemus did not want any distractions from the crowds who were always around Jesus. It is also probable that he came to Jesus at night because he did not want others to know of his interest in Jesus' religious views.

- Many people believed in Jesus because of His miracles, but often these responses were only superficial and not considered genuine by Jesus.[1]

- Jesus told Nicodemus that to enter the kingdom of God he had to repent in order to be born again. Repentance refers back to John the Baptist's ministry of baptism by water, an evidence of repentance.

- Nicodemus wanted to know how this transformation took place and Jesus responded by telling Nicodemus the story of the bronze snake on a pole, Numbers 21:4-9. It was simply by faith now as it was then.

Footnotes - Adventure 58

1. Wayne Haston, *New Testament Chronological Bible Cards* (Harrisburg: Good Soil Evangelism and Discipleship, 2013), NT-08.

2. Susan Lingo, *Written on Our Hearts*, 99.

2) Begin the Lesson

- What were some of the lessons that we learned about the "Beginnings" period of time?

- What are some of the lessons that we learned from the "Beginnings of a Nation" period of time?

- What are some of the lessons that we learned from the "Possessing the Land" period of time?

- What are some of the lessons that we learned from the "United Kingdom" period of time?

- What are some of the lessons that we learned from the "Divided Kingdom" period of time?

- What are some of the lessons that we learned from the "Taken from Home" period of time?

- What are some of the lessons that we learned from the "Return to Home" period of time?

- What are some of the lessons that we learned from the "The Early Life of Jesus Christ" period of time?

- What are some of the lessons that we learned from the "The Ministry of Jesus Christ" period of time?

Begin the Lesson Activity: Cards

The teacher can put on pieces of paper or 3 by 5 cards, the Time Period on one side of the card and the Story Line on the other side of the card or piece of paper.

The students can take a quiz with the teacher's help about matching the Story Lines on the Time Line.

3) Teach the Lesson

What would be a very hard thing for you to do? Think of the hardest thing you have ever done. What is it? Share with the class.

In today's lesson, we will learn about a religious leader who came to Jesus at night. It must have been hard for him to do this.

Tell the Story

The announcement by John the Baptist was clear: Jesus is the Messiah and He is the Lamb of God Who takes away the sin of the world.

The job of the apostles was clear: take the message of the kingdom to the entire world. They had a job to do and special authority to do it. They even were able to heal people.

It was a new day in Israel. The Messiah was present. The kingdom was coming. The apostles were out doing their job. And most of all, many people were putting their faith in Jesus. All of that did not sit well with the ruling council in Israel, the Sanhedrin. They had complete control over the religious issues until Jesus came. Now, everything was different. They even affected a lot of political decisions. The Sanhedrin was a very powerful group of men in Israel in the time of Jesus. Most of these men were opposed to Jesus. But, a few were not. One of those that was not opposed to Jesus was a man named Nicodemus.

Nicodemus had some questions for Jesus. Maybe because of the crowds and maybe because of fear, he came to Jesus at night. We really don't know why he came at night. Nicodemus could have sent a messenger to represent him, but he did not do that. He chose to come to Jesus in person at night.

Nicodemus approached Jesus with respect. After all, no one could do the miracles that Jesus was doing unless He was from God. Jesus immediately changed the direction of the conversation. Jesus changed the topic from respect to conversion. Nicodemus needed to be born again, not just to show respect for the Messiah. The religious leader was used to showing respect for the religious authority. He was not used to being told he needed to be born again. His questioned Jesus about the meaning of "born again." How could any individual be born twice?

In a radical answer, Jesus quoted from the Old Testament. He told Nicodemus that as Moses lifted up the serpent in the wilderness, so the Son of Man must also be lifted up. The Messiah was directing the religious leader's focus to one main thought: it was by faith that one is born again. And to Nicodemus and Nicodemus alone, Jesus said, "For God so loved the world that He gave His one and only Son, that whosoever believes in Him will not perish but have eternal life." This was said to one person yet it is a message for the entire world, to every one of us. It is by faith that one is born again ... it is faith in the Messiah, the Son of God, the Lord Jesus Christ.

Teacher Helps

Tell the Story Activity: 2 Triangles

To illustrate the most popular verse in the Bible, the teacher could make 2 triangles.

- The first triangle could be called the "Who" triangle. The three points of the triangle: *God*, *world*, and *Jesus Christ*.

- The second triangle could be called the "What" triangle. The three points of that triangle: *believe*, *not perish*, and *eternal life*.

The teacher should show these two triangles at the very end of the message when talking about John 3:16.

Memory Verse

John 3:16 (ESV) - For God so loved the world, that he gave his only Son, that whoever believes in him should not perish but have eternal life.

Praise and Worship

Praise and Worship styles vary greatly around the world. It is the intent of this curriculum that praise and worship songs be selected that best fit the content of this lesson. Recommendations for praise and worship are given and this music can generally be located at www.itunes.com. However, the teacher can feel free to select a similar praise and worship song.

"Worthy Is The Lamb" by Hillsong is recommended for this lesson.

Bible Activity

What if people came into this country and demanded to be made citizens on their own terms? What if they wore a flag around their shoulders? Would they become citizens of _____ because they had a flag on? Of course not! They have to follow the rules set up, or they will never become (example: Japanese) citizens.

Nicodemus wanted to become a part of God's family, a citizen in the kingdom of God. Who do you think makes the rules about what it takes to be a part of God's kingdom? Of course, God does! Yet how many people think they can make up their own way to be in God's kingdom! They think if they look a certain way on the outside, or follow a set of rules set up by men, they will be pleasing to God – not so!! Nicodemus found out he needed to be born again; He needed to believe in Jesus.

Teacher Helps

Memory Verse Activity: Scripture Scrambler[2]

Write the words to the verse on the top of a paper. Then number the paper, one number for each word in the verse. Beside the numbers, write a scrambled word to the verse. Challenge your children to unscramble each word to the verse in its correct order.

Example:

1   ofr   for

2   dgo   God

Bible Activity: Citizenship

Bring in a flag of your country, or a picture of the flag. Ask the children: "What does it take to become a citizen of (fill in country name)? Who sets up the rules for what it takes? The leaders, or the foreigners wanting to get in and live here?

4) Review the Lesson

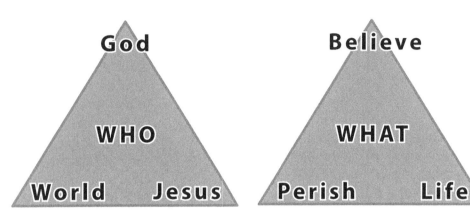

Teacher Helps

Review the Lesson Activity: 2 Triangles

To illustrate the most popular verse in the Bible, the teacher could make 2 triangles.

- The first triangle could be called the "Who" triangle. The three points of the triangle: *God*, *world*, and *Jesus Christ*.

- The second triangle could be called the "What" triangle. The three points of that triangle: *believe*, *perish*, and *eternal life*.

The two triangles are used to review this significant conversation that Jesus had with a religious leader.

5) Apply the Lesson

Nicodemus came to Jesus. He learned this: *"For God so loved the world that He gave His one and only Son, that if anyone believes on Him, he will not perish but have eternal life."* Later, Nicodemus was bold in his witness for Jesus.

Have you personally learned by faith that Jesus is the Son of God? Or, are you religious like Nicodemus? This would be a good time to put your faith in the Son of God alone for your eternal life, if you have not done so already.

Story Line: The religious man needs to be forgiven of his sin.

Adventure Number 59

John 4:1-24

> **Story Line:** The unreligious woman needs to be forgiven of her sin.

 ## 1) Study the Lesson (before class)

- Now that Jesus had begun His public ministry, there was some opposition to His message. However, it was not the right time, yet, for Jesus to confront those who opposed Him. So, Jesus travelled from Jerusalem to Galilee. He went through Samaria which was the shortest route but not the only route.

- Samaria was a separate political state under the Roman empire. The races were mixed and their religion included many forms of worship.

- Jesus came to the village, Sychar, which is located between Mount Ebal and Mount Gerazim. The Samaritans worshipped on Mount Gerizim.[1]

- This meeting happened at the sixth hour which would be noon.

- While His disciples were in town buying food, Jesus did a surprising thing. He talked to a Samaritan woman. The woman was shocked that a Jewish man would ask a drink from her. This is because most Jewish men of that day would rather go thirsty than talk to her or accept anything from her.

- Having captured her attention, Jesus caused her to be curious when He talked of "living water."

- This plot of land was probably bought by Jacob and given to Joseph many years before. But now, the Samaritan woman asked Jesus if He was greater than Jacob. She considered Jacob to be the father of her religion, even though she lived a sinful lifestyle.

- Jesus told her how to become a true worshipper of God.

- Jesus acknowledged that He was greater than Jacob and that He is the living water which anyone can have who puts their faith in Him.

Footnotes - Adventure 59

1. Wayne Haston, *New Testament Chronological Bible Cards*, NT-09.

2. Susan Lingo, *Written on Our Hearts*, 79.

3. Lynn Solem and Bob Pike, *50 Creative Training Closers*, 94.

2) Begin the Lesson

There are eight basic concepts that are emphasized throughout all of the Bible. We have studied these truths in previous lessons. Ask the children if they can name them and tell a little bit about each one. They are:

1. <u>God</u>. In the beginning, there was a very powerful God. (Lesson 1: The Eternal God; Lesson 27: The Exodus; Lesson 40: The Reign of David)

2. <u>Man</u>. God created many things. He created man and woman to be His special friends. (Lessons 3: Creation of the Universe; Lesson 4: Creation of People; Lesson 24: Moses Leads His People)

3. <u>Sin</u>. Man and woman disobeyed God. They did not do what He told them to do. (Lesson 7: Beginning of Human Sin; Lesson 33: Unbelief at Kadesh; Lesson 43: The Divided Kingdom)

4. <u>Death</u>. God punished man and woman for their disobedience. Death, in the Bible, refers to separation. (Lesson 8: The Origin of Death; Lesson 16: The Tower of Babel; Lesson 46: The Exiles of Israel and Judah)

5. <u>Christ</u>. God sent His one and only Son, His unique Son, who lived a perfect life. (Lesson 9: Promise of a Victor Over Satan; Lesson 45: Prophecies of a Coming Messiah; Lesson 52: Birth of Jesus Christ)

6. <u>Cross</u>. Jesus died on the cross for the sins of the world. (Lesson 11: Provision of Coverings; Lesson 32: The Day of Atonement; Lesson 45: Prophecies of a Coming Messiah)

7. <u>Faith</u>. If anyone places their faith in Christ, God welcomes them. (Lesson 13: Cain and Abel; Lesson 34: The Bronze Serpent; Lesson 58: The Religious Leader)

8. <u>Life</u>. God gives eternal life to those who put their faith in Him. (Lesson 5: Life in Paradise; Lesson 38: Bright Lights in an Era of Darkness; Lesson 56: Announcement by John the Baptist)

Teacher Helps

Review Activity: Eight Basic Gospel Truths - One Complete Story

The teacher should emphasize these eight gospel concepts throughout Scripture. They are foundational to telling children the one story of redemption found in the Bible. We will emphasize these eight truths regularly.

Ask the children if they can think of how these eight gospel principles are emphasized in the first 58 lessons that we have studied.

3) Teach the Lesson

Religious people need Jesus. People who are not religious also need Jesus. The woman that we will learn about is such a woman.

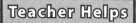

Tell the Story

Some people were keeping score of who baptized more people, John the Baptist or the disciples of Jesus. Surely, it was not something that either Jesus or John the Baptist wanted. It was not a matter of who gained more followers.

So, Jesus decided to leave the area and go back north to Galilee. His disciples went with him. To get to Galilee from Judea, they had to go through Samaria. That posed a problem. The problem was this: Most Jews hated the Samaritans and looked down on them because of their history. That was not right, but when Jews travelled north to Galilee, they did everything they could to avoid Samaria. But not Jesus, He had a divine mission.

While going through Samaria, the disciples and Jesus came to a Samaritan village and arrived at a particular well of water. Remember, they were fairly new at this job of proclaiming the kingdom. Worn out by the trip, they sat down by the well at about noon. The disciples went into town to get some food while Jesus remained alone at the well. Then, something really interesting happened. A Samaritan woman came to the well to draw some water out. Normally, a Jewish man would never start a conversation with a Samaritan woman. Not this time. Jesus asked her for some water. She seemed surprised and even asked Jesus why He was asking her for a drink.

On His divine mission, Jesus changed the conversation. He told her about the generosity of God and that if she knew about this generosity, she would be asking Him for a drink. She was shocked. How could Jesus be telling her about water when He does not even have a bucket or something to draw the water out of the well? Jesus went a step further and told her that whoever drank of the water He was talking about would never be thirsty. Her response was natural; she wanted this water.

Then, things really got interesting. Jesus told her to go get her husband and they could have this kind of water. She responded truthfully that she did not have a husband. Because Jesus knew all things, He told her that she had five husbands and was living with a completely different guy. Jesus explained to her that He was the Messiah. At about that time, the disciples arrived with the food. They were shocked that Jesus was talking to a Samaritan woman. She took the hint and left. She went back into the village and told everybody that there was Someone at the well who told her everything she had ever done. Now the people of the village were shocked. They asked her if this Person could be the Messiah and they went to the well to see for themselves.

Tell the Story Activity: In the Image of God

Remember people were created in the image of God. Ask your class, "Is it ever right to look down on anybody because of their skin color, their religion or any other reason?"

Of course not. The reason is that we were all created in the image of God. This is a great lesson to point out to your class that we are on a divine mission to proclaim the good news of the Kingdom. We are not the judge, God is.

Memory Verse

John 4:24 (ESV) - God is spirit, and those who worship him must worship in spirit and truth.

Praise and Worship

Praise and Worship styles vary greatly around the world. It is the intent of this curriculum that praise and worship songs be selected that best fit the content of this lesson. Recommendations for praise and worship are given and this music can generally be located at www.itunes.com. However, the teacher can feel free to select a similar praise and worship song.

"Worthy Is The Lamb" by Hillsong is recommended for this lesson.

Bible Activity

Review Rap

- "<u>Give</u> me" (reach hand out) – "A <u>drink</u>" (bring hand to mouth as if drinking from a cup)

- "My <u>people</u>" (point to self) – "Those <u>people</u>" (Look down, motion down with hands)

- "Mes<u>si</u>ah?" (Gesture with hands to indicate a question) – "That's <u>me</u>!" (point to self)

- "She <u>got</u> them" (Run in place) – "And <u>told</u> them" (Cup hands to mouth)

As you teach each phrase of the rap, re-tell that part of the story, and this will be a review your kids will enjoy and remember for a long time!

Teacher Helps

Memory Verse Activity: Scripture Log[2]

Make a page for children to take home that shows down the left column: Sunday, Monday, Tuesday, Wednesday, Thursday, Friday, and Saturday. Children should work on this memory verse each day and mark on their log when they practiced this verse and when they review this verse.

Bible Activity: Review Rap

Divide your class into 4 groups. Each group will learn a phrase to say "in rhythm" to tell the story. Teach the phrases one at a time, emphasizing the strong "2-beat" rhythm pattern. The emphasis should be on the syllable that is underlined. Once all 4 groups have learned their parts, start group #1, then ADD group #2, group #3, then group #4 until all 4 groups are saying their phrases and doing the motions at the same time.

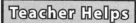

4) Review the Lesson

The teacher should divide the class up into two teams.

- One team could be the "red" team and receive red cards or pieces of paper. The other team could be the "yellow" team and receive yellow cards or pieces of paper.

- Each team has the responsibility of writing out 3 to 5 questions that they want the other team to answer.

- Each question has to pertain to the lesson today.

- After questions are written out, the other team has five to seven minutes to answer the questions. The "yellow" team will answer the questions from the "red" team and the "red" team will answer questions from the "yellow" team.

**Review Activity:
Two Team Review[3]**

After an appropriate time, the teacher will gather up the cards or pieces of paper and reward points to the best questions and best answers from each team.

It is highly advisable to have 2 adult teachers in every classroom for kids. If there are 2 adults, then one adult should be the leader of each team.

5) Apply the Lesson

Nicodemus came to Jesus. He learned this: *"For God so loved the world that He gave His one and only Son, that if anyone believes on Him, he will not perish but have eternal life."* The Samaritan woman did not HEAR this but she SAW this truth in action.

Name one or two people that you can SHOW them the love of God and then do just that this week.

Story Line: The unreligious woman needs to be forgiven of her sin.

Adventure Number 60
Matthew 4:23-25 and Luke 4:16-30

Story Line: Many people began to follow Jesus because of His teaching and miracles.

1) Study the Lesson (before class)

- When Jesus learned of John's imprisonment, He moved from Nazareth to Capernaum. This area was settled by the tribes of Zebulon and Naphtali. This fulfilled a prophecy made by Isaiah (9:1-2).

- The preaching, teaching, and healing ministry of Jesus validated Him as a prophet from God. All these actions convinced the Jewish people that God was at work.[1]

- Jesus *"went about all Galilee."* Galilee was sixty-three miles (101 kilometers) long from north to south and 33 miles (53 kilometers) wide from east to west. The historian, Josephus, estimated that 3 million people lived in the region at this time.[2]

- Thirty-five miracles are recorded in the Gospels. Many of those miracles occurred in this region.

- Many people started to follow Jesus and His fame grew nationally and internationally. Great multitudes of all sorts of people began to follow Jesus and they came from long distances, Jerusalem and Judea in the south, Jordan in the east, and Syria in the north.

- Jesus returned to His hometown, Nazareth. While there, He went into the synagogue and taught, as His normal custom was. The Luke 4 passage records that Jesus quoted from Isaiah 61:1-2, a Messianic prophecy. Jesus stopped reading in the middle of the text without reading about God's vengeance. The implications were clear to the crowd: Jesus was the Messiah and His first coming was not to bring judgment.

- The crowd was amazed at His teaching. The favorable year of the Lord was being offered to them if they repented.

Footnotes - Adventure 60

1. John Walvoord and Roy Zuck, *Bible Knowledge Commentary: New Testament*, 28.

2. John Phillips, *Exploring the Gospel of Matthew: An Expository Commentary*, 82.

2) Begin the Lesson

Teacher Helps

Adventure Number 57: Selection of Jesus' Disciples

1. What did Jesus tell the apostles to do?

2. Read Matthew 4:18-22.

3. Jesus chose twelve men to become His committed followers.

4. Ask God to guide you to follow Him.

Adventure Number 58: Jesus Meets a Religious Leader

1. Why did Nicodemus come to Jesus?

2. Read John 3:14-16.

3. Religious people need to be forgiven of their sin.

4. Pray that we would come to Jesus with a receptive heart.

Adventure Number 59: Jesus Meets an Unreligious Woman

1. What was unusual about Jesus talking to a Samaritan woman?

2. Read John 4:24.

3. Unreligious people need to be forgiven of their sin.

4. Pray that we would come to Jesus with a receptive heart.

Begin the Lesson Activity: Ask, Read, Talk, Pray

A good review strategy from 3 previous lessons will focus on four main elements.

1) Ask a question.

2) Read the Bible.

3) Talk about it.

4) Pray to God.

3) Teach the Lesson

Jesus first had a very secluded ministry. Nicodemus came to Him at night and He talked to the Samaritan woman at the well of Sychar. Now, His ministry went from seclusion to one of great popularity.

What radical changes did Jesus, the apostles, and His followers make?

Tell the Story

Jesus returned to the region of Galilee. It was His normal habit to preach and teach in the Jewish synagogues. Because of His teaching and His special healing abilities, many people began to follow Him. He was known throughout Galilee and was well known in Syria to the north, Decapolis to the east, and Judea to the south. The crowds followed Him everywhere.

On one occasion, Jesus went into the synagogue at Nazareth and read from the prophet Isaiah. The Old Testament verses that He read from were prophetic verses about the Messiah. He told them, Luke 4:18, *"The Spirit of the Lord is upon me, because he has anointed me to proclaim good news to the poor. He has sent me to proclaim liberty to the captives and recovering of sight to the blind, to set at liberty those who are oppressed, to proclaim the year of the Lord's favor."* He stopped right there. Everybody knew what He was saying because He stopped reading when Isaiah talked about judgment. Jesus came this time for redemption, not judgment. The implications were very clear to everyone at the synagogue that day: Jesus was the Messiah and He was offering redemption to them.

While Jesus was teaching in the synagogue, He told the people two stories about Elijah and Elisha. Remember, these prophets lived in the northern half of Israel and they were voices for God who did many miracles. Jesus referred to the widow of Zarephath and Naaman the Syrian who saw miracles from God. They were both Gentiles, or they were both non-Jewish. Jesus told these stories because He was offering redemption to the non-Jewish people now. That made many people mad at Jesus. They thought that if the Messiah was here, He would be for the Jews only. Instead, Jesus quoted two acts of God done by the prophets Elijah and Elisha. The crowd was so mad that they wanted to hurt Jesus but He escaped without being hurt.

Everyone was astonished at His teaching. It was amazing! On another occasion, Jesus was teaching in the synagogue in Capernaum and a man verbally abused Jesus. Jesus rebuked the man and the man returned to his senses. Everyone watched Jesus teach with authority. His fame spread throughout the land, not just in Capernaum and Nazareth. Jesus had courage to say the hard things and He rebuked this one that verbally abused Him. His teaching was unique and many more people began to follow Him.

The word was out now. Jesus taught with authority ... like no one had ever taught before. He healed people who came to Him. And, He brought a message of redemption to all people, not just the Jews.

Teacher Helps

Tell the Story Activity: Elijah and Elisha

The teacher should review with the class Lesson 44: God's Prophets: Elijah and Elisha.

- What were some of the miracles that they did?
- Where did they live?
- What else did they do?

Memory Verse

Luke 4:18 (ESV) - "The Spirit of the Lord is upon me, because he has anointed me to proclaim good news to the poor."

Praise and Worship

Praise and Worship styles vary greatly around the world. It is the intent of this curriculum that praise and worship songs be selected that best fit the content of this lesson. Recommendations for praise and worship are given and this music can generally be located at www.itunes.com. However, the teacher can feel free to select a similar praise and worship song.

"Hosanna" by Paul Baloche is recommended for this lesson.

Bible Activity

"Prove It!"

Ask your class: **"Have you ever heard anyone brag about how great they are? Sometimes people brag just to get attention. Sometimes a person tells you they can do something special, and they are telling the truth, not bragging at all. How can you tell if a person is telling the truth, or if they are bragging?"** You can ask them to "Prove it!" We are going to play a game today called "Prove it!"

Choose a child to pick one of the papers out of the basket. They should read the statement on the paper, and the class will say "Prove it!" They will then tell the class what they would have to do to prove that they can do what they claim. When all the papers have been used, end by asking this question: **"What are some things Jesus did to prove that He was truly God?"** (Miracles, amazing teaching)

Teacher Helps

Memory Verse Activity: Hop It

In large letters, write phrases of the verse on sheets of paper. On the floor, tape the papers in a mixed up fashion, but close enough for succeeding words to be reached in a step. Children should step on one word at a time in the proper order to quote the verse. Let each child have a turn of hopping on the verse.

Bible Activity: Prove It!

Ahead of time, write statements on pieces of paper that describe a special talent or ability that your children can relate to. These should all be things that could be demonstrated if they were challenged to "Prove it." For example: "I can play the piano really well" (or another instrument) or "I am the fastest runner in our class."

4) Review the Lesson

Agree/Disagree Statements (If you disagree, why do you disagree?)

1. Jesus normally preached on the street. (Disagree. He normally preached in the local synagogue).

2. Jesus was very popular because of His teaching and healing. (Agree.)

3. In the synagogue in Nazareth, Jesus quoted from the prophet Isaiah (Agree.)

4. In His message at the same synagogue, Jesus talked about two prophets, Jonah and Micah. (Disagree. Elijah and Elisha.)

5. Everybody liked Jesus. (Disagree. One time, everyone in the synagogue was mad at Jesus.)

Review Activity: Agree and Disagree Statements

Kids will have fun disagreeing or agreeing with these statements. You may want to make up some statements of your own for them to agree or disagree with.

5) Apply the Lesson

Popular ... that is what Jesus was. He was popular, not with everybody, but He was popular with many people.

Give one or two reasons why Jesus should not only be popular but also He should be Lord and Master. How can you show Jesus that He is important to you whether He is popular to others or not?

Story Line: Many people began to follow Jesus because of His teaching and miracles.

Adventure Number 61
Mark 4:35-41 and Matthew 14:22-27

Story Line: Jesus showed His power when He calmed a raging storm.

 ## 1) Study the Lesson (before class)

- The Sea of Galilee is actually a lake that is 680 feet below sea level. It is surrounded by hills and mountains. This setting often allows violent thunderstorms.[1]

- *"The other side of the lake"* was about six miles or about 9.66 kilometers. The water is about 150-200 feet (46-61 meters) deep.

- The disciples of Jesus were experienced fishermen, but when this storm arose, they panicked.

- Mark records a series of parables, then a series of the works of Jesus. The works of Jesus authenticated the words of Jesus. With four exceptions, all of the miracles of Jesus are recorded before Mark 8:27. This part of Mark's gospel shows Jesus' power over nature (4:35-41), demon possession (5:1-20), incurable physical illness (5:25-34), and death (5:21-34).[2]

- After a busy day of teaching, Jesus was asleep in the back of the boat. The twelve apostles were with him in the boat. Other boats joined them.

- The disciples called him *"Teacher,"* but they did not embrace His teaching. The disciples did not understand that Jesus had power over the wind and waves. Jesus rebuked them for their *"cowardly fear."*[1]

- Their response of *"Who is this?"* revealed they still did not understand Who Jesus was. Jesus responded, *"Do you still have no faith?"* This indicated He knew they still did not comprehend His power and authority.

Footnotes - Adventure 61

1. James Galvin, *Life Application Bible Notes*, 1625.

2. John Walvoord and Roy Zuck, *Bible Knowledge Commentary: New Testament*, 121.

3. Lynn Solem and Bob Pike, *50 Creative Training Closers*, 92.

2) Begin the Lesson

Let's review the time periods that we have studied so far:

- In order, what are these eras or time periods? (Beginnings, Beginnings of a Nation, Possessing the Land, United Kingdom, Divided Kingdom, Taken from Home, Return to Home, The Early Life of Jesus Christ, and The Ministry of Jesus Christ)

- Who are some of the people that we met in each time period?

    1) Beginnings: Adam and Eve, Lucifer, Cain, Abel, and Noah
    2) Beginnings of a Nation: Abraham, Sarah, Isaac, Rebekah, Jacob, Joseph, Moses, and Pharaoh
    3) Possessing the Land: Joshua, Gideon, and Samuel
    4) United Kingdom: Saul and David
    5) Divided Kingdom: Jeroboam, Elijah, and Elisha
    6) Taken from Home: Daniel and Ezekiel
    8) Return to Home: Ezra and Daniel
    7) The Early Life of Jesus Christ to Home: Anna, Simeon, Mary, Joseph, and Jesus
    8) The Ministry of Jesus Christ: Satan, John the Baptist, the disciples, Nicodemus, the woman at the well, and Jesus Christ

Begin the Lesson Activity: Ball Toss

Gather your class of children in a circle with a small ball. Have children take turns rolling the ball gently to each other. When a child catches the ball, have each child answer one part of the question. At this point, do not correct children if they give a wrong answer. Let each child that wants to participate and then roll the ball to another person in the class for the next question.

3) Teach the Lesson

Describe to the class one of the times that you were genuinely afraid. Let the class share times when they were also afraid.

Tell the class that this lesson deals with fear. But, more important, it deals with the power of Jesus.

In this lesson, we will learn more about the power of Jesus. What previous lessons talked about the power of God? (Lesson 1: The Eternal God, Lesson 25: The Plagues, and Lesson 27: The Exodus)

Tell the Story

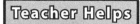

It had been a long day of teaching for Jesus. He was weary and probably needed a break from the crowds. He entered the small boat with the twelve apostles. Other boats followed them. It was supposed to be a 6 mile boat ride. Very tired, Jesus went to sleep in the back of the boat on a cushion. Some of the disciples were experienced fishermen and they knew the Sea of Galilee very well. To know the condition of this area was something they were very good at.

Once in the boat, they made their way to the other side. Other boats followed. Once they were out at sea, a huge storm arose. Since Jesus was still asleep, the disciples woke Him up and questioned Him whether He even cared if they were going down.

The wind and the waves were quite violent. It was night. Everybody was tired. Once the Teacher was awake, He told the wind and the waves to quiet down and immediately, that is what happened. The waves that had been drenching everyone were now smooth as glass. The wind that was so violent was now still. At the command of the Teacher, the wind and the waves obeyed at the moment of His command.

Well, now, everyone was attentive. The twelve questioned how the wind and the waves obeyed Jesus. They were struck with awe and amazement! At their amazement, Jesus questioned them, "Do you still have no faith?" Certainly, they did not understand that this was not the Teacher's time to die. But, now that everything was still, they were in a sense of amazement that was actually unbelief.

Faced with imminent danger and total exhaustion, Jesus demonstrated His power and authority. Faced with imminent danger and total exhaustion, the disciples demonstrated lack of faith and fear. Remember that they were experienced fishermen!

The contrast was quite obvious: the power and authority of Jesus or the experience of the fishermen. Jesus had just finished teaching people and now He was teaching His closest followers. He was teaching one very clear message: He has power. The disciples would see more of this power in the future, but for now, they knew He had power and they were amazed at this. On another occasion, they were on the same sea without Jesus and Jesus came walking on the water. Again, Jesus showed His power and authority.

Tell the Story Activity: Role Play

- Invite twelve kids in your class (if you have that many) to join you in a make believe boat.

- Let several kids role play like they are wind.

- Let several kids role play like they are waves coming into the boat.

- As each part of the story happens, have each group display their fear (disciples), their power (wind), and complete chaos that must have existed on this boat until Jesus calmed the wind and the waves.

Memory Verse

Mark 4:40 (ESV) - He said to them, "Why are you so afraid? Have you still no faith?"

Praise and Worship

Praise and Worship styles vary greatly around the world. It is the intent of this curriculum that praise and worship songs be selected that best fit the content of this lesson. Recommendations for praise and worship are given and this music can generally be located at www.itunes.com. However, the teacher can feel free to select a similar praise and worship song.

"Hosanna" by Paul Baloche is recommended for this lesson.

Bible Activity

Have you ever felt really afraid? I think we all have, at one time or another! What if you were on the playground and some big kids started picking on you? What would make you feel safe at that moment? (a friend coming to help, a teacher coming to help, etc.) If there was a robber that broke into your house, what would make you feel safe again? (The police coming to arrest the robber) Any time there is a scary situation, the thing that makes you feel safe again is when someone or something that is stronger than the scary thing comes in to help. That is exactly what happened that day on the lake with the storm! Jesus proved that He was more powerful than the wind and waves that were threatening to sink the boat. No one had ever done a miracle like that before! Jesus was the only one who could simply speak to the wind and waves and they would obey Him.

Now, do you think God put that story in the Bible just so that we could be amazed at the storm and the disciples? I think God wants us to learn a lesson that is helpful in our own lives.

Teacher Helps

Memory Verse Activity: Around the Class

Have the children sit in a circle while music is playing. Pass around a phrase of the memory verse. When the music stops, whoever is holding the phrase of the memory verse should try to quote the verse. Do this until all phrases are memorized. Then, do the same thing for the whole memory verse.

Bible Activity

Think of something that makes you afraid. It can be a big thing, or a very little thing. Whatever it is, you can know 2 things for sure. #1 is that God cares about your fears. #2 is that God is bigger and stronger than whatever you could be afraid of. Will you choose to trust God to take care of you? If you will, then write on a piece of paper the fear that you were thinking of when I asked the question earlier.

4) Review the Lesson

Volunteers from the class should list on a board or big piece of paper that everyone can see, the 5 Most Important Things To Know from this lesson.

For instance:

1. It had been a long day of teaching for Jesus.

2. The disciples called Jesus "Teacher" but they did not embrace His teaching.

3. At the command of the "Teacher," the wind and the waves went immediately silent.

4. Jesus demonstrated His power and authority over the earth.

5. The disciples were amazed at this event and Jesus questioned their faith.

Teacher Helps

Review Activity: 5 Scribes[3]

Have five different volunteers come to the front of the class to write one of the five most important things to know from this lesson. Ask the class why these are important.

5) Apply the Lesson

Jesus does not want you to be overwhelmed by your circumstances. He has the power and authority to help you, much like He helped and protected the disciples.

On a piece of paper, write down one thing that causes you to be afraid and ask God to give you faith to face your fear.

Story Line: Jesus showed His power when He calmed a raging storm.

Adventure Number 62
Luke 8:26-39

Story Line: Jesus showed His power when He cast out many evil spirits.

1) Study the Lesson (before class)

- The region of the Gerasenes was located southeast of the Sea of Galilee, near the location of the Ten Towns. These ten Greek cities belonged to no country and were self-governing. Because of their customs, the Jews would not raise pigs but the Greeks would raise pigs.

- When Jesus stepped ashore from the Sea of Galilee, He was immediately confronted by a man who was demon possessed. The demons immediately recognized Jesus. Demons are Satan's messengers. They are powerful and destructive.

- The demons shouted, *"Don't torture me."* They knew that Jesus had power over them.

- The name "Legion" is a term that refers to the Roman army which occupied that area. A "legion" in the Roman army represented 6,000 soldiers. The implication is that many demons were controlling this man.

- The "abyss" was thought to be a watery place.[1]

- At the request of the demons, Jesus cast out the demons from the man and let them enter a large herd of nearby pigs. Immediately, the pigs rushed into the water and drowned. The response of the people nearby was one of fear.

- By healing this man from demon possession, Jesus expanded His ministry into a Gentile region. His ministry would not only be to Jews but also to Gentiles. This was the first recorded witness of Jesus in a Gentile area.[2]

Footnotes - Adventure 62

1. John Walvoord and Roy Zuck, *Bible Knowledge Commentary: New Testament*, 227.

2. Ibid., 227.

3. Henrietta Mears, *What the Bible Is All About* (Ventura, CA: Gospel Light, 1986), 22.

2) Begin the Lesson

Tell your class that you are learning the one story of the Bible. While there are many stories in the Bible, they are linked to one major theme or story in the Bible. It is a story of hope. So, to help your class know that story and be able to put all the lessons together, we are going to review the lessons from the past. Ask, **"What are the main events that we have studied in the Bible?"**

- God always existed and He is very powerful.

- God created the earth and everything in it.

- Lucifer, or Satan, deceived Adam and Eve. They sinned by disobeying God.

- God sent a worldwide flood that killed everybody on the earth. God spared Noah and his family because Noah was a righteous man.

- God made special promises to Abraham.

- Jacob wrestled with the angel of God and got a new name, Israel.

- Through special plagues and deliverance, God led the Israelites out of Egypt.

- God established a moral code called the Ten Commandments that the Israelites were to obey.

- With God's help, Israel entered the Promised Land.

- God chose David to be king. He will one day send someone to be King forever.

- The kingdom was divided in two because of the sins of Solomon.

- Israel and Judah were exiled to Assyria and Babylon.

- The Jews returned from exile to build the temple and the walls.

- Between the Old and New Testaments, a lot changed.

- Jesus was born.

- Early events in the life of Jesus marked Him as a special Person.

- Jesus chose 12 men to become His committed followers.

- Many people began to follow Jesus.

- Jesus showed His great power over a storm and demons.

Teacher Helps

Begin the Lesson Activity: The Main Events

Review is a significant part of learning. Nineteen events are listed here. Write each event on a slip of paper or poster board and have children put them in chronological order. Let them work together in small teams of 2 or 3. Time how long it takes each team to put these events in the right order. Winner gets a prize.

3) Teach the Lesson

In this lesson, a man who was demon possessed experienced a transformed life. Again, we will learn that God is very powerful.

 # Tell the Story

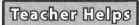

Right after Jesus rebuked the storm and the Sea of Galilee became still, Jesus and His disciples went to the opposite side of the Sea of Galilee. It was not even a Jewish area. This area was called Gerasenes and it was located on the east side of the Sea of Galilee where non-Jewish people lived. It was a Greek area but Jesus wanted to expand His ministry from Jews only to also include non-Jews. He wanted everyone to know that He was the Messiah.

So, when they landed on the other side of the Sea of Galilee, Jesus was immediately confronted by a very strange guy. This guy did not wear clothes and he did not live in a home. In fact, he lived in a cemetery. Time after time, he went into convulsions because of demons that haunted him. The guards had to put chains on him so that he would not hurt himself or other people.

When this guy saw Jesus, he shouted in a loud voice so that everybody could hear him. Jesus had already commanded the evil spirits to come out of him but the man begged Jesus to do something else. It was like the demons knew what was happening but did not want to leave the man. Jesus asked the man what his name was and he responded, "Legion," because there were lots of them. They knew their destiny was eternal torment so they begged Jesus to let them enter the pigs. They knew that Jesus had power over them. These demons knew who Jesus was and that He would determine their eternal destiny in hell. They also knew that Jesus had authority over them at this very minute. Jesus let them enter the pigs and immediately the pigs jumped into the water and died because pigs cannot swim.

Everyone in the area asked Jesus to leave. They were really afraid. They lost their pigs and they were afraid they would lose even more. But the man became normal and even wanted to follow Jesus. The man put clothes on and he acted normal. Because the other people wanted Jesus to leave, Jesus got into the boat and left. But before Jesus left, the man asked Jesus if he could go with Him. In fact, he even begged Jesus to go with Him. But, Jesus did not allow it. He had another plan for this man.

Jesus told him to go home and tell everyone what great things God had done for him. That is exactly what the man did. He proclaimed to the whole city and to his family what God had done for him.

Tell the Story Activity: Jesus Has Power Over Everything[3]

- In this part of Jesus' life, we see that Jesus has power over demons, death, and nature.

- The teacher should ask the class, **"What other lessons that we have studied show the great power of God?"** (Lesson 1: The Eternal God; Lessons 25-26: The Plagues; Lesson 36: Entering the Promised Land; and Lesson 52: The Birth of Jesus Christ.

Memory Verse

Luke 4:36 (ESV) - And they were all amazed and said to one another, "What is this word? For with authority and power he commands the unclean spirits, and they come out!"

Praise and Worship

Praise and Worship styles vary greatly around the world. It is the intent of this curriculum that praise and worship songs be selected that best fit the content of this lesson. Recommendations for praise and worship are given and this music can generally be located at www.itunes.com. However, the teacher can feel free to select a similar praise and worship song.

"Hosanna" by Paul Baloche is recommended for this lesson.

Bible Activity

Does anyone know what it means for one person to have authority over another person? Ask this question, so that you will have a good idea of what your students understand. Who are some people that are in authority over you? (Parents, teachers, grandparents, policemen, etc.) There is only one that is in authority over EVERYTHING!! Does anyone know who that is? Right, it is God!! He made the world and everything in it, and so He has authority over everything that He created. Remember last time we heard a story about Jesus speaking to the wind and waves, and they OBEYED Him!! Right away, and completely is how the storm obeyed its Creator!! Why? Because He had AUTHORITY over them! In Bible times, countries were ruled by kings. They were the highest authority in their land. People would even bow down to them to show that they respected the king's authority. Nobody in all the world has authority over God! Never have, never will!! Let's bow down to our great and wonderful God, and say words of praise to Him that show His authority. Demonstrate this: bow to the ground and say **"You are the only God, You deserve all the praise, You are all-powerful, and I will obey You."** Remind the children that we are speaking to God when we do this. You can say each phrase, and invite the children to repeat it after you. Add more of your own, Psalms is full of ideas!

Teacher Helps

Bible Memory Activity: Relay Race

Form two teams. Put the memory verse in large letters about ten yards away from the teams. Have children run to the memory verse and read the next word of the verse out loud so that everyone can hear. When each child has read his one word, go back to the team, touch the next person in line, and repeat the process until all words of the verse have been read.

Repeat this until everyone has memorized the verse.

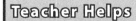

4) Review the Lesson

Divide the class into two teams. Give the teams one minute to write down as many statements as they can about this lesson, including the power of Jesus over demons. Here are a few ideas:

- The region of the Gerasenes was located on the southeast side of the Sea of Galilee.

- The region of the Gerasenes is where non-Jewish people lived.

- "Legion" is a term which refers to the Roman army. As many as 6,000 soldiers could be in a Roman legion.

- Jesus sent the demons into pigs who ran into the water.

- The people begged Jesus to leave.

- The cured man told everyone the great things that Jesus had done.

Review the Lesson Activity: One Minute List

The teacher should give two teams one minute each to list as many facts as they can about the lesson.

After the one minute has passed, compare lists and see who has more facts. Be sure that children remember that you are looking for facts.

5) Apply the Lesson

This man was a new man ... he was a changed man. Jesus had changed Him and Jesus did it alone. The demons left the man at the command of Jesus.

When Jesus changed this man, he became a bold witness for Jesus. If Jesus has changed you, in what ways can you be a bold witness for Him? List two or three people that you could do what this man did ... share the good things that Jesus has done for you.

Story Line: Jesus showed His power when He cast out many evil spirits.

99 Adventures in the Bible's Big Story Guide

Timeline: The Ministry of Jesus Christ

Adventure Number 62
Page 314

Adventure Number 63
Mark 2: 1-11; John 8:48-59 and 10:22-23

Story Line: Jesus taught that He was one with God.

1) Study the Lesson (before class)

- Jesus did many good things on the Sabbath such as healing an invalid in John 5:1-15.

- Because this took place on the Sabbath, some men began to oppose Jesus. In response to their opposition, He told them that He and His Father were always working. This made those who opposed Jesus even more upset, so much so that they wanted to kill Him.

- Jesus claimed to be one with the Father and since His opposition claimed to believe the Father, His opposition had two choices: 1) believe Jesus or 2) accuse Him of blasphemy.

- In John 8:48, the people who opposed Jesus said that He was a Samaritan. This was a term they used to belittle Him as most Samaritans were not highly regarded. Samaritans were considered a mixed race.[1]

- When accused, Jesus did not seek to justify Himself. Rather, He chose to let the Father be His judge. If the people falsely accused Him, the Father would vindicate Him and make their charges seem senseless.

- Jesus identified Himself as the "I AM" who existed before Abraham. In response, the Jews took up stones to try to kill Him. They did this because Jesus was declaring that He is God.[2]

- By acknowledging that God was His Father, Jesus taught that He was equal with God or had the same essential nature as God.

- In John 10, Jesus taught that He had the power to keep anyone who believed in Him from eternal separation from God.

- He offered security to frail sheep so they would never be lost.

Footnotes - Adventure 63

1. John Walvoord and Roy Zuck, *Bible Knowledge Commentary: New Testament*, 306.

2. Wayne Haston, *New Testament Chronological Bible Cards*, NT-13.

2) Begin the Lesson

Lay out a game board for review that looks something like this:

Time Period	Story Line	Songs	Memory Verses
100 points	200 points	300 points	400 points
100 points	200 points	300 points	400 points
100 points	200 points	300 points	400 points
100 points	200 points	300 points	400 points
100 points	200 points	300 points	400 points

Go back for each of the last 10 lessons and let the children name the time period for each lesson (100 points), the story line for each lesson (200 points), the song for each lesson (300 points), and the memory verse for each lesson (400 points).

A prize should be given to the winning team. Usually, competition is a fun thing for the children. So, keep them all involved. Depending on the size of your class, you may want to limit each child to only 1 or 2 answers. The reason for this is that a few children will answer all the questions, if you let them.

There will be a total of 10,000 points, 1000 points for each lesson (100 for the time period, 200 for the story line, 300 for the song, and 400 for the memory verse).

Begin the Lesson Activity: Bible Jeopardy

Divide the class evenly into two teams. The teams could be:

1) whoever has the most brothers and sisters

2) whoever has the fewest brothers and sisters

This game will be continued with the review at end of the lesson.

3) Teach the Lesson

The teacher should ask the class to vote on one of the following:

- Jesus is kind-of-like God.

- Jesus is not God.

- Jesus is God.

Now, let's look in the Bible and see what Jesus says about Himself.

Tell the Story

On at least three different occasions, Jesus claimed to be equal with God. One time, Jesus was teaching in a home in Capernaum which is in Galilee. It was very crowded because Jesus was very popular and people came from all over the place to hear him. Four guys had a paralyzed friend whom they wanted to get to Jesus but because of the crowd, they could not get into the house. Like many houses in those days, there was an outdoor stairway to the flat roof. The four friends took the paralyzed friend to the top and cut through the roof of grass and clay. They probably lowered him with fishing ropes. Now, everyone and especially Jesus could see the paralyzed man. When Jesus saw their faith, He said to the paralyzed man, "Son, your sins are forgiven." That did not sit well with some of the Jews who thought to themselves that only God can forgive sins. Jesus knew what they were thinking. Some thought that Jesus was blaspheming when He claimed to forgive sins. But Jesus knew that He had the authority from God to forgive sins because He was God.

On another occasion, while in the temple, the Jews called Jesus a Samaritan. That was like calling Him a bad name and belittling Him. Not only that, but they really attacked Him when they said that Jesus was demon possessed. Jesus did not attempt to justify Himself. He tried to honor His heavenly Father. Jesus told them that if they obeyed what He said to do, they would never look death in the face. Again, the Jews thought that was blasphemy. Then, Jesus referred to someone the Jews highly respected, Abraham. Abraham was their father of faith. Jesus told them that Abraham looked forward to this day and that before "Abraham was, I am." By that statement alone, Jesus was declaring that He was one with God. It may be the most radical statement in the Bible. Jesus was stating to these Jewish leaders that He existed before Abraham and was therefore God. They sought to stone Him to death which is what they did to blasphemers. But Jesus escaped their stones.

On a third occasion, it was winter in Jerusalem, probably sometime in December. The Jews wanted to know if Jesus was the Messiah so they asked Him and Jesus told them plainly, "I and the Father are one." Again, like the other time, they wanted to stone Jesus. They did not believe Jesus was one with God and they did not believe He was the Messiah. This was the last public teaching of Jesus because of all the attempts to kill Him. He withdrew to a place beyond the Jordan after this.

Tell the Story Activity: Three Scenes

- <u>Scene 1: A house.</u> Have one third of the class summarize who was there, what did Jesus say or do, and who did not like it. Why did they not like it?

- <u>Scene 2: The temple.</u> Have one third of the class summarize who was there, what did Jesus say or do, and who did not like it. Why did they not like it?

- <u>Scene 3: Winter in Jerusalem.</u> Have one third of the class summarize who was there, what did Jesus say or do, and who did not like it. Why did they not like it?

Memory Verse

John 10:28 (ESV) - I give them eternal life, and they will never perish, and no one will snatch them out of my hand.

Praise and Worship

Praise and Worship styles vary greatly around the world. It is the intent of this curriculum that praise and worship songs be selected that best fit the content of this lesson. Recommendations for praise and worship are given and this music can generally be located at www.itunes.com. However, the teacher can feel free to select a similar praise and worship song.

"Hosanna" by Paul Baloche is recommended for this lesson.

Bible Activity

Say, **"Have you ever met a famous person?"** Allow children to answer. There is a television show in America called "Undercover Boss." This is how it works: The president or owner of a very large company decides to see what it is like to work an ordinary job in his company instead of sitting in his expensive office in the big city. For example, it might be the owner of McDonald's that would "get hired" as a person that makes the hamburgers at a local McDonald's restaurant. Of course, none of the people who work there even know the name of the owner of the company; they just got a job flipping burgers to make some money. He works alongside these ordinary people, pretending to be an ordinary worker himself. He talks to the other workers and asks them what they think of working here. Imagine their surprise when at the end of this "experiment" they find out who was working with them! Did they have any idea who this person was? Maybe they saw clues along the way, if they were paying attention, but maybe they were totally unaware! Now, bring that same idea all the way up to the very highest level: What if you found out that God Himself was living and walking with you?!! Let's see what happened in that very situation, as we read God's Word today.

Teacher Helps

Memory Verse Activity: The Telephone Game

Memorize this verse using The Telephone Game. Have your class form one line, then whisper into the first person in line a phrase of this verse, have that person repeat the phrase to the next person. Do this until all have quoted the first phrase. Then do the same thing with the second phrase, the third phrase, and so on until you have memorized the verse.

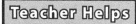

4) Review the Lesson

Continue your review game for points that you began at the start of the lesson.

- For 100 points, how many scenes did we describe? (three)
- For 200 points, what writers told about these three scenes? (Mark and John)
- For 300 points, where did these three scenes occur? (a house and the temple)
- For 400 points, what did Jesus claim? (He and the Father were one.)
- Bonus question worth 500 points: What is the theme of this lesson? (Jesus taught that He was one with God.)

Review the Lesson Activity: Bible Jeopardy

This review activity is a continuation of the review game at the beginning of the lesson.

5) Apply the Lesson

For the first time, we see that Jesus was unpopular to some people. He was opposed by some religious people. They felt so strongly about this that they wanted to kill Jesus.

Is it ever right to want to hurt someone? Of course not. It is never right to hurt someone. If there is anyone you have tried to hurt, ask them to forgive you. Jesus was opposed but He is still God and He still forgives sin.

Story Line: Jesus taught that He was one with God.

Adventure Number 64
John 9:1-41

Story Line: When Jesus healed a blind man, some religious leaders were offended.

 1) Study the Lesson (before class)

- Isaiah prophesied that the Messiah would open the eyes of the blind (Isaiah 42:7). In John chapter 8, Jesus proclaimed Himself as "the light of the world." This healing is significant because Jesus brought light to this man.

- The disciples had a theological problem. They believed that all suffering was caused by sin. They had to think that either this man sinned in his mother's womb or his parents sinned. Jesus explained that neither sinned. The man's physical blindness was not caused by sin.

- "Day" meant the time allotted by Jesus to do the will of the Father. "Night" is the time limit set to do the will of the Father by Jesus. In this case, it was the impending death of Jesus that was "night."[1]

- When Jesus placed clay, mud made with saliva, on the man's eyes, it may have reminded others that man was formed from the dust of the ground. Jesus probably used the clay as an aid to develop the man's faith, not as a medicine. From there, the man went to the Pool of Siloam on the southwest side of Jerusalem. At this pool, the man received full sight.[2]

- The Pharisees felt that Jesus had violated the Sabbath by healing on that particular day. They even accused Jesus of being a sinner.

- The Pharisees were divided in their opinion of Jesus. The healed man thought Jesus was a prophet. The man's parents were afraid to suggest any answers about the cure or the Healer.

- The Pharisees attacked the man's faith, the man's family, and reviled him.[3]

Footnotes - Adventure 64

1. John Walvoord and Roy Zuck, *Bible Knowledge Commentary: New Testament*, 307.

2. John Walvoord and Roy Zuck, *Bible Knowledge Commentary: New Testament*, 308.

3. John Phillips, *Exploring the Gospel of Luke: An Expository Commentary*, 188.

4. Mike Nappa and Michael Warden, *The Children's Worker's Encyclopedia of Bible Teaching Ideas: New Testament* (Loveland, CO: Group Publishing, 1997), 138-139.

2) Begin the Lesson

The teacher should gather all the songs that have been used in the Adventures in the Bible's Big Story and play several of them.

The class should be able to sing along with the teacher the songs that they have previously learned in this curriculum.

After the teacher has played several songs and the class and sung them, play the game, "Name That Tune." "Name That Tune" is a game in which the students will attempt to match the song with the Bible adventure that best matches the song. The teacher should use extreme graciousness to encourage the class when an answer is given.

The purpose of this activity is for kids to associate music they have learned with events in the Bible. The teacher should stay focused on this primary purpose.

Teacher Helps

Review Activity: Name That Tune

The teacher should play songs that the class has learned for the previous Bible adventures. Children should guess which adventures in the Bible's big story best match the song that is being played or sung.

If time permits, the teacher could also ask if there are phrases or words in any of the songs that the children do not understand.

3) Teach the Lesson

The teacher should ask the class to write down on a piece of paper the answer to this question, **"What makes you feel important?"** Have children write down only one thing. Ask for volunteers to share what they wrote.

Next, the teacher should say, **"Based on what we wrote on our cards, how would we define what it is to feel important?"**

Last, ask the kids to tell how would you say Jesus defined "being important?"[4]

Tell the Story

Jesus was walking down the street with His disciples when they saw a blind man. The disciples were curious about the cause of the man's blindness. They assumed that either he sinned or his parents sinned. Jesus was quick to point out that neither of them sinned. Then, Jesus changed the subject and told the disciples that they needed to work for God while it was still day. Jesus even told them when the day was, it was while He was still in the world. So, Jesus was not talking about an actual 24 hour day. He was talking about His lifetime on earth.

While talking to the disciples about working for God during the day, Jesus rubbed a mix of saliva and dirt on the man's eyes and then He told the man to wash the mix off in the Pool of Siloam on the southwest side of Jerusalem. The man did exactly what Jesus told him to do and he could instantly see! When the rest of Jerusalem saw this, they were very impressed. They knew this man had been blind from birth and that he spent much of his life begging for food on the streets. Some people objected to this man and said he was not the blind beggar but the man insisted that he was.

So, they marched him off to the Pharisees and asked him some tough questions. Most of the Pharisees said that Jesus could not be from God since He healed the blind man on the Sabbath. But, other Pharisees disagreed with the majority. They were arguing amongst themselves. Then, the Pharisees got the man's parents involved in the questioning. The parents wanted nothing to do with the Pharisees' questioning so they told them to ask their son about his healing. Well, the Pharisees brought the man back in a second time and asked him more hard questions like, "What did He do to you?" And, "How did He open your eyes?" The man thought they were interested in being the disciples of Jesus also. That really bothered the Pharisees so they threw him out on the street. They just did not believe that Jesus was from God and that He had the power to do this miracle, especially on a holy day.

Jesus found the man on the street after the Pharisees threw him out of their meeting. Jesus asked the man, "Do you believe in the Son of Man?" The man asked Jesus to point the Son of Man out to him and he would believe. Jesus told him that He was the Son of Man. The man believed right there and worshipped God. Jesus told this man that He came to make the directions of God very clear. Some Pharisees heard this also and again they were bothered. They realized that Jesus was calling them blind.

Teacher Helps

Tell the Story Activity: Important Things about Jesus

Divide the class up into two teams as you tell the story.

- <u>Team Number 1:</u> Answer this question. What important things about Jesus did the Pharisees not understand?

- <u>Team Number 2:</u> Answer this question. What important things about Jesus did the blind man understand?

After the teacher tells the story, have children write out and share 2 things from their particular question.

Memory Verse

John 8:12 (ESV) - Again Jesus spoke to them, saying, "I am the light of the world."

Praise and Worship

Praise and Worship styles vary greatly around the world. It is the intent of this curriculum that praise and worship songs be selected that best fit the content of this lesson. Recommendations for praise and worship are given and this music can generally be located at www.itunes.com. However, the teacher can feel free to select a similar praise and worship song.

"Hosanna" by Paul Baloche is recommended for this lesson.

Bible Activity

We are going to play a game called "True, true! Or No, No!!"

I will make a statement from the lesson. Some of the statements will be true, some will not. If the statement is true, everyone should say "True, true!" If it is not true, everyone should say "No, no!" Listen carefully, because some of these statements were tricky for the people to understand.
1. This man was blind because he had committed a really bad sin (No)
2. Jesus took the man to a doctor to receive medicine (No)
3. Jesus cared about the blind man (True)
4. The blind beggar was an important man in his town (No)
5. The Pharisees asked the man questions about Jesus after he had been healed (True)
6. The Pharisees were happy for the man to be able to see (No)
7. The blind man obeyed what Jesus told him to do (True)
8. The blind man believed what Jesus said, and was thankful (True)
9. Jesus said the worst kind of blindness is when your eyes don't work, like the man in this story (No)
10. The Pharisees believed what Jesus said (No)

Teacher Helps

Memory Verse Activity: Graffiti

Graffiti can also be used to help children memorize this verse. Write each word of this verse on a separate piece of paper. Then have children put the words in order in groups of 2 or 3. When each group can put the verse together in order, they will probably have this verse memorized.

4) Review the Lesson

Review the lesson in small groups. What are seven main facts or ideas that come out of this lesson? One adult leader should join each small group of kids. Let the children do most of the discovering. Help them when necessary.

- The disciples wanted to know who sinned, this man or his parents.
- Jesus healed the blind man when he rubbed a mix of saliva and dirt on the man's eyes and then the man washed this mixture off in the Pool of Siloam.
- The Pharisees did not like Jesus healing the blind man, especially on the Sabbath.
- The Pharisees were divided in their attacks on this man.
- The Pharisees questioned this man twice and his parents once.
- The blind man put his faith in the Son of Man and worshipped Him.
- The Pharisees knew Jesus thought they were blind to His works.

Review the Lesson Activity: Seven Main Facts

The teacher should have the class break up into groups of 2 or 3. Have them tell each other about the 7 main ideas in the lesson which are listed to your left. For younger children, or non-readers, the teacher should help them.

5) Apply the Lesson

For the second time, we see that Jesus was unpopular to some people. He was opposed by some religious people. This man's life was completely changed by Jesus and he worshipped Jesus.

If you are a believer, you can also worship God. Name two or three ways that you can show God that you want to worship Him.

Story Line: When Jesus healed a blind man, some religious leaders were offended.

Adventure Number 65

Luke 15:11-32 and Luke 18:9-14

Story Line: Jesus forgave a wayward son, a selfish brother, and a humble tax collector.

1) Study the Lesson (before class)

- The story of the "prodigal son" is really a story about two sons. One was a sinner and the other had a righteousness of his own. The worst of sinners saw themselves in the "despicable" son and the best of sinners saw themselves in the "righteous" son. Both needed repentance and forgiveness.

- The younger son illustrates our natural tendencies toward a sinful life of self-indulgence. The elder brother illustrates a life of self-righteousness and those who think of themselves as more deserving.[1]

- When the younger son ran out of money, he went to work with the pigs. The Jews thought pigs would defile them and would not even touch them. So, when the younger son took care of pigs, that indicated that he had reached a very low point in his life. As a Jew, he could have stooped no lower than he did.

- The younger son ran out of money, came to his senses, returned to his father in repentance, and fully expected to be hired as a servant when he returned to his father. "The father" is mentioned at least twelve times and is the central figure of this passage.

- The older brother had great difficulty in welcoming his brother. However, the father, was full of compassion and fully welcomed back his son. He even threw a great feast for his younger son.

- The purpose of the story about the tax collector and the Pharisee was that no one should trust his own righteousness and no one should have contempt for others. God welcomes the repentant sinner, regardless of their position in life. God is the standard for righteousness.

Footnotes - Adventure 65

1. Wayne Haston, *New Testament Chronological Bible Cards*, NT-15.

2) Begin the Lesson

Ask children to help you with previous memory verses. Maybe say something like, **"Who remembers what (verse) says?"**

- Adventure Number 51: Daniel 2:44
- Adventure Number 52: Luke 2:11
- Adventure Number 53: Matthew 1:16
- Adventure Number 54: Luke 2:52
- Adventure Number 55: Matthew 4:4
- Adventure Number 56: John 1:29
- Adventure Number 57: Matthew 4:19
- Adventure Number 58: John 3:16
- Adventure Number 59: John 4:24
- Adventure Number 60: Luke 4:18
- Adventure Number 61: Mark 4:40
- Adventure Number 62: Luke 4:36
- Adventure Number 63: John 10:28
- Adventure Number 64: John 8:12

Teacher Helps

Begin the Lesson Activity: Memory Verse Review

The last 14 memory verses are given here. Divide the children up into two teams and see which team can tell you the most memory verses. Bonus points should be given if they each team can recite more than the last 14 memory verses.

Give the teams five minutes and they must work together.

The teacher can provide a few helps.

3) Teach the Lesson

Imagine that your best friend has just left home and ran away. Imagine that he has chosen to get himself in a lot of trouble with his parents and the laws in your country.

What if someone very close to you did something very bad? How would you respond? Would you offer love and forgiveness? Would you tell your other friends that you are not nearly as bad as that old friend?

Today's story will help us understand God's love and forgiveness for all.

Tell the Story

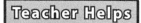

The two boys grew up in the same home with the same parents. One day, the younger boy wanted his part of the inheritance. Normally, a child waits until his parents die before he or she receives the inheritance. However, this boy wanted his inheritance sooner than that. As the younger son, he would receive one third of the inheritance while the older son would receive two thirds of the inheritance. The oldest in the family always received the most.

Well, once the younger son received the money, he left home and went to a far away land. He spent all his money on bad living. He spent the money recklessly and had nothing to show for it when he was done spending. He did not invest any of it or even use some it wisely. He just spent all the money on really bad choices.

When he ran out of money, he came to his senses. He even fed the pigs which a Jew would never do. It got so bad for him that he even wanted to eat the same food that the pigs ate. He was broke and was at the very lowest part of his life. So, he decided to come home and ask for his dad's forgiveness. He had a change of heart. He knew what he had done was wrong. When he came home, he hoped that his dad would hire him as a servant because that is all he really deserved, if even that.

When his dad saw him coming, he ran out to meet him. He embraced him, kissed him, and they wept. The father told one of the servants to fix a great celebration and feast. The younger son had come home, wanted forgiveness, and the father granted love and forgiveness to the maximum extent. There was music and dancing. There were new clothes and great food. It was a great time of rejoicing.

As usual, the older brother was out in the fields working. When he came in from the fields, he wondered what all the celebration was for. When he found out, he was so angry that he would not even go into the house. So, his father came outside to talk to him. His father explained to him that everything the dad had belonged to the older son. It was all his. He could have it. Now, that the younger son was home, it was only fitting that there would be a celebration.

The father knew how important it was to show love and forgiveness. The younger son showed repentance and a desire for forgiveness. The father granted love, mercy, and forgiveness. The older son did not give love, mercy, or forgiveness.

Tell the Story Activity: Three Important Scenes

Divide the class up into three teams as you tell the story.

- Scene 1: Contrast between the Two Sons. List two characteristics of each son.

- Scene 2: Actions of the Younger Son. Tell the class what made the younger son leave and what caused him to return.

- Scene 3: The Father's Response. Tell the class what actions you admire most about how the father handled this situation.

After the teacher tells the story, have children write out and share a few facts or observations from their particular scene.

Memory Verse

Luke 15:10 (ESV) - There is joy before the angels of God over one sinner who repents.

Praise and Worship

Praise and Worship styles vary greatly around the world. It is the intent of this curriculum that praise and worship songs be selected that best fit the content of this lesson. Recommendations for praise and worship are given and this music can generally be located at www.itunes.com. However, the teacher can feel free to select a similar praise and worship song.

"Hosanna" by Paul Baloche is recommended for this lesson.

Bible Activity

Divide your class into 2 groups. One group will imagine themselves to be the younger brother, the prodigal son. The other will be the older brother. Tell your class: "I want you to imagine that you ARE the son in this story." Describe to each group the characteristics of the son they are representing. Younger: You are selfish and want your own way. You don't care very much about following the rules. You are foolish and wasteful of your Father's money. After you have spent it all, you are very sorry, and realize how bad your actions were, and how you hurt your Father. Older: You have tried to obey the rules and work hard. You are proud that you are not like your brother. You have no patience with people who do not obey the rules. You are angry when your Father forgives your brother.

Will your actions, either good or bad, change your Father's love for you? Both sons – No (they have already behaved badly and their father still loves them. He has proven it!)

At the end of the story, are you honoring your Father? Prodigal son – Yes (he realized what he deserved and came in humility to his Father) Older son – No (he was angry with his father and told him that.)

Teacher Helps

Bible Memory Activity

Review the verse a few times then divide the children into two or more teams. Have the teams form lines across from a chalk or white board or piece of paper on a chair. Place something to write with at the board in front of each team. Have the first child of each team run to the board and write the first word of the verse, then run back to the line. The next child of the team will write the next word and it will continue until the verse is completed.

Bible Activity

Did you show honor and respect for your Father? Prodigal son – No (he wasted his father's hard earned money, dishonored the family by his sinful behavior, left the family for the wrong reasons) Older son – No (he scolded his father for showing grace & forgiveness to his brother).

4) Review the Lesson

Have children simplify the lesson into 10 words or less using their own words. What are their answers? When children simplify the story of the lesson into ten words or less, they will probably say something like these possibilities:

- This parable tells about God's love and forgiveness.
- The older brother was self-righteous.
- The younger brother was repentant and wanted forgiveness.
- Both sons needed love and forgiveness.
- The younger son ran out of money but gained common sense.
- The contrast between the two sons is very obvious.
- The father welcomed home the wayward son.

Teacher Helps

Review the Lesson Activity: Simplify

Simplify can be a useful game for the children. The teacher can give each team of 2 or 3 kids about 1-2 minutes to come up with the most significant 10 words of this lesson.

5) Apply the Lesson

Perhaps there is someone that you haven't forgiven that needs your forgiveness. You have harbored bitterness and anger over what they have done to you or someone in your family. The issue is not: can you forgive them? The issue is: will you forgive them?

Also, have you wandered away from God and need His love and forgiveness? The heavenly Father is full of grace and forgiveness. He abundantly forgives all those who call on His name. For those who ask, Jesus Christ offers forgiveness and life to those who repent of their sin.

Story Line: Jesus forgave a wayward son, a selfish brother, and a humble tax collector.

Adventure Number 66
Luke 16:19-31

Story Line: Worms and fire are forever. Repent!

 ## 1) Study the Lesson (before class)

- Jesus strongly warned people not to turn others away from believing in God.
- The punishment for turning away from God would be very severe.
- The reference to hell is a picture of a garbage dump where there were continual fires and maggots or worms. It is a picture of excruciating pain and suffering.
- The worms represent internal torment and the fire represents external torment. Hell is a place of unending torment for the unbeliever.
- The rich man in Luke 16 was in great torment as he experienced the flames of hell. He even wanted Abraham to warn his brothers about the reality of this horrific place.
- The rich man still seemed to see Lazarus as inferior to him.
- Jesus' response was quite simple: to avoid the place of eternal torment, hell, one should listen to and pay attention to the Scriptures.
- People in the life after this one on earth have some kind of body.
- Some people will go to a place of comfort and security. Some people will go to a place of torment and agony.
- When people die, they do not simply go to sleep and are unconscious. They do not just burn up or are annihilated.
- The Bible warns people how to avoid this place of torment.
- To repent is what needs to be done to avoid the place of torment.

Footnotes - Adventure 66

1. Lynn Solem and Bob Pike, *50 Creative Training Closers*, 70.

2) Begin the Lesson

Think back over the all of our lessons that we have studied and see if we can put the lessons in order. Here are the themes for some of the lessons:

1) God is very strong.

5) Life in the garden was full of pleasure.

10) Sin affected God's creation in many negative ways.

15) The people were evil. God sent a flood. Noah trusted and obeyed God.

20) God told Abraham to sacrifice Isaac. God provided a ram instead.

25) God sent plagues in Egypt to set free the Israelites.

30) God told the Israelites to build a tent where they could meet Him and offer sacrifices.

35) People who followed God were to be completely loyal and obedient to Him.

40) God chose David to be a king. God will one day reveal a Man to be King forever.

45) Prophets told about Jesus 700 years before He came to earth.

50) The Jews returned to Jerusalem to rebuild the walls.

55) Satan tempted Jesus. Jesus did not sin.

60) Many people began to follow Jesus because of His teaching and miracles.

65) Jesus told a story how a loving Father forgave a wayward son, a selfish brother, and a humble tax collector.

Teacher Helps

Begin the Lesson Activity: Theme Review

The teacher should write these statements on pieces of paper and then mix them up. Do not put the number of the lesson on the piece of paper. Divide the children into 2 or 3 teams, depending on the size of the class. Time how long it takes each team to put the statements in the correct order. Do not number the slips of paper.

3) Teach the Lesson

Ask children to fill in the rest of this sentence, " Hell is a place _____

_____.

Let the children explain to you what their perception of hell is. Then, explain to them that you are going to look into the Bible to see what the Bible says about hell.

Timeline:
The Ministry of Jesus Christ

Tell the Story

There was a certain rich man. He had expensive clothes and spent money on whatever he wanted. This man lived in total luxury. There was also a poor man. His name was Lazarus. The only food that Lazarus ate was the scraps or leftovers from whatever the rich man did not eat. Lazarus probably waited at the garbage dump to get the scraps of food so that he did not go hungry. The best friends of Lazarus were the dogs that he ate with.

Both of the men died. The rich man was in great pain when he looked up and saw Lazarus and Abraham together. They were in a safe and peaceful place. The rich man called out to Abraham and begged him to send Lazarus with just a drop of water to cool him down. The rich man was fiery hot and in lots of pain and agony. Abraham reminded the rich man that he had lived in luxury and Lazarus lived in poverty. Besides, Abraham pointed out to him that there was this impassable gulf between them. No one could pass from one side to the other. The rich man resorted to begging. He begged Abraham to send Lazarus to warn his five brothers. Even in great pain, the rich man still looked down on Lazarus.

Abraham told the rich man that the rich man's five brothers had Moses and the prophets, the Bible of that day. The brothers could listen to Moses and the prophets if they needed a warning. The rich man was sure that his brothers weren't listening to the Bible but that if someone were raised from the dead, they would surely listen. Abraham assured the rich man that Moses and the prophets were sufficient warning for the five brothers who were still alive.

The destinies of the two men were sealed. The rich man had a life of luxury but did not listen to the Scriptures. He certainly did not obey them. He ended up in a place of torment, not because he was rich and rich people need to be punished sometime. He ended up in a place of torment because he did not listen to Moses and the prophets.

On the other hand, poor Lazarus had eternal happiness, not because he was poor and needed relief. He was rewarded in eternity because he did listen to Moses and the prophets. His friends used to be the dogs. Now, his friend for eternity was Abraham in a very happy place. Lazarus now had peace and security. He had eternal comfort.

When Jesus told this story, He was reminding His followers that there is a place of torment for eternity and there is a place of security and happiness.

Teacher Helps

Tell the Story Activity: The Teachings of Jesus about Hell

Have children look up these teachings of Jesus about hell and give a one word description of hell from each passage.

- Matthew 8:11-12
- Matthew 13:40-42
- Matthew 22:13
- Matthew 23:33
- Matthew 25:30, 41, 46
- Mark 9:47-48

What can you conclude about hell from the teachings of Jesus?

Memory Verse

Matthew 25:46 (ESV) - And these will go away into eternal punishment, but the righteous into eternal life.

Praise and Worship

Praise and Worship styles vary greatly around the world. It is the intent of this curriculum that praise and worship songs be selected that best fit the content of this lesson. Recommendations for praise and worship are given and this music can generally be located at www.itunes.com. However, the teacher can feel free to select a similar praise and worship song.

"Hosanna" by Paul Baloche is recommended for this lesson.

Bible Activity

This is a good lesson to act out as a drama. Choose students to be Abraham, Lazarus, Rich man, angels, 5 brothers, people in heaven, people in hell. (Involve all students) After telling the story, have students act it out. If possible, have some "props" to use – simple clothing to represent wealth (for the rich man), poverty (such as rags to tie around Lazarus' "sores"), red, orange, and yellow paper to wave (representing the fire of hell). Use your imagination, and encourage the kids to be creative in their drama, and use of props. The teacher should be the narrator, filling in the gaps to keep it moving smoothly along. As the narrator tells the story, the children play the part being described. Remind the children that hell is a real place with real suffering.

Teacher Helps

Memory Verse Activity: Bean Bag Toss

With masking tape, mark off a large square on the floor, about 36 inches. Connect the opposite corners inside the square with tape to form an "X." If you have space and many students, make a second square. Give each section a number value (1,2,3,4). A bit of a distance away, put a line of tape to mark where the student will throw from. Divide into two teams. Each student takes a turn throwing a bean bag into one of the sections. (You may make a bean bag by putting beans in a sock and closing it tight with a rubber band. Take the long part of the sock and fold it over the bean section.) If they can say the verse correctly, their team scores the amount of the section where the bean bag was thrown.

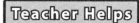

4) Review the Lesson

The teacher should have the class think of the main ideas of the lesson that they want to take home. Then they should number off 1 through 5. Number 1 should say tell the main thing that he or she learned from the lesson. All five groups should get an opportunity to share the main thing they learned from this lesson.

Ideas might include:
- Hell is a real place that is full of torment and agony.
- Heaven is a real place of comfort and security.
- People have bodies that live on after this life, either in a place of torment or in a place of paradise.
- After death, people do not just burn up or cease to exist. Nor do they experience some type of reincarnation.

Review the Lesson Activity: Repetition[1]

The teacher should allow about 5 minutes for children to share the main thing that they learned. If more than 5 children are in the class, allow for each of the groups to share with each other.

5) Apply the Lesson

Jesus taught and healed people. He offered them comfort. On some occasions, he challenged their beliefs. Regarding hell, the religious leaders were confronted by Jesus. Jesus did this on several occasions.

The rich man and his five brothers refused to listen to the Scriptures. Is there any part of Scripture that you are refusing to listen to? If so, you need to repent, turn from your disobedience, confess your sin to God, and live a life that pleases the Lord.

> **Story Line: Worms and fire are forever. Repent!**

Adventure Number 67
Matthew 4:23-24 and John 11:1-45

Story Line: Jesus Christ has power over death.

1) Study the Lesson (before class)

- Jesus Christ not only preached, He did many miracles. His miracles became known all over the country of Israel, even to neighboring countries.

- When Jesus healed the people, it authenticated His role as a prophet.

- The miracles of Jesus were supposed to lead a person to repentance from his/her sins, not just better health.

- Large crowds began to follow Jesus because of His miracles.

- Lazarus was a special friend of Jesus who lived in Bethany, which was located near Jerusalem. You can only read about Lazarus in two chapters in the Bible, John 11 and 12.

- Lazarus had become very sick and his sisters, Mary and Martha, sent for Jesus. They knew Jesus could heal their brother because they saw Him heal many other people. Jesus and His disciples were not near Bethany.

- However, when Jesus got the word that Lazarus was sick, He did not come immediately. He delayed for two days and said that this sickness was for the glory of God.

- Mary and Martha did not understand His delay of two days. In that time, Lazarus had died. By the time Jesus got to Bethany, Lazarus had been dead for four days.

- Jesus raised Lazarus from the dead when He arrived and told the family of Lazarus, *"I am the resurrection and the life."* They knew that Jesus had power over sickness, even death.

Footnotes - Adventure 67

1. Susan Lingo, *Written on Our Hearts*, 92.

2) Begin the Lesson

Teacher Helps

Eight essential truths have emerged from the Bible's big story of hope. Challenge children to know the eight truths, know them in order, and be able to give a brief description of each.

1. <u>God</u>. In the beginning, there was a very powerful God.

2. <u>Man</u>. God created people to be His special friends.

3. <u>Sin</u>. Man and woman disobeyed God.

4. <u>Death</u>. God punished man and woman for their disobedience. Death, in the Bible, refers to separation.

5. <u>Christ</u>. God sent His one and only Son who lived a perfect life.

6. <u>Cross</u>. Jesus died on the cross for the sins of the world.

7. <u>Faith</u>. If anyone places their faith in Christ, God welcomes them.

8. <u>Life</u>. God gives eternal life to those who put their faith in Him.

Begin the Lesson Activity: Eight Essential Truths

Write the eight essential truths on pieces of paper and place them face down. Do the same with the brief descriptions. Now, create 2 or 3 teams and have them put the truths and descriptions in the correct order. Time them and give a reward to the winning team.

Remind the class where these truths can be found in Scripture.

3) Teach the Lesson

The death of a friend or family member can be a very sad experience. If children want to tell of the death of a friend or family member, let them. If children do not want to say anything, that is fine. Perhaps the teacher could share an experience or two about the death of a friend or family member.

The lesson for today is about the death of a brother. It was a sad experience. In this lesson, we will see how Jesus has more power than death.

In what other lessons that we have studied did God have lots of power? (Lesson 1 - The Eternal God, Lesson 27 - Crossing the Red Sea, Lesson 61 - Jesus Has Power Over a Stormy Sea, and Lesson 62 - Jesus Has Power Over Many Demons).

Tell the Story

Teacher Helps

There once was a family of two sisters and one brother. They were special friends of Jesus. They were not disciples or apostles, but they knew Jesus very well. Mary, one of the sisters, even worshipped Jesus once by pouring expensive oils on His feet. Mary and her sister, Martha, sent a message to Jesus that their brother, Lazarus, was very sick. Now, Jesus loved all of them.

When Jesus got the word that Lazarus was very sick, He told His friends that this sickness was not fatal He also told them that this sickness was for the glory of God. So, Jesus continued teaching for two more days, even though Lazarus was very sick. After He completed His teaching, Jesus told the disciples that all of them would go to Judea and see Lazarus. The disciples thought Jesus was out of His mind. After all, they were trying to kill Him in Jerusalem and Judea. Jesus and the disciples went to Bethany, about 2 miles or 3.2 kilometers from Jerusalem. They were far enough away from Jerusalem to be not sought after by His potential assassins.

Jesus told the disciples, again, that He had to work while it was light. In other words, He had to work for God while He could before He died. Then, he told them that Lazarus was asleep and the disciples thought that was a good thing. After all, if Lazarus was really sick, he needed rest. But, that is not what Jesus meant. Then, He told them that Lazarus had died. Nobody knew that, except for Jesus. Thomas told them that since Jesus would not change His mind about going close to Jerusalem, that he would die with Jesus. Although Thomas later doubted, he showed great loyalty to Jesus by going to Jerusalem with Him at a very dangerous time.

When Jesus got close to the house of Mary, Martha, and Lazarus, Martha ran out to meet Him. She told Him that if He had been there, then her brother would not have died. Jesus announced to her, *"I am the resurrection and the life, he who believes in Me will not die."* Now, by this time, Mary ran out to the edge of Bethany and met Jesus. She said the same thing that Martha said a few minutes earlier. She told Jesus that if He had been there sooner, then their brother would not have died. Jesus was very sad because of their unbelief but He told them again that all of them would see the glory of God. When they got to the tomb where Lazarus was laid, Jesus told them to roll the stone away to the entrance of the tomb. Someone said that Lazarus would stink since he had been in the tomb for four days. But, Jesus prayed and then shouted in a loud voice, *"Lazarus, come out."* Instantly, Lazarus came out. He was alive. Jesus showed His friends that He had power over death.

Tell the Story Activity: Belief or Unbelief

The teacher should tell children to raise their hand or stand when they see belief or unbelief on the part of Jesus' friends or disciples.

Have the children explain why they see belief in Jesus or doubt in Jesus.

Memory Verse

John 11:25 (ESV) - Jesus said to her, "I am the resurrection and the life. Whoever believes in me, though he die, yet shall he live."

Praise and Worship

Praise and Worship styles vary greatly around the world. It is the intent of this curriculum that praise and worship songs be selected that best fit the content of this lesson. Recommendations for praise and worship are given and this music can generally be located at www.itunes.com. However, the teacher can feel free to select a similar praise and worship song.

"Arise My Love" by Newsong is recommended for this lesson.

Bible Activity

Has someone you knew well died and gone to heaven? (Teacher can share an experience of losing a family member or friend) Allow children time to share. How did you feel when you lost that person that meant so much to you? On the other hand, 5 minutes after that person was in the presence of God, how do you think THEY were feeling? What were they thinking about? What were you thinking about? What a big difference in perspective! (explain the meaning of perspective – it's HOW you see a certain thing. Two people can both look at the same event, and see two totally different things, all based on different perspectives) Talk about the difference between being in heaven, and being on earth. In today's story, we will learn how very differently Mary, Martha, Jesus, and Lazarus viewed this situation, let's join them!

After the lesson, re-visit this discussion. Ask the children: "What were Mary & Martha thinking and feeling? What was Lazarus most likely thinking and feeling? What was Jesus thinking? Who had the accurate view of Lazarus' death and coming back to life?

Teacher Helps

Memory Verse Activity: Scripture Card Battle[1]

Divide your class up into groups of 2 or 3. Give each group a set of cards. On each card is one word from the memory verse. Groups should try to put the words of the memory verse in the right order.

4) Review the Lesson

"Who" Questions:

1. Who were Mary and Martha?

2. Who was Lazarus?

"What" Questions:

1. What happened to Lazarus?

2. What did Thomas announce to the other disciples?

"When" Questions:

1. When did Jesus come to see Lazarus?

2. When did Lazarus rise from the dead?

"Where" Questions:

1. Where did Mary, Martha, and Lazarus live?

2. Where was Jesus when He got word that Lazarus was sick?

"Why" Questions:

1. Why were the disciple afraid to go to Jerusalem?

2. Why was Jesus not afraid to go to Jerusalem?

Teacher Helps

Review Activity: The Investigative Cube

Divide the class up into two teams. Make a cube with these labels on each side of the cube: who, what, when, where, why. When the cube is rolled to one team, they will answer the type of question that is face up on the cube. For instance, if the "why" is face up on the cube, then that team will answer a "why" question. Teachers can make up their own questions from the lesson, only they must pertain to this lesson.

5) Apply the Lesson

Jesus demonstrated that He has power over death. Ask children, "Is there anyone in this room that has power over death? If there anyone outside this room that has demonstrated he has power over death?"

The teacher should ask the class to put their faith in the power of Jesus.

Story Line: Jesus Christ has power over death.

Adventure Number 68

John 12:12-46 and Zechariah 9:8-9

Story Line: An enthusiastic crowd welcomed Jesus when He arrived in Jerusalem.

1) Study the Lesson (before class)

- A large crowd had gathered in Jerusalem for the Feast of the Passover. Previously, Jesus had rejected the role of a political reign, but as Jesus entered Jerusalem, the crowd began to think that this might be the time that His reign would begin. They shouted *"Hosanna"* which means *"please save"* or *"save now."*[1]

- If Jesus wanted to raise the suspicions of the Romans, He would have ridden into Jerusalem on a war horse. However, when He rode into Jerusalem on a donkey, he disarmed the Romans. A king riding on a donkey would pose no threat.[2] The entry of Jesus into Jerusalem was prophesied by Zechariah hundreds of years earlier.

- *"Daughter of Zion"* (verse 15) is a poetic way of referring to the people of Jerusalem.[3]

- When these events happened, the disciples did not grasp them as they were happening. However, when Jesus rose from the dead, they understood.

- Eyewitnesses to the raising of Lazarus from the dead added more energy to the already enthusiastic crowd. The Romans realized that this large crowd was getting out of control.

- The kernel of wheat illustration that Jesus taught was a prophecy of His coming death. His death would bring a great harvest.

- Then, Jesus issued another prophecy. He said that He would be *"lifted up from the earth."* This prophecy in verse 32 indicated that He would die and rise from the dead.

Footnotes - Adventure 68

. John Walvoord and Roy Zuck, *Bible Knowledge Commentary: New Testament*, 314.

2. John Phillips, *Exploring the Gospel of John: An Expository Commentary*, 232.

3. John Walvoord and Roy Zuck, *Bible Knowledge Commentary: New Testament*, 317.

4. Susan Lingo, *Written on Our Hearts*, 99.

2) Begin the Lesson

Time Period	People	Event
Beginnings	God	God made all things.
Beginnings	Adam and Eve	Sin
Beginnings	Noah	Worldwide flood
Beginnings	wicked people	Confused languages
Beginnings of a Nation	Abraham	Special promises by God
Beginnings of a Nation	Moses	Plagues
Possessing the Land	Joshua	Enter Promised Land
Possessing the Land	Gideon	Cycles of sin
United Kingdom	David	A special King forever
Divided Kingdom	Elijah and Elisha	Special prophets in Israel
Taken from Home	Jeremiah, Daniel, Ezekiel	Israel sent to Assyria
Return to Home	Nehemiah and Ezra	Israel returned to land
Return to Home	Daniel	400 years of change
Early Life of Jesus	Mary and Joseph	the birth of Jesus
Ministry of Jesus Christ	12 disciples	Jesus called 12 apostles
Ministry of Jesus Christ	Jesus	Miracles of Jesus
Ministry of Jesus Christ	Blind man	Healing power of Jesus
Betrayal and Death	Jesus Christ	Entry into Jerusalem

Teacher Helps

Begin the Lesson Activity: Match Time Periods, People, and Events

The teacher should form three stacks of paper. One stack should be the "time period" stack. 18 different eras should be underneath this "time period" piece of paper. Do the same thing for "people" and "event." Then mix them up and have the children arrange them so that they have the correct time period with the correct people with the correct event. For instance, when matched correctly, Beginnings, God, and God made all things should all be in the same group.

3) Teach the Lesson

At this point in time, Jesus was very popular. If you were going to have a "Popularity Contest" in your class, what are some things that make people popular?

What are some good things about being popular?

What are some bad things about being popular?

 # Tell the Story

 **Teacher Helps**

The plot to kill Jesus and Lazarus grew and grew. The main Jewish leaders did not like it that so many of the Jews were becoming followers of Jesus. The next day, at the Feast of the Passover, the crowd heard that Jesus was coming to Jerusalem. So, they gathered palm branches as Jesus entered the city of David and they shouted "Save now!" Earlier, at the request of Jesus, the disciples secured a donkey for Jesus to ride into Jerusalem. They did not know it at the time but this was fulfilling a prophecy that Zechariah wrote hundreds of years earlier.

Jesus was becoming a very popular person. Many people thought that He was going to set up His kingdom at this time. He had rejected this idea in the past but now seemed like a good time. The Jewish religious leaders were afraid because Jesus had become so popular that they were losing many of their followers. The Romans were worried because this "Jesus movement" was getting out of hand. On one hand, so many of the people were greatly enthused about the popular Jesus. But, not everybody felt that way, especially the Jewish religious leaders and the Roman government.

Once inside Jerusalem, Jesus declared two prophecies that most people missed … maybe everybody missed them. He told the people that a kernel of wheat had to fall into the ground and die before it could yield a great harvest. He spoke this because He knew He was about to die, even though He was very popular at the time. Jesus also told the people that He would be lifted up from the earth. He spoke this to tell of His coming resurrection after His death. The disciples understood all of this after the resurrection but when it happened, they were clueless. They had no idea.

Some Greeks wanted to see Jesus so they sent word through several of Jesus' disciples. Jesus responded to them that the time for Him to be glorified was here. Upon saying that, a voice from heaven reinforced what Jesus had just told the disciples. The voice said, "I have glorified my name and I will glorify it again." When the crowd heard this voice, they grew even more thunderous.

After Jesus said these things, He withdrew from the crowd and hid Himself. He was wildly popular amongst the crowds, yet they did not believe in Him. They loved His popularity but they did not know who He really was. Isaiah wrote about this 700 years earlier when he wrote, *"Lord, who has believed our report and to whom is the arm of the Lord revealed?"* Now, Jesus knew He was in His final days on earth. His death was quickly approaching.

Tell the Story Activity: A Kernel of Wheat

The teacher should bring a kernel of wheat to class. When this kernel of wheat is planted, it appears to die. But, after it germinates and grows above the ground, many more seeds are produced. They can be used to plant again or used for bread.

Emphasize to the class that a kernel of wheat is small. It must first be buried in the ground before it can reproduce itself many times over.

Memory Verse

John 12:24 (ESV) - Truly, truly, I say to you, unless a grain of wheat falls into the earth and dies, it remains alone; but if it dies, it bears much fruit.

Praise and Worship

Praise and Worship styles vary greatly around the world. It is the intent of this curriculum that praise and worship songs be selected that best fit the content of this lesson. Recommendations for praise and worship are given and this music can generally be located at www.itunes.com. However, the teacher can feel free to select a similar praise and worship song.

"Arise My Love" by Newsong is recommended for this lesson.

Bible Activity

"Digging Deeper"

If possible, bring a small hand-held trowel to class to use as a visual help in this activity. The teacher should make a statement, and if you can "dig deeper" to find the greater meaning, raise your hand and you can hold the shovel as you give us all the answer.

1. Jesus asked his disciples to bring a donkey for Him to ride on into Jerusalem. (This was a fulfillment of a prophecy written by Zechariah hundreds of years earlier. The donkey was a poor person's way to ride, not a king.)

2. Jesus said a kernel of wheat had to fall to the ground and die to produce a harvest. (He was speaking of His own death.)

3. The crowds of people waved palm branches and praised Him as He rode into Jerusalem. (They loved the miracles, but didn't truly believe or know Who He was.)

4. Jesus said He would be lifted up from the earth. (He was talking about His resurrection after He would die.)

Teacher Helps

Memory Verse Activity: Scripture Scrambler[4]

Write the words to a verse on the top of a paper. Then number the paper, one number for each word in the verse. Beside the numbers, write a scrambled word to the verse. Challenge your children to unscramble each word to the verse in its correct order.

Example:

1   lyrtu   truly

2   ssnleu   unless

Bible Activity

This story is full of things that were full of meaning beyond what was easy to see. Just like a worker in a gold mine, or coal mine has to dig down deep to get the gold, coal, or whatever they are looking for, we also have to dig deep into God's word to find out what He wants us to know.

4) Review the Lesson

Based on the lives of those who followed Jesus, rate yourself on this grid:

- Following Jesus' example   1   2   3   4   5   6
- Understanding God's Word   1   2   3   4   5   6
- Faith in Jesus   1   2   3   4   5   6
- Ready to deny selfish desires   1   2   3   4   5   6
- Give glory to God   1   2   3   4   5   6
- Stay away from bad relationships 1   2   3   4   5   6
- Respond to God's leading   1   2   3   4   5   6
- Overall commitment to God   1   2   3   4   5   6

Review Activity: Grid for Growth

The teacher should instruct the class of children that the example of Jesus should help us evaluate our own lives.

Children should fill out this chart (1= low; 6 = high).

5) Apply the Lesson

Some people followed Jesus because He was popular. Some people followed Jesus because they had put their faith in Him.

Have you put your faith completely in Jesus Christ? Are you following Him because of what He can do for you or because of your faith in Him?

Story Line: An enthusiastic crowd welcomed Jesus when He arrived in Jerusalem.

Adventure Number 69
Matthew 23:37 - 24:31

Story Line: Two days after Jesus' triumphal entry, He taught about future events.

1) Study the Lesson (before class)

- Jesus entered the city of Jerusalem with great sorrow. He knew He would be rejected. However, there would come a time when He would be welcomed (Zechariah 12:10). When Jesus said, *"Blessed is He who comes in the name of the Lord,"* He was referring to Psalm 118:26. This is probably a reference to the beginning of His millennial rule on earth.

- As Jesus left the temple area, He told the disciples that not one of these temple stones would remain. This prompted a discussion with the disciples. Two direct questions were asked of Jesus. 1) When will this happen? and 2) What will be the sign of Your coming and the end of the age?

- The first response of Jesus to these questions was that the disciples should not let anyone mislead them. Looking for signs could easily lead to deception. This period will be characterized by people claiming to be Jesus Christ, and by wars, famines, and earthquakes.

- The signs of Matthew 24:4-8 correspond with the seven seals in Revelation 6.

- The *"abomination of desolation"* spoken of by Daniel (9:27) and referred to here by the Lord could be referring to the time when the antichrist will enter the temple, set up an image of himself, and direct everyone to worship it (2 Thessalonians 2:4; Revelation 13:14-15).

- Immediately after this time of distress, the Lord will return to earth accompanied by great signs from heaven. Christ's coming will be obvious to everyone.[1]

Footnotes - Adventure 69

1. John Walvoord and Roy Zuck, *Bible Knowledge Commentary: New Testament*, 77.

2. Susan Lingo, *Written on Our Hearts*, 79.

3. Lynn Solem and Bob Pike, *50 Creative Training Closers*, 94.

2) Begin the Lesson

There are eight basic concepts that are emphasized throughout all of the Bible. We have studied these truths in previous lessons. Ask the children if they can name them and tell a little bit about each one. They are:

1. <u>God</u>. In the beginning, there was a very powerful God. (Lesson 1: The Eternal God; Lesson 27: The Exodus; Lesson 40: The Reign of David)

2. <u>Man</u>. God created many things. He created man and woman to be His special friends. (Lessons 3: Creation of the Universe; Lesson 4: Creation of People; Lesson 24: Moses Leads His People)

3. <u>Sin</u>. Man and woman disobeyed God. They did not do what He told them to do. (Lesson 7: Beginning of Human Sin; Lesson 33: Unbelief at Kadesh; Lesson 43: The Divided Kingdom)

4. <u>Death</u>. God punished man and woman for their disobedience. Death, in the Bible, refers to separation. (Lesson 8: The Origin of Death; Lesson 16: The Tower of Babel; Lesson 46: The Exiles of Israel and Judah)

5. <u>Christ</u>. God sent His one and only Son, His unique Son, who lived a perfect life. (Lesson 9: Promise of a Victor Over Satan; Lesson 45: Prophecies of a Coming Messiah; Lesson 52: Birth of Jesus Christ)

6. <u>Cross</u>. Jesus died on the cross for the sins of the world. (Lesson 11: Provision of Coverings; Lesson 32: The Day of Atonement; Lesson 45: Prophecies of a Coming Messiah; Lesson 56: Announcement by John)

7. <u>Faith</u>. If anyone places their faith in Christ, God welcomes them. (Lesson 13: Cain and Abel; Lesson 34: The Bronze Serpent; Lesson 58: The Religious Leader; Lesson 61: Jesus Has Power Over a Stormy Sea)

8. <u>Life</u>. God gives eternal life to those who put their faith in Him. (Lesson 5: Life in Paradise; Lesson 38: Bright Lights in an Era of Darkness; Lesson 56: Announcement by John the Baptist)

Teacher Helps

Review Activity: Eight Basic Gospel Truths - One Complete Story

The teacher should emphasize these eight gospel concepts throughout Scripture. They are foundational to telling children the one story of redemption found in the Bible. We will emphasize these eight truths regularly.

Ask the children if they can think of how these eight gospel principles are emphasized in the first 68 lessons that we have studied.

3) Teach the Lesson

Are you ever troubled by what will happen at the end of time? The disciples were troubled also and asked Jesus about the end times.

Tell the Story

On the Mount of Olives, Jesus looked over the city of Jerusalem with His disciples; He wept. He was so burdened for the people. He wanted the people of Jerusalem and all of Israel to welcome Him and worship Him. In fact, He came to His own and His own did not receive Him.

When Jesus left the temple area, He commented to His disciples that not one stone of the buildings in the temple area would be left standing on the other. This might have been hard to believe because Solomon's Colonnade or long sequence of columns was 1562 feet long (476 meters). There were 160 columns that stretched a 921 foot (281 meters) length. Surely, if this was destroyed, something really went wrong. This statement aroused their curiosity about the future again. So, one of the disciples asked Him, *"When will this happen?"* Another question came to Him, *"What will be the sign of Your coming and of the end of the age?"*

Immediately, Jesus told them to watch out for deceivers. That was His first response. There would come people who claimed to be the Christ but were really imposters. Everyone should watch out for these imposters. The next thing He told them was that there would be wars, rumors of wars, famines, and earthquakes. There will be lots of hatred. But, the good news of the kingdom will be preached around the world and then the end would come.

Then, He told them to be ready to run to the mountains when they saw the desolation of the temple. It would be a very troublesome time. Probably, the antichrist would enter the temple, put up an image of himself, and force everyone to worship him. The antichrist is the exact opposite of Jesus Christ only he will force people to worship Him. Jesus referred to words that Daniel spoke hundreds of years earlier. The apostle John would write about these same events also.

In the end times, there was going to be trouble like never before. If these days were not cut short, no one would survive. So, Jesus left them with an encouraging word. Because of those who would become believers, the perilous times at the end of the age would be cut short.

Jesus closed with this illustration. He told His followers that the Master was going to show up. He would not show up when they expected it but He would show up. They should be ready for His arrival, whenever that would be. Anyone who claimed to be a follower of Christ should always be ready and always be vigilant. Jesus, the Master, would come back.

Teacher Helps

Tell the Story Activity: A Replica of the Temple

The teacher should create a replica of the temple or show a picture of the temple area.

Memory Verse

Matthew 24:24 (ESV) - For false christs and false prophets will arise and perform great signs and wonders, so as to lead astray, if possible.

Praise and Worship

Praise and Worship styles vary greatly around the world. It is the intent of this curriculum that praise and worship songs be selected that best fit the content of this lesson. Recommendations for praise and worship are given and this music can generally be located at www.itunes.com. However, the teacher can feel free to select a similar praise and worship song.

"Arise My Love" by Newsong is recommended for this lesson.

Bible Activity

"Get Ready!" We are going to play an imaginary game today. Everyone close your eyes and imagine this: You mother and father have gone out to the store to buy food for the family. They will be gone for several hours, and they have left you a list of jobs to do before they get home. We will imagine 2 different attitudes and actions that you might choose.

1) You decide that you will lay around or play games for a long time, because you don't need all the time to do the jobs. You watch your favorite TV program, then you fall asleep. When you wake up, you realize that your mom and dad could be home at any moment, and you haven't even started the jobs! Oh no!! How do you feel? (allow children to respond – possible answers: afraid, hurrying, trying to take shortcuts so you can finish, hoping you don't get caught, ashamed that you might disappoint them)

2) You decide to do the jobs first thing, and you have plenty of time to do all the jobs really well. Actually, when you have finished the list, you notice that there are some weeds that need to be pulled up in the garden, so you do that extra job, to surprise your mom and dad. Soon it is almost time for them to be home, how do you feel? (possible answers: happy, glad that you will make your parents happy, can't wait to see them and show how you have obeyed)

Teacher Helps

Memory Verse Activity: Scripture Log²

Make a page for children to take home that shows down the left column: Sunday, Monday, Tuesday, Wednesday, Thursday, Friday, and Saturday.

Across the top, put practice times and review times.

Children should work on this memory verse each day and mark on their log when they practiced this verse and when they review this verse. Bring this log to class with you next week.

This type of activity will encourage Scripture memory and obedience throughout the week, not just as part of the lesson.

4) Review the Lesson

The teacher should divide the class up into two teams.

- One team could be the "red" team and receive red cards or pieces of paper. The other team could be the "yellow" team and receive yellow cards or pieces of paper.

- Each team has the responsibility of writing out 3 to 5 questions that they want the other team to answer.

- Each question has to pertain to the lesson today.

- After questions are written out, the other team has five to seven minutes to answer the questions. The "yellow" team will answer the questions from the "red" team and the "red" team will answer questions from the "yellow" team.

Teacher Helps

Review Activity: Two Team Review[3]

After an appropriate time, the teacher will gather up the cards or pieces of paper and reward points to the best questions and best answers from each team.

It is highly advisable to have 2 adult teachers in every classroom for kids. If there are 2 adults, then one adult should be the leader of each team.

5) Apply the Lesson

Jesus knew what the future held. Name two things that you are concerned about regarding the future. Now, commit those to Jesus and trust Him for the things that concern you about the future. He knows the future and He is concerned about the future of the world as well as your personal future. Pray to Him and ask Him to give you peace and confidence in Him.

Story Line: Two days after Jesus' triumphal entry, He taught about future events.

Adventure Number 70
Luke 22:7-20 and John 14:1-27

Story Line: Jesus gave His disciples valuable instructions and comforting promises.

1) Study the Lesson (before class)

- The last meal that Jesus ate with His disciples is referred to as the Passover meal. Yet, John refers to the time when Jesus died as the exact time that lambs were slain for the Passover meal (John 19:14). Probably, the Passover was an eight day celebration. It was really Passover week.[1]

- It would be traditional for women to carry the water so when a man was carrying water, he must have stood out. It was at this man's house that the disciples and Jesus would have this last meal. Evidently, the man was a believer. Even in preparation for His death, Jesus was doing miraculous signs.[2]

- The Passover celebration commemorated the escape of Israel from Egypt when a lamb was slain and the blood of the lamb was placed on the doorposts of each believing family.

- Jesus taught the disciples that the eating of bread and the drinking of the wine were the symbolic beginning of the New Covenant. The symbolism showed that the body and blood of Jesus were necessary for the beginning of the New Covenant.

- The wine and the bread were symbolic of the broken body and shed blood of the Lamb of God who would take away the sins of the world. Jesus declared to the apostles that this was His last meal with them.

- The New Covenant provided for the regeneration of the Jewish nation as well as those who came to faith in the Lamb of God. Believers in the church age also participate in this.[3]

Footnotes - Adventure 70

1. John Walvoord and Roy Zuck, *Bible Knowledge Commentary: New Testament*, 258.

2. James Galvin, *Life Application Bible Notes*, 1734.

3. John Walvoord and Roy Zuck, *Bible Knowledge Commentary: New Testament*, 259.

2) Begin the Lesson

Teacher Helps

Adventure Number 67: The Power of Jesus Over Death

1. What did Jesus mean when He said He was the resurrection?

2. Read John 11:25.

3. Jesus Christ has power over death.

4. Thank God that Jesus conquered death.

Adventure Number 68: The Triumphal Entry of Jesus

1. Why did Jesus ride into Jerusalem on a donkey?

2. Read Zechariah 9:8-9.

3. An enthusiastic crowd welcomed Jesus into Jerusalem.

4. Pray to follow Christ, even when it is not popular.

Adventure Number 69: A Prophetic Talk on the Mount of Olives

1. What future events did Jesus tell His disciples about?

2. Read Matthew 24.

3. Two days after His triumphal entry, Jesus talked to His disciples about future events.

4. Pray that we would recognize His ability to know future events.

Begin the Lesson Activity: Ask, Read, Talk, Pray

A good review strategy from 3 previous lessons will focus on four main elements.

1) Ask a question.

2) Read the Bible.

3) Talk about it.

4) Pray to God.

3) Teach the Lesson

Have you ever felt afraid of the future? What are some events that make you feel fearful? This lesson will let us see that Jesus Christ has very comforting things to say about the future.

Tell the Story

It was a great time of celebration in Jerusalem. Many people were in town for the week-long celebration of the Passover. Lots of people were excited to see Jesus and they were hoping He would do some special miracle for them. But, not everybody was excited to see Jesus. The Jews were still trying to figure out a way to kill Jesus. That is when it happened ... Satan entered Judas, one of the twelve apostles. So, Judas left the other apostles and conferred with the religious leaders who were trying to kill Jesus. They could not believe this ... one of Jesus' own followers was betraying Him! He was so popular that they never thought it would happen like this.

The day came to eat the Passover lamb. This reminded everybody when Israel was in Egypt and they escaped. By faith, they put the blood of a lamb on the doorposts and the angel passed over every home that had the blood of the lamb on the doorposts. Jesus told Peter and John to prepare the meal and they immediately wanted to know where they were going to eat the meal. Jesus told Peter and John that they would see a man carrying a jug of water and they should ask him if they could use his house. In those days, it would be very unusual to see a man carrying a jug of water. Women did this almost all the time.

Well, they found the man and he showed them a large room on the second story of his house. They could eat the Passover meal there. When all the apostles and Jesus arrived to eat the meal, Jesus told them how much He was looking forward to eating this meal with them. Taking bread, he blessed it, broke it, and gave it to them, saying, *"This is my body, given for you. Eat it in my memory."* He did the same with the cup after supper, saying, *"This cup is the new covenant written in my blood, blood poured out for you."*

Then, Jesus warned them that one of them would betray Him. The betrayer was present at the table. Immediately, the apostles began quizzing each other and they became suspicious of each other. They thought, "Which one of us would betray Him?" Jesus told Peter that He was praying for him and Peter responded back to the Lord and told Him that he would do anything for Jesus. Jesus told him that before the rooster crowed three times, that Peter would have denied Jesus three times.

While in the upper room, Jesus also told His apostles about the peace that He would leave with them. He told them that He was going to prepare a special place for them where they could be with Him. He also told them that He was the only truth, the only way, and the only way to find life.

Tell the Story Activity: Celebration

The teacher should bring in a special meal or snack for a celebration. Let the children eat the snack or meal before telling the story. Then, tell the story about Jesus' last supper with the apostles.

Timeline: Betrayal and Death

Memory Verse

John 14:6 (ESV) - Jesus said to him, "I am the way, and the truth, and the life. No one comes to the Father except through me."

Praise and Worship

Praise and Worship styles vary greatly around the world. It is the intent of this curriculum that praise and worship songs be selected that best fit the content of this lesson. Recommendations for praise and worship are given and this music can generally be located at www.itunes.com. However, the teacher can feel free to select a similar praise and worship song.

"Arise My Love" by Newsong is recommended for this lesson.

Bible Activity

"Jesus' Last Supper with His Disciples"

Well guess what? For those of us that have Jesus as our Savior, we are going on a really big trip one day! We will be going to heaven!! If you were going on a special trip here on earth, you could find out what it will be like in many ways. Maybe you have been there before. Maybe you know someone who has been there, and you could ask them about the place. If not, you could look on the internet to find out what it is like. For our trip to heaven, we have some clues about what it will be like from God Himself! He has told us in the Bible that it will be so wonderful that no one can even imagine how great it is. He tells us that He is preparing it for us. God is preparing it for us!! Let's see how many other things we can think of that God's word has told us about heaven. The teacher should allow time for responses: streets of gold, gates of pearl, perfect, no sin, no tears, no death, always with Jesus, etc. Make a list for all to see of what God's word says about heaven. Jesus knew he was going to suffer and die, and He also knew that He was going to be in heaven soon. It gave Him great peace, and it can give us great peace also.

Teacher Helps

Memory Verse Activity: Hop It

In large letters, write phrases of the verse on sheets of paper. On the floor, tape the papers in a mixed up fashion, but close enough for succeeding words to be reached in a step. Children should step on one word at a time in the proper order to quote the verse. Let each child have a turn of hopping on the verse.

Bible Activity: Jesus' Last Supper with His Disciples

Have you ever gone on a big trip? It is so exciting to think about how wonderful it will be! Maybe you are going to visit a friend or relative. Maybe you are going for a special holiday.

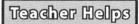

4) Review the Lesson

Agree/Disagree Statements (If you disagree, why do you disagree?)

1. The Passover was normally a week long celebration. (Agree.)

2. It was customary for men to carry water in this time. (Disagree. Normally, women carried the water.)

3. The Passover was done as a remembrance of crossing the Red Sea. (Disagree. It commemorated when the Israelites placed the blood of a lamb on the doorposts and escaped death.)

4. Jesus told Peter and John to prepare the Passover Meal. (Agree.)

5. When Jesus told the apostles that one of them would betray Him, they all knew it was Judas. (Disagree. They were all suspicious of each other.)

Review Activity: Agree and Disagree Statements

Kids will have fun disagreeing or agreeing with these statements. You may want to make up some statements of your own for them to agree or disagree with.

5) Apply the Lesson

Imagine a big house ... a very big house ... a very big house that is lavishly prepared. Now, imagine that this house is prepared just for you. Jesus told the disciples that He was going to prepare a very special place for them.

What can you do to prepare to enter this place that Jesus has prepared?

Story Line: Jesus gave His disciples valuable instructions and comforting promises.

Adventure Number 71
Matthew 26:1-56

THEME: Judas betrayed Jesus.

1) Study the Lesson (before class)

- There was a deliberate plot to kill Jesus. Without this plot, there would have been no charges brought against Jesus.

- Matthew and Mark record this story to have happened right after the last supper. The contrast is obvious: the devotion of Mary and the betrayal by Judas.[1]

- Judas probably betrayed Jesus because he expected a political overthrow of the Roman government. Judas was the treasurer for the group of disciples. When he realized Jesus would not establish His kingdom as Judas expected, Judas chose to betray Jesus for 30 pieces of silver, the redemptive price of a slave.[2]

- Judas betrayed Jesus with a kiss in the garden, a sign to the Roman soldiers that this was Jesus whom they should arrest.

- Judas pointed out Jesus not because it was hard to recognize Jesus but because Judas would become the formal accuser in a trial of law.

- Peter cut off the ear of a servant of the high priest, Malchus. Peter was trying to prevent defeat. However, Peter did not realize that Jesus had to die to gain victory.

- The kingdom of God was not to go forward with swords but with faith and obedience.

- The religious leaders could have arrested Jesus anytime but they chose to do it at night because the crowds were usually gone at night.

- The Jewish council recommended death which was approved by the Romans.

Footnotes - Adventure 71

1. James Galvin, *Life Application Bible Notes*, 1598.

2. John Walvoord and Roy Zuck, *Bible Knowledge Commentary: New Testament*, 82.

3. Lynn Solem and Bob Pike, *50 Creative Training Closers*, 52.

Timeline: Betrayal and Death

2) Begin the Lesson

Let's review the time periods that we have studied so far:

- In order, what are these eras or time periods? (Beginnings, Beginnings of a Nation, Possessing the Land, United Kingdom, Divided Kingdom, Taken from Home, Return to Home, The Early Life of Jesus Christ, and The Ministry of Jesus Christ)

- Who are some of the people that we met in each time period?

    1) Beginnings: Adam and Eve, Lucifer, Cain, Abel, and Noah
    2) Beginnings of a Nation: Abraham, Sarah, Isaac, Rebekah, Jacob, Joseph, Moses, and Pharaoh
    3) Possessing the Land: Joshua, Gideon, and Samuel
    4) United Kingdom: Saul and David
    5) Divided Kingdom: Jeroboam, Elijah, and Elisha
    6) Taken from Home: Daniel and Ezekiel
    7) Return to Home: Ezra and Daniel
    8) The Early Life of Jesus Christ to Home: Anna, Simeon, Mary, Joseph, and Jesus
    9) The Ministry of Jesus Christ: Satan, John the Baptist, the disciples, Nicodemus, the woman at the well, and Jesus Christ
    10) Betrayal and Death of Jesus Christ: Jesus Christ, His disciples, and Judas

Begin the Lesson Activity: Ball Toss

Gather your class of children in a circle with a small ball. Have children take turns rolling the ball gently to each other. When a child catches the ball, have each child answer one part of the question. At this point, do not correct children if they give a wrong answer. Let each child that wants to participate and then roll the ball to another person in the class for the next question.

3) Teach the Lesson

Think of a friend who has betrayed you. You trusted them and then they turned on you. You thought they were your friend, but when you needed them, they left you and even told lies about you.

Jesus Christ also had a friend like that.

Tell the Story

On Wednesday, Jesus told the disciples about the last times. He had told them that in the end of time, some would be bound for the fires of hell and some would be live in the happiness of heaven. Those who believe and do acts of mercy would be the kind of people that would be headed for heaven. He was telling them that you do not have to have money and you do not have to have some kind of special abilities. You just have to see deep spiritual and physical needs and meet them. Those people, He taught, are the kind that will be in heaven.

After He had finished telling them this, He told them that He would be betrayed and crucified. Then, a woman put a lot of expensive perfume on the feet of Jesus. The disciples were furious. They thought that this perfume could have been sold and the money used to feed the poor. Jesus rebuked the disciples and told them that He would not be with them much longer. At about that time, Judas was looking for just the right time to betray Jesus. He had agreed with the Pharisees on a price to betray Jesus ... 30 pieces of silver.

On Thursday, they began to look for a place to have supper for the Feast of Unleavened Bread. Jesus told them of a place that would host this special dinner. So, that night, all the disciples and Jesus met together for the last meal. Jesus told them about His body which would be broken and His blood which would be spilled out on the ground. He passed around a loaf of bread which symbolized His broken body. Everyone ate. Then, He passed around a cup of wine which symbolized His blood which would be spilled out on the ground. Everyone drank. Then, Jesus told the disciples that one of them would betray Him. Judas asked if it was he.

After dinner, the disciples and Jesus went a short distance to the Mount of Olives to pray. But, Judas got the Roman soldiers so that he could betray Jesus and get that money. While Jesus was praying in a garden on the Mount of Olives, His disciples could not stay awake. Even after Jesus told them several times to stay awake, they still went to sleep. That was until Judas came with the Roman soldiers who took Jesus away. Judas had told the Roman soldiers that the one whom Judas kissed was Jesus. Then, the soldiers would definitely know who they were supposed to take into custody. Jesus did not resist their arrest but Peter took a sword and cut off one of the servant's ears. In mercy, Jesus healed the ear of this servant of the high priest. When the Roman soldiers arrested Jesus, the rest of the disciples ran away and deserted Jesus.

Teacher Helps

Tell the Story Activity: Chronology of the Last Week in the Life of Jesus Christ

The teacher should divide the class up into two teams. The goal of each team is to give the correct order of events in the last week of Jesus before His crucifixion.

- Jesus raises a friend in Bethany from the dead.

- The disciples get a donkey from Bethphage, just like Jesus told them.

- Jesus rides into Jerusalem on a donkey.

- Jesus tells His disciples about end times.

- A woman puts expensive perfume on the feet of Jesus

- Last Supper

- Jesus and His disciples go to pray on the Mount of Olives.

- Judas betrays Jesus.

Timeline: Betrayal and Death

Memory Verse

Matthew 26:56 (ESV) - But all this has taken place that the Scriptures of the prophets might be fulfilled. Then all the disciples left him and fled.

Praise and Worship

Praise and Worship styles vary greatly around the world. It is the intent of this curriculum that praise and worship songs be selected that best fit the content of this lesson. Recommendations for praise and worship are given and this music can generally be located at www.itunes.com. However, the teacher can feel free to select a similar praise and worship song.

"Arise My Love" by Newsong is recommended for this lesson.

Bible Activity

If possible, bring a dictionary to class. Also bring at least six small treats, but keep that part a secret! Before class, write each of the following words on a separate piece of paper or card: betray, humility, treasurer, agony, darkness, submit. Ask for volunteers to choose a card, then look up the word that is on the card. They should then read the definition to the class. The teacher (or student if they are able to do this) should write the definition of each word on its respective card. After defining these words, say: we are going to listen for each of these words (or ideas) during the story today. When you hear one of these words either said, or described, hold up the card with that word on it. Once the story is finished, go back and talk about each of these key words and concepts.

Teacher Helps

Memory Verse Activity: Around the Class

Have the children sit in a circle while music is playing. Pass around a phrase of the memory verse. When the music stops, whoever is holding the phrase of the memory verse should try to quote the verse. Do this until all phrases are memorized. Then, do the same thing for the whole memory verse.

4) Review the Lesson

Volunteers from the class should list on a board or big piece of paper that everyone can see, the 5 Most Important Things To Know from this lesson.

For instance:

1. Jesus warned people about going to hell on Wednesday.

2. On Thursday, the disciples and Jesus had their Last Supper at a special placed designated by Jesus.

3. Judas betrayed Jesus for 30 pieces of silver.

4. The disciples could not stay awake in the garden when they were supposed to be praying.

5. Jesus did not retaliate with violence when He was arrested by the Roman soldiers.

Review Activity: 5 Scribes[3]

Have five different volunteers come to the front of the class to write one of the five most important things to know from this lesson. Ask the class why these are important.

5) Apply the Lesson

In Lesson 45, we learned that Jesus would be betrayed. In what ways was Jesus betrayed by Judas and the other disciples? The teacher should read Isaiah 53 and remind the class that this part of Scripture was now going to be fulfilled. Isaiah wrote this 700 years before Jesus was born. The betrayal of Jesus was something that God knew would happen.

THEME: Judas betrayed Jesus.

Adventure Number 72
Matthew 27:1-24

Story Line: Jesus was innocent but the crowds shouted, "Crucify Him!"

1) Study the Lesson (before class)

- The Jewish religious leaders had to convince the Roman authorities to crucify Jesus because they did not have the authority to do it themselves.

- To be sentenced to die, Jesus had to be brought before the Roman governor, Pilate. Pilate governed from Caesarea but happened to be in Jerusalem for a special occasion. Pilate had one accusation brought against Jesus, that He claimed to be the King of the Jews. The Jews arrested Jesus for blasphemy but that charge meant nothing to the Romans. If Jesus called Himself a King, then the Romans would act.

- Judas realized that he was wrong to betray Jesus but by that time it was too late. He decided to get rid of the money which only reminded him of his sinful actions.

- Neither Pontius Pilate, the governor of the Roman province of Judea, nor Herod Antipas, the Jewish ruler of the region of Galilee, found any guilt in Jesus. But to satisfy the Jews, Pilate delivered Jesus to be crucified.[1]

- When Pilate asked Jesus if He was the King of the Jews, the answer came back positive. Pilate realized that this King was no threat to the Roman empire and tried to release Jesus. However, the crowd would have nothing to do with that.

- Because it was Passover, it was a custom to release a criminal. A notorious criminal named Barabbas and Jesus were the possibilities for a release. Pilate thought the Jewish people would pick Jesus whom they loved. However, the crowd wanted nothing to do with that and shouted *"Crucify Him!"* When Pilate wanted further confirmation from the crowd, they only shouted louder *"Crucify Him!"*[2]

Footnotes - Adventure 72

1. Wayne Haston, *New Testament Chronological Bible Cards*, NT-22.

2. John Walvoord and Roy Zuck, *Bible Knowledge Commentary: New Testament*, 87.

2) Begin the Lesson

Remind your class that you are learning the one story of the Bible. While there are many stories in the Bible, they are linked to one major theme or story in the Bible. It is a story of hope. So, to help your class know that story and be able to put all the lessons together, we are going to review the lessons from the past. Ask, **"What are the main events that we have studied in the Bible?"**

- God always existed and He is very powerful.
- God created the earth and everything in it.
- Lucifer, or Satan, deceived Adam and Eve.
- God spared Noah and his family because Noah was a righteous man.
- God made special promises to Abraham.
- Jacob wrestled with the angel of God and got a new name, Israel.
- God led the Israelites out of Egypt.
- God established a moral code called the Ten Commandments
- God chose David to be king. He will one day send someone to be King forever.
- The kingdom was divided in two because of the sins of Solomon.
- Israel and Judah were exiled to Assyria and Babylon.
- The Jews returned from exile to build the temple and the walls.
- Between the Old and New Testaments, a lot changed.
- Jesus was born.
- Early events in the life of Jesus marked Him as a special Person.
- Jesus chose 12 men to become His committed followers.
- Jesus showed His great power over a storm and demons.
- Jesus entered Jerusalem with shouts of praise from the crowds.
- Judas betrayed Jesus.

Teacher Helps

Begin the Lesson Activity: The Main Events

Review is a significant part of learning. Nineteen events are listed here. Write each event on a slip of paper or poster board and have children put them in chronological order. Let them work together in small teams 2 or 3. Time how long it takes each team to put these events in the right order. Winner gets a prize.

3) Teach the Lesson

Some people are very demanding. They want things and they want them now. Have you ever met someone who was very demanding? How did that make you feel to be around them?

Some people in Jerusalem were very demanding. They even wanted the death of Jesus, even though He did nothing wrong.

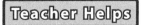

Tell the Story

Thursday night was certainly eventful for Jesus. Jesus had the Last Supper with His disciples where He reminded them of His upcoming crucifixion. Judas betrayed Jesus. The disciples could not stay awake long enough to pray with Jesus. The Roman soldiers came to arrest the Christ. In fear, the disciples all fled. Then, the Roman soldiers took Jesus to several unfair judges.

The Roman soldiers were joined by the Jewish police. Together, they tied up Jesus and took Him to Annas, who had been the high priest. Peter followed from a distance to watch where they took Jesus. When someone identified Peter as a follower of Jesus, he immediately denied it. After Jesus appeared before Annas, the soldiers and police took Him to the current high priest, Caiphas, and the entire Jewish Council. There they tried to find charges against Jesus that would guarantee His death. One person after another brought false accusations against Jesus, but nothing was believable.

After that, the Roman soldiers and Jewish police took Jesus to Pilate, the governor of Judea. The accusations of the people focused on something that Jesus said earlier, that He was a king. The people thought this might incite the Roman governor. So, Pilate asked Jesus if He was a king to which Jesus responded, "You have said so." During the interrogation, Pilate found out that Jesus was from Galilee. After further questioning, Pilate told the Jewish leaders that he found no fault in Jesus Christ. Because Jesus was from Galilee, Pilate sent Jesus to Herod, the ruler of Galilee, who just happened to be in Jerusalem at the time. When Herod questioned Jesus, Jesus refused to answer Him. Now, the Roman soldiers were engaged in mocking Jesus and making fun of Him. They even put a royal robe on Him and pretended Jesus was a false king. Herod joined in on this mockery and eventually sent Jesus back to Pilate, the governor of Judea.

Now, while Jesus appeared the second time in front of Pilate, the people joined in the mockery. They told Pilate, "Put Him to death on a cross!" They were loud and forceful. They kept shouting, "Put Him to death on a cross!" Three times, Pilate told the crowd that he found no fault in Christ. But the people persisted and eventually their voices prevailed.

Pilate declared his own innocence and sent Jesus away to be put to death on a cross. Before Pilate sent Him away, Pilate had Jesus beaten and whipped. In mockery, the soldiers placed a crown of thorns on the head of Jesus. Then, they led Him away to Golgotha, where they would crucify Him.

Tell the Story Activity: 5 Court Rooms

Between Thursday night and Friday morning, Jesus appeared before at least 5 different courts who judged Him:

- Annas (John 18:12-24)
- Caiphas (Matthew 26:57-64)
- Pontius Pilate (Luke 23:1-6)
- Herod (Luke 23:8-11)
- Pontius Pilate again (Luke 23:13-23 and Matthew 27:24-26)

"Crucify Him"

When the crowd shouted, "Crucify Him," they were actually saying "Put Him to death on a cross."

Memory Verse

1 Corinthians 5:7 (ESV) - For Christ, our Passover lamb, has been sacrificed.

Praise and Worship

Praise and Worship styles vary greatly around the world. It is the intent of this curriculum that praise and worship songs be selected that best fit the content of this lesson. Recommendations for praise and worship are given and this music can generally be located at www.itunes.com. However, the teacher can feel free to select a similar praise and worship song.

"Arise My Love" by Newsong is recommended for this lesson.

Bible Activity

Ask the children: **"Have you ever been accused of something that you didn't do?"** (Allow time to respond) **How did that make you feel? When Jesus was accused of doing wrong, was He guilty?** (No) **Had Jesus ever done anything wrong?** (No) **Did He try to argue with His accusers? Why not? Let's see what that might have felt like…** Choose one child that volunteers to be the "accused." The teacher will lead the "accusing" of the volunteer. Tell the class that anyone who wants to may bring an accusation, but the volunteer is not to answer in his/her defense. Possible accusations: "Joe stole some food from the market" or "Mary got in trouble at school for hitting someone, and I think we should tell her parents" (Be creative, and get the other kids to join in on each accusation – such as "yes, I saw them do it!" or "that's not all they did, I know something even worse!" After the volunteer has been accused of 2-3 things, ask for a different volunteer to be accused. Let several children have a turn. If you run short of volunteers, let the kids accuse you (teacher) of a few things. Emphasize that it is hard to not defend yourself when you know you have done nothing wrong.

Say: **"We were just playing a little game here, with no consequences."** How much harder would it be if this had been REAL? What if you were accused and you knew you would get a really bad spanking if the teacher believed the story? Or what if you were on trial in a court and the punishment was death? That would be a different story!

Teacher Helps

Bible Memory Activity: Relay Race

Form two teams. Put the memory verse in large letters about ten yards away from the teams. Have children run to the memory verse and read the next word of the verse out loud so that everyone can hear. When each child has read his one word, go back to the team, touch the next person in line, and repeat the process until all words of the verse have been read.

Bible Activity

Make a cross out of construction paper. Learn the Bible verse. The students will then need to sit in chairs in a circle. Everyone must close their eyes. Place the cross under a chair. That student then has a chance to say the verse. If the child can say the verse, he or she gets to place the cross under someone else's chair. Continue until everyone gets a turn.

4) Review the Lesson

Divide the class into two teams. Give the teams one minute to write down as many statements as they can about the appearance of Jesus before unjust judges. Here are a few ideas:

- After the arrest of Jesus, the disciples all fled. Peter followed from a distance but still denied that he knew Jesus when someone asked him about his friendship with Jesus.

- Jesus first appeared before Jewish priests, Annas and Caiphas.

- Then, Jesus appeared before a Roman governor, Pilate.

- The Roman soldiers, the Roman governors, the Jewish leaders, and the Jewish people all mocked and ridiculed Jesus.

- Pilate declared his own innocence, but still had Jesus sentenced to die even though Pilate knew that Jesus had done nothing wrong.

Review the Lesson Activity: One Minute List

The teacher should give two teams one minute each to list as many facts as they can about the lesson.

After the one minute has passed, compare lists and see who has more facts. Be sure that children remember that you are looking for facts.

5) Apply the Lesson

Does it seem fair to you that a guilty person, Barabbas, was acquitted and an innocent person, Jesus Christ, was declared guilty and sent to die? No, it does not seem fair. Justice would soon take place at the cross. It did not seem like justice was happening in these courts. Name one way that justice would soon occur.

Apply the Lesson Activity: Justice

Justice occurred when Jesus died on the cross and forgave sins; 1 John 1:9.

Story Line: Jesus was innocent but the crowds shouted, "Crucify Him!"

99 Adventures in the Bible's Big Story

Timeline: Betrayal and Death

Adventure Number 72
Page 364

Adventure Number 73

Luke 23:26-38 and 1 Corinthians 5:7

Story Line: Jesus died on a cross for our sins.

1) Study the Lesson (before class)

- Crucifixion was a common way to put a criminal to death. However, it was a cruel and usually slow method. A Roman citizen could not be crucified. Crucifixion was reserved for the worst criminals.
- Simon, from northern Africa, was forced to carry the cross when Jesus could not.
- From the sixth hour, noon, until the ninth hour, 3 p.m., there was darkness on the earth.
- The curtain in the Temple torn in half, from top to bottom. This was symbolic, indicating that the common person now had free access to the presence of God.
- Luke verifies that Jesus gave His life, it was not taken from Him. Repeatedly, Luke affirms the innocence of Jesus. In one of the references, Pilate reported that Herod found Jesus innocent also. The centurion at the cross declared that Jesus was innocent.[1]
- A Roman soldier called Jesus a righteous man and showed that Jesus was not guilty of the crimes He was charged with. The Roman soldier praised God.
- Luke notices that many people who observed the death of Jesus mourned for Him.
- No gospel writer records any instance of any woman who opposed Jesus.
- Jesus was crucified on Golgotha, probably a hill outside Jerusalem along a main road.
- The Roman poet Cicero wrote, *"Crucifixion is the most cruel and most hideous of tortures."*[2]

Footnotes - Adventure 73

1. Roy B. Zuck, *A Biblical Theology of the New Testament* (Chicago: Moody Press, 1994), 127.

2. Wayne Haston, *New Testament Chronological Bible Cards*, NT-23.

2) Begin the Lesson

Lay out a game board for review that looks something like this:

Time Line	Story Line	Songs	Memory Verses
100 points	200 points	300 points	400 points
100 points	200 points	300 points	400 points
100 points	200 points	300 points	400 points
100 points	200 points	300 points	400 points
100 points	200 points	300 points	400 points

Go back for each of the last 10 lessons and let the children name the time line for each lesson (100 points), the story line for each lesson (200 points), the song for each lesson (300 points), and the memory verse for each lesson (400 points).

A prize should be given to the winning team. Usually, competition is a fun thing for the children. So, keep them all involved. Depending on the size of your class, you may want to limit each child to only 1 or 2 answers. The reason for this is that a few children will answer all the questions, if you let them.

There will be a total of 10,000 points, 1000 points for each lesson (100 for the time line, 200 for the story line, 300 for the song, and 400 for the memory verse).

Teacher Helps

Begin the Lesson Activity: Bible Jeopardy

Divide the class evenly into two teams. The teams could be:

1) whoever has the most brothers and sisters

2) whoever has the fewest brothers and sisters

This game will be continued with the review at end of the lesson.

3) Teach the Lesson

People use the cross for different reasons. Some people use the cross for jewelry. Some people use the cross for religious reasons. Other people use the cross for protection from accidents.

What does the Christian cross mean to you?

What does the Christian cross mean to your friends?

Tell the Story

On Thursday night and Friday morning, the pressure had mounted on Pilate to do something; either to release Jesus which would infuriate the Jews or he could crucify Jesus as the crowds now demanded. He chose the latter.

So, Jesus went from Pilate's judgment to a place just outside Jerusalem called Skull Hill or Golgotha. He had to carry his own cross which weighed about 100 pounds. He had been beaten and whipped with sharp glass, small pieces of bone, and metal. He had been disfigured so that no one could even recognize Him. He had been stripped of His clothes. On this walk from Pilate to Golgotha, Jesus was derided, belittled, and mocked.

When they arrived at Golgotha, Jesus was placed on this cross. It was now about nine in the morning on Friday. One Roman poet said that the cross was "the most cruel and most hideous of tortures." While Jesus was on the cross, the Roman soldiers divided up His clothes and gambled for them. They offered Jesus a mild painkiller but He refused it.

Usually, death on a cross was slow and took a long time. Sometimes it even took days to die. Some yelled to Jesus, *"Save yourself."* Some mocked Him and said, *"He bragged about tearing the temple down in three days and now He cannot even save Himself."* Others jeered Him and made fun of Him. From noon to 3 in the afternoon, the earth was completely dark. Then at 3 in the afternoon, Jesus groaned out loud, *"My God, My God, why have You abandoned Me?"* Then, He breathed His last breath. At that very moment, there was a great earthquake. Not only that, but the curtain in the temple ripped in two from top to bottom at the same time. One of the Roman soldiers who was guarding Jesus said, *"This has to be the Son of God."*

Later in the afternoon, a man named Joseph went to Pilate and asked if he could take the body of Jesus and place it in a tomb. Pilate granted Joseph's request and so Joseph covered the body of Jesus with clean linens and placed the body in a tomb. It was a brand new tomb and they rolled a large rock in front of the tomb to protect the body of Jesus.

It was just like Isaiah had written 700 years earlier when he wrote about the death of the Christ, *"Surely he has borne our griefs and carried our sorrows; yet we esteemed him stricken, smitten by God, and afflicted. But he was pierced for our transgressions; he was crushed for our iniquities; upon him was the chastisement that brought us peace, and with his wounds we are healed."*

Tell the Story Activity: People at the Cross

The teacher could interview volunteers in the class who would describe how it felt to be at Skull Hill or Golgotha:

- Mary, the mother of Jesus
- The disciples
- A Roman soldier
- A mocker in the crowd
- Simon
- Joseph (who asked Pilate for the body of Jesus)

Memory Verse

1 Peter 3:18 (ESV) - For Christ also suffered once for sins, the righteous for the unrighteous, that he might bring us to God, being put to death in the flesh but made alive in the spirit.

Praise and Worship

Praise and Worship styles vary greatly around the world. It is the intent of this curriculum that praise and worship songs be selected that best fit the content of this lesson. Recommendations for praise and worship are given and this music can generally be located at www.itunes.com. However, the teacher can feel free to select a similar praise and worship song.

"Arise My Love" by Newsong is recommended for this lesson.

Bible Activity

"Show and Know." Bring in as many objects as you can to "show" the children, so they will "know" what really happened on the day of Jesus' crucifixion. Example – 6" long nails, a crown of thorns made from a thorny bush such as a rose bush, dirty rags, a leather whip if you can find or make one, a hollow stick that could be used to beat a criminal.

Optional Activity: Make a "Punishment Substitution" chart. Explain to the class that they will sign this chart and take it home. At home they will explain it to their parents, and if it is acceptable with them, they will take turns bearing the punishment for anything that anyone else in their family does wrong. For example, if Johnny signs up for the first week, and his brother leaves a toy out in the rain and is grounded from TV for a week, Johnny has to take that punishment instead of his brother, even though he didn't do anything wrong. Make a chart for each child, and put enough spaces on it for each person in the family to be the "sin substitute" for one week. Talk about the unfairness of the system, but that Jesus was not concerned about standing up for His own rights, He was concerned about making us right with God! He wanted us to be in heaven with Him one day! Encourage your students to sign up for the first week of this exercise themselves. Their family members can learn from them how it should be done.

Teacher Helps

Memory Verse Activity: The Telephone Game

Memorize this verse using The Telephone Game. Have your class form one line, then whisper into the first person in line a phrase of this verse, have that person repeat the phrase to the next person. Do this until all have quoted the first phrase. Then do the same thing with the second phrase, the third phrase, and so on until you have memorized the verse.

Bible Activity: Punishment Substitution

Week 1 - _____

Week 2 - _____

Week 3 - _____

Week 4 - _____

Week 5 - _____

Week 6 - _____

4) Review the Lesson

Continue your review game for points that you began at the start of the lesson.

- For 100 points, who carried the cross of Jesus? (Simon)
- For 200 points, when was Jesus put on the cross? (9 a.m. on Friday)
- For 300 points, how many criminals were crucified with Jesus? (two)
- For 400 points, who asked Pilate for the body of Jesus after He died? (Joseph)
- Bonus question worth 500 points: What is the theme of this lesson? (Jesus died on a cross for our sins.)

Review the Lesson Activity: Bible Jeopardy

This review activity is a continuation of the review game at the beginning of the lesson.

5) Apply the Lesson

Jesus Christ bore our sins in His body on the cross. He was humiliated and tortured for everyone. The prophecies of the Old Testament (Isaiah 52, 53, and Psalm 22) all clearly were written about Jesus Christ hundreds of years before His actual death.

Next week, we are going to talk about the significance of His death. But, go home, think about it, and come back next week. Your assignment, should you choose to accept it: What is the significance of the death of Jesus Christ on the cross?

Story Line: Jesus died on a cross for our sins.

Adventure Number 74
Luke 23:39-47

Story Line: Jesus Christ forgave a guilty man.

1) Study the Lesson (before class)

- Luke's gospel contains the word "sinner" more than all the other gospels combined. It is found in Matthew five times, Mark also uses "sinner" five times, John uses it four times, but Luke uses the word "sinner" sixteen times. At the cross, there was a sinner who wanted forgiveness.[1]

- Two sinners were nailed to crosses and Jesus was on a cross between them. One of the sinners hurled malicious insults at Jesus and blasphemed Jesus or reviled Him.

- The other sinner recognized that Jesus was God, Luke 23:40. That sinner, a thief, made a magnificent confession. And here, on the cross, Jesus could display that salvation does not happen because a person is good. Obviously, this sinner was not good.[2]

- Jesus also showed that salvation is not a matter of doing good works. This sinner obviously had no time left for good works and could not earn the grace of God.

- Jesus immediately answered the thief on the cross. On that day, the thief would join Jesus in glory. Forgiveness was full and complete. It was not earned.

- Jesus offered His assurance that this would happen. It was not merely a kind response to a dying request. It was the assurance that God could and would offer forgiveness when anyone, such as a thief, would only ask and put his faith in Jesus Christ.

- Luke's record of the crucifixion contains imagery from the Psalms and Isaiah. Five such allusions exist (Luke 23:34 alluding to Isaiah 53:12, Luke 23:35 alluding to Psalm 22:6-7, Luke 23:36 alluding to Psalm 69:21-22. Luke 23:46 alluding to Psalm 31:5, and Luke 23:46 to Psalm 22:1).[3]

Footnotes - Adventure 74

1. John Phillips, *Exploring the Gospel of Luke: An Expository Commentary*, 291.

2. Ibid., 292.

3. Roy B. Zuck, *A Biblical Theology of the New Testament*, 128.

2) Begin the Lesson

The teacher should gather all the songs that have been used in the Adventures in the Bible's Big Story and play several of them.

The class should be able to sing along with the teacher the songs that they have previously learned in this curriculum.

After the teacher has played several songs and the class and sung them, play the game, "Name That Tune." "Name That Tune" is a game in which the students will attempt to match the song with the Bible adventure that best matches the song. The teacher should use extreme graciousness to encourage the class when an answer is given.

The purpose of this activity is for kids to associate music they have learned with events in the Bible. The teacher should stay focused on this primary purpose.

3) Teach the Lesson

Can it be that simple?

Suppose you were reading the Bible for the first time and you read about a very evil man who never performed good deeds, yet God promised to receive this man into God's wonderful paradise simply because the man uttered a brief and simple expression of faith.

What would you think?

Teacher Helps

Review Activity: Name That Tune

The teacher should play songs that the class has learned for the previous Bible adventures. Children should guess which adventures in the Bible's big story best match the song that is being played or sung.

If time permits, the teacher could also ask if there are phrases or words in any of the songs that the children do not understand.

Tell the Story

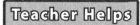

The place was Skull Hill. The time was shortly after noon on a Friday. The event was the crucifixion of three people, two criminals and Someone who had done nothing wrong. That Someone was Jesus Christ and His cross was located in the middle. A criminal was on either side of Him. All three were experiencing excruciating pain. That is what happens when someone dies on a cross ... pain that is unbearable. The Romans used this kind of death penalty to humiliate the worst of criminals.

While Jesus and the two criminals were hanging in unbearable pain on the cross, the two criminals began what probably would be their last talk, ever. They talked about the Christ who was between them. One criminal told Jesus, "Come down off the cross if You were really the Messiah. Save yourself and us too!" The other criminal told him to be quiet. He explained to the other criminal that they were both getting what they deserved, the death penalty. But Jesus had done nothing wrong.

Then, the criminal who defended Jesus turned to Jesus and said, *"Remember me when you enter your kingdom."* Jesus simply responded, *"Today, you will be with Me in paradise."* It was that simple ... a statement of "faith" by the repentant criminal and he was guaranteed by Jesus a place in paradise. He had done nothing to deserve this and he could do nothing in the future. Yet, Jesus saw his repentant heart and He heard his statement of faith.

Just a few simple words by an evil man. No act of righteousness, no position of religious responsibility, and certainly no merit of his own could earn this criminal a place in eternal bliss.

Simple faith ... that was all. It was just like in the days of Moses when Moses held up a bronze snake and those who had been bitten by poisonous snakes could be healed by faith if they just looked at the bronze snake that Moses held up.

Simple faith ... that was all. It was just like in the days of Abraham when Abraham believed God and it was credited to him as righteousness.

Simple faith ... that was all. It was just like in the days of Cain and Abel when Abel by faith brought his best offering and God accepted it.

Simple faith ... even from a criminal. Jesus Christ was looking for faith in Him and repentance from evil deeds. The one criminal had both ... paradise!

Tell the Story Activity: Newspaper Reporters

The teacher could ask for three volunteers to write an article for the newspaper and submit his or her article for publication next week. The reporters should include interviews with:

- Jesus
- The two criminals

Next week, have children read their newspaper article and try to publish it somehow, if only for your own class.

Memory Verse

Luke 23:42 (ESV) - And he said, "Jesus, remember me when you come into your kingdom."

Praise and Worship

Praise and Worship styles vary greatly around the world. It is the intent of this curriculum that praise and worship songs be selected that best fit the content of this lesson. Recommendations for praise and worship are given and this music can generally be located at www.itunes.com. However, the teacher can feel free to select a similar praise and worship song.

"Arise My Love" by Newsong is recommended for this lesson.

Bible Activity

Bring in a variety of different keys, and (if possible) a lock that fits one of them. Have keys that look different from each other. Show the keys to the class, then ask the kids: **"What are some things that people think are the key to someday having a home in heaven?"** Possible answers: doing good things, being baptized, going to church, being a good person, giving money to charities, etc. Explain that just like a lock has only one key that will open it, the key to heaven is only one truth, which is found in God's word, the Bible. Tell the first part of the story, about the thief on the cross being promised a home in heaven with Jesus. Refer back to the answers that were given at the beginning of class. "Did the thief on the cross do any good things (mention some good things they could relate to, such as visiting sick people in the hospital, helping feed hungry people, etc.) Hold up the first key and say: "That must not have been the key to heaven." Did he go to church? No. Did he get baptized? No. Each time, hold up another key and say: **"That must not have been the key to heaven."**

So then, if none of these things are the keys to heaven, what DID he do? Go back and re-read the passage and help the children see that it was his repentance and faith in Jesus that was the key to having a home in heaven. If you have a lock that fits one of the keys, show it at this time, and say: "Just like this key is the only one that will open this lock, repentance (being truly sorry for your sins) and faith in Jesus is the only thing that God will accept."

Teacher Helps

Memory Verse Activity: Graffiti

Graffiti can also be used to help children memorize this verse. Write each word of this verse on a separate piece of paper. Then have children put the words in order in groups of 2 or 3. When each group can put the verse together in order, they will probably have this verse memorized.

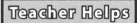

4) Review the Lesson

Review the lesson in small groups. What are seven main facts or ideas that come out of this lesson? One adult leader should join each small group of kids. Let the children do most of the discovering. Help them when necessary.

- Two criminals that were crucified with Jesus deserved death.
- Jesus had done nothing wrong and did not deserve this death penalty.
- The pain on the cross was unbearable.
- The two criminals began a discussion about Jesus Christ.
- One criminal mocked Jesus and told Him to come down off the cross.
- The other criminal turned to Jesus in faith.
- Jesus welcomed the repentant criminal into eternal paradise.

Review the Lesson Activity: Seven Main Facts

The teacher should have the class break up into groups of 2 or 3. Have them tell each other about the 7 main ideas in the lesson which are listed to your left. For younger children, or non-readers, the teacher should help them.

5) Apply the Lesson

Last week, the assignment was to determine what the significance of the death of Jesus Christ was. The teacher should discuss that with the class.

The significance of the death of Jesus Christ is this: He has the power and ability to welcome into eternal happiness those who come to Him by faith alone. Simple faith in Who He is and what He has done, that is it!

Story Line: Jesus Christ forgave a guilty man.

Adventure Number 75
Luke 24:1-12 and 36-43

Story Line: Jesus rose from the dead. Jesus has power over death.

1) Study the Lesson (before class)

- The women brought spices to the tomb as a symbol of love and respect.[1]

- When the women got to the tomb, they found the large stone rolled away from the entrance and the body missing. Two men dressed in gleaming clothes, certainly angels, appeared to them and told them that Jesus Christ had risen from the dead, just as He said He would.

- The women entered the tomb boldly but soon were filled with doubts. Who had tampered with the tomb? Who had removed the body? Was it the priests? Had they taken that blessed body away to desecrate it?[2]

- While the women remembered what Jesus said, the men didn't. In fact, Peter ran to the empty tomb and when he got there, he wondered how this could happen.

- Then, Jesus appeared on a road to two people. He did not have an imaginary body, like a ghost, because the disciples could touch Him and He ate food. Yet, He did not have a body like ours because He was able to appear or disappear. He had a glorified, perfect body which is immortal.

- When Jesus rose from the dead, He did what no other person had ever done or will ever do. He conquered death. This is proof that He is the great "Satan Crusher" of Genesis 3:15.

- When Jesus rose from the dead, He showed His followers all the facts from the Old Testament that demonstrated He was indeed the Messiah.

- Because of His death and resurrection, the message of repentance and forgiveness was to be proclaimed to the world by those who believed His message.

Footnotes - Adventure 75

1. James Galvin, *Life Application Bible Notes*, 1598.

2. John Phillips, *Exploring the Gospel of Luke: An Expository Commentary*, 296.

2) Begin the Lesson

Ask children to help you with previous memory verses. Maybe say something like, **"Who remembers what (verse) says?"**

- Adventure Number 61: Mark 4:40
- Adventure Number 62: Luke 4:36
- Adventure Number 63: John 10:28
- Adventure Number 64: John 8:12
- Adventure Number 65: Luke 15:10
- Adventure Number 66: Matthew 25:46
- Adventure Number 67: John 11:25
- Adventure Number 68: John 12:24
- Adventure Number 69: Matthew 24:24
- Adventure Number 70: John 14:6
- Adventure Number 71: Matthew 26:56
- Adventure Number 72: 1 Corinthians 5:7
- Adventure Number 73: 1 Peter 3:18
- Adventure Number 74: Luke 23:42

Begin the Lesson Activity: Memory Verse Review

The last 14 memory verses are given here. Divide the children up into two teams and see which team can tell you the most memory verses. Bonus points should be given if each team can recite more than the last 14 memory verses.

Give the teams five minutes and they must work together.

The teacher can provide a few helps.

3) Teach the Lesson

The teacher should prepare the classroom for a party. The class is going to have a celebration today. The teacher should have party music playing as the class comes in. There could be snacks and maybe even special gifts for each person.

The teacher should tell the class that today is a day to celebrate. In Bible times, the disciples were sad when Jesus died. But, their sadness turned to celebration. Why?

 ## Tell the Story

Teacher Helps

After Jesus was placed in the new tomb on Friday afternoon, the city settled down. There was great sadness by some who had followed Jesus. On Sunday morning, several women went to the cemetery where Jesus was buried. For some unknown reason, they even took with them burial spices that they had prepared for the body of Jesus. When they got to the tomb, two men appeared to them out of nowhere. A very bright light surrounded them. They had to be angels. The women were amazed and fell down. The angels even questioned the women. *"Why are you looking for the Living One in a cemetery?"* The angels reminded the women of something Jesus said earlier while they were in Galilee. Jesus told them that He would be handed over to sinners, killed on a cross, and then raised from the dead. When the angels reminded them of the words of Jesus, it all made sense to them. They remembered what Jesus told them.

So much for the city settling down! The women hurried back to tell the men the good news ... Jesus had risen from the dead, just like He said He would! When they told the apostles, they didn't believe a word of what they said. However, Peter and John ran to the tomb. John ran faster than Peter. When Peter arrived at the tomb, he was puzzled. He looked in the empty tomb and saw a few grave clothes ... that was it.

Later, Jesus appeared to two men on a road to Emmaus, about 7 miles from Jerusalem. He also appeared to Peter. The risen Christ had now appeared to at least five women, two men on the road to Emmaus, and Peter.

Jesus Christ had risen from the dead. He was the great Satan Conqueror that God promised to Adam and Eve. His promises came true. Death had lost its power. In the moment of His resurrection, God the Father demonstrated that He is more powerful than Satan.

At first the disciples thought the resurrection of Jesus was a fairy tale. They did not believe it. Then, they were puzzled about the early reports from the women and went to check out the reports. Later, they encountered the resurrected Christ and saw personally for themselves that He had risen from the dead. Lastly, the disciples devoted themselves to serving Jesus Christ as the Lord and Master of their lives. They knew that He had lived, died, and conquered death. They knew that He was God and they gave their lives to serve Him based on two simple facts: Jesus Christ rose from the dead and He has power over death!

Tell the Story Activity: Mary Magdalene

The teacher should ask for volunteers. These volunteers are needed to act out this story.

- Mary Magdalene and four other women

- Peter, John, and other disciples

- An angel

After the teacher has told the story, have these volunteers reenact the story.

Timeline: Victory and Life

Memory Verse

Luke 24:6 (ESV) - He is not here, but has risen. Remember how he told you, while he was still in Galilee.

Praise and Worship

Praise and Worship styles vary greatly around the world. It is the intent of this curriculum that praise and worship songs be selected that best fit the content of this lesson. Recommendations for praise and worship are given and this music can generally be located at www.itunes.com. However, the teacher can feel free to select a similar praise and worship song.

"Arise My Love" by Newsong is recommended for this lesson.

Bible Activity

As Christians we celebrate one day of the year more than any other. Do you know what day that is? Easter! Easter is the day when Jesus rose from the dead. A rich man named Joseph asked to bury the body of Jesus. Friends brought spices to take care of the burial customs. The Jewish custom at that time was to take strips of linen and wrap them around the body of a dead person, and then the burial spices were poured over the strips of linen and hardened in place like a plaster cast would on a broken arm today. Hold up the stick (or pencil) and say, let's pretend this stick is an arm or leg. If you have a band-aid, wrap it around the stick with the sticky side OUT so that it doesn't stick to the stick. Tell the rest of the story, and when you get to the part where the disciples found the grave clothes empty, slip the bandage off the stick and hold it up so they can see the hollow area where the stick used to be. The clothes were there, but Jesus was gone, He had risen!!

Teacher Helps

Bible Memory Activity

Review the verse a few times then divide the children into two or more teams. Have the teams form lines across from a chalk or white board or piece of paper on a chair. Place something to write with at the board in front of each team. Have the first child of each team run to the board and write the first word of the verse, then run back to the line. The next child of the team will write the next word and it will continue until the verse is completed. Allow all teams to finish before playing again.

4) Review the Lesson

Have children simplify the lesson into 10 words or less using their own words. What are their answers? When children simplify the story of the lesson into ten words or less, they will probably say something like these possibilities:

- Jesus Christ rose from the dead.
- Jesus Christ is alive.
- Death has no power over Jesus.
- After three days, Jesus rose again.
- Jesus appeared to many people after His resurrection.
- The tomb could not hold the Christ.
- Jesus has more power than Satan.
- Jesus is the great Satan Conqueror.

Review the Lesson Activity: Simplify

Simplify can be a useful game for the children. The teacher can give each team of 2 or 3 kids about 1-2 minutes to come up with the most significant 10 words of this lesson.

5) Apply the Lesson

The resurrection of Jesus Christ is proof that God offers good news to all who will put their faith in Him. He is the Almighty Creator who desires to have a personal relationship with each of us. As Adam and Eve sinned, so all of us have sinned and fallen short of the glory of God. Our punishment is physical, spiritual, and eternal death in the Lake of Fire. But, God demonstrated His love toward us in that while we were still sinners, Christ died for us. He rose again so that we could have life. Put your trust in Him!

Story Line: Jesus rose from the dead. Jesus has power over death.

Adventure Number 76
Luke 24:13-35 and 1 Corinthians 15:3-8

Story Line: Jesus appeared to many people after His resurrection.

 1) Study the Lesson (before class)

- Because this was Passover week, there were many Jews in Jerusalem from all over the nation of Israel. The death and resurrection of Jesus not only affected the disciples, the entire nation was interested. News about the death of Jesus spread all over the Roman empire.[1]

- In I Corinthians 15:3, Paul says he is merely passing along the information he had previously received, so the creed must be dated prior to A. D. 55. When exactly did Paul learn of the creed? The most probable explanation is found in Galatians 1, where Paul says he spent about two weeks with Peter and James confirming the message of the Gospel. Paul says this event took place three years after his conversion. So at a maximum, the creed existed three years after Paul's conversion, which is generally thought to have happened one or two years after Jesus' death. This is amazing evidence, but for the creed to exist at Paul's Jerusalem meeting, it had to have started even earlier.

- We do not have any written documentation from the life of Alexander the Great until 300 years after his death, yet we have a consensus of scholars that people claimed to see the risen Jesus a mere 2 years after the event!

- Like Paul, James knew the fate of those who turned from Judaism to Christianity. After becoming one of the most prominent leaders in the early church, James was martyred for his faith. So, we have 2 examples of men who did not believe in Jesus and shortly after His death came to believe that He was God incarnate. They made this radical change in belief despite knowing that their decision would cause significant persecution, possibly even a gruesome death.

Footnotes - Adventure 76

1. James Galvin, *Life Application Bible Notes*, 1742.

2. Lynn Solem and Bob Pike, *50 Creative Training Closers*, 70.

2) Begin the Lesson

Let's think back over the all of our lessons that we have studied and see if we can put the lessons in order. Here are the themes for some of the lessons:

1) God is very strong.

5) Life in the garden was full of pleasure.

10) Sin affected God's creation in many negative ways.

15) The people were evil. God sent a flood. Noah trusted and obeyed God.

20) God told Abraham to sacrifice Isaac. God provided a ram instead.

25) God sent plagues in Egypt to set free the Israelites.

30) God told the Israelites to build a tent where they could meet Him and offer sacrifices.

35) People who followed God were to be completely loyal and obedient to Him.

40) God chose David to be a king. God will one day choose a Man to be King forever.

45) Prophets told about Jesus 700 years before He came to earth.

50) The Jews returned to Jerusalem to rebuild the walls.

55) Satan tempted Jesus. Jesus did not sin.

60) Many people began to follow Jesus because of His teaching and miracles.

65) God forgave a wayward son, a selfish brother, and a humble tax collector.

70) Jesus gave His disciples valuable instructions and comforting promises.

75) Jesus rose from the dead. Jesus has power over death.

Begin the Lesson Activity: Story Line Review

The teacher should write these statements on pieces of paper and then mix them up. Do not put the number of the lesson on the piece of paper. Divide the children into 2 or 3 teams, depending on the size of the class. Time how long it takes each team to put the statements in the correct order. Do not number the slips of paper.

3) Teach the Lesson

Discuss this statement with your class: *"If Christ is risen, nothing else matters. And if Christ is not risen – nothing else matters."* - Jaroslav Pelikan

Let's learn about people who were dramatically affected by the resurrection of Jesus Christ.

Tell the Story

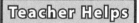

As Jesus died on the cross, Jesus asked John to take care of His mother. He did this, presumably, because James, the Lord's half brother, was not there. He had fled. James was not grieving the death of Jesus, he was not even there. Paul was not grieving the death of Jesus. In fact, Paul heavily persecuted Christians. These men later gave their lives for Jesus Christ. James was killed for his faith by Herod in Jerusalem and Paul died in a lonely jail cell in Rome. What changed?

Women were the first eyewitnesses at the empty tomb. In those days, women were not credible sources of truth. If Paul and the gospel writers were making up a lie, they would not have stated that women were the first eyewitnesses at the empty tomb. No reliable author would do that. To state that women were the first eyewitnesses at the tomb means that Paul and the other gospel writers knew the testimony of these women was true.

Paul's letter to the Corinthians stated that the risen Christ appeared to several individuals, a small group, and a large group. Without identifying them, Paul stated to the Corinthians that most of them were still alive. If Paul and the gospel writers were making up a myth, they would not state that so many people who saw the risen Christ were still alive. There would be too much contradictory evidence if this story was a myth. In essence, Paul is saying, "If you doubt that Jesus rose from the dead, feel free to go talk to all of these eyewitnesses. They were there when He appeared and can tell you about it."

The two men on the road to Emmaus knew that the tomb was empty but they did not understand the significance of the empty tomb. They were filled with sadness and confusion. However, the risen Christ met these men on the road and explained to them from all the Scriptures all things concerning Himself. At the end of this discussion, they were convinced that Jesus was the Christ and that He had risen from the dead.

The quantity of the witnesses, over 500, leads us to believe that Christ rose from the dead. The early church experienced significant growth because they knew that Jesus Christ had risen from the dead. Men and women were witnesses of this fact. Large numbers of people were witnesses of this fact. Those who had abandoned the Lord now gave their lives for Him. Why? They knew that Jesus Christ had risen from the dead. Those who would not travel to Skull Hill went to various parts of the world with this Good News. Why? They knew that Jesus Christ had risen from the dead.

Tell the Story Activity: Eyewitness Reporters

The teacher should ask for volunteers to name all the people who were eyewitnesses to the resurrection of Christ.

What do we know about them <u>before</u> the resurrection?

- Doubt
- Confusion
- Abandoned Christ

What do we know about them <u>after</u> the resurrection?

- Confidence
- Solidarity
- Gave their lives for the risen Christ

Memory Verse

Luke 24:27 (ESV) - And beginning with Moses and all the Prophets, he interpreted to them in all the Scriptures the things concerning himself.

Praise and Worship

Praise and Worship styles vary greatly around the world. It is the intent of this curriculum that praise and worship songs be selected that best fit the content of this lesson. Recommendations for praise and worship are given and this music can generally be located at www.itunes.com. However, the teacher can feel free to select a similar praise and worship song.

"Arise My Love" by Newsong is recommended for this lesson.

Bible Activity

Activity – Courtroom

Today the class is going to pretend that they are in a courtroom, with a judge. The case before the class today is: "True or False: Did Jesus really rise from the dead?"

Appoint one child to be the judge. Others can be witnesses, others can be a jury, or whatever legal process is normal in the place where your children live. The judge should say: "I now call this court to order, to hear the case of "Did Jesus really rise from the dead?" Each witness comes forward and states a fact about the resurrection from the lesson (See "tell the story" section for ideas.) The students should share as if they were really there (example: "I saw Jesus myself"- as one of the 500 witnesses, or "I was one of the disciples who met Jesus in the upper room after He came back to life.")

After all have spoken, the judge will say: "I find this fact to be supported by overwhelming evidence. Jesus really did rise from the dead!"

Teacher Helps

Memory Verse Activity: Bean Bag Toss

With masking tape, mark off a large square on the floor, about 36 inches. Connect the opposite corners inside the square with tape to form an "X." If you have space and many students, make a second square. Give each section a number value (1,2,3,4). A bit of a distance away, put a line of tape to mark where the student will throw from. Divide into two teams. Each student takes a turn throwing a bean bag into one of the sections. (You may make a bean bag by putting beans in a sock and closing it tight with a rubber band. Take the long part of the sock and fold it over the bean section.) If they can say the verse correctly, their team scores the amount of the section where the bean bag was thrown.

4) Review the Lesson

The teacher should have the class think of the main ideas of the lesson that they want to take home. Then they should number off 1 through 5. Number 1 should say tell the main thing that he or she learned from the lesson. All five groups should get an opportunity to share the main thing they learned from this lesson.

Ideas might include:
- Many people were eyewitnesses of the resurrected Christ.
- Men and women reported what they saw concerning the resurrected Christ.
- Men who had abandoned Christ at the crucifixion gave their lives to the resurrected Christ.
- Jesus died, was buried, and rose again for our sins.

Teacher Helps

Review the Lesson Activity: Repetition[2]

The teacher should allow about 5 minutes for children to share the main thing that they learned. If more than 5 children are in the class, allow for each of the groups to share with each other.

5) Apply the Lesson

When the two men on the road to Emmaus from Jerusalem realized who the resurrected Christ was, they learned from Him that *"repentance and forgiveness of sins should be proclaimed in His name to all the nations."*

- Find one person to share the good news.

- Tell one person that there is a God who forgives sins if they repent.

Story Line: Jesus appeared to many people after His resurrection.

Adventure Number 77

Matthew 28:16-20, Mark 16:15: Luke 24:44-48; John 20:21; Acts 1:8

Story Line: Many times, Jesus told His followers to take His message to all people.

1) Study the Lesson (before class)

- On at least three different occasions after His resurrection, Jesus commanded His disciples to take the message of His death, burial, and resurrection to the world.[1]
- Key elements of the Great Commission passages are:
    - The disciples were sent by Jesus Christ.
    - It was assumed by the Lord that the disciples would be going.
    - Proclamation or delivering the good news was commanded.
    - The disciples were to take the Gospel to every nation.
    - True repentance by people and forgiveness by God were at the heart of the message.
    - The message came from understanding the Scriptures.
    - The disciples had authority from God to go with the message to the entire world.
    - The message was divine in origination, global in scope, Christ-centered, Scripture-based, Trinitarian, and has the help of the resurrected Christ.
- Great Commission roots are also found in the Old Testament. Passages such as Genesis 12:1-3 and Psalm 96:3 exhort God's people to declare God's message to the nations.
- "The promise of Genesis 12:3 comes true as the missionaries of the Christian church extend the message of the gospel to all the families of the earth." -John Piper[2]

Footnotes - Adventure 77

1. Wayne Haston, *The Roots of Faith New Testament Workbook*, 27-C.

2. Ibid.

3. Susan Lingo, *Written on Our Hearts*, 92.

2) Begin the Lesson

Eight essential truths have emerged from the Bible's big story of hope. Challenge children to know the eight truths, know them in order, and be able to give a brief description of each.

1. <u>God</u>. In the beginning, there was a very powerful God.

2. <u>Man</u>. God created people to be His special friends.

3. <u>Sin</u>. Man and woman disobeyed God.

4. <u>Death</u>. God punished man and woman for their disobedience. Death, in the Bible, refers to separation.

5. <u>Christ</u>. God sent His one and only Son who lived a perfect life.

6. <u>Cross</u>. Jesus died on the cross for the sins of the world.

7. <u>Faith</u>. If anyone places their faith in Christ, God welcomes them.

8. <u>Life</u>. God gives eternal life to those who put their faith in Him.

Teacher Helps

Begin the Lesson Activity: Eight Essential Truths

Write the eight essential truths on pieces of paper and place them face down. Do the same with the brief descriptions. Now, create 2 or 3 teams and have them put the truths and descriptions in the correct order. Time them and give a reward to the winning team.

Remind the class where these truths can be found in Scripture.

3) Teach the Lesson

The teacher should ask the class, **"What are some important messages that your parents or your teachers have given you?"** Let the children discuss some of the most important things they have been told.

Then, the teacher should ask them, **"Did you ever have to be reminded to do what you were told to do?"** Again, let the children discuss this.

Today's lesson is about a very important message that Jesus Christ gave to His followers. By many people, it is called the Great Commission. The word "commission" means *"authority to act for, in behalf of, or in place of another; a task or matter entrusted to one as an agent for another."* Jesus has given believers a task to do. What is that task?

Tell the Story

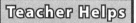

At least 500 people had seen the resurrected Christ. They knew that He was alive. Now what were they supposed to do? Did Jesus Christ have a task for them? Did He just expect them to sit around in the Upper Room until He came back for them like He said that He would do?

No ... no ... no! He had a job for them. He tasked them on at least three different occasions to do the same job. After the resurrection, Jesus met the 11 disciples on top of a mountain in Galilee. Jesus had set up the appointment and the eleven met Him. When they got to the mountain, Jesus met them and they worshipped Him. On top of the mountain in Galilee, Jesus told the disciples that He had authority to give them their next task. That task was to make disciples of all the nations. He would be with them ... He would not leave them alone. He even gave them three specifics ideas on how to make disciples: go, baptize, and teach.

On another occasion, the eleven disciples were reclining at a table. A couple of guys had told them that Jesus was alive. They had seen and talked to Him. But the eleven did not believe them. Shortly after that, Jesus appeared to them and rebuked the eleven for not believing. He wanted them to have faith in Him but they did not, at least, not yet. Then, Jesus told them to go into all the world and proclaim the good news to all people. Just like Jesus did up north in Galilee, He gave them a job to do. Jesus told them that as the Father sent Him, so Jesus was sending the disciples. He was sending them to the people of the world with a message of forgiveness.

The last time that the disciples saw the resurrected Christ was while they were on the Mount of Olives, just outside of Jerusalem. Jesus appeared to them again. They wondered about the coming kingdom of Jesus. "Was this the time that Jesus would set up His kingdom on earth?" they thought. Again, Jesus told them that He had a job for them to do. They were to be His witnesses in Jerusalem, Judea, Samaria, and to the ends of the earth. The disciples were to spread the message to an ever widening circle. The message was not only for their own city, Jerusalem, it was for their regional area of Judea. The message was not only for their city and their region, it was also for the outcasts of Samaria. The message was not only for their city, their region, and some nearby outcasts, it was for the entire world. The disciples had a job to do. It is called the "Great Commission" or the great job of telling other people about Jesus Christ. Kids can do the same job. They can go to other kids and adults with the wonderful message that brings hope ... hope to anyone who will put their faith in Jesus and repent of their sin!

Tell the Story Activity: 3 Locations of the Great Commission

The teacher should note that at least three locations are given regarding the great commission.

Jesus met the disciples on a mountain in Galilee.

- Matthew 28:16-20

Mark, Luke and John all talk about an upper room. It is possible that these three writers were not describing the same situation.

- Luke 24:44-48
- John 20:21
- Mark 16:15

Luke tells Theophilus that the disciples were on the Mount of Olives when the Lord met them.

- Acts 1:8

Memory Verse

Matthew 28:19 (ESV) - Go therefore and make disciples of all nations, baptizing them in the name of the Father and of the Son and of the Holy Spirit.

Praise and Worship

Praise and Worship styles vary greatly around the world. It is the intent of this curriculum that praise and worship songs be selected that best fit the content of this lesson. Recommendations for praise and worship are given and this music can generally be located at www.itunes.com. However, the teacher can feel free to select a similar praise and worship song.

"Jesus, Thank You" by Sovereign Grace Music is recommended for this lesson.

Bible Activity

Tell Good News

Ask your class if anyone had something really great happen this week. Allow responses. Children love to share what is going on in their lives. Talk about how exciting it is to share good news. What if you knew the secret to curing cancer (or another disease your children can relate to)? Would you keep the great news to yourself? No! Of course not!

What if you couldn't explain it perfectly? Would you say nothing at all? No! It's too important to keep to yourself! What if you knew the only way people could be sure of going to heaven when they die? Isn't eternity more important than living a few more years here on earth? Yes! So why don't we share the good news of the gospel with people? Most likely the idea of fear will come up. Let's practice telling the story so we will be ready when someone needs to hear it from us.

Pass out the 8 words that are the essential truths to 8 kids. Let them tell the story together. Encourage them to practice at home, so they can be ready to share the best news of all.

Teacher Helps

Memory Verse Activity: Scripture Card Battle[3]

Divide your class up into groups of 2 or 3. Give each group a set of cards. On each card is one word from the memory verse. Groups should try to put the words of the memory verse in the right order.

4) Review the Lesson

"Who" Questions:

1. Who saw the resurrected Christ?

2. Who was in the upper room?

"What" Questions:

1. What did Jesus tell the disciples that their job was?

2. What did Jesus tell them on the Mount of Olives?

"When" Questions:

1. When did Jesus appear to the disciples?

2. When did the disciples wonder about the coming kingdom of Jesus?

"Where" Questions:

1. Where is Galilee?

2. Where is the Mount of Olives?

"Why" Questions:

1. Why can kids do the same job of sharing the good news?

2. Why did some of the disciples not believe that Jesus had risen from the dead?

Teacher Helps

Review Activity: The Investigative Cube

Divide the class up into two teams. Make a cube with these labels on each side of the cube: who, what, when, where, why. When the cube is rolled to one team, they will answer the type of question that is face up on the cube. For instance, if the "why" is face up on the cube, then that team will answer a "why" question. Teachers can make up their own questions from the lesson, only they must pertain to this lesson.

5) Apply the Lesson

There is a job to do for all of us. That job is called the Great Commission and it was given to us by Jesus Christ. Ask, "What kids will be willing to tell the story of Jesus Christ?"

Let kids volunteer and then help them tell the eight basic truths.

Story Line: Many times, Jesus told His followers to take His message to all people.

Timeline: Victory and Life

Adventure Number 78

1 Corinthians 15:3-8 and Acts 1:6-11

Story Line: Jesus returned to heaven to prepare a place for believers.

 ## 1) Study the Lesson (before class)

- Psalm 16:10 and Isaiah 53:8-10 verify that Jesus Christ had to die for our sins and be raised from the dead.

- The gospel is clearly stated in 1 Corinthians 15:3-8. Jesus Christ died for our sins, was buried, and rose again.

- The fact that He was buried verified His death. The fact that He was seen by others verified His resurrection.

- The 500 brothers mentioned in 1 Corinthians 15 as having seen Jesus were those who received the Great Commission in Matthew 28:18-20 and Acts 1:3-11. Since most of these were still alive when Paul wrote 1 Corinthians, they could be consulted about the resurrection and ascension of Jesus.[1]

- Paul (Acts 9:3-6) and James (John 7:5 and Acts 11:14) probably both came to faith in Christ because of resurrection appearances by Jesus. The resurrection of Jesus was not just a theoretical appearance by those who wanted to have faith in Jesus.

- The people who believed in God were told to make disciples of all the nations (Matthew 28:18-20). However, they were to wait for the power of the Holy Spirit (Acts 1:8). The power of God was reserved for those who would work for Him.

- The disciples wanted to know when His kingdom would come to earth. But Jesus wanted His disciples to be witnesses of Him first. The kingdom would come later, working for Him was a priority.

Footnotes - Adventure 78

1. John Walvoord and Roy Zuck, *Bible Knowledge Commentary: New Testament*, 542.

2. Susan Lingo, *Written on Our Hearts*, 99.

2) Begin the Lesson

Teacher Helps

Time Line	People	Event
Beginnings	God	God made all things.
Beginnings	Adam and Eve	Sin
Beginnings	Noah	Worldwide flood
Beginnings	wicked people	Confused languages
Beginnings of a Nation	Abraham	Special promises by God
Beginnings of a Nation	Moses	Plagues
Possessing the Land	Joshua	Enter Promised Land
Possessing the Land	Gideon	Cycles of sin
United Kingdom	David	A special King forever
Divided Kingdom	Elijah and Elisha	Special prophets in Israel
Taken from Home	Jeremiah, Daniel, Ezekiel	Israel sent to Assyria
Return to Home	Nehemiah and Ezra	Israel returned to land
Return to Home	Daniel	400 years of change
Early Life of Jesus	Mary and Joseph	The birth of Jesus
Ministry of Jesus Christ	12 disciples	Jesus called 12 apostles
Ministry of Jesus Christ	Jesus	Miracles of Jesus
Opposition	Blind man	Healing power of Jesus
Betrayal and Death	Jesus Christ	Entry into Jerusalem
Victory and Life	Resurrected Christ	Empty tomb

Begin the Lesson Activity: Match Time Line, People, and Events

The teacher should form three stacks of paper. One stack should be the "time line" stack. 18 different time lines should be underneath this "time line" piece of paper. Do the same thing for "people" and "event." Then mix them up and have the children arrange them so that they have the correct time period with the correct people with the correct event. For instance, when matched correctly, beginnings, God, and God made all things should all be in the same group.

3) Teach the Lesson

Jesus Christ left believers with a job to do. That job was to take the good news to the world. However, Jesus left earth and also had a job to do.

What possible jobs do you think Jesus could do in heaven?

Tell the Story

The resurrected Christ was preparing to leave the earth. He knew that He had 40 days to deliver His final messages to His special friends. He told them several times that He had a job for them to do. They were to spread the good news that He died, was buried, and rose again. They were to take that message around the world. Everybody needed to know this message, not just the Jews.

On the fortieth day after His resurrection, He was preparing to leave them. He gave them their final assignment: wait in Jerusalem for the promised Holy Spirit. But, before He left, the disciples had a question for Him. In the past, they had wanted to know who was the greatest ... which one of them would be in charge when Jesus left. Even their mothers got involved in this discussion. But this question was about the setting up of His kingdom. The disciples were curious. Was this the time for the kingdom of Christ on earth? If it was, they were ready for it. They knew that Jesus had all power. He had just conquered death. No one had ever done that before.

The response of Jesus was interesting. He told them that they do not get to know when the kingdom is coming. What they needed to do was stay focused on the task He had already given them and would give them one more time. "You shall be my witnesses," He told them. These were His last words. Then, He left and ascended to heaven right in front of them. It had to be an awesome sight to see Jesus rise from the ground and disappear into the clouds!

When Jesus got to heaven, He sat down at the right hand of the Father. He promised to pray regularly for believers and that is what He is doing right now. He sat at the most privileged place ... the right hand of God Almighty! One thousand years earlier, David said this would happen.

Now, Jesus is a High Priest forever.

He is a sympathetic High Priest ... He understands our weaknesses because He was tempted like we are.

He is a sufficient High Priest ... He can save completely those who come to faith in Him.

He is a faithful High Priest ... Because of the blood that He shed, God accepted His payment for our sins. Jesus is the great High Priest!

Teacher Helps

Tell the Story Activity: One Lord, One Faith, One Job

The teacher should tell the class to listen for the last words of Jesus Christ to His disciples.

Ask your class before and after the "Tell the Story" section, **"What did Jesus tell His disciples to do?"**

- "Be my witnesses."

Ask your class after the "Tell the Story" section, **"What is Jesus doing right now for believers?"**

- Praying

- Saving those who put their faith in Him

- Understanding our weaknesses

Memory Verse

Acts 1:8 (ESV) - But you will receive power when the Holy Spirit has come upon you, and you will be my witnesses in Jerusalem and in all Judea and Samaria, and to the end of the earth.

Praise and Worship

Praise and Worship styles vary greatly around the world. It is the intent of this curriculum that praise and worship songs be selected that best fit the content of this lesson. Recommendations for praise and worship are given and this music can generally be located at www.itunes.com. However, the teacher can feel free to select a similar praise and worship song.

"Jesus, Thank You" by Sovereign Grace Music is recommended for this lesson.

Bible Activity

Bring in a history book, if possible. Look at a historical event with which your children would be familiar. (Example: a political leader's life, a war in your country that happened many years ago, even a sporting event that happened before the children were born, as long as it is something that is accepted as fact by your students.) Give some facts about the event you have chosen, and then ask the children: Are these facts true or false? (true) How do you know? (It is in the history books, records) How do you know that these people got it right? (You have to trust them, they were there.) Could you write a book about this event yourself? (You could, but you would have to do research to make sure you got the facts right.) How about something that happened at school in your class yesterday? Could you write a story about that? (Yes.) Which one would be easier? (The event at school.) Why? BECAUSE YOU WERE THERE!! People that are eyewitnesses to an event are the most believable. Let's count up how many people in the Bible were eyewitnesses when Jesus went back to heaven. Read 1 Corinthians 15:3-8.

Teacher Helps

Memory Verse Activity: Scripture Scrambler[2]

Write the words to a verse on the top of a paper. Then number the paper, one number for each word in the verse. Beside the numbers, write a scrambled word to the verse. Challenge your children to unscramble each word to the verse in its correct order.

Example:

1   eecevir   receive

2   nhew   when

3   wpreo   power

4   aeudj   Judea

4) Review the Lesson

Based on the lives of those who followed Jesus, rate yourself on this grid:

- Following Jesus' example   1   2   3   4   5   6
- Understanding God's Word   1   2   3   4   5   6
- Willing to be a missionary   1   2   3   4   5   6
- Ready to share my faith   1   2   3   4   5   6
- Know eight essential truths   1   2   3   4   5   6
- Told others 8 essential truths   1   2   3   4   5   6
- Respond to God's leading   1   2   3   4   5   6
- Overall commitment to God   1   2   3   4   5   6

Review Activity: Grid for Growth

The teacher should instruct the class of children that the example of Jesus should help us evaluate our own lives.

Children should fill out this chart (1= low; 6 = high).

5) Apply the Lesson

There is a job to do for all of us. That job is called the Great Commission and it was given to us by Jesus Christ. Ask, **"What kids will be willing to tell the story of Jesus Christ?"**

Let kids volunteer and then help them tell the eight basic truths.

Apply the Lesson Activity: Eight Essential Truths

This application is the same as the last lesson for one very important reason. All believers must be busy at the job Christ has given us to do, kids included. All kids can be Kid Missionaries (KMs)!

> **Story Line: Jesus returned to heaven to prepare a place for believers.**

Adventure Number 79
Acts 2:14-42

> **Story Line: The disciples of Jesus told other people why they should trust Jesus.**

 ## 1) Study the Lesson (before class)

- Peter told other people that the miracles of Jesus were God's way of verifying that Jesus is God.

- The crucifixion of Jesus was not an accident. It was God's plan to have Jesus die on the cross for the sins of all humans.

- Death could not keep its grip on Jesus and He conquered death. This was another sign that Jesus was the Messiah. Peter told others that death could not stop Jesus.

- The body of Jesus was not left to rot in a grave. It was resurrected and glorified. This verified the resurrection and ascension of Jesus.

- The prophecy of Psalm 16:8-11 verified the resurrection and ascension of Jesus.

- The presence of "David's tomb" in Acts 2:25-31 emphasizes that David was talking about someone else's resurrection, not his own.

- The witnesses (verse 32) verified the resurrection and ascension of Jesus.

- The supernatural events (verse 33) of Pentecost verified the resurrection and ascension of Jesus.

- The resurrection and ascension of Jesus verified that Jesus is David's greater Son (Psalm 110:1; Acts 2:34-35).

- The apostles spoke of seeing the resurrected Christ five different times; (v. 32; 3:15; 5:32; 10:39-41; 13:30-31).

Footnotes - Adventure 79

1. Susan Lingo, *Written on Our Hearts*, 79.

2. Lynn Solem and Bob Pike, *50 Creative Training Closers*, 94.

2) Begin the Lesson

There are eight basic concepts that are emphasized throughout all of the Bible. We have studied these truths in previous lessons. Ask the children if they can name them and tell a little bit about each one. They are:

1. <u>God</u>. In the beginning, there was a very powerful God. (Lesson 1: The Eternal God; Lesson 27: The Exodus; Lesson 40: The Reign of David)

2. <u>Man</u>. God created many things. He created man and woman to be His special friends. (Lesson 3: Creation of the Universe; Lesson 4: Creation of People; Lesson 24: Moses Leads His People)

3. <u>Sin</u>. Man and woman disobeyed God. They did not do what He told them to do. (Lesson 7: Beginning of Human Sin; Lesson 33: Unbelief at Kadesh; Lesson 43: The Divided Kingdom)

4. <u>Death</u>. God punished man and woman for their disobedience. Death, in the Bible, refers to separation. (Lesson 8: The Origin of Death; Lesson 16: The Tower of Babel; Lesson 46: The Exiles of Israel and Judah)

5. <u>Christ</u>. God sent His one and only Son, His unique Son, Who lived a perfect life. (Lesson 9: Promise of a Victor Over Satan; Lesson 45: Prophecies of a Coming Messiah; Lesson 52: Birth of Jesus Christ)

6. <u>Cross</u>. Jesus died on the cross for the sins of the world. (Lesson 11: Provision of Coverings; Lesson 32: The Day of Atonement; Lesson 45: Prophecies of a Coming Messiah; Lesson 56: Announcement by John; Lesson 73: The Crucifixion of Jesus)

7. <u>Faith</u>. If anyone places their faith in Christ, God welcomes them. (Lesson 13: Cain and Abel; Lesson 34: The Bronze Serpent; Lesson 58: The Religious Leader; Lesson 61: Jesus Has Power Over a Stormy Sea: Lesson 74: Why Jesus Died on the Cross)

8. <u>Life</u>. God gives eternal life to those who put their faith in Him. (Lesson 5: Life in Paradise; Lesson 38: Bright Lights in an Era of Darkness; Lesson 56: Announcement by John the Baptist; Lesson 75: The Resurrection of Jesus Christ)

Teacher Helps

Review Activity: Eight Basic Gospel Truths - One Complete Story

The teacher should emphasize these eight gospel concepts throughout Scripture. They are foundational to telling children the one story of redemption found in the Bible. We will emphasize these eight truths regularly.

Ask the children if they can think of how these eight gospel principles are emphasized in the first 78 lessons that we have studied.

3) Teach the Lesson

What would keep you from telling your friends about Jesus Christ?

Timeline: The Church

Tell the Story

Jesus Christ had died ... we know that. He rose again three days later ... we know that. He ascended into heaven forty days later ... we know that. Now, ten days after Jesus Christ ascended into heaven, Peter gave a speech to an international audience in Jerusalem and as a result, there was a great number of people who became believers.

Here is how it happened. A large number of followers of Jesus were assembled in one place at 9 in the morning. Instantly, they began speaking in other languages. Nobody understood what was going on. Some thought they might be drunk. Other were just plain confused. How could Galileans be speaking all these different languages? All the languages had this in common: they were all telling about the wonders that God had done and they were praising God.

Then, Peter stood up to address the large crowd. He was backed by the other 11 apostles. The first thing Peter did was quote the Old Testament prophet, Joel. Joel had prophesied that God would pour out His Spirit on every kind of people in the end times or the last days. It was not like everything Joel said was coming true this particular day, but it was starting to come true. Peter then told them the well thought out plan of God.

The plan looked like this: Jesus was betrayed by men who took the law into their own hands. These men nailed Jesus Christ to the cross where He died a very painful death. But, God took the death ropes from Jesus Christ and raised Him from the dead. Death could not contain Jesus Christ. Again, Peter quoted the Old Testament ... this time he quoted David. David said in one of the Psalms, "For you will not abandon my soul to Hades, or let your Holy One see corruption." In a way, David was telling us that Jesus Christ would be resurrected. He would not stay in the grave or Hades.

Peter's audience did not know what to do. They were deeply sensitive to the fact that this Jesus was now resurrected and He was alive. Peter told this group of people to repent or to turn from their sin. This Jesus was both Lord and Christ and He had the power to forgive their sin if they would only repent from their sin and place their faith in Jesus Christ. Repeatedly, Peter told this group to get out of this sick culture of sinful living. Change! That day alone, about 3,000 people took Peter at his word and became believers. They committed themselves to the Christian faith.

Teacher Helps

Tell the Story Activity: Map

The teacher should tell the class that people from these countries could hear the gospel in their own language.

- Parthians - near the Persian Gulf
- Medes - south of the Caspian Sea
- Elamites - part of the Persian empire
- Mesopotamia - Syria
- Judea - Israel
- Cappadocia - Asia Minor
- Pontus - Asia Minor
- Asia
- Phrygia and Pamphilia - two provinces in Asia Minor
- Egypt - Africa
- Libya - Africa
- Crete - Mediterranean Sea
- Arabs - Middle East

Memory Verse

Acts 2:38 (ESV) - And Peter said to them, "Repent and be baptized every one of you in the name of Jesus Christ for the forgiveness of your sins.

Praise and Worship

Praise and Worship styles vary greatly around the world. It is the intent of this curriculum that praise and worship songs be selected that best fit the content of this lesson. Recommendations for praise and worship are given and this music can generally be located at www.itunes.com. However, the teacher can feel free to select a similar praise and worship song.

"Jesus, Thank You" by Sovereign Grace Music is recommended for this lesson.

Bible Activity

Give each student a small card or piece of paper. Ask this question: **"What is the best news you could possibly think of?"** Write your answer on your card. (Get them started thinking with some ideas, if needed, such as the cure for a disease, end of a war, favorite sports team won the big game, and suggestions like this.)

"Now just think if that news were really true, and you were the first to know about it! What would you want to do?" (Tell people.) Allow time for the children to share what is on their paper. How exciting to be able to share wonderful news with other people! That's exactly how Peter felt so many years ago.

Teacher Helps

Memory Verse Activity: Scripture Log[1]

Make a page for children to take home that shows down the left column: Sunday, Monday, Tuesday, Wednesday, Thursday, Friday, and Saturday.

Across the top, put practice times and review times.

Children should work on this memory verse each day and mark on their log when they practiced this verse and when they review this verse. Bring this log to class with you next week.

This type of activity will encourage Scripture memory and obedience throughout the week, not just as part of the lesson.

4) Review the Lesson

The teacher should divide the class up into two teams.

- One team could be the "red" team and receive red cards or pieces of paper. The other team could be the "yellow" team and receive yellow cards or pieces of paper.

- Each team has the responsibility of writing out 3 to 5 questions that they want the other team to answer.

- Each question has to pertain to the lesson today.

- After questions are written out, the other team has five to seven minutes to answer the questions. The "yellow" team will answer the questions from the "red" team and the "red" team will answer questions from the "yellow" team.

Teacher Helps

Review Activity: Two Team Review[2]

After an appropriate time, the teacher will gather up the cards or pieces of paper and reward points to the best questions and best answers from each team.

It is highly advisable to have 2 adult teachers in every classroom for kids. If there are 2 adults, then one adult should be the leader of each team.

5) Apply the Lesson

There is a job to do for all of us. That job is called the Great Commission and it was given to us by Jesus Christ. Ask, "What kids will be willing to tell the story of Jesus Christ?"

Let kids volunteer and then help them tell the eight basic truths.

Apply the Lesson Activity: Eight Essential Truths

This application is the same as the last two lessons. All believers must be busy at the job has given us to do, kids included. All kids can be Kid Missionaries (KMs)!

> **Story Line: The disciples of Jesus told other people why they should trust Jesus.**

Adventure Number 80

Acts 2:42-47; 4:1-12; 5:42

Time Line: The followers of Jesus met to pray, worship, read the Bible, fellowship, and witness.

1) Study the Lesson (before class)

- After Peter proclaimed the good news of Jesus Christ and 3,000 became new believers, the early church sought out ways to incorporate these new believers into the church.

- While these 3,000 were new believers, they continued steadfastly. They persevered. There is no record of any of them turning their back on the faith.[1]

- The early church devoted themselves to four basic disciplines.

    1) <u>Biblical teaching</u>. *"The doctrines of the apostles"* refers to the teaching or doctrines that the apostles proclaimed. It does not mean that the apostles had their own doctrine.[2]

    2) <u>Fellowship</u>. The early believers shared things that they had in common. The early church shared their prayers together, they shared their struggles together, and they even shared their property.

    3) <u>Breaking of bread or the Lord's Supper</u>. The Lord's last request before He went to the cross was, *"Do this in remembrance of Me."* The disciples incorporated that into their fellowship. In their fellowship, they remembered His broken body and shed blood.

    4) <u>Prayers</u>. The newly converted followers were committed to a love for prayer and they persevered in it.

- The early church was also devoted to <u>evangelism</u>. Two distinctions marked their evangelism. First, that Jesus Christ was resurrected. God had raised Jesus Christ from the dead. Second, that Jesus Christ is the one and only way to God. There were not multiple paths to God.[3]

<u>Footnotes - Adventure 80</u>

1. James Galvin, *Life Application Bible Notes*, 1890.

2. Albert Barnes, *Barnes' Notes on the New Testament* (Austin, TX: Wordsearch Corporation, 2007), Acts 2.

3. Wayne Haston, *The Roots of Faith New Testament Workbook*, 30-C.

2) Begin the Lesson

Adventure Number 77: The Great Commission

   1. What did Jesus tell His disciples to do?

   2. Read Matthew 28:19.

   3. Jesus Christ gave His disciples a job to do.

   4. Ask God to help us make disciples of all nations.

Adventure Number 78: The Ascension of Jesus Christ

   1. Jesus left the earth and ascended to heaven. Who was watching?

   2. Read Acts 1:6-11.

   3. While the disciples were watching, Jesus ascended into the clouds.

   4. Pray that we would follow the last instructions of the ascended Lord.

Adventure Number 79: Peter Proclaims the Good News

   1. Why did Peter start preaching?

   2. Read Acts 2:14-22.

   3. The disciples of Jesus told other people why they should trust Jesus.

   4. Pray that we would be faithful to share the Good News.

> **Teacher Helps**
>
> **Begin the Lesson Activity: Ask, Read, Talk, Pray**
>
> A good review strategy from 3 previous lessons will focus on four main elements.
>
> 1) Ask a question.
>
> 2) Read the Bible.
>
> 3) Talk about it.
>
> 4) Pray to God.

3) Teach the Lesson

If you were to start your own church, what are some things that you think would be vital to the success of the church?

What are the most important aspects of your children's ministry at church?

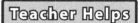

Tell the Story

Now, the church really grew ... 3,000 people were added in one day! That is a lot of people to add to one church in one day. The apostles had their work cut out for themselves. The last job that the Lord gave them to do was to make disciples of all the nations. They had converts that needed to be guided into discipleship. Five basic functions helped these converts to live the Christian life.

The Word of God was a basic function of the early church to help these converts live the Christian life. The apostles taught and the people listened. In fact, they not only listened, they persevered in the apostles' teaching. They kept on listening and they continued to want more of this Biblical teaching.

The early church also continued in fellowship. That is, they shared things in common. They shared a lot of things that they had in common. They shared their prayers and their struggles. They shared their possessions and they shared their faith. They were growing in their unity. They could not have fellowship unless they were united in the things they had in common. Whatever happened to one, happened to all. It was like they were bonded together and it helped them to live the Christian life.

They continued in the breaking of bread. The last request of Jesus Christ before He went to the cross was that they would remember His broken body and shed blood. The apostles were continuing this last request of Jesus. They wanted their focus to be on the person and work of Jesus Christ. The Lord's Supper was their way of remembering who Jesus was and what He did.

They also continued in prayers together. The Lord told them that His house should be called a house of prayer and they took that admonition seriously. They prayed about everything and prayer was a basic function that the early church enjoyed very much and it helped them to live the Christian life.

The early church focused on evangelism. They wanted everyone to know that this Jesus who was recently crucified was now resurrected. He was no longer dead. They also wanted everyone to know that there was "no other Name under heaven by which we must be saved." There were not a lot of paths to God, there was only one path to God and that was through the person of Jesus Christ. He was the only Mediator, not one among many.

Life in the early church was exciting and growing. There were many new converts who wanted to live the Christian life.

Tell the Story Activity: Living the Christian Life

The teacher should ask the class to write or tell how they will try to make these five basic functions of the Christian life part of their life. Have volunteers share and then write out their thoughts for each of the five. Then, encourage kids to be a member of the Faithful Five.

- Bible teaching
- Fellowship
- Breaking of bread
- Prayers
- Evangelism

Memory Verse

Acts 2:42 (ESV) - And they devoted themselves to the apostles' teaching and the fellowship, to the breaking of bread and the prayers.

Praise and Worship

Praise and Worship styles vary greatly around the world. It is the intent of this curriculum that praise and worship songs be selected that best fit the content of this lesson. Recommendations for praise and worship are given and this music can generally be located at www.itunes.com. However, the teacher can feel free to select a similar praise and worship song.

"Jesus, Thank You" by Sovereign Grace Music is recommended for this lesson.

Bible Activity

Life and Ministry in the Early Church

Building a church – ahead of time, make "pieces" of a church out of brown paper. They should look like building blocks as much as possible. On each piece, write one of the elements used in today's "Tell the Story" section. If you have a large class and enough paper, make several of each thing, such as "Bible Teaching", "Fellowship", and the other three.

Ask these questions:

"How is a church built? With bricks and wood and stone? Yes, the building is made from these things, but the real church is made up of people, no matter where they meet for a church service. How was the first church in the New Testament built?" Allow children to give the 5 things found in today's lesson. Talk about how your church fulfills each of these. As they answer, invite them to come up and place one of the building blocks on the floor. Have them "build" a church-like picture on the floor.

Teacher Helps

Memory Verse Activity: Hop It

In large letters, write phrases of the verse on sheets of paper. On the floor, tape the papers in a mixed up fashion, but close enough for succeeding words to be reached in a step. Children should step on one word at a time in the proper order to quote the verse. Let each child have a turn of hopping on the verse.

4) Review the Lesson

Agree/Disagree Statements (If you disagree, why do you disagree?)

1. The new church grew by 3,000 in one year. (Disagree. They grew 3,000 in one day.)

2. The early church listened intently to the teaching of the apostles. (Agree.)

3. The young church did not think it was a good idea to share their possessions with everyone else. (Disagree. They thought this was a good idea.)

4. The new church practiced the Lord's Supper every week. (Disagree. The Bible does not tell us how often they did this.)

5. Evangelism was something that only the apostles were supposed to do. (Disagree. Many people were sharing the good news.)

Review Activity: Agree and Disagree Statements

Kids will have fun disagreeing or agreeing with these statements. You may want to make up some statements of your own for them to agree or disagree with.

5) Apply the Lesson

Let's develop a Fabulous Five for Families. Pick one of the five functions. Tell someone else in the class which one you picked. Then, tell each other in the class how you plan on making one of these functions more important in your life. Have kids share with each other and then pray for them as they grow in living the Christian life.

Time Line: The followers of Jesus met to pray, worship, read the Bible, fellowship, and witness.

Adventure Number 81
Acts 8:1-39

> **Story Line:** Philip told the gospel to a Samaritan man and an Ethiopian official.

1) Study the Lesson (before class)

- The Ethiopian man in Acts 8 was a Gentile black man (probably) who lived 1,500 miles from Jerusalem in a country that was polytheistic. He was a government official who was a eunuch. A eunuch had special worship restrictions under the Mosaic law.[1]

- Stephen had just been stoned to death for his faith. Saul was right there congratulating the killers and giving his approval. That set off a terrific persecution. Many believers, with the exception of the apostles, were scattered and had to leave their homes in Jerusalem.

- Because of persecution, Philip went to Samaria, north of Jerusalem, to proclaim the gospel. However, he was led of the Lord to Gaza, southwest of Jerusalem, to tell the Ethiopian official about Christ.

- There was a close connection between Stephen (Acts 6-7) and Philip (Acts 8). Both are mentioned in Acts 6:5 because they belonged to the Seven. Even their names follow the same narrative from Acts 6:8-8:40.

- The Lord directed Philip to a specific location, the "desert road." Then and there, Philip met a specific man who was reading Isaiah 53 but did not understand what he was reading.

- Philip seized the opportunity with the Ethiopian official. The official's lack of understanding about Isaiah 53:7-8 allowed Philip to tell the good news from Isaiah 53. The Ethiopian official became a believer and was immediately baptized.

- Philip used the Old Testament to lead this Ethiopian official to faith in Jesus Christ.

Footnotes - Adventure 81

1. Wayne Haston, *The Roots of Faith New Testament Workbook*, 31-C.

2. Lynn Solem and Bob Pike, *50 Creative Training Closers*, 52.

2) Begin the Lesson

Let's review the time periods that we have studied so far:

- In order, what are these eras or time periods? (Beginnings, Beginnings of a Nation, Possessing the Land, United Kingdom, Divided Kingdom, Taken from Home, Return to Home, The Early Life of Jesus Christ, and The Ministry of Jesus Christ)

- Who are some of the people that we met in each time period?

    1) Beginnings: Adam and Eve, Lucifer, Cain, Abel, and Noah
    2) Beginnings of a Nation: Abraham, Sarah, Isaac, Rebekah, Jacob, Joseph, Moses, and Pharaoh
    3) Possessing the Land: Joshua, Gideon, and Samuel
    4) United Kingdom: Saul and David
    5) Divided Kingdom: Jeroboam, Elijah, and Elisha
    6) Taken from Home: Daniel and Ezekiel
    8) Return to Home: Ezra and Daniel
    7) The Early Life of Jesus Christ to Home: Anna, Simeon, Mary, Joseph, and Jesus
    8) The Ministry of Jesus Christ: Satan, John the Baptist, the disciples, Nicodemus, the woman at the well, and Jesus Christ
    9) Betrayal and Death of Jesus Christ: Jesus Christ, His disciples, and Judas
    10) Victory and Life: The Resurrected Christ, Peter, and the apostles
    11) The Church: Jesus Christ and Peter

Begin the Lesson Activity: Ball Toss

Gather your class of children in a circle with a small ball. Have children take turns rolling the ball gently to each other. When a child catches the ball, have each child answer one part of the question. At this point, do not correct children if they give a wrong answer. Let each child that wants to participate and then roll the ball to another person in the class for the next question.

3) Teach the Lesson

Persecution caused many people in the early church to leave their homes. If you did not have to leave your home or if you had to leave your home, would you be willing to share some good news about Jesus Christ? Why? Why not?

Tell the Story

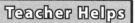

Stephen had just been stoned to death because of his faith in Jesus Christ. Saul was applauding the killers and thought it was a good idea. Because of that, an awful persecution began. Many believers in Jerusalem had to leave their homes. Stephen's friend, Philip, left his home and went to Samaria to proclaim the good news of Jesus Christ. Samaria was north of Jerusalem. In Samaria, Simon held everybody captive with his magic. The young and the old all were in awe of his magical abilities. While Philip was in Samaria, many people came to faith in Christ and forgot about Simon. Even, Simon came to faith in Christ and was baptized. Simon was a magician and was even known as the "great wizard."

After the "great wizard" came to faith in Christ, he wanted to buy the talents that the apostles had. He was rebuked by Peter and John. They told him that the gift of God could not be obtained with money.

Peter and John went back to Jerusalem. On their way, they proclaimed the good news to other towns and villages in Samaria. On the other hand, the Lord directed Philip to a desert road. There was an Ethiopian official there who was reading the Old Testament and he could not understand it. The part that he was reading said, "Like a sheep he was led to the slaughter and like a lamb before its shearer is silent, so he opens not his mouth. In his humiliation justice was denied him. Who can describe his generation? For his life is taken away from the earth." The official invited Philip on to his chariot and asked, *"Tell me, please, who is the prophet talking about, himself or someone else?"*

Again, Philip seized the opportunity and shared with the Ethiopian eunuch how to place his faith in Jesus Christ which is exactly what he did. Then, the eunuch stopped the chariot and Philip baptized him. It was a special miracle from God that the Ethiopian official put his faith in Christ. Then, another special miracle happened. Suddenly, the Lord took Philip away and the Ethiopian official never saw him again. But, he went on his way rejoicing about his new found faith in Christ.

So, to the north of Jerusalem, at least one entire Samaritan village came to faith in Christ. To the southwest of Jerusalem, one Ethiopian man came to faith in Christ. The gospel was going out to the fringes of Jerusalem. The believers were proclaiming the good news in unusual places and to non-Jewish people.

Tell the Story Activity: Two Proclamations - One Purpose

As the teacher tells this story, give the class a listening assignment. That assignment is this:

- What do Philip's two witnessing opportunities have in common?

- What do Philip's two witnessing opportunities not have in common?

Memory Verse

Isaiah 53:7 (ESV) - Like a sheep he was led to the slaughter and like a lamb before its shearer is silent, so he opens not his mouth.

Praise and Worship

Praise and Worship styles vary greatly around the world. It is the intent of this curriculum that praise and worship songs be selected that best fit the content of this lesson. Recommendations for praise and worship are given and this music can generally be located at www.itunes.com. However, the teacher can feel free to select a similar praise and worship song.

"Jesus, Thank You" by Sovereign Grace Music is recommended for this lesson.

Bible Activity

Dramatization – **"Let's pretend we were there on that desert road so many years ago."** Choose one child to play the part of Philip, one to be the Ethiopian official, one to be the chariot driver, Peter, John, and perhaps a few others on the chariot. Peter, John, and Philip start out by preaching and teaching together in Samaria. Scene two is on the desert road with Philip and the Ethiopian. Guide the children to "act out" the story. Help them feel the emotions of that very special and unique time in the early church. Be sure to emphasize the rejoicing that took place when someone came to faith in Christ.

Teacher Helps

Memory Verse Activity: Around the Class

Have the children sit in a circle while music is playing. Pass around a phrase of the memory verse. When the music stops, whoever is holding the phrase of the memory verse should try to quote the verse. Do this until all phrases are memorized. Then, do the same thing for the whole memory verse.

4) Review the Lesson

Teacher Helps

Volunteers from the class should list on a board or big piece of paper that everyone can see, the 5 Most Important Things To Know from this lesson.

For instance:

1. An entire village in Samaria came to faith in Christ.

2. God directed Philip to share the good news about Jesus Christ.

3. It was important for Samaritans and Ethiopians to hear the good news.

4. Philip obeyed when the Lord sent him somewhere.

5. When Philip shared the good news, he used the Scriptures.

Review Activity: 5 Scribes[2]

Have five different volunteers come to the front of the class to write one of the five most important things to know from this lesson. Ask the class why these are important.

5) Apply the Lesson

Philip obeyed the Lord when the Lord showed him where to go and what to say.

Name one or two people that you think the Lord may be showing you need to hear the good news. Pray for them. Share the good news with them. You may even want to use the "eight basic truths" to help them learn about Jesus and perhaps put their faith in Jesus.

Story Line: Philip told the gospel to a Samaritan man and an Ethiopian official.

Adventure Number 82
Acts 9:1-19

Story Line: God radically changed the life of Saul.

1) Study the Lesson (before class)

- Luke recorded Saul's conversion three times; Acts 9, 22, and 26.

- Saul was from Jerusalem but traveled as far away as Damascus to persecute Christians. Stephen's challenge (Acts 7) may have caused a renewed effort on the behalf of Saul to eliminate Christians. If Stephen's message was accurate, the Law would be obsolete, the very thing Saul was clinging to because of his Jewish beliefs.[1]

- Saul was confronted by the resurrected Christ. When this happened, Saul asked two questions: *"Who are you?"* and *"What do you want me to do?"* Saul's conversion was radical and dramatic. Many conversions are quiet and not as dramatic.

- The men travelling with Saul heard the sound but did not understand the voice. Saul heard and understood the voice. He also saw a dazzling bright light.

- Saul's *"thorn in the flesh"* (2 Corinthians 12:7) was probably poor eyesight. This scene may have been the beginning of his loss of sight.

- By means of a vision, Ananias was told to find Saul on Straight Street which was one of two parallel streets that connected the eastern wall and the western wall in Damascus. The house of Judas was on Straight Street.

- The believers were first called "saints" in the book of Acts (1:13). *Hagios*, or "set apart ones" is also used in Romans 1:1; Ephesians 1:1; and Philippians 1:1.[2]

Footnotes - Adventure 82

1. John Walvoord and Roy Zuck, *Bible Knowledge Commentary: New Testament*, 375.

2. John Walvoord and Roy Zuck, *Bible Knowledge Commentary: New Testament*, 376.

2) Begin the Lesson

Tell your class that you are learning the one story of the Bible. While there are many stories in the Bible, they are linked to one major theme or story in the Bible. It is a story of hope. So, to help your class know that story and be able to put all the lessons together, we are going to review the lessons from the past. Ask, **"What are the main events that we have studied in the Bible?"**

- God always existed and He is very powerful. He created the earth and everything in it.

- Lucifer, or Satan, deceived Adam and Eve. They sinned.

- God spared Noah and his family because Noah was a righteous man.

- God made special promises to Abraham.

- Jacob wrestled with the angel of God and got a new name, Israel.

- God established a moral code called the Ten Commandments.

- God chose David to be king. He will one day appoint someone to be King forever.

- Israel and Judah were exiled to Assyria and Babylon.

- The Jews returned from exile to build the temple and the walls.

- Between the Old and New Testaments, a lot changed.

- Jesus was born.

- Early events in the life of Jesus marked Him as a special Person.

- Jesus chose 12 men to become His committed followers.

- Jesus showed His great power over a storm and demons.

- Jesus entered Jerusalem with shouts of praise from the crowds.

- Judas betrayed Jesus.

- Jesus died, was buried, and rose again.

- Jesus appeared to many people.

- Jesus ascended to heaven.

Teacher Helps

Begin the Lesson Activity: The Main Events

Review is a significant part of learning. Nineteen events are listed here. Write each event on a slip of paper or poster board and have children put them in chronological order. Let them work together in small teams 2 or 3. Time how long it takes each team to put these events in the right order. Winner gets a prize.

3) Teach the Lesson

Conversion begins with the change of mind that results in a faith response. Our heart changes to reflect life that is different.

Can you think of anyone who has had a radical change of life because they converted to Christianity?

Tell the Story

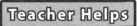

In the history of the church, other than Jesus Christ, probably no one affected Christianity more than Saul. Saul was breathing down the throats of the believers with hatred. He went near and far to persecute them, even have them put to death. Saul was a religious man. He studied under one of the most important Jewish teachers in Jerusalem. He was devoted to the Old Testament law. He was also a Pharisee, which meant that not only was he religious, he was very religious. But, when it came to Christians, Saul had no tolerance. They were the opposition and they needed to be persecuted, even killed. Such was what happened to Stephen. They stoned him to death and Saul was right there.

One day, just outside of Damascus, Saul was intent on finding and hurting more Christians when he saw a dazzling light and heard a voice. He understood the voice but his travelling companions did not understand the voice. They did see the light, though. The voice from heaven asked Saul, *"Saul, why are you out to get me?"* Apparently, Saul recognized that the voice was from God and he responded, *"Who are you, Lord?"* The voice from heaven responded, "I am Jesus, the One you are hunting down."

Then, Saul asked his second question, *"What do you want me to do?"* The voice from heaven told him where to go. Since Saul was temporarily blinded, his travelling companions took him to Damascus where he stayed at the house of Judas on Straight Street. In a dream, God instructed a believer in Damascus to find and help Saul. This believer's name was Ananias and he was really afraid. He knew what Saul had done to Christians. Everyone knew that. But, he obeyed the voice of the Lord, went to Straight Street, found the house of Judas, and talked to Saul. As soon as he started talking to Saul, Saul regained his sight. Immediately, Saul rose to his feet, was baptized, and then ate a hearty meal.

Saul stayed with the believers in Damascus for a brief time then he got right to work. Saul began preaching that Jesus was the Christ. None of the believers knew what to do. They were greatly surprised! They knew Saul had been trying to destroy the church; now he was openly acknowledging that Jesus was the Christ. It was a radical transformation to say the least.

After Saul had preached the gospel for a long time, the Jews wanted to kill him. They looked at him like a traitor who had turned his back on them. Once he was hurting Christians, now he was honoring their Lord.

Tell the Story Activity: Two Important Questions for Everyone to Answer

As the teacher tells this story, have children listen for those two important questions. Have them also discuss how they would answer those two important questions if God asked them.

- Who are you, Lord?

- What do you want me to do?

Memory Verse

Acts 9:15 (ESV) - But the Lord said to him, "Go, for he is a chosen instrument of mine to carry my name before the Gentiles and kings and the children of Israel."

Praise and Worship

Praise and Worship styles vary greatly around the world. It is the intent of this curriculum that praise and worship songs be selected that best fit the content of this lesson. Recommendations for praise and worship are given and this music can generally be located at www.itunes.com. However, the teacher can feel free to select a similar praise and worship song.

"Jesus, Thank You" by Sovereign Grace Music is recommended for this lesson.

Bible Activity

Divide the children into two groups and have the first group identify what they learn about Saul before He encounters Jesus on the road. The second group should identify what indicates the differences found in Saul after his encounter with Jesus.

Immediately following the reading of Acts 9:1-19, have a volunteer retell the story to the best of their recollection. Ask someone from the first group to describe Saul before He meets Jesus, and then ask for volunteer from second group to describe Saul after meeting Jesus.

Teacher Helps

Bible Memory Activity: Relay Race

Form two teams. Put the memory verse in large letters about ten yards away from the teams. Have children run to the memory verse and read the next word of the verse out loud so that everyone can hear. When each child has read his one word, go back to the teach, touch the next person in line, and repeat the process until all words of the verse have been read.

Repeat this until everyone has memorized the verse.

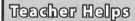

4) Review the Lesson

Divide the class into two teams. Give the teams one minute to write down as many statements as they can about the conversion of Saul. Here are a few ideas:

- Saul went from Jerusalem to Damascus to persecute Christians.

- Saul's travelling companions saw the light and heard a voice, but they could not understand the voice.

- Saul saw a bright light and heard the voice. He could understand what the voice from heaven was saying.

- Saul asked the Lord two important questions: Who are you, Lord? and What do you want me to do?

- Ananias was afraid to help Saul because he knew what Saul had done to other Christians.

Review the Lesson Activity: One Minute List

The teacher should give two teams one minute each to list as many facts as they can about the lesson.

After the one minute has passed, compare lists and see who has more facts. Be sure that children remember that you are looking for facts.

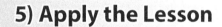

5) Apply the Lesson

Those who have been converted to faith in Christ want to show that in their daily lives.

Name one way that believers can reflect in their daily lives how they have been converted to faith in Christ.

Story Line: God radically changed the life of Saul.

Adventure Number 83
Acts 10:1-48

> **Story Line: No person should be called common or unclean.**

 ## 1) Study the Lesson (before class)

- This Caesarea was located on the Mediterranean Sea coast. It was 32 miles from Joppa, the largest and most important port city on the Mediterranean in Israel. Caesarea served as a capital of the Roman province of Judea. This city was the first city to have Gentile Christians and a non-Jewish church.[1]

- The Roman officer was a centurion. He had the command of 100 soldiers. Cornelius was stationed in Caesarea but would probably return to Rome soon. Therefore, his conversion was a major hurdle to taking the gospel to Rome.

- Cornelius had a dream in the middle of the afternoon that a messenger from God would come to him. The next day, Peter was hungry and fell into a trance. In that trance, God showed Peter that he should not call any person common or unclean. That happened three times.

- While Peter was pondering the meaning of this trance, the sovereign God arranged for three visitors from Cornelius to show up at the place where Peter was staying. The next day, they began the two day trip. Peter took some believers from Joppa with him.[2]

- Cornelius was religious and sincere. However, he was spiritually separated from God. Peter made it clear that the ministry of Christ results in judgment or salvation. The key element of salvation was faith in Jesus Christ.

- Cornelius and his family put their faith in Jesus Christ for forgiveness of sins and were later baptized. God shows no partiality but honors faith from any person in all nations.

Footnotes - Adventure 83

1. James Galvin, *Life Application Bible Notes*, 1838.

2. John Walvoord and Roy Zuck, *Bible Knowledge Commentary: New Testament*, 380.

2) Begin the Lesson

Lay out a game board for review that looks something like this:

Time Line	Story Line	Songs	Memory Verses
100 points	200 points	300 points	400 points
100 points	200 points	300 points	400 points
100 points	200 points	300 points	400 points
100 points	200 points	300 points	400 points
100 points	200 points	300 points	400 points

Go back for each of the last 10 lessons and let the children name the time line for each lesson (100 points), the story line for each lesson (200 points), the song for each lesson (300 points), and the memory verse for each lesson (400 points).

A prize should be given to the winning team. Usually, competition is a fun thing for the children. So, keep them all involved. Depending on the size of your class, you may want to limit each child to only 1 or 2 answers. The reason for this is that a few children will answer all the questions, if you let them.

There will be a total of 10,000 points, 1000 points for each lesson (100 for the time line, 200 for the story line, 300 for the song, and 400 for the memory verse).

Teacher Helps

Begin the Lesson Activity: Bible Jeopardy

Divide the class evenly into two teams. The teams could be:

1) whoever has the most brothers and sisters

2) whoever has the fewest brothers and sisters

This game will be continued with the review at end of the lesson.

3) Teach the Lesson

The teacher should ask, "What do you have to do to go to heaven?"

- Is being sincere enough?

- Is being religious enough?

- Is being God-fearing enough?

Today's lesson will look at someone who was all of these but, from God's perspective, it was not enough.

 # Tell the Story

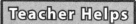

It all happened about 3 o'clock in the afternoon. Cornelius was a man who worshipped God, helped people, and prayed a lot. He was an Italian officer in charge of 100 soldiers in Caesarea, the Roman capital of Judea. Most Roman soldiers were not good like this man was. Anyway, Cornelius had a vision and this vision was from God. In the vision, God told Cornelius to send men to Joppa to find Peter who was staying with Simon who was a tanner in Joppa.

So, Cornelius sent two servants and one soldier on a mission. He told them everything about the vision that he just had. The three messengers left Caesarea and headed for Joppa, a journey of two days. Once they got to Joppa, they found Simon's house.

What made this really interesting was that Peter had just had a vision from God. In Peter's vision, he saw a huge blanket being lowered from heaven by four ropes. On the blanket were all kinds of animals, birds, and reptiles. Peter was told to kill them and eat them. Normally, a Jew like Peter would not do that. These foods were not kosher foods. On top of that, this happened three times and then the blanket was taken up to heaven. Peter was curious ... he did not understand what all this meant until the three visitors from Caesarea knocked on the door. God told Peter to go with these visitors to Caesarea.

The next day, the three visitors, Peter, and some believers from Joppa went to Joppa to see Cornelius. When Peter met Cornelius, Cornelius explained the vision that he had from God. That is when it all made sense to Peter. He told them clearly that God does not have favorites. It does not make a difference who you are or where you are from. You see, Peter was an uneducated Jewish fisherman and Cornelius was a highly educated Roman soldier. Normally, these men would never be friends. But because God powerfully ruled in these circumstances, the men became friends and Peter shared the good news of Jesus Christ.

Peter told Cornelius and his family that Jesus was nailed to a tree and died. But, three days later, God raised Him from the dead. Many witnesses saw this and were commissioned by Jesus to tell the good news of His death, burial, and resurrection. And these eyewitnesses not the only witnesses; the prophets from the Old Testament also told of the forgiveness that this Messiah would offer. Cornelius believed the good news of forgiveness through Jesus Christ and was later baptized. Even though Cornelius was a worshipper of God, he needed the forgiveness that only Jesus could give him.

Tell the Story Activity: Blanket with Various Foods

The teacher should bring a blanket with all kinds of food that the class would not eat, if this is possible.

Tell the class that Peter looked at these foods that he would never eat. The lesson was not about food, it was about people.

Ask the class, **"Are there people you do not like or think that they are inferior to you?"**

God does not want us to look down on anyone.

Memory Verse

Acts 10:43 (ESV) - To him all the prophets bear witness that everyone who believes in him receives forgiveness of sins through his name.

Praise and Worship

Praise and Worship styles vary greatly around the world. It is the intent of this curriculum that praise and worship songs be selected that best fit the content of this lesson. Recommendations for praise and worship are given and this music can generally be located at www.itunes.com. However, the teacher can feel free to select a similar praise and worship song.

"Jesus, Thank You" by Sovereign Grace Music is recommended for this lesson.

Bible Activity

Activity: What matters to God, and what does not matter to God.

Divide your class into several groups (the number and size of the groups will vary depending on the size of your class).

Each group will have 3 minutes to think of as many things as they can to answer this question: "What things do not matter to God, that sometimes matter too much to us?" Possible answers – where a person lives, where they are from, what kind of clothes they wear, how much money they have, how smart they are, the color of their skin, hair, etc.

After 3 minutes have passed, go around the room and let each group tell one of the things they came up with. Continue to have each group tell another thing until they are out of ideas. Wrap it up by reminding the children that *"Man looks on the outward appearance, but God looks on the heart."*

Teacher Helps

Memory Verse Activity: The Telephone Game

Memorize this verse using The Telephone Game. Have your class form one line, then whisper into the first person in line a phrase of this verse, have that person repeat the phrase to the next person. Do this until all have quoted the first phrase. Then do the same thing with the second phrase, the third phrase, and so on until you have memorized the verse.

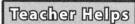

 ## 4) Review the Lesson

Continue your review game for points that you began at the start of the lesson.

- For 100 points, where did Cornelius live at this time? (Caesarea)

- For 200 points, who was Peter visiting? (Simon the Tanner)

- For 300 points, how many times did Cornelius have his vision (once) and how many times did Peter have his vision? (three times)

- For 400 points, how many people did Cornelius send to Joppa? (three; two servants and one soldier)

- Bonus question worth 500 points: What is the theme of this lesson? (No person should be called common or unclean.)

Review the Lesson Activity: Bible Jeopardy

This review activity is a continuation of the review game at the beginning of the lesson.

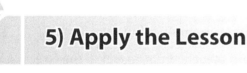 ## 5) Apply the Lesson

Some people say that all that matters is if you believe and are a good person. Cornelius believed in God, prayed, and did good deeds. However, all this was not enough for his salvation.

The eight words that we have learned that summarize the one story of God are: God, man, sin, death, Christ, cross, faith, and life. This story shows us that faith in who Jesus Christ is and what He did is essential.

Doing good is not good enough or else Cornelius did not need God's forgiveness.

Story Line: No person should be called common or unclean.

Adventure Number 84
Acts 11:19-30

Story Line: A new church got started in Antioch of Syria.

 ## 1) Study the Lesson (before class)

- At Antioch, Syria, for the first time in the history of the church, believers actually evangelized Gentiles. The Samaritans of Acts 8 were partly Jewish. The Ethiopian eunuch (Acts 8) was actually on his own reading Isaiah 53. And even Cornelius (Acts 10) actually took the initiative in getting the gospel from Peter.[1]

- Because of the martyrdom of Stephen (Acts 8:1-2), the gospel spread to many places. The death of Stephen helped the gospel to move out to Samaria, Phoenicia, Cyprus, and Antioch.

- The gospel went from Jerusalem to Antioch, a major cosmopolitan city in the Roman Empire, and a blended Jewish-Gentile church was founded that sent out missionaries.[2]

- Antioch of Syria was the third largest city in the Roman empire. Only Rome and Alexandria were larger in population. It was a major commercial hub and very multicultural.

- Some Christ-followers from Judea went there and preached the gospel to the Greek-speaking Gentiles and many people believed in Christ.

- The Jerusalem church sent Barnabas to visit the church in Antioch. When he saw the mix of people, including many Gentiles, he brought Saul there to help teach them.

- The Antioch church became a model for other churches by commissioning Saul and Barnabas to be missionaries.[3]

- The blessing to all the nations began with Abraham (Genesis 12) and continued through the rest of the Scriptures.

Footnotes - Adventure 84

1. John Walvoord and Roy Zuck, *Bible Knowledge Commentary: New Testament*, 382.

2. Wayne Haston, *New Testament Chronological Bible Cards*, NT-34.

3. Ibid.

2) Begin the Lesson

The teacher should gather all the songs that have been used in the Adventures in the Bible's Big Story and play several of them.

The class should be able to sing along with the teacher the songs that they have previously learned in this curriculum.

After the teacher has played several songs and the class and sung them, play the game, "Name That Tune." "Name That Tune" is a game in which the students will attempt to match the song with the Bible adventure that best matches the song. The teacher should use extreme graciousness to encourage the class when an answer is given.

The purpose of this activity is for kids to associate music they have learned with events in the Bible. The teacher should stay focused on this primary purpose.

Teacher Helps

Review Activity: Name That Tune

The teacher should play songs that the class has learned for the previous Bible adventures. Children should guess which adventures in the Bible's big story best match the song that is being played or sung.

If time permits, the teacher could also ask if there are phrases or words in any of the songs that the children do not understand.

3) Teach the Lesson

If you were going to start a church, who would you tell first? Who would you invite to be the leader or leaders of your new church? Today's story is going to give us a good idea of how to start a new church and something about its leadership.

Tell the Story

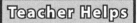

Stephen's death started it all. A great persecution arose against the believers at that time. It was like it became acceptable to punish Christians for no good reason at all. So, lots of believers left Jerusalem. They went to far away places like Phoenicia and Antioch. Some travelled to a far away place in Africa called Cyrene. They even went to an island in the Mediterranean Sea. The believers were probably hoping to keep their faith and not lose their lives. It was a strategic move that helped the growth of the church.

We do not even know their names, but some believers went to Antioch in Syria. They started telling non-Jews, or Gentiles, about Jesus Christ and many of them placed their faith in Jesus. That was the beginning of a new church in the third largest city in the Roman empire. So many people turned to faith in Christ that the Jerusalem church found out about it. As a precaution, they sent Barnabas to check out this new group of believers. Barnabas was a good man who led a life that followed God completely. More and more people came to faith in Christ.

Barnabas needed help. So, he went looking for Saul who was living in Tarsus, in what is now called Turkey. The two of them led the body of believers in Antioch for a whole year. The message of the Master was their main concern. They chose to get the message out of the death, burial, and resurrection of Jesus Christ. Many of the people who saw the resurrected Christ were still alive and perhaps some of them were in the area. They knew that Jesus Christ was nailed to the cross, was buried, and that He rose again from the dead. That is what they put their faith in ... faith in Who Jesus was (God), and faith in what He had done (paid the price for their sin on the cross). Their faith was so strong in this message that believers were first called "Christians" in Antioch of Syria.

Eventually, Saul and Barnabas got even more help from three other leaders. Together, the five of them led the growing congregation in Antioch. The church leadership team now consisted of a Jew from Cyprus (Barnabas), a black man from Africa (Simeon), a Roman from northern Africa, a Jewish man who was probably from Galilee (Manaen), and a highly educated Jew from Turkey (Saul). God had put His stamp of approval on the new church. It was pretty amazing!

One day, these five elders in the church were praying and fasting. The Holy Spirit told them to set apart two of them, Paul and Barnabas, for a very special work. They would become missionaries sent out by the Antioch church.

Tell the Story Activity: Names of the First Church Planters

The teacher should tell the story and ask the class to tell who the names of the first church planters are.

Answer: we do not know their names. They were just a group of believers who spread the message of Jesus Christ. The early believers were active in sharing their faith. The Jerusalem church sent Barnabas, an established leader. However, the names of the first church planters are not known to this day. God can use people who are not well-known.

Memory Verse

Acts 11:24 (ESV) - For Barnabas was a good man, full of the Holy Spirit and of faith. And a great many people were added to the Lord.

Praise and Worship

Praise and Worship styles vary greatly around the world. It is the intent of this curriculum that praise and worship songs be selected that best fit the content of this lesson. Recommendations for praise and worship are given and this music can generally be located at www.itunes.com. However, the teacher can feel free to select a similar praise and worship song.

"Jesus, Thank You" by Sovereign Grace Music is recommended for this lesson.

Bible Activity

Ahead of time, find out names of 5-10 people that were famous 50-75 years ago that your students have probably not heard of. You should choose a variety of types of fame: political, sports, and national heroes. The goal is to help children realize that earthly fame is fleeting, but people that do things for God will have a reward in eternity.

Ask the children: **"Who do you know that is very famous?"** Have them tell why each person is famous. Write the names that they give on a paper, or on a board at the front of the classroom, if possible. Make a list on one side of the board, leaving room on the other side. After you have at least 5 names that the children have given, begin to write the names you chose of the people that were famous 50-75 years ago. Ask the class if anyone has ever heard of..(read the names one by one). After you have finished your list, briefly tell what each person was known for.

Objective: **"The 5 elders in our story today were named in the Bible. Even people that are very famous today will someday be forgotten. God will never forget those that love Him and serve Him."**

Teacher Helps

Memory Verse Activity: Graffiti

Graffiti can also be used to help children memorize this verse. Write each word of this verse on a separate piece of paper. Then have children put the words in order in groups of 2 or 3. When each group can put the verse together in order, they will probably have this verse memorized.

4) Review the Lesson

Review the lesson in small groups. What are seven main facts or ideas that come out of this lesson? One adult leader should join each small group of kids. Let the children do most of the discovering. Help them when necessary.

- Stephen's death started a large persecution of the church.
- Believers fled from Jerusalem and went as far away as Africa and Cyprus.
- Antioch was the third largest city in the Roman empire. Only Rome and Alexandria were larger.
- The names of the first church planters are not known.
- The Jerusalem church sent Barnabas to verify what was going on in Antioch.
- Barnabas went and found Saul to help him lead this church.
- Barnabas and Saul found three other qualified men to help lead this church.

Review the Lesson Activity: Seven Main Facts

The teacher should have the class break up into groups of 2 or 3. Have them tell each other about the 7 main ideas in the lesson which are listed to your left. For younger children, or non-readers, the teacher should help them.

5) Apply the Lesson

Spreading the message of Jesus Christ was the way the early church grew.

Go to one or two people that you can tell this same message. Use the eight essential truths to help you explain this simple but life changing message.

Story Line: A new church got started in Antioch of Syria.

Timeline: The Church

99 Adventures in the Bible's Big Story

*Adventure Number 84
Page 424*

Adventure Number 85
Acts 13:4 - 14:27

Story Line: The church in Antioch sent out the first missionaries.

1) Study the Lesson (before class)

- Paul and Barnabas accepted the new assignment from God. They chose to bring an assistant with them, John Mark. John Mark was a cousin of Barnabas. The assignment was to take the message of the gospel to other countries.

- Their first destination was Cyprus, the home country of Barnabas. Cyprus was where Saul was first called Paul. Salamis, on the eastern coast of Cyprus, was the first stop. Evidently, there was a large Jewish population in Salamis. From Salamis, they went to Paphos, a trip of about 100 miles or 160 kilometers.

- At Paphos, they encountered Bar-Jesus, a fraudulent wizard. Paul confronted this sorcerer and the governor immediately placed his faith in Jesus Christ as a result. At this point, Paul seems to take the lead over Barnabas, except when they were in Jerusalem.[1]

- From Cyprus, they went to Perga in Pamphilia (southern Turkey). It was here that John Mark left the team and went back to Jerusalem. Paul thought John Mark lacked courage and commitment but later came to respect him and acknowledge that he needed John Mark for the work (2 Timothy 4:11).

- From Perga, they headed north to Pisidian Antioch. When invited to speak at the synagogue, Paul read two portions of Scripture from the Old Testament. First, from Moses and then from the prophets. The result was explosive.[2]

- On their way home, Paul and Barnabas retraced their journey to encourage new believers along the way.[3]

Footnotes - Adventure 85

1. John Walvoord and Roy Zuck, *Bible Knowledge Commentary: New Testament*, 388.

2. Lawrence O. Richards, *The Teacher's Commentary*, 780.

3. Wayne Haston, *New Testament Chronological Bible Cards*, NT-35.

4. Bill Greig, *Gospel Light's Really Big Book of Bible Games* (Ventura, CA: Gospel Light, 2006), 262.

2) Begin the Lesson

Ask children to help you with previous memory verses. Maybe say something like, **"Who remembers what (verse) says?"**

- Adventure Number 71: Matthew 26:56
- Adventure Number 72: 1 Corinthians 5:7
- Adventure Number 73: 1 Peter 3:18
- Adventure Number 74: Luke 23:42
- Adventure Number 75: Luke 24:6
- Adventure Number 76: Luke 24:27
- Adventure Number 77: Matthew 28:19
- Adventure Number 78: Acts 1:8
- Adventure Number 79: Acts 2:38
- Adventure Number 80: Acts 2:42
- Adventure Number 81: Isaiah 53:7
- Adventure Number 82: Acts 9:15
- Adventure Number 83: Acts 10:43
- Adventure Number 84: Acts 11:24

Teacher Helps

Begin the Lesson Activity: Memory Verse Review

The last 14 memory verses are given here. Divide the children up into two teams and see which team can tell you the most memory verses. Bonus points should be given if they each team can recite more than the last 14 memory verses.

Give the teams five minutes and they must work together.

The teacher can provide a few helps.

3) Teach the Lesson

If you were going to start a missionary emphasis, who would you invite to come to your missionary emphasis? Who would you invite to be the leader or leaders of your new mission? What kind of qualities would you be looking for in this man or woman?

Today's story is going to give us a good idea of how to start a missions emphasis and something about its leadership.

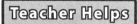

Tell the Story

The church in Antioch of Syria was the first ... no other church had ever sent out missionaries before, not even the church in Jerusalem. The Holy Spirit directed them to select two of their leaders to become missionaries. Paul and Barnabas would be the first missionaries while Simon, Lucius, Manaen, and perhaps others stayed back in Antioch to oversee the church.

Here is how the first missionary journey got started. Paul and Barnabas left Antioch and went to the nearest port city. From there, they sailed to the island of Cyprus. While Barnabas had been living in Jerusalem before he came to the church in Antioch, he was originally from Cyprus. So, he knew just the right places to go. Once they landed in Cyprus, they went to the synagogue at Salamis and proclaimed the Word of God. John Mark also went along as an assistant to Paul and Barnabas. It was at Cyprus, that Saul's name was changed to Paul.

From Salamis, they went to Paphos where the governor of the island wanted to hear the Word of God. One magician wanted to stop this from happening but Paul rebuked the magician. After that, the governor became a believer in Jesus Christ. Not only did he become a believer, he was full of enthusiasm over the message of hope in Jesus Christ. Then, the missionary team headed north to Perga which is the very southern part of modern day Turkey. When they got to Perga, John Mark quit and went home to Jerusalem. Paul thought he lacked courage and commitment.

From Perga, they went further north to Pisidian Antioch in the mountains. At Pisidian Antioch, Paul read from the Law and the Prophets. He wanted them to understand the Old Testament message about Jesus Christ. That message was that God raised Jesus Christ from the dead. Paul quoted from Psalms 2 and 16 as well as something that Isaiah wrote. He wanted the people to know that the Old Testament told all about Jesus. A great number of people converted to faith in Jesus Christ.

Paul and Barnabas went several other places and then headed for home. They retraced their trip so that they could encourage new disciples to stay faithful to the Lord. By the grace of God, they launched out and made it home safely. Once they got back to their home church in Antioch of Syria, they reported to the believers all the good things that God was doing in the nations of the world. They told in detail how the door of faith was wide open to the peoples of the world. After their report, they stayed in Antioch for quite a while.

Tell the Story Activity: Map

It would be good for the teacher to locate a map to show the class the general direction that Paul and Barnabas took on the first missionary journey.

Memory Verse

Acts 13:47 (ESV) - I have made you a light for the Gentiles, that you may bring salvation to the ends of the earth.

Praise and Worship

Praise and Worship styles vary greatly around the world. It is the intent of this curriculum that praise and worship songs be selected that best fit the content of this lesson. Recommendations for praise and worship are given and this music can generally be located at www.itunes.com. However, the teacher can feel free to select a similar praise and worship song.

"Jesus, Thank You" by Sovereign Grace Music is recommended for this lesson.

Bible Activity

Story segments – Ahead of time, make up papers with these verses written out:

- Acts 13:1-5
- Acts 13:6-8
- Acts 13:9-12
- Acts 13:13-19
- Acts 13:20-25
- Acts 13:26-29
- Acts 13:30-37
- Acts 13:38-41
- Acts 13:48-52

Divide your class into 9 groups. Depending on the size of your class, you might have several children in each group, or if you have a small class, each child may have more than one passage to work on.

Teachers or assistants may also choose to be involved, depending on the age of your students. Their job is to re-read the story and then draw a picture showing what happened in those verses. It should be very simple, no great artwork required!

Teacher Helps

Bible Memory Activity

Review the verse a few times then divide the children into two or more teams. Have the teams form lines across from a chalk or white board or piece of paper on a chair. Place something to write with at the board in front of each team. Have the first child of each team run to the board and write the first word of the verse, then run back to the line. The next child of the team will write the next word and it will continue until the verse is completed. Allow all teams to finish before playing again.

Bible Activity

Allow the groups about 10 minutes to prepare their drawings, then 1 minute each to describe the scene to the class. Post the artwork around the room and let early arrivers to the next class try to tell the story to you by looking at the pictures.

4) Review the Lesson

Have children simplify the lesson into 10 words or less using their own words. What are their answers? When children simplify the story of the lesson into ten words or less, they will probably say something like these possibilities:

- Paul and Barnabas were the first missionaries.
- The first missionaries went to Cyprus then Turkey.
- The first missionaries proclaimed Jesus.
- Many non-Jewish people became believers in Christ.
- John Mark quit.
- Paul and Barnabas retraced their path when headed for home.
- The church in Antioch sent out the first missionaries.
- Saul became Paul in Cyprus.

Teacher Helps

Review the Lesson Activity: Simplify

Simplify can be a useful game for the children. The teacher can give each team of 2 or 3 kids about 1-2 minutes to come up with the most significant 10 words of this lesson.

5) Apply the Lesson

The teacher should have the class line up in two lines about 30 feet apart. The first team member sits cross-legged and rests hands on the ground. The second team member wraps his or her legs around the waist of the first team member. The third and the fourth members do the same. Together, they have a message that they must deliver at the finish line. That message is to proclaim the good news of Jesus Christ but they must work together.

First team across the finish line wins. Work together to get the message to the finish line.[4]

Story Line: The church in Antioch sent out the first missionaries.

Adventure Number 86
Acts 15:1-35

> **Story Line: False teachers were trying to add requirements to the Gospel.**

 ## 1) Study the Lesson (before class)

- Some people believed that they needed to obey the law of Moses as a requirement for salvation. They insisted that circumcision was necessary for justification. Paul and Barnabas strongly disagreed. [1]

- Paul and Barnabas travelled from Antioch to Jerusalem. Their travels took them through Phoenicia and Samaria. In these regions, Paul and Barnabas shared in detail what God was doing among the Gentiles. All the believers rejoiced greatly.

- When Paul and Barnabas arrived in Jerusalem, a "Jerusalem Council" convened to settle the issue of salvation by faith alone. After hearing Peter's view and the ministry report of Paul and Barnabas, James concluded that the Gentile Christians did not need to obey the law of Moses in order to be justified. That decision was relayed back to the church in Antioch where the false teachers came from. [2]

- Peter argued that the Holy Spirit was given to the Gentiles (Acts 10:44-46) just like He was to the Jews (Acts 2:4; 11:15).

- After Peter spoke, Paul and Barnabas told of the miraculous things God had done among the Gentiles.

- James, evidently the lead pastor at the Jerusalem church, issued a summary statement. The Jerusalem Council probably wanted more than the experiences of Paul, Barnabas, and Peter. So, James gave the witness of Scripture as he quoted from Amos 9:11-12.

- The leaders of the Jerusalem church and the whole church confirmed that Gentiles who turned to God should not have any more requirements to add to their faith for their salvation.

Footnotes - Adventure 86

1. John Walvoord and Roy Zuck, *Bible Knowledge Commentary: New Testament*, 393.

2. Wayne Haston, *New Testament Chronological Bible Cards*, NT-36.

3. Lynn Solem and Bob Pike, *50 Creative Training Closers*, 70.

2) Begin the Lesson

Let's think back over the all of our lessons that we have studied and see if we can put the lessons in order. Here are the story lines for some of the lessons:

1) God is very strong.

5) Life in the garden was full of pleasure.

10) Sin affected God's creation in many negative ways.

15) The people were evil. God sent a flood. Noah trusted and obeyed God.

20) God told Abraham to sacrifice Isaac. God provided a ram instead.

25) God sent plagues in Egypt to set free the Israelites.

30) God told the Israelites to build a tent where they could meet Him and offer sacrifices.

35) People who followed God were to be completely loyal and obedient to Him.

40) God chose David to be a king.

God will one day appoint a Man to be King forever.

45) Prophets told about Jesus 700 years before He came to earth.

50) The Jews returned to Jerusalem to rebuild the walls.

55) Satan tempted Jesus. Jesus did not sin.

60) Many people began to follow Jesus because of His teaching and miracles.

65) God forgave a wayward son, a selfish brother, and a humble tax collector.

70) Jesus gave His disciples valuable instructions and comforting promises.

75) Jesus rose from the dead. Jesus has power over death.

80) The followers of Jesus met to pray, worship, read the Bible, and fellowship.

85) False teachers were trying to add requirements to the Gospel.

Teacher Helps

Begin the Lesson Activity: Story Line Review

The teacher should write these statements on pieces of paper and then mix them up. Do not put the number of the lesson on the piece of paper. Divide the children into 2 or 3 teams, depending on the size of the class. Time how long it takes each team to put the statements in the correct order. Do not number the slips of paper.

3) Teach the Lesson

Many people think that it is important to have faith and do something good to go to heaven. Why would somebody believe that being a good person or obeying the Bible would be important to go to heaven?

Timeline: The Church

Tell the Story

Teacher Helps

It was not long before false teachers came into the church at Antioch. They taught that to be a believer, you had to obey certain parts of the law of Moses. It was very important to them because they were Jewish. However, Paul and Barnabas strongly disagreed.

The argument got so strong that the church decided to send Barnabas, Paul, and a few others to Jerusalem to see what the apostles and elders of the church thought. On their way from Antioch to Jerusalem, Barnabas and Paul shared what God was doing among the non-Jewish people. Everyone was so happy.

When Paul and Barnabas arrived in Jerusalem, they were warmly received by the apostles and elders. Then, a council convened. Peter started first. He began by telling everyone what God was doing among the Gentiles. Peter told the Jerusalem Council that the Holy Spirit was given to the Gentiles just like the Holy Spirit had been given to the Jews. His views were very significant since he was very close to the Lord and was one of the apostles himself.

Some of the false teachers spoke up. The debate got very heated. It went back and forth for quite a while. Paul and Barnabas shared what God was doing among the non-Jewish people in the countries where they had preached and proclaimed. It got so quiet you could hear a pin drop. The room was totally quiet.

Finally, to break the silence, James got up to speak. Apparently, he was the leader of the church in Jerusalem. James said that God had made it very clear that racial outsiders, or non-Jews, should be included and that Jews should not make it more difficult for the Gentiles to become believers. The words of James were piercing and seemed to solve the debate. Peter, Barnabas, Paul, and James all agreed that salvation was by faith alone, not faith and obeying some parts of the Law of Moses.

The apostles and elders all agreed and it seemed good to the whole church. The first major doctrinal problem had been solved. To make sure everyone knew about their decision, the church at Jerusalem sent Paul and Barnabas back to the Antioch church with a written letter informing the church of their decision. Several believers also went with Paul and Barnabas. When the church in Antioch heard the news, they were greatly relieved and pleased.

Tell the Story Activity: Council Time

The teacher should form a council with two teams. Team A should discuss why they think it is important to believe God and do good works for salvation. Team B should discuss why this is not what the Bible teaches.

The teacher should be the moderator. This council time should not make fun of people or put them down. It should focus on the issue of salvation by grace or not by grace.

Memory Verse

Acts 15:7 (ESV) - Peter stood up and said to them, "Brothers, you know that in the early days God made a choice among you, that by my mouth the Gentiles should hear the word of the gospel and believe."

Praise and Worship

Praise and Worship styles vary greatly around the world. It is the intent of this curriculum that praise and worship songs be selected that best fit the content of this lesson. Recommendations for praise and worship are given and this music can generally be located at www.itunes.com. However, the teacher can feel free to select a similar praise and worship song.

"Jesus, Thank You" by Sovereign Grace Music is recommended for this lesson.

Bible Activity

"Prayer of Faith" Activity

Ask the children this question: **"What (or Who) are you trusting with your soul? What are you trusting to take you safely to heaven someday? How do we talk to God?"**

Today we will write a letter to God, expressing our faith in Him alone for our salvation. Of course we won't put the letter in the mail, but if you were writing a letter to God, what would it say? Take a few minutes to talk about the importance of expressing our thoughts to God in prayer. Writing your thoughts down is a good way to think about what you really believe. It is just another way to communicate.

Give the children some suggestions about how they might start. Emphasize that writing a letter to God is just like praying, it is simply talking to God. Don't feel like you have to use fancy words, just tell God what is in your heart. If they would like to share with the class, allow a few children to read their letters.

Teacher Helps

Memory Verse Activity: Bean Bag Toss

With masking tape, mark off a large square on the floor, about 36 inches. Connect the opposite corners inside the square with tape to form an "X." If you have space and many students, make a second square. Give each section a number value (1,2,3,4). A bit of a distance away, put a line of tape to mark where the student will throw from. Divide into two teams. Each student takes a turn throwing a bean bag into one of the sections. (You may make a bean bag by putting beans in a sock and closing it tight with a rubber band. Take the long part of the sock and fold it over the bean section.) If they can say the verse correctly, their team scores the amount of the section where the bean bag was thrown.

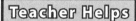

4) Review the Lesson

The teacher should have the class think of the main ideas of the lesson that they want to take home. Then they should number off 1 through 5. Number 1 should say tell the main thing that he or she learned from the lesson. All five groups should get an opportunity to share the main thing they learned from this lesson.

Ideas might include:
- God wants Jews and non-Jews to have faith in Jesus Christ.
- Salvation is not a "faith + obedience" issue. It is a faith alone issue.
- Although there were false teachers, the church leaders and apostles solved their first doctrinal problem with unity among the leadership.
- Paul and Barnabas were used by God to spread the Gospel and bring right doctrine to the church.
- Peter, James, Paul, and Barnabas led the early church.

Review the Lesson Activity: Repetition[3]

The teacher should allow about 5 minutes for children to share the main thing that they learned. If more than 5 children are in the class, allow for each of the groups to share with each other.

5) Apply the Lesson

To become a believer in Christ, one must admit that salvation is by faith alone and not because of works. The teacher should apply the lesson with the words of Galatians 2:16 which was written by Paul shortly after the Jerusalem Council. *"We know that a person is not justified by works of the law but through faith in Jesus Christ, so we also have believed in Christ Jesus, in order to be justified by faith in Christ and not by works of the law, because by works of the law no one will be justified."*

Story Line: False teachers were trying to add requirements to the Gospel.

Adventure Number 87

Acts 16:1- 18:22

Story Line: Paul and his companions went to Syria, Turkey, and Greece.

1) Study the Lesson (before class)

- Paul and Barnabas had a strong disagreement about who should be on the second missionary team. Barnabas wanted to include John Mark who had deserted them on the first missionary journey and Paul felt just the opposite. Eventually, both made missionary journeys. Barnabas took John Mark and went to Cyprus. Paul took Silas and went to Syria, modern day Turkey, and Greece. Later, Paul spoke well of Barnabas so the disagreement did not stop their friendship (1 Cor. 9:6; Col. 4:10).[1]

- Neither Peter, Barnabas, or John Mark are seen again in the book of Acts. Silas was one of the representatives from the Jerusalem church that took the decision of the council to the church in Antioch. He was also a Roman citizen, a prophet, and he probably knew the Greek language. Together, Paul and Silas strengthened the church on the second missionary journey.

- Early in the second missionary journey, Paul was introduced to Timothy, a second generation convert. The mother and grandmother of Timothy had become believers. Apparently, his father was a Greek but not a believer. Timothy became one of Paul's most trusted associates.

- After travelling through modern day Turkey, the Lord spoke to Paul in a vision, *"Come to Macedonia and help us."* So, Paul and his companions left for Macedonia (northern Greece) where they went to Philippi and Berea.

- After their time in Macedonia, Paul went to Athens where he debated the Athenian philosophers. He also went to Corinth where he stayed for over a year and a half. After that, he went to Jerusalem and then Antioch.

Footnotes - Adventure 87

1. John Walvoord and Roy Zuck, *Bible Knowledge Commentary: New Testament*, 396.

2. Susan Lingo, *Written on Our Hearts*, 79.

3. Bill Greig, *Gospel Light's Really Big Book of Bible Games*, 262.

2) Begin the Lesson

Teacher Helps

Eight essential truths have emerged from the Bible's big story of hope. Challenge children to know the eight truths, know them in order, and be able to give a brief description of each.

1. <u>God</u>. In the beginning, there was a very powerful God.

2. <u>Man</u>. God created people to be His special friends.

3. <u>Sin</u>. Man and woman disobeyed God.

4. <u>Death</u>. God punished man and woman for their disobedience. Death, in the Bible, refers to separation.

5. <u>Christ</u>. God sent His one and only Son who lived a perfect life.

6. <u>Cross</u>. Jesus died on the cross for the sins of the world.

7. <u>Faith</u>. If anyone places their faith in Christ, God welcomes them.

8. <u>Life</u>. God gives eternal life to those who put their faith in Him.

Begin the Lesson Activity: Eight Essential Truths

Write the eight essential truths on pieces of paper on place them face down. Do the same with the brief descriptions. Now, create 2 or 3 teams and have them put the truths and descriptions in the correct order. Time them and give a reward to the winning team.

Remind the class where these truths can be found in Scripture.

3) Teach the Lesson

In Paul's second missionary journey, the class will learn about certain people that Paul and his companions cared for and became good friends with. People such as Silas, Timothy, Lydia and others are introduced to us in the second missionary journey. Paul's friends lived in different countries.

What are some characteristics of friendships that you think Paul looked for while he was travelling?

- Reliable witnesses?

- Good travellers?

- Godly attitudes?

Timeline:
The Church

Tell the Story

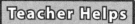

Shortly after the letter from the Jerusalem Council was read to the church in Antioch, Paul and Barnabas discussed the idea of going back to the churches of the first missionary journey and see how they were doing. It seemed like a good idea to both of them. One big difference though: Barnabas wanted to take his cousin, John Mark, who had deserted them on the first missionary journey and Paul would have nothing to do with him. So, they each went their own way. Barnabas and John Mark went to Cyprus. Paul and his new travelling companion, Silas, went to modern day Turkey.

Early in the journey of Paul and Silas, they met a young man named Timothy. He was a believer who had a believing mother and grandmother. Timothy became a travelling companion of Paul and became one of his most trusted friends and ministry partners. When this missionary team got to western Turkey, the Lord appeared to Paul in a vision. Paul saw a man from Macedonia, northern Greece, and that man said, "Come over to Macedonia and help us." Now, that was different than what Paul thought would happen on this second missionary journey. He had only planned to go to strengthen the churches of the first journey. But, God opened a much bigger door for their ministry which led them to Greece and eventually Europe.

They sailed across the Aegean Sea from Turkey to Greece and looked for a place of prayer. They found a place of prayer and they also found a lady who sold expensive clothes. Her name was Lydia. She became a believer in the town of Philippi. But, as usual, some troublemakers came into town and stirred up the people against Paul and Silas. It got them thrown into jail but they still praised God. One night, there was an earthquake and all the prisoners chains were released. The jailer was afraid but Paul told him that all the prisoners were still in the jail. That got the jailer's attention and he asked Paul, "What must I do to be saved?" Paul told him, *"Believe on the Lord Jesus Christ and you will be saved."* Eventually, the whole family of the jailer came to put their faith in Jesus Christ.

After this, Paul went to Athens where he was greatly disturbed at all the pagan gods. He even held a debate with their philosophers. Then, he went to Corinth and evidently thought it was really important that he stay there for awhile. So, he stayed in Corinth for over a year-and-a-half. He was strengthening the church and many people were coming to faith in Jesus. It was time for the second missionary journey to be over so Paul travelled back to Caesarea first and then to his home in Antioch.

Tell the Story Activity: Map

It would be good for the teacher to locate a map to show the class the general direction that Paul and Silas took on the second missionary journey.

Memory Verse

Acts 16:31 (ESV) - Believe in the Lord Jesus, and you will be saved.

Praise and Worship

Praise and Worship styles vary greatly around the world. It is the intent of this curriculum that praise and worship songs be selected that best fit the content of this lesson. Recommendations for praise and worship are given and this music can generally be located at www.itunes.com. However, the teacher can feel free to select a similar praise and worship song.

"Jesus, Thank You" by Sovereign Grace Music is recommended for this lesson.

Bible Activity

Divide the children into 5 groups:
1. The No-Eyes (Cover eyes with hands)
2. The No-Ears (Plug ears with fingers)
3. The No-Voice (Cover mouths with hands)
4. The No-Hands (Hold hands behind backs)
5. The No-Feet (Sit on the floor cross-legged)

Say: Let's sing our praise song again and see if we can praise God in different ways. If you are a member of the No-Eyes group, you'll have to praise God with your eyes closed. If you are in the No-Voice group, you may clap or move around, but you cannot use your voice, etc. Sing the song once again. Be sure the children "obey" the rules. After the song is done, ask:

*Was it difficult or easy to praise God with the limitations?

*Did you find a way to praise God anyway?

Say: **"Sometimes we feel like Paul and Silas felt, tied up in difficult circumstances. Just as Paul and Silas found a way to praise God, we can find ways and reasons to praise God no matter what we are going through, and no matter where we are."** If there is time, sing the praise song again.

Teacher Helps

Memory Verse Activity: Scripture Card Battle[2]

Divide your class up into groups of 2 or 3. Give each group a set of cards. On each card is one word from the memory verse. Groups should try to put the words of the memory verse in the right order.

Bible Activity

Invite the children to sing a familiar praise song with you. It could be "Jesus Loves Me," or any other simple song that the children know well. Encourage the children to clap and move to the music.

4) Review the Lesson

"Who" Questions:

1. Who did Paul meet on this journey that became his close friend?

2. Who did Paul travel with?

"What" Questions:

1. What did Paul do in the Philippian jail?

2. What did Paul do in Athens?

"When" Questions:

1. When did Paul decide to go to Greece or Macedonia?

2. When did Paul leave for this second missionary journey?

"Where" Questions:

1. Where is Macedonia?

2. Where are Athens and Corinth?

"Why" Questions:

1. Why did Paul stay in the Philippian jail?

2. Why did Paul debate the Greek philosophers in Athens?

Teacher Helps

Review Activity: The Investigative Cube

Divide the class up into two teams. Make a cube with these labels on each side of the cube: who, what, when, where, why. When the cube is rolled to one team, they will answer the type of question that is face up on the cube. For instance, if the "why" is face up on the cube, then that team will answer a "why" question. Teachers can make up their own questions from the lesson, only they must pertain to this lesson.

Apply the Lesson Activity: Gospel Teamwork

The teacher should have the class line up in two lines about 30 feet apart. The first team member sits cross-legged and rests hands on the ground. The second team member wraps his or her legs around the waist of the first team member. The third and the fourth members do the same.

5) Apply the Lesson

Together, they have a message that they must deliver at the finish line. That message is to proclaim the good news of Jesus Christ but they must work together. First team across the finish line wins. Work together to get the message to the finish line.[3]

Story Line: Paul and his companions went to Syria, Turkey, and Greece.

Adventure Number 88
Acts 18:23-19:41

Story Line: Paul spent a great amount of time in the pagan city of Ephesus.

1) Study the Lesson (before class)

- Once Paul arrived in Antioch, it appears that he spent very little time there and left on his third missionary journey. Immediately, he headed toward Ephesus where he spent 2 to 3 years of this four year missionary journey. This third missionary journey probably lasted from 53 to 57 A.D.[1]

- Ephesus, one of the largest cities in the Roman empire, was the center for the Artemis or Diana cult and magical arts. The second missionary journey began with Paul meeting Timothy, a lifelong friend. The third missionary journey began with Paul meeting Apollos in Ephesus. Apollos was an outstanding Bible teacher.

- The Temple of Artemis was one of the seven wonders of the ancient world. The temple was four times as big as the Parthenon in Athens.

- In Ephesus, the fear of God fell on many people and the believers burned their magical arts books. Demetrius, a silversmith in Ephesus, started a riot in protest of Paul's influence against the Artemis cult.[2]

- Miracles through Paul were similar to those through Peter. Both men had God's hand of blessing on them.

- The result was great fear and a high esteem for the name of Jesus. Many Christians had been openly involved in sorcery and spiritism. But now, they openly confessed their wickedness. Many people publicly burned their sorcery books. The value of these sorcery books was about 50,000 pieces of silver, a very large sum of money.

- The strategy of Demetrius was to stir up love of money and greed. He did not quarrel with the doctrine that Paul preached.

Footnotes - Adventure 88

1. James Galvin, *Life Application Bible Notes*, 1868.

2. John Walvoord and Roy Zuck, *Bible Knowledge Commentary: New Testament*, 409.

3. Susan Lingo, *Written on Our Hearts*, 99.

4. Bill Greig, *Gospel Light's Really Big Book of Bible Games*, 262.

2) Begin the Lesson

Time Line	People	Event
Beginnings	God	God made all things.
Beginnings	Adam and Eve	Sin
Beginnings	Noah	Worldwide flood
Beginnings	wicked people	Confused languages
Beginnings of a Nation	Abraham	Special promises by God
Beginnings of a Nation	Moses	Plagues
Possessing the Land	Joshua	Enter Promised Land
Possessing the Land	Gideon	Cycles of sin
United Kingdom	David	A special King forever
Divided Kingdom	Elijah and Elisha	Special prophets in Israel
Taken from Home	Jeremiah, Daniel, Ezekiel	Israel sent to Assyria
Return to Home	Nehemiah and Ezra	Israel returned to land
Return to Home	Daniel	400 years of change
Early Life of Jesus	Mary and Joseph	The birth of Jesus
Ministry of Jesus Christ	12 disciples	Jesus called 12 apostles
Ministry of Jesus Christ	Jesus	Miracles of Jesus
Opposition	Blind man	Healing power of Jesus
Betryal and Death	Jesus Christ	Entry into Jerusalem
Victory and Life	Resurrected Christ	Empty tomb
The Church	Jesus and the apostles	The Jerusalem church

Teacher Helps

Begin the Lesson Activity: Match Time Line, People, and Events

The teacher should form three stacks of paper. One stack should be the "time line" stack. 18 different time lines should be underneath this "time line" piece of paper. Do the same thing for "people" and "event." Then mix them up and have the children arrange them so that they have the correct time line with the correct people with the correct event. For instance, when matched correctly, beginnings, God, and God made all things should all be in the same group.

3) Teach the Lesson

When Paul preached in Ephesus, he got in trouble with people who made silver idols. The sellers of these silver idols also sold magic books. They got very mad at Paul.

What would make the makers of these silver idols so upset?

Tell the Story

Paul had just returned from the second missionary journey and he was ready to go again. After a brief time in Antioch, he left for Phrygia and Galatia in central modern-day Turkey. But, his goal was Ephesus. Ephesus was a major trade center and it was the center of pagan idolatry. In fact, many of the believers had adopted the pagan practices in Ephesus as their own life choices. Things like practicing magic and worshipping silver idols of the goddess Artemis were important, even to some of the Christians.

The temple for Artemis was huge. It measured 239 feet (73 meters) by 418 feet (127 meters). It was four times bigger than the Acropolis in Athens. The temple was a magnet for money. Lots of people were buying and selling stuff related to Artemis. It was how they stayed financially secure. And because Ephesus was such a major city with over 200,000 people, the money that Artemis worship brought to the city was very significant.

When Paul got to Ephesus, he preached and many became believers. Paul became so famous that people took their handkerchiefs and scarves with the hopes that if this clothing touched Paul, then they would be healed of some illness. In fact, the magic sorcerers in Ephesus tried to copy this and say they were of Paul. The seven sons of a certain man in Ephesus tried this and an evil spirit spoke back to them. The evil spirit said, "I know Jesus and I've heard of Paul, but who are you?" The evil spirit beat up the magicians and even ripped their clothes off.

Some Ephesian citizens thought their city was falling apart. If Rome heard about these riots, then soldiers would come and put a stop to their business. They were afraid that their very profitable business would come to an end. People ran into the street shouting, "Great is Artemis of the Ephesians." Worried about the riots, the town clerk settled everybody down. After that, Paul left for Greece. He had challenged the worldview of the Ephesians. Many of the believers repented and gave up their magic books and idols. They even burned a lot of them.

The preaching of Paul had convicted believers not to accept the worship of Artemis or the money that people made from selling Artemis idols. The believers now had a different lifestyle or worldview. They no longer tolerated false idols and many of the believers completely turned to the Lord and worshipped only the Master, Jesus. In the end, the cleansed church became more powerful and growing.

Tell the Story Activity: Map

It would be good for the teacher to locate a map to show the class the general direction that Paul took on the third missionary journey.

Memory Verse

Acts 19:19 (ESV) - And a number of those who had practiced magic arts brought their books together and burned them in the sight of all.

Praise and Worship

Praise and Worship styles vary greatly around the world. It is the intent of this curriculum that praise and worship songs be selected that best fit the content of this lesson. Recommendations for praise and worship are given and this music can generally be located at www.itunes.com. However, the teacher can feel free to select a similar praise and worship song.

"Jesus, Thank You" by Sovereign Grace Music is recommended for this lesson.

Bible Activity

Bring a dictionary to class, or a device that has internet access. Help the students look up the words "sorcery," "witchcraft," and "magic". The people in Ephesus had a big problem with sorcery and magic.

- Why would these things be wrong for Christians? Make a list on the board of the answers they give. Many superstitions are based on sorcery, witchcraft, or magic. These beliefs are based on fear and lies, not God's word.

- What are some superstitions that people believe today? Write answers on the board.

If possible, give a scripture verse that deals with false beliefs that are given. Remind the students to always compare statements or actions with what is taught in God's word.

Teacher Helps

Memory Verse Activity: Scripture Scrambler[3]

Write the words to a verse on the top of a paper. Then number the paper, one number for each word in the verse. Beside the numbers, write a scrambled word to the verse. Challenge your children to unscramble each word to the verse in its correct order.

Example:

1 rbneum   number

2 oesht   those

3 gciam   magic

4 kobos   books

4) Review the Lesson

Teacher Helps

Based on the lives of those who followed Jesus, rate yourself on this grid:

- Following Jesus' example   1   2   3   4   5   6
- Understanding God's Word   1   2   3   4   5   6
- Willing to be a missionary   1   2   3   4   5   6
- Ready to share my faith   1   2   3   4   5   6
- Choices I make   1   2   3   4   5   6
- Told others 8 essential truths   1   2   3   4   5   6
- Willing to forsake evil deeds   1   2   3   4   5   6
- Overall commitment to God   1   2   3   4   5   6

Review Activity: Grid for Growth

The teacher should instruct the class of children that the example of Jesus should help us evaluate our own lives.

Children should fill out this chart (1= low; 6 = high).

5) Apply the Lesson

Together, they have a message that they must deliver at the finish line. That message is to proclaim the good news of Jesus Christ but they must work together. First team across the finish line wins. Work together to get the message to the finish line.[4]

Apply the Lesson Activity: Gospel Teamwork

The teacher should have the class line up in two lines about 30 feet apart. The first team member sits cross-legged and rests hands on the ground. The second team member wraps his or her legs around the waist of the first team member. The third and the fourth members do the same.

> **Story Line: Paul spent a great amount of time in the pagan city of Ephesus.**

Adventure Number 89
Acts 26:1-31

Story Line: Paul was arrested for his faith and appeared before several Roman judges.

1) Study the Lesson (before class)

- Herod Agrippa II's great uncle was Herod Antipas who actually met Jesus Christ during his trial but failed to come to faith in Christ. Agrippa II heard the gospel from Paul but considered it mild entertainment. Agrippa II was the last ruler of the Herod dynasty which lasted from 40 B.C. to 100 A.D. He mediated between Rome and Palestine.[1]

- Paul had already presented his reasons for placing his faith in Jesus Christ before Festus (Acts 25:6-12). He was now ready to address Agrippa. His presentation can be easily broken down into three key segments.

  - First, Paul told Agrippa about his life before coming to Christ (Acts 26:1-11). Paul was a member of the Pharisees, a very strict religious group of Jews. Paul was so convinced that the Pharisees were right and the Christian beliefs were wrong that he went to great lengths to persecute Christians, even casting his vote to put them to death.

  - Second, Paul told Agrippa about his faith story, how he came to faith in Christ (Acts 26:12-17). Paul's life changed on the Damascus Road when he heard a voice and saw a light. When Paul's life changed, five things happened that Agrippa needed to hear: 1) eyes were opened, 2) turned from darkness to light, 3) turned from the power of Satan to power of God, 4) received forgiveness, and 5) received a place with those who were set apart for God.[2]

  - Third, Paul told Agrippa about his faith story after he trusted Christ. Paul was obedient to the heavenly vision and now he was going to tell both small and great about his newfound faith in Christ.

Footnotes - Adventure 89

1. James Galvin, *Life Application Bible Notes*, 1883.

2. Wayne Haston, *The Roots of Faith New Testament Workbook*, 39-B.

3. Susan Lingo, *Written on Our Hearts*, 79.

4. Lynn Solem and Bob Pike, *50 Creative Training Closers*, 94.

2) Begin the Lesson

Teacher Helps

There are eight basic concepts that are emphasized throughout all of the Bible. We have studied these truths in previous lessons. Ask the children if they can name them and tell a little bit about each one. They are:

1. <u>God</u>. In the beginning, there was a very powerful God. 1-The Eternal God; 27-The Exodus; 40-The Reign of David; Lesson 83-The Conversion of Saul.

2. <u>Man</u>. God created many things. He created man and woman to be His special friends. 3-Creation of the Universe; 4-Creation of People; 24-Moses Leads His People; 83-Conversion of Cornelius.

3. <u>Sin</u>. Man and woman disobeyed God. They did not do what He told them to do. 7-Beginning of Human Sin; 33-Unbelief at Kadesh; 43-The Divided Kingdom; 88-Paul's Third Missionary Journey.

4. <u>Death</u>. God punished man and woman for their disobedience. Death, in the Bible, refers to separation. 8-The Origin of Death; 16-The Tower of Babel; 46:-The Exiles of Israel and Judah.

5. <u>Christ</u>. God sent His one and only Son, His unique Son, who lived a perfect life. 9-Promise of a Victor Over Satan; 45-Prophecies of a Coming Messiah; 52-Birth of Jesus Christ; 75- The Resurrection of Jesus Christ; 78-The Ascension of Jesus Christ.

6. <u>Cross</u>. Jesus died on the cross for the sins of the world. 11-Provision of Coverings; 32-The Day of Atonement; 45-Prophecies of a Coming Messiah; 56-Announcement by John; 73-The Crucifixion of Jesus.

7. <u>Faith</u>. If anyone places their faith in Christ, God welcomes them. 13-Cain and Abel; 34-The Bronze Serpent; 58-The Religious Leader; 61-Jesus Has Power Over a Stormy Sea: 74-Why Jesus Died on the Cross; 86-The Jerusalem Council.

8. <u>Life</u>. God gives eternal life to those who put their faith in Him. 5-Life in Paradise; 38-Bright Lights in an Era of Darkness; 56-Announcement by John the Baptist; 75-The Resurrection of Jesus Christ; Lesson 83-The Conversion of Saul.

Review Activity: Eight Basic Gospel Truths - One Complete Story

The teacher should emphasize these eight gospel concepts throughout Scripture. They are foundational to telling children the one story of redemption found in the Bible. We will emphasize these eight truths regularly.

Ask the children if they can think of how these eight gospel principles are emphasized in the first 88 lessons that we have studied.

3) Teach the Lesson

What is your faith story? Can you tell it to us?

Tell the Story

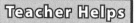

It was in the coastal city of Caesarea that Paul had to go in front of Festus, a newly appointed governor of the area. The Jews were upset that Paul kept talking about Jesus and His resurrection so they took Paul to court where Festus presided. Festus admitted that he did not understand Paul's belief in the resurrection.

King Agrippa, great grandson of Herod the Great, and his wife, Bernice, were in Caesarea to greet Festus. Because there were 5,000 Roman soldiers stationed in Caesarea, there were lots of high ranking officers and very important people. To hear Paul would be an opportunity for Herod and Bernice to show off their position. So, a few days later, Festus told Agrippa that he had a man on his hands who was left here as a prisoner by the previous governor, Felix. Festus admitted that he did not know what to do with him so Agrippa agreed to hear Paul personally.

The next day, Agrippa and Bernice went to the Great Hall in Caesarea to hear Paul. They made a grand entrance with all the top military people at their side. Once everyone was seated in the Great Hall, Agrippa had Paul tell him his story.

Paul told Agrippa what his life was like before he came to faith in Christ. He was a very religious man, a devout Pharisee. A Pharisee kept every part of the Old Testament law. Not only did he keep every part of the Old Testament law, he persecuted those who did not. He even considered some to be worthy of death.

Then, Paul told Agrippa that he was travelling on the Damascus Road when suddenly a very bright light shone down from heaven and a voice from heaven spoke to him. Paul responded with two questions, *"Who are you, Lord?"* and *"What do you want me to do?"* Paul instantly became a believer in Christ and the people he used to persecute he now welcomed.

After Paul became a true believer, he acknowledged what the Old Testament prophets and Moses said would happen; these Scriptures said the Christ would suffer and rise from the dead. Paul was only telling people what was prophesied hundreds of years earlier. That was why he was in prison. The Jews did not like it that Paul was telling them about Christ. Agrippa thought about it and told Paul that he almost persuaded him to become a Christian also. Agrippa rose from his judge's chair and told everyone that Paul had done nothing to deserve death or imprisonment.

Tell the Story Activity: Developing Your Own Faith Story

As the teacher tells the faith story of Paul, have the children write down what Paul was like before he became a Christian, how he became a Christian, and what his life was like after he became a Christian.

Have them make three columns on a sheet of paper.

- Column 1 - Before Paul Became a Christian

- Column 2 - How Paul Became a Christian

- Column 3 - What Paul's Life Was Like After He Became a Christian

Now, encourage kids to do the same for themselves. Write out their own faith story, if they have a faith story.

Memory Verse

Acts 26:18 (ESV) - (I am sending you) to open their eyes, so that they may turn from darkness to light and from the power of Satan to God.

Praise and Worship

Praise and Worship styles vary greatly around the world. It is the intent of this curriculum that praise and worship songs be selected that best fit the content of this lesson. Recommendations for praise and worship are given and this music can generally be located at www.itunes.com. However, the teacher can feel free to select a similar praise and worship song.

"Jesus, Thank You" by Sovereign Grace Music is recommended for this lesson.

Bible Activity

Telling My Faith Story

During this activity, the students will continue to develop their own faith story for retelling to others. They should make 3 columns on their faith story paper, just like they did on the paper they made to write down Paul's faith story. Have them practice by telling their faith story to a friend right there in class. The teacher might begin this session by telling their own faith story to the class. If there are students that are brave enough, let them tell their story to the class. Remind the students that we are "blessed to be a blessing." We have received the good news of the gospel, we need to share it!

Teacher Helps

Memory Verse Activity: Scripture Log[3]

Make a page for children to take home that shows down the left column: Sunday, Monday, Tuesday, Wednesday, Thursday, Friday, and Saturday.

Across the top, put practice times and review times.

Children should work on this memory verse each day and mark on their log when they practiced this verse and when they reviewed this verse. Bring this log to class with you next week.

This type of activity will encourage Scripture memory and obedience throughout the week, not just as part of the lesson.

4) Review the Lesson

The teacher should divide the class up into two teams.

- One team could be the "red" team and receive red cards or pieces of paper. The other team could be the "yellow" team and receive yellow cards or pieces of paper.

- Each team has the responsibility of writing out 3 to 5 questions that they want the other team to answer.

- Each question has to pertain to the lesson today.

- After questions are written out, the other team has five to seven minutes to answer the questions. The "yellow" team will answer the questions from the "red" team and the "red" team will answer questions from the "yellow" team.

Teacher Helps

Review Activity: Two Team Review[4]

After an appropriate time, the teacher will gather up the cards or pieces of paper and reward points to the best questions and best answers from each team.

It is highly advisable to have 2 adult teachers in every classroom for kids. If there are 2 adults, then one adult should be the leader of each team.

5) Apply the Lesson

Help children in the class develop their own faith story. Realize that they may not have a story of faith to tell. Some may not want to tell.

Have the class write out or tell: 1) what they have done that was not pleasing to God, 2) how they came to faith in Jesus Christ, and 3) how wonderful it is to be a true Christian.

Apply the Lesson Activity: Faith Story

The teacher may want to assign this part of the lesson and discuss it next week.

Story Line: Paul was arrested for his faith and appeared before several Roman judges.

Adventure Number 90
Jude 3-20 and Colossians 1:15-22

Story Line: The faith was really important to the early believers.

 1) Study the Lesson (before class)

- Persecution and martyrdom in the last half of the first century.[1]
    - A.D. 64 - The Roman emperor Nero burned Rome and blamed Christians.
    - A.D. 66-68 - Apostles Peter and Paul were executed by Nero.
    - A.D. 70 - Roman General Titus destroyed Jerusalem and the temple.
    - A.D. 80 - Rabbi Gamaliel II drove Christians from synagogues.
    - A.D. 81-96 - Roman Emporer Domitian was a persecutor of Christians.
    - A.D. 90 (about) - Domitian exiled the apostle John to the island of Patmos.
    - A.D. 96 - Last Bible book (Revelation) written by John on Patmos.
- Every apostle, except John, was executed.
    - James - beheaded by Herod Agrippa I
    - Peter - crucified upside down
    - Paul - beheaded by Nero in Rome
    - Andrew - crucified by a Roman governor
    - Philip - stoned to death
    - Nathanael - burned at the stake or beheaded
    - Thomas - speared to death in India
    - Matthew - burned at the stake or beheaded
    - James the Less - stoned to death
    - Simon the Zealot - sawn into pieces
    - Judas Thaddeus - crucified, axed, or stoned to death
    - John - exiled on Patmos where he lived in a cave

Footnotes - Adventure 90

1. Wayne Haston, *The Roots of Faith New Testament Workbook*, 40-B.

2) Begin the Lesson

Teacher Helps

Adventure Number 87: Paul's Second Missionary Journey

1. What did Paul tell the Philippian jailer to do?

2. Read Acts 16:31.

3. Believe on the Lord Jesus is the only way to heaven.

4. Thank Jesus that He is the way, the truth, and the life.

Adventure Number 88: Paul's Third Missionary Journey

1. What was so unique about the city of Ephesus?

2. Read Acts 19:19.

3. God does not want believers involved in idol worship.

4. Pray that believers would worship only the Lord Jesus Christ.

Adventure Number 89: Paul Before Roman Judges

1. What did Paul tell Agrippa?

2. Read Acts 26:18.

3. Paul became a believer by faith.

4. Pray that we could give our testimony to anyone.

Begin the Lesson Activity: Ask, Read, Talk, Pray

A good review strategy from 3 previous lessons will focus on four main elements.

1) Ask a question.

2) Read the Bible.

3) Talk about it.

4) Pray to God.

3) Teach the Lesson

Toward the end of the apostles' lives, many were seriously concerned that false teachers were already teaching in the church.

Why would false teachers want to come into the church and change the doctrine or teachings of the church?

Tell the Story

"The faith" was critical to the early teaching of the church. "The faith" represented the **essential teachings of Jesus and the apostles, centered around who Jesus is and what He accomplished through His death and resurrection.** Many of the apostles were greatly concerned that false teachers were creeping into the church with their false doctrines. The church had grown so fast and so many new things were happening around the Christian world that it was easy for false teachers to become prominent in the church.

Jude was a half-brother of Jesus. He wrote about these false teachers when he said believers should "contend" or agonize for the faith that was once delivered for all the believers. Jude was concerned about "the faith." The faith was **essential teachings of Jesus and the apostles, centered around who Jesus is and what He accomplished through His death and resurrection.** Jude told believers to work hard or agonize about these truths. He was concerned that some false teachers would come in and believers would just accept this false teaching and not do anything about it.

One group of false teachers said that God was remote and distant from mankind. That was certainly wrong. God was not remote or distant from us humans. He wants to have a personal relationship with everyone.

One group came in and said that the material world was bad and the spiritual world was good. That group was also wrong. There was nothing evil about the material world.

Another group came in and said that the body of Jesus was not a real or physical body. That group was really wrong. Remember, they pierced His body and it bled. He ate food. It had to be a real body.

There were other groups that claimed to have a corner on the truth. The apostles were very concerned about this. That is why it is important to stick exclusively to "the faith." The faith ... the real faith ... **essential teachings of Jesus and the apostles, centered around who Jesus is and what He accomplished through His death and resurrection.**

The apostle John said it like this, *"Every spirit that confesses that Jesus Christ has come in the flesh is from God."* The apostle Paul said it like this, *"He (Jesus) is before all things and in Him all things hold together."* The apostle Peter said it like this, *"He himself (Jesus) bore our sins in his body on the tree, that we might die to sin and live to righteousness."*

Teacher Helps

Tell the Story Activity: The Faith

As the teacher should have the class tell what "the faith" represents. They can use their own words. Have the kids write down or tell each other what "the faith" is.

"The faith" is highlighted with bold letters three times in this story. Can children tell the teacher and each other what the apostles believed about "the faith?"

- 1 John 4:2
- Colossians 1:17
- 1 Peter 3:24

Memory Verse

Colossians 1:19 (ESV) - For in him all the fullness of God was pleased to dwell.

Praise and Worship

Praise and Worship styles vary greatly around the world. It is the intent of this curriculum that praise and worship songs be selected that best fit the content of this lesson. Recommendations for praise and worship are given and this music can generally be located at www.itunes.com. However, the teacher can feel free to select a similar praise and worship song.

"Jesus, Thank You" by Sovereign Grace Music is recommended for this lesson.

Bible Activity

Real or Fake?

Find a picture of counterfeit money and print several copies of it to bring in to class. Also print a picture of a genuine piece of money, but don't show it at first. Ask the students: **"Is this a picture of a real piece of money, or is it fake?"** Allow children to answer.

If they think it is fake, have them tell why. After a few minutes, bring out the picture of the genuine money and have them compare the real thing with the counterfeit. See if they can tell the difference. Ask: **"What makes it easier to tell which is the real thing?"** Answer: **"Comparing it with the real thing."**

Parallel teaching: how can we tell what is true teaching or false teaching? (By comparing it with God's Word, or original truth.)

Teacher Helps

Memory Verse Activity: Hop It

In large letters, write phrases of the verse on sheets of paper. On the floor, tape the papers in a mixed up fashion, but close enough for succeeding words to be reached in a step. Children should step on one word at a time in the proper order to quote the verse. Let each child have a turn of hopping on the verse.

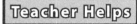

4) Review the Lesson

Agree/Disagree Statements (If you disagree, why do you disagree?)

1. The early church always knew who the false teachers were. (Disagree. False teachers kept trying to spread false doctrine.)

2. Jude was not a half brother of Jesus. (Disagree. He was a half brother of Jesus.)

3. Several apostles wrote about "the faith." (Agree.)

4. "The faith" is believing who Jesus is and what He accomplished through His death and resurrection. (Agree.)

5. Early believers were so concerned about "the faith" that they were willing to give their lives for "the faith." (Agree.)

Review Activity: Agree and Disagree Statements

Kids will have fun disagreeing or agreeing with these statements. The teacher may want to make up some statements for them to agree or disagree with.

5) Apply the Lesson

Name the two main truths about "the faith" and repeat them to a friend.

1. Jesus is the Son of God who lived in the flesh on the earth.

2. Jesus Christ died for the sins of all men. Through His death and resurrection, anyone can have eternal life.

Apply the Lesson Activity: Repeat the Faith Story

Send kids home with the assignment of telling someone what "the faith" is all about.

Story Line: The faith was really important to the early believers.

Adventure Number 91
1 Thessalonians 4:13-18 and John 14:1-3

Story Line: Jesus will return for those who have believed in Him.

 ## 1) Study the Lesson (before class)

- In his first letter to the Thessalonians, Paul assured them that they would not experience the wrath of God (1:10 and 5:9). The fact of deliverance from the wrath of God is not questioned. The timing of the deliverance is uncertain.[1]

- The church at Thessalonica had just been started and was under attack for what they believed.

- Paul responded to the concerns of the people in this church: he did not want them to be ignorant. Surely, God wanted these believers to know what would happen to their loved ones.

- There is absolutely no hope for those who are unbelievers. But, there is great hope for those who are believers. In fact, believers are to encourage each other about this blessed hope that one day those of us who know Christ will be with Him in heaven.

- "Those who have fallen asleep" is not teaching a semi-conscious departure. Sleep is used to describe those who have died.

- The inspired writers of the New Testament saw the second coming of Christ as a very important truth. It is mentioned 318 times in the 260 chapters of the New Testament; an average of one reference every twenty-five verses.[2]

- When the Lord comes back, He will issue a loud command accompanied by the sound of a trumpet. The dead in Christ will rise first, then those who are alive with follow.

Footnotes - Adventure 91

1. Roy B. Zuck, *A Biblical Theology of the New Testament*, 294.

2. John Phillips, *Exploring First Thessalonians: An Expository Commentary*, 112.

2) Begin the Lesson

Tell your class that you are learning the one story of the Bible. While there are many stories in the Bible, they are linked to one major theme or story in the Bible. It is a story of hope. So, to help your class know that story and be able to put all the lessons together, we are going to review the lessons from the past. Ask, **"What are the main events that we have studied in the Bible?"**

- God always existed and He is very powerful. He created the earth and everything in it.
- Lucifer, or Satan, deceived Adam and Eve. They sinned.
- God spared Noah and his family because Noah was a righteous man.
- God made special promises to Abraham.
- Jacob wrested with the angel of God and got a new name, Israel.
- God established a moral code called the Ten Commandments.
- God chose David to be king. He will one day appoint someone to be King forever.
- Israel and Judah were exiled to Assyria and Babylon.
- The Jews returned from exile to build the temple and the walls.
- Between the Old and New Testaments, a lot changed.
- Jesus was born.
- Early events in the life of Jesus marked Him as a special Person.
- Jesus chose 12 men to become His committed followers.
- Jesus showed His great power over a storm and demons.
- Jesus entered Jerusalem with shouts of praise from the crowds.
- Judas betrayed Jesus.
- Jesus died, was buried, and rose again.
- Jesus appeared to many people.
- Jesus ascended to heaven.
- The church continues to grow and proclaim His message.

Teacher Helps

Begin the Lesson Activity: The Main Events

Review is a significant part of learning. Nineteen events are listed here. Write each event on a slip of paper or poster board and have children put them in chronological order. Let them work together in small teams 2 or 3. Time how long it takes each team to put these events in the right order. Winner gets a prize.

3) Teach the Lesson

This series of lessons is called "99 Adventures in the Bible's Big Story" What kind of things bring you real hope? Is it a person? Is it a possession? Is it a game?

Tell the Story

Before Jesus left the earth, He promised that He would come back again. While He was gone, He said He would be preparing a wonderful place in heaven where believers will live. Even more special than that, it will last forever.

A long time ago, some people in northern Greece were worried about this. They wondered what happened to believers who die. Where do they go? What do they do? These were some of their concerns. Paul also told them that the dead in Christ would rise first.

Here is how it will work. Jesus has already gone to heaven. Some day, He will come back again for believers just like He said He would. We know this because He has never lied and always tells the truth. He will keep His promise. There will be a trumpet sound signalling His return. When He comes back, He will gather all believers in the air. The dead in Christ will rise first and then we which are alive will go with them. Then, we will always be with the Lord. There will not be "in between" stages. Either believers will be here on earth or with the Lord in heaven.

This should be a great hope for all believers. In fact, this is sometimes called by some people "the blessed hope." That means that there is hope that is blessed or happy. It is a happy hope to know that Jesus has a place for us in heaven where we will be with Him all the time. There won't be any tears. There won't be any pain. There won't be any sickness. There won't even be death. Death will be gone forever. Remember when we talked about the "Satan Crusher?" That is the person who crushed the head of that old serpent which is Satan. Jesus has done that and believers will not have any more sadness. It will be a wonderful place of happiness!

For nearly 2,000 years, believers have waited and hoped for Jesus to come back. Many people thought He would come back sooner. But, the fact that He has not come back yet does not mean that He is not coming back again. It only means He has not come back yet. When He chooses to come back, that will be a great day. Anyone who has this hope in Christ is happy or blessed.

The eternal home of the believer will be with Jesus. He will give believers a body that will not be subject to decay or disease. He will give believers a body that is not subject to death. He will transform our earthly body to be like His glorious body. What a blessed hope!

Teacher Helps

Tell the Story Activity: Two Funerals

The teacher should ask the class these questions at the end of telling the story.

What words would describe a person died and who has no hope?

What words would describe a person who died with great hope?

Memory Verse

John 14:3 (ESV) - And if I go and prepare a place for you, I will come again and will take you to myself, that where I am you may be also.

Praise and Worship

Praise and Worship styles vary greatly around the world. It is the intent of this curriculum that praise and worship songs be selected that best fit the content of this lesson. Recommendations for praise and worship are given and this music can generally be located at www.itunes.com. However, the teacher can feel free to select a similar praise and worship song.

"There Is A Hope" by Keswick is recommended for this lesson.

Bible Activity

You know that she will be gone ALL afternoon, because she has lots of shopping to do, and also she is going to visit your grandmother for a while. You think: "There is a TV show I really want to watch, and if I do ALL these jobs first, I will miss it. I could do some of the jobs, just until time for the show, and after the show I will finish the jobs." So, even though your mother has given you very specific instructions, you decide that you know best, and you do one job, then sit down to watch TV. The program lasts for an hour, so you should have plenty of time before your mom gets home. All of a sudden, when the show is only half over, you hear the front door open, and in walks your mom!!! Oh no!!! There you are, watching TV, and most of your jobs still are unfinished! Imagine the surprise and disappointment on your mom's face when she realizes you have disobeyed her. Then imagine YOUR surprise and disappointment to hear what she has to say: "I'm so sorry that you have disobeyed me and not finished your work. I'm also sorry that you will not be able to go over to your best friend's house for the rest of the day." What??!! I didn't know about that! I know you didn't, says your mom. I saw his/her mom at the store and she invited you to come over. They are having a big party with lots of food, games, and later they are going swimming. I told her that I would come right home to get you, and then go visit grandma afterwards. But since you chose to disobey, now you will have to stay here and finish your jobs.

Teacher Helps

Memory Verse Activity: Around the Class

Have the children sit in a circle while music is playing. Pass around a phrase of the memory verse. When the music stops, whoever is holding the phrase of the memory verse should try to quote the verse. Do this until all phrases are memorized. Then, do the same thing for the whole memory verse.

Bible Activity

Have you ever been at home while your parents were at work, or had gone somewhere for a few hours? Let's imagine that you are home on a Saturday afternoon, and your mom told you that you had a few jobs to do while she was gone. Make up a list of jobs that would be appropriate for your class. Not only that, but she said that you must complete all the jobs before you are allowed to play any games, watch TV, read a book, or anything else.

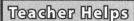

4) Review the Lesson

Divide the class into two teams. Give the teams one minute to write down as many statements as they can about the return of Jesus for believers. Here are a few ideas:

- Before Jesus left the earth, He promised that He would come back again.

- Some day, Jesus will come back again for believers just like He said He would.

- There will be a trumpet sound signalling the return of Jesus.

- For nearly 2,000 years, believers have waited and hoped for Jesus to come back.

- The eternal destiny of the believer will be with Jesus.

- It is a happy hope to know that Jesus has a place for us in heaven where we will be with Him all the time.

Review the Lesson Activity: One Minute List

The teacher should give two teams one minute each to list as many facts as they can about the lesson.

After the one minute has passed, compare lists and see who has more facts. Be sure that children remember that you are looking for facts.

5) Apply the Lesson

The "blessed hope" should cause each person to examine himself or herself. It ought to make us think that Jesus could come back today.

What is one thing that you could give up if you knew that Jesus were coming back to day?

Story Line: Jesus will return for those who have believed in Him.

Adventure Number 92
Romans 14:10-12; 1 Corinthians 3:15; and 2 Corinthians 5:10

Story Line: Believers will be evaluated and rewarded for faithful service.

1) Study the Lesson (before class)

- After Jesus returns for believers and before He returns as King, He will evaluate the lives of those who have trusted Him and will reward them for faithful service.

- True believers in Jesus will not face condemning judgment, but the integrity of their lives will be assessed.

- Every true Christian will appear before the Judgment Seat of Christ to give account of his or her life. Rewards will be given to those whose lives pass the test of God's scrutiny. Some unfaithful Christians will receive no rewards.

- There is a popular notion of a "Great Judgment Day" when believers and unbelievers will all appear together before God's throne, to await His decision regarding their eternal destiny. That view fails to understand the distinctions between the judgments of believers and unbelievers.[1]

- In Paul's first letter to the Corinthians, he wrote about this evaluation time as it related to Christian teachers (1 Corinthians 3:12-15). In his second letter, he affirmed that all Christians will be evaluated (2 Corinthians 5:10). He said basically the same thing to the church in Rome (Romans 14:12).[2]

- Salvation is not an issue for this evaluation time because it is by grace that believers have been saved (Ephesians 2:8-9).

- Good deeds will receive a good evaluation (1 Corinthians 4:5 and Ephesians 6:8). Worthless deeds will receive a negative evaluation (1 Corinthians 3:15 and Colossians 3:25).

Footnotes - Adventure 92

1. Wayne Haston, *New Testament Chronological Bible Cards*, NT-43.

2. John Walvoord and Roy Zuck, *Bible Knowledge Commentary: New Testament*, 566.

2) Begin the Lesson

Lay out a game board for review that looks something like this:

Time Line	Story Line	Songs	Memory Verses
100 points	200 points	300 points	400 points
100 points	200 points	300 points	400 points
100 points	200 points	300 points	400 points
100 points	200 points	300 points	400 points
100 points	200 points	300 points	400 points

Go back for each of the last 10 lessons and let the children name the time line for each lesson (100 points), the story line for each lesson (200 points), the song for each lesson (300 points), and the memory verse for each lesson (400 points).

A prize should be given to the winning team. Usually, competition is a fun thing for the children. So, keep them all involved. Depending on the size of your class, you may want to limit each child to only 1 or 2 answers. The reason for this is that a few children will answer all the questions, if you let them.

There will be a total of 10,000 points, 1000 points for each lesson (100 for the time line, 200 for the story line, 300 for the song, and 400 for the memory verse).

Teacher Helps

Begin the Lesson Activity: Bible Jeopardy

Divide the class evenly into two teams. The teams could be:

1) whoever is wearing something red or blue

2) everyone else

The teacher should divide the teams evenly.

This game will be continued with the review at end of the lesson.

3) Teach the Lesson

Imagine that you have a loving father and a loving mother. You have done something that displeases them. What will their response be?

- A. Correct you lovingly

- B. Remove you completely from the family and tell you to never come home again.

Our lesson today will look at how our loving heavenly Father evaluates our behavior, if we belong to His family.

99 Adventures in the Bible's Big Story

Timeline: Future Events

Adventure Number 92 Page 461

Tell the Story

As a boy, I grew up in a home with two loving parents. They always took care of me and they always made sure I had enough to eat and warm clothes to wear. They even worked many jobs so that I could grow up in a loving home. They worked hard and loved fairly.

One day, I decided to disobey them. Instead of going to school, I played games with my friends. My parents thought I was at school. I put on my school clothes and pretended like I was going to school. My friends and I had a wonderful day playing. We all stayed out of school ... it was so much fun. What we did not know was that the school principal called each of our parents and asked them why we were not in school that day. I came home at the normal time when school ended and my parents asked me how school went that day. I told them that school went "good," not knowing that they knew I was not in school.

My parents sat down with me and told me they knew that I was not in school that day. Then, they asked me again. "How did school go today?" I had to respond truthfully what my friends and I did. I told them that I did not go to school today. I played games with my friends. My parents did not like it at all that I did not go to school that day. In fact, they even told me I could not play with my friends for the next two weeks. They hoped that I would learn my lesson ... school was important and telling the truth was even more important.

I let my parents down that day. I lied to them and tried to conceal my "fun and games" day with my friends. I acknowledged to them that I had done wrong. I would not do it again. My parents still loved me. My parents still provided good meals for me. My parents still gave me warm clothes to wear. They did not tell me that they were through with me. They did not tell me to get out of the house and never come back again.

That is how the heavenly Father evaluates a believer. A believer is rewarded for the good things he has done with his life and corrected for the things that were not done to please Him. He never removes any believer out of the family, never! When a believer stands in front of the heavenly Judge for what is done in this life, that believer can trust that this heavenly Judge will give a righteous and fair evaluation. He will not sentence the believer to an eternal life of doom or even hell. He will give to each believer rewards for what is done well in this life. That is how the heavenly Father treats those that are His children.

Tell the Story Activity: Monologue

The teacher may want to tell his or her own story instead of this one. The goal is help children see that the heavenly Father evaluates a believer. The heavenly Father does not judge or condemn a believer.

Memory Verse

2 Corinthians 5:10 (ESV) -For we must all appear before the judgment seat of Christ, so that each one may receive what is due for what he has done in the body, whether good or evil.

Praise and Worship

Praise and Worship styles vary greatly around the world. It is the intent of this curriculum that praise and worship songs be selected that best fit the content of this lesson. Recommendations for praise and worship are given and this music can generally be located at www.itunes.com. However, the teacher can feel free to select a similar praise and worship song.

"There Is A Hope" by Keswick is recommended for this lesson.

Bible Activity

The Bible refers to these rewards as crowns. Do you wish you could "see how you are doing?" When God judges, He knows every single thing that has happened, even what people were thinking. No one will be able to deceive Him, or pretend that they are not guilty. Let's see if we can get a little peek at what might be on our "heavenly report cards." I will ask you to grade yourself on several things that are important to God. If you see that you are not doing as well as you would like, then now is the time to make changes and improvements, before the "heavenly report card" is written.

  1. Sharing the good news of the gospel (1 Thessalonians 2:19-20).

  2. Being faithful to God (doing what is right), even when people make fun of you (1 Corinthians 9:24-25).

  3. Teaching others the Bible. This can be as simple as sharing your Sunday School lesson with a friend, or someday being a pastor or teacher (1 Peter 5:1-4).

  4. Enduring temptation, and choosing God's ways (James 1:12).

If you have time, you could even make a simple crown for a craft.

Teacher Helps

Memory Verse Activity: The Telephone Game

Memorize this verse using The Telephone Game. Have your class form one line, then whisper into the first person in line a phrase of this verse, have that person repeat the phrase to the next person. Do this until all have quoted the first phrase. Then do the same thing with the second phrase, the third phrase, and so on until you have memorized the verse.

Bible Activity: Heavenly Report Card

When you go to school, you get a report card at the end of the year. When we get to heaven, those that are believers will be judged in a similar way, receiving rewards for good things, or losing rewards for bad things.

Timeline: Future Events

4) Review the Lesson

Continue your review game for points that you began at the start of the lesson.

- For 100 points, will a believer be condemned ever? (No.)
- For 200 points, will a believer ever be evaluated by Jesus Christ? (Yes.)
- For 300 points, will believers and unbelievers be judged at the same time? (No.)
- For 400 points, how will God evaluate a believer? (Lovingly and fairly.)
- Bonus question worth 500 points: What is the theme of this lesson? (Believers will be evaluated and rewarded for faithful service.)

Teacher Helps

Review the Lesson Activity: Bible Jeopardy

This review activity is a continuation of the review game at the beginning of the lesson.

5) Apply the Lesson

There are rewards for faithful service to the heavenly Father, but only for believers. There is no condemnation for those who belong to Jesus Christ.

Perhaps there is a child in the class that is outside of faith in Christ and will never be evaluated like this. He or she will be judged and condemned. Would that person like to become a Christian right now?

Those who are truly believers need to show their heavenly Father that they are trying to love Him and obey Him daily.

Story Line: Believers will be evaluated and rewarded for faithful service.

Adventure Number 93
Daniel 9:24-27; Matthew 24:15-21; and Revelation 6-19

Story Line: Seven years of tribulation will come to the earth.

1) Study the Lesson (before class)

- God's judgment upon the Jewish people will not be completed until a future period of seven years of tribulation.

- The greatest observable sign during the tribulations will be the abomination which causes desolation. The abomination was spoken of by Daniel (9:27). It refers to the disruption of Jewish worship which will be restarted during the tribulation.[1]

- Daniel 9:26 tells about the death of the Messiah. He will be killed by His own people. His earthly reign on earth will come later.

- Daniel's 70th week will continue until Jesus Christ returns to the earth. Because Jesus said this will be a time of "great distress," it is often called the tribulation.

- The middle 14 chapters of the book of Revelation contain some very frightening details about the fulfillment of Daniel's 70th week.

- The Olivet Discourse (Matthew 24-25), which Jesus gave shortly before His crucifixion, elaborated on the fulfillment of Daniel's 70th week.[2]

- Daniel was exiled in Babylon during the 70 years of exile, a time of punishment by God on the Jewish people. Daniel was praying when the angel came to him with a vision about seventy weeks which explained God's future plan for the Jewish people.[3]

- In the tribulation, the antichrist will set up an image of himself for everyone to worship which will make worship in the temple abominable.

Footnotes - Adventure 93

1. John Walvoord and Roy Zuck, *Bible Knowledge Commentary: New Testament*, 77.

2. Wayne Haston, *New Testament Chronological Bible Cards*, NT-44.

3. Wayne Haston, *The Roots of Faith New Testament Workbook*, 44-B.

2) Begin the Lesson

The teacher should gather all the songs that have been used in the Adventures in the Bible's Big Story and play several of them.

The class should be able to sing along with the teacher the songs that they have previously learned in this curriculum.

After the teacher has played several songs and the class and sung them, play the game, "Name That Tune." "Name That Tune" is a game in which the students will attempt to match the song with the Bible adventure that best matches the song. The teacher should use extreme graciousness to encourage the class when an answer is given.

The purpose of this activity is for kids to associate music they have learned with events in the Bible. The teacher should stay focused on this primary purpose.

Review Activity: Name That Tune

The teacher should play songs that the class has learned for the previous Bible adventures. Children should guess which adventures in the Bible's big story best match the song that is being played or sung.

If time permits, the teacher could also ask if there are phrases or words in any of the songs that the children do not understand.

3) Teach the Lesson

Satan has a lot of power but he does not have as much power as God has. In today's lesson, we will see that Satan will start a very distressful time on earth.

Tell the Story

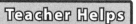

It was a bleak time when it all happened. There were lots of terrible days. But a new ruler came to power and he commanded the attention of the his own country and the world. He gained more and more power until eventually most of the world was ready to turn control of their governments over to this ruler. Not everybody felt this way, but there was growing momentum for his worldwide reign.

At first, things started to get better. There was peace for a short while. But, then it all happened. He went to the temple in Jerusalem and proclaimed that not only would he rule the world, but everyone in the world would worship him. He even put pictures up so that people would not forget what he looked like and remember to worship him.

He was the exact opposite of Jesus Christ ... he was even called the antichrist, and that is what he was, the opposite of Christ. Now, he made war against those who worshipped Jesus Christ. His worldwide following made it very hard for believers and many were put to death.

In the middle of his covenant with the world, he went to the Jewish temple. That is when things got really bad. It was called the abomination of desolation by Daniel hundreds of years before it even happened. Daniel told about this seven years when there would be unparalleled trouble and great distress. Shortly before He went to the cross, Jesus Christ told about this time of tribulation. He told the believers to make sure that they were not led astray by this leader. John devoted half of his last book, the Revelation, to this seven year period of time. The end times appeared to be near and there seemed to be no hope.

Despite this ruler's apparent success, his reign would be short-lived. This ruler was a monster who made it so bad that some people would want to run for the hills and hide from him; women who were pregnant would find this time especially hard. There was trouble in the world from this monster like the world had never seen before and would never see again.

The future gets better after this but you will have to wait till next week for me to tell you that there is a Ruler who is coming who will annihilate the monster. Although this monster claimed to be a god, he really was not. Although this monster wanted everyone to worship him forever, it will not happen. Wait and you will find out what happens.

Tell the Story Activity: Deception

The teacher should label this leader as a deceiver. Ask, **"What kind of things do deceivers do?" What kind of things would a person do who is trying to take the place of Jesus Christ?"**

Bring in models of deception, like fake money or imitation food.

Memory Verse

2 Thessalonians 2:4 (ESV) - Who opposes and exalts himself against every so-called god or object of worship, so that he takes his seat in the temple of God, proclaiming himself to be God.

Praise and Worship

Praise and Worship styles vary greatly around the world. It is the intent of this curriculum that praise and worship songs be selected that best fit the content of this lesson. Recommendations for praise and worship are given and this music can generally be located at www.itunes.com. However, the teacher can feel free to select a similar praise and worship song.

"There Is A Hope" by Keswick is recommended for this lesson.

Bible Activity

Is it real, or is it fake? Bring in several items that you have the "real thing" and also a "fake copy" to display. For example, a real flower and a plastic one, or a real piece of fruit and a plastic one. Use your own imagination to think of other possible ideas. If you are able, it would even be good to create a "fake" piece of paper money. Use a copy machine to copy a piece of money, cut it out to the proper size, and use that, along with the real money as an example. Hold up the real and fake things, and ask the class to tell you which one is real. Did you know that when people are trained to spot counterfeit money, they don't get training on what counterfeit money looks like? They study the real thing so much that when they see a fake, it is easy to recognize. The same thing is true in our world today. There are so many fake things that all claim to be real. We need to spend a lot of time reading and studying the Bible, so that when a fake idea or person comes along, we are able to compare what they are saying to the truth found in God's Word. Only then will be able to see the fakes for what they are.

Teacher Helps

Memory Verse Activity: Graffiti

Graffiti can also be used to help children memorize this verse. Write each word of this verse on a separate piece of paper. Then have children put the words in order in groups of 2 or 3. When each group can put the verse together in order, they will probably have this verse memorized.

4) Review the Lesson

Review the lesson in small groups. What are seven main facts or ideas that come out of this lesson? One adult leader should join each small group of kids. Let the children do most of the discovering. Help them when necessary.

- One ruler in the world will gain more and more power.
- The time of trouble caused by this monster will be unparalleled in world history.
- Daniel prophesied in chapter 9 that this time of unparalleled world trouble would happen.
- Jesus discussed this time of unparalleled trouble with his disciples in Matthew 24 and 25 at the Olivet Discourse.
- John devoted half of his book, the Revelation, to this time of unparalleled trouble.
- The antichrist will not be the ultimate victor or world leader.

Teacher Helps

Review the Lesson Activity: Seven Main Facts

The teacher should have the class break up into groups of 2 or 3. Have them tell each other about the 7 main ideas in the lesson which are listed to your left. For younger children, or non-readers, the teacher should help them.

5) Apply the Lesson

Deception is a mark of the devil, Satan himself. It always has been. Name one or two things that you might have done that were deceptive or not telling the whole truth. Once you name those deceptive ways, acknowledge them before God as sin, and thank Jesus Christ that He is the truth.

Story Line: Seven years of tribulation will come to the earth.

Adventure Number 94
Revelation 19:11-19 and Revelation 20:1-6

Story Line: Jesus will return to rule the earth with those who have believed in Him.

 1) Study the Lesson (before class)

- The second coming of Christ to the earth is a well established doctrine throughout Scripture (Psalm 2:1-9; 24:7-10; 96:10-13; 110; Isaiah 9:6-7; Jeremiah 23:1-8; Ezekiel 37:15-28; Daniel 2:44-45; 7:13-14; Hosea 3:4-5; Amos 9:11-15; Micah 4:7; Zechariah 2:10-12; 12; 14:1-9; Matthew 19:28; 24:27-31; 25:6, 31-46; Mark 13:24-27; Luke 12:35-40; 17:24-37; 18:8; 21:25-28; Acts 1:10-11; 15:16-18; Romans 11:25-27; 2 Thessalonians 2:8; 2 Peter 3:3-4; Jude 14-15; Revelation 1:7-8; 2:25-28; 16:15; 22:20).[1]

- The events described in Revelation 20 are chronologically sequential to the second coming of Christ in Revelation 19 and portray a literal earthly kingdom ruled by Jesus for 1,000 years.[2]

- The rapture, which was talked about in the lesson 92, is not the same as this event. None of the details of the second coming are the same as those of the rapture. In the rapture, Christ is never said to come to the earth. The passages of the second coming have Christ actually setting His feet on the earth and ruling from the earth.

- The white horse is symbolic of coming triumph. The rider of the horse is named Faithful and True, it could only be the Lord Jesus.[3]

- The eyes of Jesus are like blazing fire tells us that He is coming to judge sin. The many titles and crowns that He is wearing means that He has the authority to judge sin.

- When Christ returns to the earth, He will lock up Satan for one thousand years so that Satan will not deceive the nations anymore.

- Satan will be unbound for a brief period of time at the end of Christ's rule on earth with believers.

Footnotes - Adventure 94

1. John Walvoord and Roy Zuck, *Bible Knowledge Commentary: New Testament*, 976.

2. Roy B. Zuck, *A Biblical Theology of the New Testament*, 241.

3. Albert Barnes, *Barnes' Notes on the New Testament*, Revelation 21.

2) Begin the Lesson

Ask children to help you with previous memory verses. Maybe say something like, **"Who remembers what (verse) says?"**

- Adventure 60: Luke 4:18
- Adventure 61: Mark 4:40
- Adventure 62: Luke 4:36
- Adventure 63: John 10:28
- Adventure 64: John 8:12
- Adventure 65: Luke 15:10
- Adventure 66: Matthew 25:46
- Adventure 67: John 11:25
- Adventure 68: John 12:24
- Adventure 69: Matthew 24:24
- Adventure 70: John 14:6
- Adventure 71: Matthew 26:56
- Adventure 72: 1 Corinthians 5:7
- Adventure 73: 1 Peter 3:18
- Adventure 74: Luke 23:42
- Adventure 75: Luke 24:6
- Adventure 76: Luke 24:27
- Adventure 77: Matthew 28:19
- Adventure 78: Acts 1:8
- Adventure 79: Acts 2:38
- Adventure 80: Acts 2:42
- Adventure 81: Isaiah 53:7
- Adventure 82: Acts 9:15
- Adventure 83: Acts 10:43
- Adventure 84: Acts 11:24
- Adventure 85: Acts 13:47
- Adventure 86: Acts 15:7
- Adventure 87: Acts 16:31
- Adventure 88: Acts 19:19
- Adventure 89: Acts 26:18
- Adventure 90: Colossians 1:19
- Adventure 91: Matthew 16:18
- Adventure 92: John 14:3
- Adventure 93: 2 Corinthians 5:10
- Adventure 94: 2 Thess. 2:4

Teacher Helps

Begin the Lesson Activity: Memory Verse Review

The last 35 memory verses are given here. Divide the children up into two teams and see which team can tell you the most memory verses. Bonus points should be given if they each team can recite more than the last 35 memory verses.

Give the teams five minutes and they must work together.

The teacher can provide a few helps.

3) Teach the Lesson

In our last lesson, we looked at a very flawed leader. In fact, he was a monster who was called the antichrist. Before we study today's lesson, what do you think a wise or even perfect leader looks like? What are the kinds of things a wise and perfect leader will do?

Tell the Story

The monster called the antichrist had proclaimed himself as God and everyone in the world had to worship him. The antichrist had abruptly stopped the worship of God by Jews in the temple. Jesus would no longer stand for that deception.

He left the wonders of heaven. He was riding a beautiful and strong white horse. He was clothed in a robe that had been soaked in blood. On His robe was written, *"King of Kings and Lord of Lords."* He had a special name that nobody knew but they addressed Him as *"Word of God."* His eyes were like a blazing fire. With Him were millions of heavens armies and they were dressed in dazzling white robes. He wore a great crown on His head. It was an incredible sight to see the King of Kings and all those who accompanied Him.

The battle was about to begin. It was the *"Word of God"* and millions of heavens armies against the Beast, the False Prophet, and all who worshipped them. The Beast and his wicked priest, the False Prophet were taken directly to the Lake of Fire by the Word of God. In the Lake of Fire, these two monsters will spend the rest of eternity. They were completely and totally defeated. Everyone else was killed by the sword that came from the mouth of the Word of God. It was a feast for all the birds as they fed on all that dead flesh.

This battle was an awesome display of the wrath of God against those who defy Him. Even though He is a gracious and loving God, His anger burns against those who defy Him and He punished them with eternal punishment. Most of the world followed the Beast and the False Prophet. Yet, once again, God showed His sovereignty and His power. When that final battle began, all the world leaders thought they could choose who they would follow and worship on their own. When the "Word of God" came, the battle was quick and decisive. All those who followed Satan were defeated and punished.

The Word of God, Jesus Christ, had won the battle. Satan would have no more power for his worldwide rebellion. He was cast into the Lake of Fire and punished forever. All those who followed Satan, including the Beast and the False Prophet were also killed. Jesus Christ reigned supreme and sovereignly. As in the beginning of creation, the Powerful One had won again over that great deceiver, Satan.

Teacher Helps

Tell the Story Activity: The Coming of Jesus Christ

As the teacher tells this story, have kids remember:

- one thing that Jesus Christ looks like.

- one thing that Jesus Christ does.

- one thing about the last battle.

Memory Verse

Revelation 19:11 (ESV) - Then I saw heaven opened, and behold, a white horse! The one sitting on it is called Faithful and True, and in righteousness he judges and makes war.

Praise and Worship

Praise and Worship styles vary greatly around the world. It is the intent of this curriculum that praise and worship songs be selected that best fit the content of this lesson. Recommendations for praise and worship are given and this music can generally be located at www.itunes.com. However, the teacher can feel free to select a similar praise and worship song.

"There Is A Hope" by Keswick is recommended for this lesson.

Bible Activity

The year was 1815, and France was fighting with much of Europe for domination. There was a fierce battle between the army of Wellington and the army of Napoleon. This battle would prove to be the biggest turning point of the war. On the one side, the European allied nations were trying to hold on to the land they called their own. The battle was long and hard, and on the other side of a river where the battle was taking place, a group of people waited to find out what the outcome of the battle had been. The signal would come from flashes of light that were sent in a code. Finally the signal started to come through! One by one the letters were spelled out: "W-e-l-l-i-n-g-t-o-n" (Have the first child hold up his/her sign) "Here comes the next word!" "D-e-f-e-a-t-e-d" (Have the second child hold up their sign.) Just then a thick fog settled in over the river, and no more lights could be seen. It's all over, Napoleon will come and take us as prisoners and there is no one to defend us! But wait! The fog had lifted, and the signal came again: "W-e-l-l-i-n-g-t-o-n" (Have the first child hold up their sign.) "Here comes the next word!" "D-e-f-e-a-t-e-d" (Have the second child hold up their sign) "N-a-p-o-l-e-o-n" (Have the third child hold up his/her sign.) YES!!! Wellington had DEFEATED Napoleon!! The whole meaning changed when they saw the rest of the message! At first, they thought that Wellington (their leader) had been defeated by Napoleon, but then they learned the end of the message, THEY HAD WON!!!!

Teacher Helps

Memory Verse Activity: Graffiti

Graffiti can also be used to help children memorize this verse. Write each word of this verse on a separate piece of paper. Then have children put the words in order in groups of 2 or 3. When each group can put the verse together in order, they will probably have this verse memorized.

Bible Activity

Before class, make 3 signs. On the first one, in big letters, write "Wellington." On the second write "defeated." On the third, write "Napoleon." Give the signs to 3 different children, and instruct them as to when they should hold up their sign.

4) Review the Lesson

Have children simplify the lesson into 10 words or less using their own words. What are their answers? When children simplify the story of the lesson into ten words or less, they will probably say something like these possibilities:

- The Beast and False Prophet are defeated by Jesus.
- Satan is finally destroyed.
- The Lake of Fire received those who follow Satan.
- Jesus Christ is very strong in battle.
- Those who believe in Christ will reign forever.
- Jesus Christ is the Word of God.
- Jesus is faithful, true, and powerful.
- Satan is unfaithful, deceptive, and has limited power.

Review the Lesson Activity: Simplify

Simplify can be a useful game for the children. The teacher can give each team of 2 or 3 kids about 1-2 minutes to come up with the most significant 10 words of this lesson.

5) Apply the Lesson

Those who followed Satan will be ultimately defeated and sent to eternity in a very bad place called hell.

You choose whom you will follow and worship. Will you follow, worship, and obey the faithful, true, and all-powerful One?

Or, will you choose to follow, worship, and obey the unfaithful and deceptive one called Satan. It is your choice … whom will you choose?

> **Story Line: Jesus will return to rule the earth with those who have believed in Him.**

Adventure Number 95
Daniel 2:44-45 and Revelation 20:1-6

Story Line: Jesus will reign on the earth for 1000 years.

1) Study the Lesson (before class)

- If taken literally, the 20th chapter of Revelation is fairly easy to understand. However, over the years, three major interpretations have developed.[1]

  - 1) *Postmillenialism*. According this view, the thousand years represents the triumph of the gospel leading up to the second coming of Christ. The return of Christ will follow the millenium. This is an optimistic view that Christ will reign on earth through the work of the church. This view has been largely discarded because of the rise of anti-Christian movements in the 20th and 21st centuries.

  - 2) *Amillenialism*. Amillenialism denies that there is any literal millenium or reign of Christ on earth. The reign is either those who put their trust in Christ or those in heaven. Both this view and the first view are not literal.

  - 3) *Premillenialism*. This view of Revelation 20 says that the literal 1,000 year reign of Christ will follow His second coming. The second coming precedes the millennial reign and is therefore premillenial. Many Bible passages speak of a literal second coming followed by a rule of righteousness on earth (Psalm 2; 24; 72; 96; Isaiah 2; 9:6-7; 11-12; 63:1-6; 65-66; Jeremiah 23:5-6; 30:8-11; Dan. 2:44; 7:13-14; Hosea 3:4-5; Amos 9:11-15; Micah 4:1-8; Zephaniah 3:14-20; Zechariah 8:1-8; 14:1-9; Matthew 19:28; 25:31-46; Acts 15:16-18; Romans 11:25-27; Jude 14-15; Revelation 2:25-28; 19:11-20:6).

- The resurrection of Jesus gave hope that He will return to earth to establish His promised kingdom.[2]

Footnotes - Adventure 95

1. John Walvoord and Roy Zuck, *Bible Knowledge Commentary: New Testament*, 978.

2. Wayne Haston, *New Testament Chronological Bible Cards*, NT-46.

3. Lynn Solem and Bob Pike, *50 Creative Training Closers*, 70.

2) Begin the Lesson

Let's think back over the all of our lessons that we have studied and see if we can put the lessons in order.

1) God is very strong.

5) Life in the garden was full of pleasure.

10) Sin affected God's creation in many negative ways.

15) The people were evil. God sent a flood. Noah trusted and obeyed God.

20) God told Abraham to sacrifice Isaac. God provided a ram instead.

25) God sent plagues in Egypt to set free the Israelites.

30) God told the Israelites to build a tent where they could meet Him and offer sacrifices.

35) People who followed God were to be completely loyal and obedient to Him.

40) God chose David to be a king. God will one day appoint a Man to be King forever.

45) Prophets told about Jesus 700 years before He came to earth.

50) The Jews returned to Jerusalem to rebuild the walls.

55) Satan tempted Jesus. Jesus did not sin.

60) Many people began to follow Jesus because of His teaching and miracles.

65) God forgave a wayward son, a selfish brother, and a humble tax collector.

70) Jesus gave His disciples valuable instructions and comforting promises.

75) Jesus rose from the dead. Jesus has power over death.

80) The followers of Jesus met to pray, worship, read the Bible, and fellowship.

85) False teachers were trying to add requirements to the Gospel.

90) The faith was really important to early believers.

Teacher Helps

Begin the Lesson Activity: Story Line Review

The teacher should write these statements on pieces of paper and then mix them up. Do not put the number of the lesson on the piece of paper. Divide the children into 2 or 3 teams, depending on the size of the class. Time how long it takes each team to put the statements in the correct order. Do not number the slips of paper.

3) Teach the Lesson

What would it be like if Satan was imprisoned forever? What would it be like if Jesus Christ ruled on earth?

Tell the Story

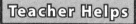

The battle was over. The Word of God, Jesus Christ, had won the battle! Yeah! Then, Jesus Christ commanded an angel to take that old serpent, the devil, and throw him into a great place of captivity. He would not be able to deceive the people of the world anymore during the next thousand years.

The next thing that John saw was believers who had been beheaded during the tribulation for their witness. These people refused the mark of the beast and they did not worship the beast or his false prophet. God was rewarding them now for their faithfulness to Him and He let them reign with Jesus on the earth for the next thousand years. These believers had received a new body ... a resurrected body ... so that they could reign with Jesus Christ.

You see kids, Daniel told about this kingdom thousands of years before it will happen. Daniel wrote, *"And in the days of those kings the God of heaven will set up a kingdom that shall never be destroyed, nor shall the kingdom be left to another people. It shall break in pieces all these kingdoms and bring them to an end, and it shall stand forever, just as you saw that a stone was cut from a mountain by no human hand, and that it broke in pieces the iron, the bronze, the clay, the silver, and the gold. A great God has made known to the king what shall be after this. The dream is certain, and its interpretation sure."* Now, after the four kingdoms will come another kingdom, the kingdom of the great God we have been learning about. This kingdom will not be broken and it will not come to an end. You can be sure of this.

For the next thousand years after the second coming of Christ, there will be peace and safety. There will be a rule of righteousness as Jesus Christ will be the king on earth. Satan will not be around to deceive and lie to the people of the earth ... he will be in prison. This reign of Christ on earth will be a perfect reign. It will all be about following the only true King who is Jesus Christ. All the things that Satan does now to ruin this earth will not happen then.

We know that it will be a thousand years. John said that six different times in this part of the Bible. According to John, he was sure of the length of this reign of Christ. Think about it ... six times the thousand year reign of Christ is talked about in this chapter. That is a lot of times. We are going to learn later what happens after this thousand years, but we can be sure that Jesus will rule for a thousand years on earth and that His rule as king will be perfect.

Tell the Story Activity: Two Scenes

As the teacher tells this story, have kids remember:

- What was it like for Satan during this time?

- What is like for the people of the earth during this period of time?

If possible, show the picture of this story and ask kids to tell you what they see in this picture. They should say things that they see like the lion and the sheep lying down together.

Memory Verse

Revelation 20:6 (ESV) - Blessed and holy is the one who shares in the first resurrection! Over such the second death has no power, but they will be priests of God and of Christ, and they will reign with him for a thousand years.

Praise and Worship

Praise and Worship styles vary greatly around the world. It is the intent of this curriculum that praise and worship songs be selected that best fit the content of this lesson. Recommendations for praise and worship are given and this music can generally be located at www.itunes.com. However, the teacher can feel free to select a similar praise and worship song.

"There Is A Hope" by Keswick is recommended for this lesson.

Bible Activity

Do you ever like to imagine things? Sometimes people call this "daydreaming." You are not asleep, but you are imagining something in your mind. We are going to imagine together in class about a time that has not come yet, but the Bible tells us it will come someday. We don't know when it will be, but we know FOR SURE that it will come, because the Bible tells us so, and God never lies. One day, Jesus will return to earth as a king. Who remembers how He came the first time? (as a little baby) Next time He comes, it will be to rule over the earth as the king. Let's just imagine what the world with Jesus as the king. Close your eyes and think about a world where the devil is nowhere to be found. There would be no temptation to sin. No bad guys. No bad things to watch on TV. No one trying to hurt each other. No fighting. What else can you imagine that would be a part of life like that? (allow for answers) What would not be a part of the world? What would be different from the first time He came? If you have time and supplies, give the children a blank piece of paper to draw a picture of what they think the world would look like during the 1,000 year reign of Christ.

Teacher Helps

Memory Verse Activity: Bean Bag Toss

With masking tape, mark off a large square on the floor, about 36 inches. Connect the opposite corners inside the square with tape to form an "X." If you have space and many students, make a second square. Give each section a number value (1,2,3,4). A bit of a distance away, put a line of tape to mark where the student will throw from. Divide into two teams. Each student takes a turn throwing a bean bag into one of the sections. (You may make a bean bag by putting beans in a sock and closing it tight with a rubber band. Take the long part of the sock and fold it over the bean section.) If they can say the verse correctly, their team scores the amount of the section where the bean bag was thrown.

Timeline: Future Events

4) Review the Lesson

The teacher should have the class think of the main ideas of the lesson that they want to take home. Then they should number off 1 through 5. Number 1 should say tell the main thing that he or she learned from the lesson. All five groups should get an opportunity to share the main thing they learned from this lesson.

Ideas might include:
- Satan will be imprisoned for 1,000 years after the second coming of Jesus Christ.
- Jesus will rule on earth for 1,000 years with those who have been martyred for their witness during the tribulation.
- The reign of Jesus on earth will be a perfect reign.
- Daniel told about this time thousands of years before it happened.
- John says six times that this reign on earth is for 1,000 years in Revelation 20.

Review the Lesson Activity: Repetition[3]

The teacher should allow about 5 minutes for children to share the main thing that they learned. If more than 5 children are in the class, allow for each of the groups to share with each other.

5) Apply the Lesson

From our very first lessons, we have learned that Jesus Christ is very powerful. In today's lesson, we learned that He is so powerful that He can imprison Satan for 1,000 years while Jesus reigns on earth.

The power of God can be used to destroy Satan and it can be used to rule in our lives. Name one or two things that you want the power of God to rule over your life. These are things in which you need God's power.

Story Line: Jesus will reign on the earth for 1000 years.

Timeline: Future Events

Adventure Number 96
Hebrews 2:14-15 and Revelation 20:7-10

Story Line: Satan will be cast into the lake of fire forever.

1) Study the Lesson (before class)

- The millenium, the rule and reign of Jesus Christ on earth for 1,000 years will follow His second coming to earth. It will be a time of great blessing.

- At the end of the 1,000 years, Satan will be loosed from his prison and he will try to deceive the nations into following him instead of Jesus Christ.

- Satan's release will produce a worldwide rebellion against the earthly rule of Jesus Christ. The armies involved in this battle are so large in number that they are described *"like the sand on the seashore."*

- Many will profess salvation in Jesus Christ during His 1,000 year reign. But when Satan is released, the shallowness of their profession will cause them to be deceived.

- In this final battle, nations will come from all directions. Gog and Magog may be a reference to those who will lose the battle.

- The armies will surround the city which God loves, Jerusalem. The result is immediate fire coming down from heaven.

- After Satan's followers are destroyed, Satan and his angels will be thrown into the Lake of Fire. In the Lake of Fire, they will experience eternal torment.

- The lake of burning sulfur is not annihilation because the beast and the false prophet are there and have been there for about 1000 years after their final judgment.

Footnotes - Adventure 96

1. Bill Greig, *Gospel Light's Really Big Book of Bible Games*, 262.

2) Begin the Lesson

Teacher Helps

Eight essential truths have emerged from the Bible's big story of hope. Challenge children to know the eight truths, know them in order, and be able to give a brief description of each.

1. <u>God</u>. In the beginning, there was a very powerful God.

2. <u>Man</u>. God created people to be His special friends.

3. <u>Sin</u>. Man and woman disobeyed God.

4. <u>Death</u>. God punished man and woman for their disobedience. Death, in the Bible, refers to separation.

5. <u>Christ</u>. God sent His one and only Son who lived a perfect life.

6. <u>Cross</u>. Jesus died on the cross for the sins of the world.

7. <u>Faith</u>. If anyone places their faith in Christ, God welcomes them.

8. <u>Life</u>. God gives eternal life to those who put their faith in Him.

Begin the Lesson Activity: Eight Essential Truths

Write the eight essential truths on pieces of paper on place them face down. Do the same with the brief descriptions. Now, create 2 or 3 teams and have them put the truths and descriptions in the correct order. Time them and give a reward to the winning team.

Remind the class where these truths can be found in Scripture.

3) Teach the Lesson

Ask the class, **"Do you remember when we studied the 'Satan Crusher' lesson from Genesis 3?"** See if any of them remember the promise that God made in Genesis 3:15. Reminder: Lesson 9 (Promise of a Victor Over Satan) is the lesson that we learned a very important truth. "God promised to send a special Person who would crush Satan."

Now, we will see how Jesus Christ will destroy Satan forever. Satan will be cast into the lake of fire to be tormented for eternity. But, God told Adam and Eve thousands of years ago about the "Satan Crusher."

The final defeat of Satan and his destiny in hell will follow the thousand year reign of Christ on the earth.

Timeline: Future Events

Tell the Story

The thousand year reign of Christ on earth was now over and Satan was let go from his cell. He was no longer imprisoned. And do you know what he did? He did the same old thing that he used to do. He went back to deceiving the people from all over the world. It was same trick he used on Adam and Eve and millions of other people. And for some reason, even though the millennial reign of Christ was a beautiful thing, many of the people of the nations followed that great deceiver.

Once again, Satan was leading a worldwide rebellion. He gathered more and more followers through deception and lies. Remember how he tempted Adam and Eve to believe that God was not really good. Well, that is probably what he will do again at this time. Millions of people will listen to him and follow him. In fact, so many people will follow him that his followers will be almost countless in number.

The armies of Satan will surround Jerusalem and the great King Jesus. That is all it will take for Jesus to call down fire from heaven and destroy Satan for the very last time. In the past, Satan had been defeated. Time and time again, he would rise up from his defeat and challenge Jesus and His followers with his worldwide rebellion. This time, Satan was thrown into the lake of fire. And for the first time, this is where he will stay forever. He will join the Beast and the False Prophet from the tribulation. They had been in this awful place for a thousand years and now their contemptible leader, Satan, will join them forever.

Now, Satan will have an eternal home in the Lake of Fire. No more deception from Satan. No more lies from Satan. He will be imprisoned in his new cell block where there is eternal torment. He will never get out of his cell again. He will not be able to lead a worldwide rebellion any more. His once powerful army will be defeated, destroyed, and sent to a place where there are worms and maggots. It will not be any fun and there will be no friends in this eternal place of agony.

For thousands of years, the evil one had tempted people to become a follower of his … to obey him … to question the goodness of God. This torment of Satan will be everlasting. This torment of Satan will be conscious. And this torment will be God's final dealing with Satan. There will be no more wars. This will be the final end of Satan. The war will be over. Satan will be imprisoned forever in hell. "The offspring of the woman" will have completely and finally crushed the serpent's head.

Tell the Story Activity: Satan's Doom

As the teacher tells this story, have kids remember:

- Lesson 9: Promise of a Victor Over Satan. *God promised to send a special Person who would crush Satan.*

- Lesson 52: The Birth of Jesus Christ. *God's Son was born. His name was Jesus.*

- Lesson 55: Temptations by Satan. *Satan tempted Jesus. Jesus did not sin.*

- Lesson 73: The Crucifixion of Jesus. *Jesus died on the cross for our sins.*

- Lesson 75: The Resurrection of Jesus. *Jesus rose from the dead. Jesus has power over death.*

Memory Verse

Revelation 20:10 (ESV) - The devil who had deceived them was thrown into the lake of fire and sulfur where the beast and the false prophet were, and they will be tormented day and night forever and ever.

Praise and Worship

Praise and Worship styles vary greatly around the world. It is the intent of this curriculum that praise and worship songs be selected that best fit the content of this lesson. Recommendations for praise and worship are given and this music can generally be located at www.itunes.com. However, the teacher can feel free to select a similar praise and worship song.

"There Is A Hope" by Keswick is recommended for this lesson.

Bible Activity

Have you ever gone fishing? How do you know what kind of bait to put on your hook? (Worms, other little fish, or something else – the point you need to get the children to see is that you have to use bait that is appealing to the fish you want to catch.) Expert fishermen know just the right bait that will "catch" the fish they want. What if you put a piece of valuable jewelry on the hook? Would the fish really want to bite it? How about a bottle of wine, do you think they would go for that? (of course not!) But what if, instead of you going fishing, it was the devil looking to "Catch" someone, and that someone was not a fish, but a person? What kind of "bait" would the devil use? Not a worm, for sure! He would choose something that would tempt the person, like expensive jewelry, or alcohol, or fame, or something else. From the beginning of time, when he tempted Adam and Eve in the garden, he has been a deceiver, and even at the end of time, he hasn't changed his ways. Let's see what that old serpent is up to at the end of time.

Teacher Helps

Memory Verse Activity: Scripture Card Battle[1]

Divide your class up into groups of 2 or 3. Give each group a set of cards. On each card is one word from the memory verse. Groups should try to put the words of the memory verse in the right order.

4) Review the Lesson

"Who" Questions:

1. Who is the Beast?

2. Who did Satan tempt at the end of the 1000 year reign of Christ?

"What" Questions:

1. What did Satan do at end of the 1000 year reign of Christ?

2. What are characteristics of this punishment?

"When" Questions:

1. When were the Beast and the False Prophet thrown into the lake of fire?

2. When was Satan thrown into the lake of fire?

"Where" Questions:

1. Where was the central city of the 1000 year reign of Christ?

2. Where did Satan attack?

"Why" Questions:

1. Why does Satan keep deceiving people?

2. Why will there be no more war?

Teacher Helps

Review Activity: The Investigative Cube

Divide the class up into two teams. Make a cube with these labels on each side of the cube: who, what, when, where, why. When the cube is rolled to one team, they will answer the type of question that is face up on the cube. For instance, if the "why" is face up on the cube, then that team will answer a "why" question. Teachers can make up their own questions from the lesson, only they must pertain to this lesson.

5) Apply the Lesson

Nobody wants to be punished. Nobody wants to be punished forever. Nobody wants to be punished forever in torment. Satan is doomed to this punishment. Eternal punishment is something you can avoid. There is only one way to avoid this punishment and that is through the death, burial, and resurrection of Jesus Christ.

> **Story Line: Satan will be cast into the lake of fire forever.**

Adventure Number 97

2 Thessalonians 1:8-9 and Revelation 20:11-15

Story Line: Unbelievers will be cast into the lake of fire forever.

1) Study the Lesson (before class)

- The events of the Great White Throne judgment clearly follow the 1,000 year reign of Christ; Revelation 20:1-6.

- The Great White Throne is different than the throne mentioned 30 times in Revelation. The purpose of the Great White Throne is to judge the dead. All people will stand before God at this throne.

- From other Scriptures, we know that dead believers have been judged at the Bema Seat and are now with the Lord.

- Old Testament saints have been raised and will not be judged. Therefore, we must conclude that the Great White Throne is to judge the wicked dead.

- Their works will be the basis for their judgment. Their works will not save them, but will demonstrate their lost state, deserving of punishment.

- According to verse 5, the wicked dead will not be raised until after the 1,000 years. They will have no part in the first resurrection.

- The teaching of eternal punishment is clear in Scripture. Unbelievers will be cast into the Lake of Fire forever where Satan and his angels already are.

- The teaching of Scripture shows two possibilities: spending eternity in heaven with the Lord Jesus Christ or suffering in the Lake of Fire with Satan. There is no other option.

- Satan's power will not last forever. He will be doomed eternally. Those who are not believers will also suffer eternal punishment.

Footnotes - Adventure 97

1. Susan Lingo, *Written on Our Hearts*, 99.

2) Begin the Lesson

Time Line	People	Event
Beginnings	God	God made all things.
Beginnings	Adam and Eve	Sin
Beginnings	Noah	Worldwide flood
Beginnings	wicked people	Confused languages
Beginnings of a Nation	Abraham	Special promises by God
Beginnings of a Nation	Moses	Plagues
Possessing the Land	Joshua	Enter Promised Land
Possessing the Land	Gideon	Cycles of sin
United Kingdom	David	A special King forever
Divided Kingdom	Elijah and Elisha	Special prophets in Israel
Taken from Home	Jeremiah, Daniel, Ezekiel	Israel sent to Assyria
Return to Home	Nehemiah and Ezra	Israel returned to land
Return to Home	Daniel	400 years of change
Early Life of Jesus	Mary and Joseph	The birth of Jesus
Ministry of Jesus Christ	12 disciples	Jesus called 12 apostles
Ministry of Jesus Christ	Jesus	Miracles of Jesus
Opposition	Blind man	Healing power of Jesus
Betrayal and Death	Jesus Christ	Entry into Jerusalem
Victory and Life	Resurrected Christ	Empty tomb
The Church	Jesus and the apostles	The Jerusalem church
Future Events	Satan and Jesus	Tribulation

Teacher Helps

Begin the Lesson Activity: Match Time Line, People, and Events

The teacher should form three stacks of paper. One stack should be the "time line" stack. 18 different eras should be underneath this "time line" piece of paper. Do the same thing for "people" and "event." Then mix them up and have the children arrange them so that they have the correct era with the correct people with the correct event. For instance, when matched correctly, beginnings, God, and God made all things should all be in the same group.

Timeline: Future Events

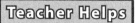

3) Teach the Lesson

Wear a robe and hold a gavel. Ask: **"Have you ever been in a courtroom? Have you seen a TV show with courtroom scenes? The judge sits behind a big desk. It is a little scary -- especially when you realize he has the authority to put someone in prison. Our Bible story today tells of a very scary courtroom scene where Jesus is the judge."**

Tell the Story

Shortly after Satan has been judged and thrown into the lake of fire, this is what will happen. The eternal Judge will open the records of life. Those who have put their trust in Christ will not be around for this judgment. They have already received their rewards. When these records are opened and read, those who have not put their faith in Christ will be judged by what they have done. They will be cast into hell. No one will be saved by their deeds. It is very clear from Scripture that only those who have a personal relationship with Jesus will escape this judgment.

When this punishment is finished, God will be done with judgment. The lake of fire is the final destination of everything and everybody that is wicked. Satan will be in the lake of fire. The beast will be in the lake of fire. The false prophet will be in the lake of fire. Demons will be in the lake of fire. Death will be in the lake of fire. The grave will be in the lake of fire. All those whose names were not found in the Lamb's Book of Life will be in the lake of fire.

It is by faith that we are identified with Jesus Christ. Those who do not confess Him as Lord will have no hope, no second chance, no other means of appeal. This judgment will be final and it will be eternal. It will also be a place of great agony. It is for those who chose not to trust Jesus Christ and not be identified with Him.

This judgment takes places at the Great White Throne. It is called great because it is elevated. It is called white because it is shining. At this elevated throne that is white, a holy and just God will not allow sin to go unpunished. God is merciful, kind, and loving. However, He is also holy and just.

Tell the Story Activity: What is God Like?

As the teacher tells this story, have kids write down or recall what God is like. For instance:

- God is *loving*. He loves people. God is *holy*. He hates sin.

- God is *merciful*. He provides a way for people to avoid punishment. God is a God of *wrath*. His holy anger hates sin.

- God is *long-suffering*. He often delays the execution of His wrath. God is *just*. His will must be executed against sin.

Timeline: Future Events

Memory Verse

Revelation 20:15 (ESV) - And if anyone's name was not found written in the book of life, he was thrown into the lake of fire.

Praise and Worship

Praise and Worship styles vary greatly around the world. It is the intent of this curriculum that praise and worship songs be selected that best fit the content of this lesson. Recommendations for praise and worship are given and this music can generally be located at www.itunes.com. However, the teacher can feel free to select a similar praise and worship song.

"There Is A Hope" by Keswick is recommended for this lesson.

Bible Activity

I was in God's throne room and saw a great big white throne and the risen Jesus—to Whom God had given all authority to judge—seated on it. Earth and sky ran from His presence but could find no place to hide.

Then I saw the Sea giving up all who had died there. Death and Hell turned their dead over, also. I saw all who had died, important people and not-so-important people, stand before that throne! Books were opened, including the most important one: the Book of Life. The dead were judged by what they had done as recorded in the books. Then Death and Hell were thrown into Fire Lake. This is the second death (Fire Lake). Anyone whose name was not found written in the Book of Life was thrown into Fire Lake. All those who refuse to know God (by not believing the Good News of Jesus and trusting Him) will suffer for what they've done. Their punishment will be eternal separation from Jesus and His awesome power. If they refuse Him when they have the opportunity, they will forever be separated from Him.

Listen carefully; this is so important: anyone who believes Jesus and believes the Father who actually put Him in charge, has real, lasting life and will not be condemned to the second death. These believers have passed from the world of the dead to the world of the living. In our final story we will learn about their future.

Teacher Helps

Memory Verse Activity: Scripture Scrambler[1]

Write the words to a verse on the top of a paper. Then number the paper, one number for each word in the verse. Beside the numbers, write a scrambled word to the verse. Challenge your children to unscramble each word to the verse in its correct order.

Bible Activity

While he was a prisoner, God gave John a peek into the future through a fascinating vision; it was as if he was taken to heaven. He could see what was going to happen there and what was going to happen on earth—as if he was watching it happen right in front of his eyes! He wrote it all down in a book. Part of his vision included what would happen after Satan was thrown in Fire and Brimstone Lake.

4) Review the Lesson

Teacher Helps

Based on the lives of those who followed Jesus, rate yourself on this grid:

- Following Jesus' example   1   2   3   4   5   6
- Understanding God's Word   1   2   3   4   5   6
- Willing to be a missionary   1   2   3   4   5   6
- Ready to share my faith   1   2   3   4   5   6
- Choices I make   1   2   3   4   5   6
- Told others 8 essential truths 1   2   3   4   5   6
- Willing to forsake evil deeds 1   2   3   4   5   6
- Overall commitment to God   1   2   3   4   5   6

Review Activity: Grid for Growth

The teacher should instruct to the class of children that the example of Jesus should help us evaluate our own lives.

Children should fill out this chart (1= low; 6 = high).

5) Apply the Lesson

Nobody wants to be punished. Nobody wants to be punished forever. Nobody wants to be punished forever in torment. Satan is doomed to this punishment. Eternal punishment is something you can avoid. There is only one way to avoid this punishment and that is through the death, burial, and resurrection of Jesus Christ.

> **Story Line: Unbelievers will be cast into the lake of fire forever.**

99 Adventures in the Bible's Big Story

Timeline: Future Events

Adventure Number 98
2 Peter 3:3-7 and Matthew 24:35

> **Story Line: God will destroy the heavens and earth with intense fire.**

 ## 1) Study the Lesson (before class)

- Near the time of the Great White Throne judgment of unbelievers, God will destroy the current sin-contaminated earth and its heavens with a roaring fire and intense heat.

- Up to this point in history, Noah's flood was the greatest God-inflicted catastrophe the earth had ever known. But the flood was nothing compared to a future catastrophe, the destruction of the earth and its skies by fire.

- In order to purge the earth of its contamination by sin, the heavens and earth will be consumed by a roaring fire.[1]

- When the heavens are destroyed, the text probably does not mean that the place where God lives is destroyed. Rather, the meaning is more likely the heavens as they appear to the human eye. If the earth and its atmosphere are destroyed, as Peter affirms, then the heavens would be radically altered also.

- "By the same word" refers solely to the will of God. He has only one command to give and all will be destroyed.[2]

- 2 Peter 3:7, 10, and 12 are the only places in the New Testament that the final destruction is pictured by fire.

- Judgments associating fire with the return of the Lord are found in the Old Testament (Isaiah 66:15-16 and Malachi 4:1).[3]

- In the days of Noah, judgment came through water, the universal flood. In the end times, judgment will come through fire.

Footnotes - Adventure 98

1. Wayne Haston, *New Testament Chronological Bible Cards*, NT-49.

2. Albert Barnes, *Barnes' Notes on the New Testament*, 2 Peter 3:17.

3. John Walvoord and Roy Zuck, *Bible Knowledge Commentary: New Testament*, 876.

4. Susan Lingo, *Written on Our Hearts*, 79.

2) Begin the Lesson

There are eight basic concepts that are emphasized throughout all of the Bible. We have studied these truths in previous lessons. Ask the children if they can name them and tell a little bit about each one. They are:

1. <u>God</u>. In the beginning, there was a very powerful God. 1-The Eternal God; 27-The Exodus; 40-The Reign of David; Lesson 83-The Conversion of Saul.

2. <u>Man</u>. God created many things. He created man and woman to be His special friends. 3-Creation of the Universe; 4-Creation of People; 24-Moses Leads His People; 83-Conversion of Cornelius.

3. <u>Sin</u>. Man and woman disobeyed God. They did not do what He told them to do. 7-Beginning of Human Sin; 33-Unbelief at Kadesh; 43-The Divided Kingdom; 88-Paul's Third Missionary Journey; Lesson 94-A Future Period of Tribulation.

4. <u>Death</u>. God punished man and woman for their disobedience. Death, in the Bible, refers to separation. 8-The Origin of Death; 16-The Tower of Babel; 46:-The Exiles of Israel and Judah; Lesson 98-The Great White Throne Judgment.

5. <u>Christ</u>. God sent His one and only Son, His unique Son, who lived a perfect life. 9-Promise of a Victor Over Satan; 45-Prophecies of a Coming Messiah; 52-Birth of Jesus Christ; 75- The Resurrection of Jesus Christ; 78-The Ascension of Jesus Christ; Lesson 96-The Earthly Kingdom of Jesus Christ.

6. <u>Cross</u>. Jesus died on the cross for the sins of the world. 11-Provision of Coverings; 32-The Day of Atonement; 45-Prophecies of a Coming Messiah; 56-Announcement by John; 73-The Crucifixion of Jesus.

7. <u>Faith</u>. If anyone places their faith in Christ, God welcomes them. 13-Cain and Abel; 34-The Bronze Serpent; 58-The Religious Leader; 61-Jesus Has Power Over a Stormy Sea: 74-Why Jesus Died on the Cross; 86-The Jerusalem Council; Lesson 90-Final Years of the First Century A.D.

8. <u>Life</u>. God gives eternal life to those who put their faith in Him. 5-Life in Paradise; 38-Bright Lights in an Era of Darkness; 56-Announcement by John the Baptist; 75-The Resurrection of Jesus Christ; Lesson 83-The Conversion of Saul; Lesson 95-The Return of Jesus as King.

Teacher Helps

Review Activity: Eight Basic Gospel Truths - One Complete Story

The teacher should emphasize these eight gospel concepts throughout Scripture. They are foundational to telling children the one story of redemption found in the Bible. We will emphasize these eight truths regularly.

Ask the children if they can think of how these eight gospel principles are emphasized in the first 98 lessons that we have studied.

Timeline: Future Events

3) Teach the Lesson

Imagine a nuclear bomb or bombs all over the whole world. What would that be like?

Probably, you are imagining great amount of heat, lots of fire, and a completely decimated earth and its atmosphere.

Tell the Story

All the galaxies, all the heavens, the earth, and everything in the earth were formed or created with the Word of God. We learned that in the very beginning of our lessons. God made the atmosphere, He made the stars, He made the sun, the moon, all the fish, all the birds, all the trees, all the bushes; He made everything. He formed all of this by His own word. His word is very powerful. It can create something when there is nothing there.

Remember this ... God can create something from nothing!

When God's creation became exceeding wicked with lots of violence, God punished His creation with the flood. By His own word, He sent a worldwide flood. The only people who lived through the flood were Noah and his family. Of course, the animals all went in the ark, two at a time. God's word is very powerful in punishment, even punishing His own creation.

Remember this also ... God can punish anything, even His own creation!

At the very end of time, God will destroy the heavens and the earth with a great fire. It would kind of be like a massive nuclear bomb that affected the entire earth, just like the flood affected the entire earth. The earth and the heavens will be destroyed by this fire. It will annihilate everything. God knows that sin has contaminated all this and He wants to get rid of this contamination. He will burn it and destroy it, even though He once saw it as good and called it "good." This fire will be the visible evidence of His judgment on sin.

Lastly, remember this ... God will punish anything that is "sin contaminated."

Tell the Story Activity: Judgments from God

The teacher should recall with the help of the class other judgments that we have studied. Conclusion: God always punishes sin and its contaminating effects.

- Lesson 8: The Origin of Death
- Lesson 10: Sin Has Negative Effects
- Lesson 15: The Great Flood
- Lesson 16: The Tower of Babel
- Lesson 34: The Bronze Serpent
- Lesson 66: Jesus Teaches about Hell

Memory Verse

Matthew 24:35 (ESV) -Heaven and earth will pass away, but my words will not pass away.

Praise and Worship

Praise and Worship styles vary greatly around the world. It is the intent of this curriculum that praise and worship songs be selected that best fit the content of this lesson. Recommendations for praise and worship are given and this music can generally be located at www.itunes.com. However, the teacher can feel free to select a similar praise and worship song.

"There Is A Hope" by Keswick is recommended for this lesson.

Bible Activity

The powerful Word of God can do anything! Let's see how many things we can think of that God's word was responsible for. Allow time for responses and be ready to give some examples to help them get started. Possible ideas: each thing created in Genesis 1-2, the plagues in Egypt, the crossing of the Red Sea, miracles in the OT and NT, the destruction of the earth and the heavens, etc.

Make a list at the front of the room that everyone can see. If you have time, play a game where one or more students comes to the front of the room and silently chooses one of the examples that has been written down earlier. They will act out that scene and see who can guess what they are depicting.

If you would like, you can divide the class into 2 teams, boys against girls, and keep score for who gets the most right answers. Emphasize that God has power over everything on earth and in heaven, because He created it all! Also remind the children that God is good and loving, and He never uses His great power in a selfish or unwise way. When He judges sin with His great power, it is for the good of those that love and obey His good commands.

Teacher Helps

Memory Verse Activity: Scripture Log[4]

Make a page for children to take home that shows down the left column: Sunday, Monday, Tuesday, Wednesday, Thursday, Friday, and Saturday.

Across the top, put practice times and review times.

Children should work on this memory verse each day and mark on their log when they practiced this verse and when they review this verse. Bring this log to class with you next week.

This type of activity will encourage Scripture memory and obedience throughout the week, not just as part of the lesson.

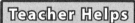

4) Review the Lesson

The teacher should divide the class up into two teams.

- One team could be the "red" team and receive red cards or pieces of paper. The other team could be the "yellow" team and receive yellow cards or pieces of paper.

- Each team has the responsibility of writing out 3 to 5 questions that they want the other team to answer.

- Each question has to pertain to the lesson today.

- After questions are written out, the other team has five to seven minutes to answer the questions. The "yellow" team will answer the questions from the "red" team and the "red" team will answer questions from the "yellow" team.

Review Activity: Two Team Review

After an appropriate time, the teacher will gather up the cards or pieces of paper and reward points to the best questions and best answers from each team.

It is highly advisable to have 2 adult teachers in every classroom for kids. If there are 2 adults, then one adult should be the leader of each team.

5) Apply the Lesson

God created with His word. He has punished with His word. He will punish with His word when the earth and heavens are destroyed by fire.

Describe one thing about the judgment of God that makes you want to avoid this judgment.

Story Line: God will destroy the heavens and earth with intense fire.

Adventure Number 99
Revelation 21:1 - 22:5

> **Story Line: Everyone who has trusted Jesus will enter an eternal paradise with God.**

 1) Study the Lesson (before class)

- After God's great judgment, He will create a new heaven and a new earth. (Romans 8:18-21; 2 Peter 3:7-13)

- These verses describe a scene that is happy and triumphant for the redeemed church. All its conflicts shall have ceased and its enemies shall have been destroyed.[1]

- God has planned that those who live eternally with Him will not know any kind of sickness, pain, or sorrow. Only joy and happiness will be present in the eternal glories of His presence.

- The new Jerusalem is as tall as it wide and long. With its design and with its Designer, it will be a perfect place to live forever. The special walls and the special gates will be magnificent to look at and glorious in their appearance.

- God's glory will illuminate the city making it a place of holiness and righteousness. The city will be complete without sin and evil.

- Only those whose names are written in the Lamb's Book of Life will live in the new Jerusalem. That is, only those who have put their faith in the Lord Jesus Christ will live there.

- There is no need for a temple or a church for the Lord Himself will be present there.

- The concluding words of John are also appropriate to the conclusion of the entire Bible. The angel affirms to John the reliability of these words. The appropriate response to these words is worship of God.[2]

Footnotes - Adventure 99

1. Albert Barnes, *Barnes' Notes on the New Testament*, Revelation 21.

2. Roy B. Zuck, *A Biblical Theology of the New Testament*, 242.

2) Begin the Lesson

This fun game should be planned as a final review activity for all the lessons. Divide the class into two teams and use cards that the teacher has made up for all 99 adventures. The cards that the teacher designs should have something on the card (like a picture, the Bible verse, the story line, or something like this) that designates the story. The teacher will need two sets of cards, if possible.

There will be 198 cards (2 sets of 99 adventure cards) should be scattered around the teaching room or teaching rooms. The teacher should scatter the cards as much as possible for children to find. Do not let the kids see you scatter the cards.

Rules for the game are as follows:

- Each team should go looking for the cards in the designated area.

- Kids can bring back only 1 card at a time.

- If 2 of the same card are brought back, then the team that has these should give one of the cards to the team that has none.

- Once all the cards are found, each team should work together to put the stories in order.

- First team to put all 99 cards in order will win a prize.

Teacher Helps

Review Activity: 99 Pictures - One Complete Story

The teacher should make this closing review activity a fun way to review. Make sure all kids are involved in the collection of the cards. Also, make sure they work together when putting them in order. All kids must participate or they will lose points for their team.

3) Teach the Lesson

This last story ends with wonderful news. Since the sin contaminated earth and heavens are gone, God has provided a new sin-free paradise where He lives.

Imagine what you think this new paradise will be like. Now, have the class share 5-8 ideas of what this new paradise will be like.

Now, let us look at the Biblical record of this new paradise.

Tell the Story

The first earth and everything in it are gone. Now, God will make a brand new earth and a brand new heaven. Let me tell you what it will be like. I think you will really like it.

There won't be any more sadness, no more tears in this place. Have you ever been sad or unhappy? Well, you won't be sad in this new earth. There won't be anybody dying. Have your parents or a good friend ever died? It won't ever happen again in this new earth. Anybody ever had some pain? You won't feel any pain here. It will be a "pain-free zone." There will be peace, life, and happiness. You will really like this place. And those who have trusted Jesus will be able to live here forever! It won't just be a temporary home. It will be a forever home.

Let me tell you what this home will look like. It will be bright and shining. There will be no darkness. Anyone ever afraid of the darkness? You won't ever have to think about it in this place because there will be no darkness, ever! It will be a massive place to live; 1,400 miles (2,253 kilometers) long by 1,400 miles (2,253 kilometers) wide by 1,400 miles (2,253 kilometers) tall. It will be full of ruby-red gems and emerald-green gems. It is full of blue-sapphire gems and purple-colored gems. It is full of golden gems and yellow gems. All of these magnificent stones will provide a fabulous array of colors for our new home. But it gets even better, there will a crystal river flowing from the throne of God right down the main street of this new home. Ripe fruits will be on both sides of the river and everyone will be able to enjoy the fruits in this new home.

This new home won't need sun, moon, or stars because God is there. He will be that bright and shining light and it will never get dark because He will always be there. And nothing dirty or defiled will ever get into our new home. There won't be pollution or anything bad that could hurt us.

The throne of God will be right in the middle. We will be able to talk to Him and worship Him all the time. It won't be boring and it won't be dull. It will be the greatest thing ever. Just think of it: a beautiful new home where there is peace and safety forever ... a beautiful new home where there is love and happiness forever!

But, this new home is only for those who have put their trust in Jesus. Because of their trust in Jesus, God will provide and protect believers forever in their new home.

Teacher Helps

Tell the Story Activity: The Lamb's Book of Life

The teacher should create a book that says "The Lamb's Book of Life" on the front of it. Tell kids that this book is not the real one, it is one that we will imagine. Have blank pages on this inside of this folder or book.

The teacher should ask the children, **"Is your name written down in a book like this in heaven?"** Emphasize that the pages are blank. The only way that it can be written down in heaven is if you have placed your trust and faith in Jesus Christ alone.

Memory Verse

Revelation 22:5 (ESV) - And night will be no more. They will need no light of lamp or sun, for the Lord God will be their light, and they will reign forever and ever.

Praise and Worship

Praise and Worship styles vary greatly around the world. It is the intent of this curriculum that praise and worship songs be selected that best fit the content of this lesson. Recommendations for praise and worship are given and this music can generally be located at www.itunes.com. However, the teacher can feel free to select a similar praise and worship song.

"There Is A Hope" by Keswick is recommended for this lesson.

Bible Activity

Have a child look up and read I Corinthians 2:9, if possible. If your children are too young, the teacher should read this verse out loud. Then ask the following questions: (After each question, allow 3-4 children to give an answer, then say together: "Heaven will be better than that!")

1. What is the most beautiful city in the world?

2. What is the best tasting food you have ever had?

3. What is the most beautiful music you have ever heard?

4. What is the best weather to enjoy?

5. What is the happiest thing on earth that you most enjoy doing?

The Bible teaches that we can't even imagine how wonderful heaven will be! It sure is fun to imagine it, though!

Let's make a list of things that the Bible says will NOT be in heaven....

Sin, sadness, tears, death, pain (all the bad stuff).

Teacher Helps

Memory Verse Activity: Hop It

In large letters, write phrases of the verse on sheets of paper. On the floor, tape the papers in a mixed up fashion, but close enough for succeeding words to be reached in a step. Children should step on one word at a time in the proper order to quote the verse. Let each child have a turn of hopping on the verse.

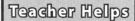

4) Review the Lesson

1. <u>God</u>. In the beginning, there was a very powerful God.

2. <u>Man</u>. God created many things. He created man and woman to be His special friends.

3. <u>Sin</u>. Man and woman disobeyed God. They did not do what He told them to do.

4. <u>Death</u>. God punished man and woman for their disobedience. Death, in the Bible, refers to separation.

5. <u>Christ</u>. God sent His one and only Son, His unique Son, who lived a perfect life.

6. <u>Cross</u>. Jesus died on the cross for the sins of the world.

7. <u>Faith</u>. If anyone places their faith in Christ, God welcomes them.

8. <u>Life</u>. God gives eternal life to those who put their faith in Him.

9. <u>Conclusion</u>: God wants to offer eternal life to those who trust who Jesus is (God) and what He did (died on the cross for our sins). He will then offer eternal life to those who trust Him.

**Review Activity:
8 Words or Concepts -
One Complete Story**

There are eight basic concepts that are emphasized throughout all of the Bible. We have studied these truths in previous lessons. Ask the children if they can name them and tell a little bit about each one.

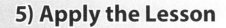

5) Apply the Lesson

This new home is reserved only for some special people. You don't have to be rich or famous to live in this new home. You don't have to be a special sports hero or political leader to live in this new home. You just have to place your faith in Jesus Christ believing that He died for your sins. If you will make this faith commitment, Jesus will give you a place to live in this new home.

Story Line: Everyone who has trusted Jesus will enter an eternal paradise with God.

Made in the USA
Las Vegas, NV
28 June 2024